# Commercial Liability Underwriting

# Volume II

# Commercial Liability Underwriting
## Volume II

LARRY D. GAUNT, Ph.D., CPCU
*Professor of Risk Management and Insurance*
*Georgia State University*

NUMAN A. WILLIAMS, Ph.D., CPCU, CLU, AU
*Professor of Insurance*
*Ball State University*

EVERETT D. RANDALL, CPCU, CLU, AU, APA
*Assistant Vice President*
*Insurance Institute of America*

INSURANCE INSTITUTE OF AMERICA
HAEC STUDIA ADOLESCENTIAM ALUNT
1924

Third Edition • 1990

INSURANCE INSTITUTE OF AMERICA
*720 Providence Road, Malvern, Pennsylvania 19355-0770*

*Third Edition • June 1990*

Library of Congress Catalog Number 90-80136
International Standard Book Number 0-89462-051-7

*Printed in the United States of America*

# Table of Contents

# CHAPTER 7

# Underwriting General Liability Insurance, I

Organizations can be held liable for injuries and damages arising out of exposures such as the existence of a premises, operations conducted, products sold or manufactured, operations completed, contracts entered into, libel, slander, and the work of independent contractors. These are essentially the nonauto, nonprofessional exposures faced by a business organization. This chapter and the two that follow analyze these exposures and discuss how they may be underwritten.

The coverage that applies to these exposures is provided through the Insurance Services Office (ISO) commercial general liability (CGL) policy. The rules of the ISO *Commercial Lines Manual* (*CLM*) are followed in classifying and rating these exposures. These rules and the CGL are used as the basis for the discussion of general liability exposures in this chapter and in Chapters 8 and 9.

By way of introduction to the terms used in this discussion, some definitions should be highlighted.

There are three terms that are used almost interchangeably—exposure base, premium base, and rating base. All three terms are correct. Payroll for example, is (1) a variable that can serve as one measure of the *exposure* assumed by the insurer, (2) used in determining the final *premium* for the policy, and (3) used in *rating* the policy. In certain circumstances, one of the terms may be more appropriate than the other two. For example, when describing the rating process, the term rating base is probably preferred. In more general, risk management terms, exposure base would probably be best. The terms are used interchangeably in this text, using the one most appropriate for the discussion at hand. When referring to manual rules or guidelines, the terminology used in the manual is the terminology used in the text.

## COMMERCIAL LINES MANUAL

Various sources have published manuals for property and liability insurance. Because of the need for continuity and consistency of rulings and interpretations, the National Bureau of Casualty Underwriters in 1961 compiled and issued a compendium called *Manuals of Liability Insurance*. This contained eleven subsections defining rules and classifications for the coverage parts detailed therein, as well as two supplements, and supplementary pages necessary for individual company uses.

The formation of ISO in 1971 further centralized the activities of bureaus and rating organizations. In 1973, ISO issued a larger version of the *Manuals of Liability Insurance*. The major change in this edition was the introduction of five-digit classification code numbers.

Statistical needs dictated the change to five-digit code numbers. However, this change somewhat complicated the underwriter's task since the workers compensation codes remained as four-digit numbers. There was still much shifting from one manual to the next in an effort to correlate premises and operations exposures and coverage parts to products and completed operations exposures and coverage parts. The earlier four-digit codes rarely corresponded for the premises and operations and the products classes. While some of the new codes did correspond for those coverage parts, the majority of codes did not track so well. Nor was terminology parallel in some instances. Often it was a matter of dispute as to which premises and operations codes went with which products and completed operations codes.

In 1978, the Insurance Services Office issued a *Commercial Lines Manual (CLM)* that provides uniformity in format and language for the nine lines of insurance within its scope. This uniformity simplifies the task of multi-line account rating and eliminates much of the confusion caused by variations in the old manuals. The *CLM* also facilitates uniform application of rules across state lines. And in addition to combining the rules and rates for nine commercial lines into one manual, the *CLM* also states the rules in simplified language.

In order to avoid repeating itself, the *CLM* rearranges the material found in the previous manuals for separate lines of insurance. The new arrangement makes the *CLM* more compact than the total of the manuals it replaces. It also facilitates uniformity among separate lines.

The massive simplification project in the mid-eighties produced major changes in the classification and rating structure. These changes necessitated a complete revision of the *Commercial Lines Manual*, which was implemented in 1985. While its effective date in particular states varies according to regulatory approval, this version of the manual is usually called the November 1985 *Commercial Lines Manual* or simply the new *CLM*.

The new *CLM* contains the simplified "Classification Table" that resulted from the Commercial Lines Policy and Rating Simplification Project. Each classification has a new, unique code that applies for both premises-operations coverage and products-completed operations coverage. Division Six—General Liability reflects the extensive changes in policywriting and rating rules for general liability. Changes appear in several other parts of the new *CLM* as well. For example, for commercial property, Division Five—Fire was rewritten to parallel policy simplification, recognize automated policy issuance requirements, reduce rating steps, and to simplify rules and rating procedures. In Division Two—Boiler and Machinery, Division Three—Crime, and Division Eight—Inland Marine, the new *CLM* has a new arrangement: a separate section in each division contains the country-wide rates that were formerly included in the countrywide rules.

The main parts to the *CLM* are the "Classification Table" and the separate divisions containing the special rules and rates for each of nine lines of insurance. These parts of the *CLM* are intended to apply throughout the country. In addition, state rates and state exceptions to the general *CLM* rules are printed on state pages. The state pages also indicate effective dates for the introduction of new rules and new policy forms within each state. State exception pages may also show an exception to the common general rules.

## "Classification Table"

The "Classification Table" provides the necessary rating and classification information for crime, fire and allied lines, general liability, and multiple-lines insurance. These are the lines that use a written description of the insured's operations as a basis for classification and rating. The "Classification Table" does not apply to the other lines of insurance included in the *CLM* because they involve unique approaches to classification. Rules for using the "Classification Table" in connection with general liability classifications are discussed later.

## Nine Lines of Insurance Divisions

The remaining part of the manual is divided into nine sections pertaining to the nine lines of insurance incorporated into the *CLM*.

**4—Commercial Liability Underwriting**

Each division has its own rules and rates. These divisions are as follows:

Division One—Automobile
Division Two—Boiler and Machinery
Division Three—Crime
Division Four—Farm
Division Five—Fire and Allied Lines (including Glass)
Division Six—General Liability
Division Seven—Professional Liability
Division Eight—Inland Marine
Division Nine—Multiple Line

Each division has a separate explanatory memorandum, general index of applicable forms and endorsements, table of contents, and rules and procedures related to the specific insurance lines detailed therein.

Manual pages are numbered to reflect the structure of the *CLM*. Pages for each division can be identified by a letter code system:

| *Code* | *Section* |
|---|---|
| CS | Classification Table |
| CA | Commercial Auto |
| BM | Boiler and Machinery |
| CR | Crime |
| FR | Farm |
| CF | Commercial Fire and Allied Lines |
| CG | General Liability |
| PL | Professional Liability |
| IM | Inland Marine |
| CP | Commercial Package Policy Subdivision of Multiple Line Division |
| BP | Businessowners Policy Subdivision of Multiple Line Division |

Thus, CS-112 identifies page 112 of the "Classification Table" section. Rate pages or state exception pages are found within each of the nine divisions and have an additional letter code preceding the number. These secondary letter codes are as follows:

A—Additional Rules
E—Exceptions to Common and General Rules
R—Rate Pages
RA—Rate Adjustment Pages (Commercial Fire)
RC—Class Rate Pages (Commercial Fire)
T—Territory Pages
RE—Earthquake Rate Pages (Commercial Fire)

S—Supplemental Pages (where applicable)
RX—Rating Examples Pages (Crime and Commercial Fire) or Transition Program Information (General Liability)
CWR—Country Wide Rates
AS—Alarm Systems Appendix (Crime)
SV—Safes and Vaults Appendix (Crime)

Thus, CG-R-005 signifies the fifth state rate page in the general liability division.

Dates shown at the bottom of the pages are printing dates and are not necessarily the effective date. The manual revision notice accompanying a new or revised page states the effective date. Effective dates may vary when rates and rules must be filed in that particular state by the individual company or when the company chooses to make an independent filing.

## SIMPLIFIED COMMERCIAL LINES POLICIES

Generally, commercial lines policies may be written in two different ways—as (1) monoline and (2) package policies.

At one time, state regulations prohibited insurers from writing more than one line of insurance. A company providing fire insurance could not also write liability insurance. Thus, policy forms and underwriting practices developed to reflect each separate line of insurance. Commercial policies providing liability coverage alone, for example, may be called single or *monoline policies*.

The removal of legal restrictions has made it possible to combine different kinds of insurance in one policy. These *commercial package policies* can be designed to meet the typical insurance needs of a business. The combination of coverages greatly simplifies the task of obtaining the necessary insurance. Not only was obtaining coverage made simpler, but so were the policies themselves—they were rewritten in the eighties in an easier-to-read format and language. Package policies may include both property coverage and liability coverage. It is important for the underwriter to understand the coverages afforded and how various endorsements or schedules may modify the package policy to broaden or limit coverage.

The uniform format of the simplified policies eliminates redundant information and makes it easier to locate important information in the policy. Each line has one set of forms and one set of manual rules. In a simplified commercial lines policy, all the forms and endorsements for a particular line of insurance compose a coverage part. A typical *coverage part* consists of the following:

- One or more lines of business declarations
- One or more coverage forms
- Any applicable endorsements
- In some cases, a separate *conditions* or *general provisions form* (conditions are included in the auto and general liability coverage forms)

The coverage part becomes a monoline policy with the attachment of the following:

- *Common policy declarations* (which may be combined with the line of business declarations to make one form)
- *Common policy conditions*

Exhibit 7-1 illustrates a commercial general liability monoline policy. The important fact to remember about a monoline policy is that it includes only one coverage part.

The coverage part becomes part of a *package policy* when combined with the following:

- One or more other coverage parts
- Common policy declarations
- Common policy conditions[1]

Exhibit 7-2 illustrates the contents of the commercial package policy (CPP). The common policy declarations and conditions appear in every commercial package policy. For both monoline and package policies, the same forms and rules apply.

## Common Policy Conditions

The common policy conditions apply to all coverage parts included in the policy. These conditions relate to cancellation, charges, examination of books and records, inspections and surveys, premiums, and transfer of rights and duties.

A new term, *first named insured,* appears in the common policy conditions to emphasize that for policies with more than one named insured, the first named insured has the following responsibilities and characteristics:

- Responsibility for the payment of premiums
- Authorization to make changes
- Sole authorization to cancel a policy
- The only one designated to receive notice of cancellation
- Sole authorization to receive any return premiums

**Exhibit 7-1**
Commercial General Liability Monoline Policy*

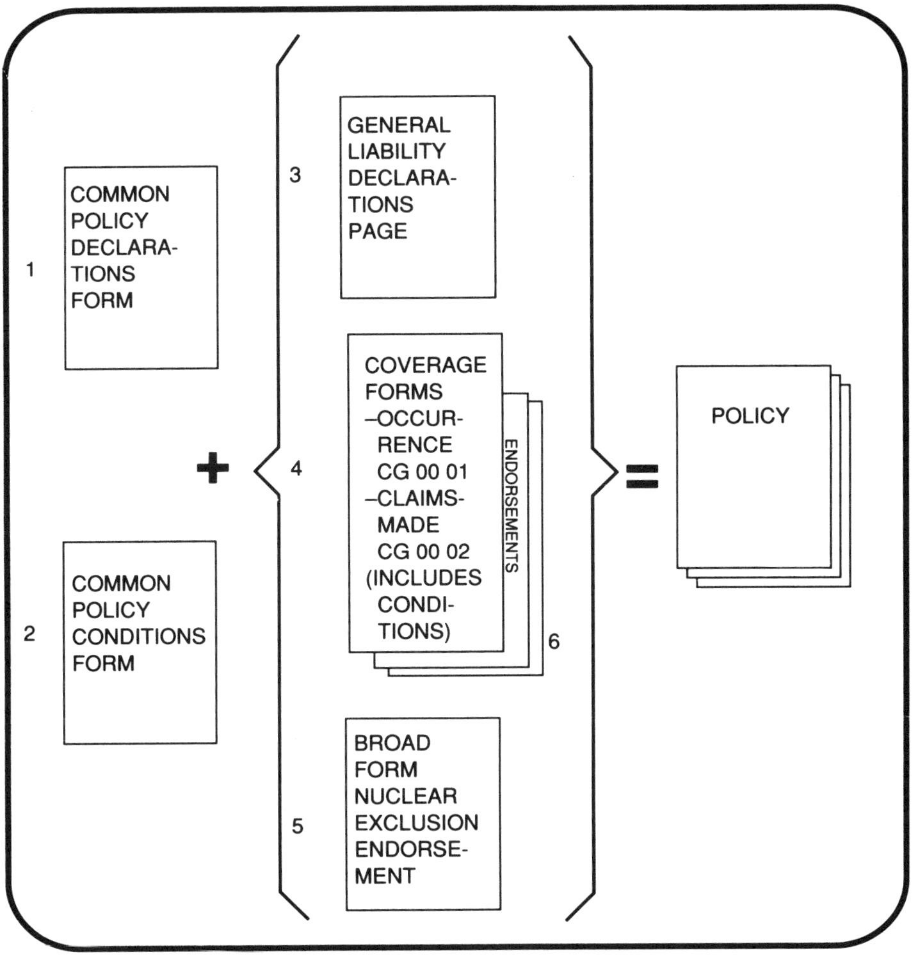


*Adapted with permission from *Workshop Leader's Guide*, ISO Commercial Lines Policy and Rating Simplification Project© Insurance Services Office, 1985, p. 52.

## Common Policy Declarations

Exhibit 7-3 shows a sample common policy declarations page. This page gives the policy number and the specific information identifying the insured and the coverage. The first item specifies the named insured, shows the insured's address, explicitly states the policy period, and describes the type of business insured. The coverage parts included in the policy are indicated by showing the advance premium charges for

**Exhibit 7-2**
Contents of the Commercial Package Policy (CPP)*

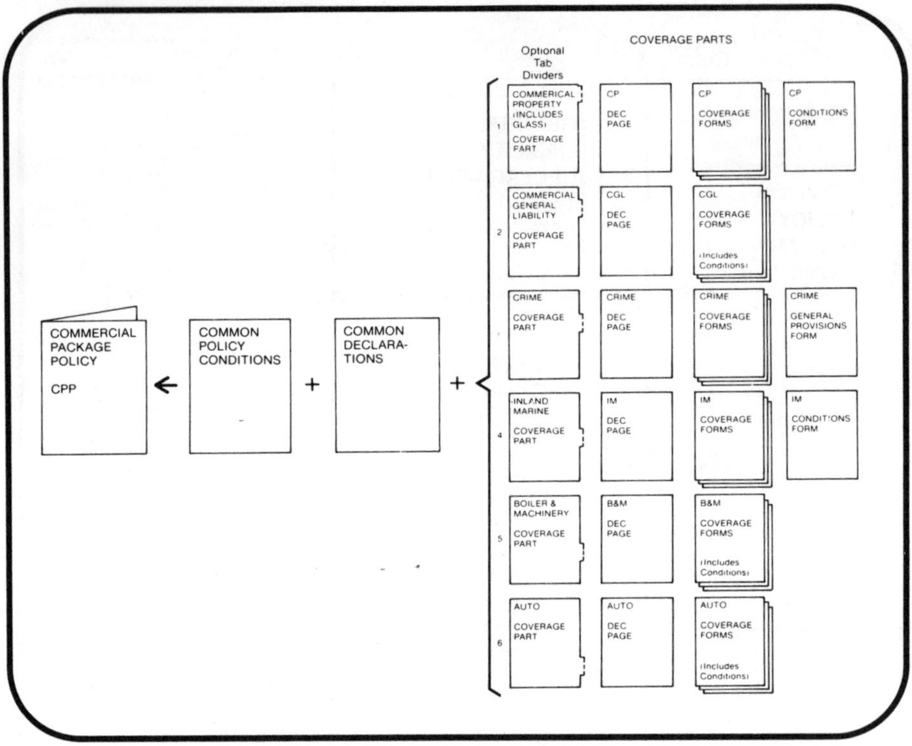


*Copyright, Insurance Services Office, Inc. Reprinted with permission.

each coverage. The common policy declarations page also lists by number all forms included in the policy.

## GENERAL LIABILITY CLASSIFICATION

General liability exposures must be classified so that each type of business operation pays its share of insured losses. The *Commercial Lines Manual* lists the classifications and stipulates the procedures for assigning classifications to insureds with general liability policies. The list of classifications appears in the "Classification Table," which is a separate section of the *CLM.*

### The Classification Table

The "Classification Table" pages of the *Commercial Lines Manu-*

**Exhibit 7-3**
Common Policy Declarations

Policy No. ______

| Company Name Area | Producer Name Area |
|---|---|

Named Insured ______

Mailing Address ______

______

Policy Period: From ______ to ______ at 12:01 A.M. Standard Time at your mailing address shown above.

Business Description ______

In return for the payment of the premium, and subject to all the terms of this policy, we agree with you to provide the insurance as stated in this policy.

This policy consists of the following coverage parts for which a premium is indicated. This premium may be subject to adjustment.

| | PREMIUM |
|---|---|
| Boiler and Machinery Coverage Part | $______ |
| Commercial Auto Coverage Part | $______ |
| Commercial Crime Coverage Part | $______ |
| Commercial General Liability Coverage Part | $______ |
| Commercial Inland Marine Coverage Part | $______ |
| Commercial Property Coverage Part | $______ |
| Farm Coverage Part | $______ |
| ______ | $______ |
| TOTAL | $______ |

Premium shown is payable:
$______ at inception. $ ______ ______

______

______

Forms applicable to all Coverage Parts: ______
(Show numbers.)

______

______

Countersigned ______ (Date) BY ______ (Authorized Representative)

NOTE: Officers' Facsimile signatures may be inserted here, on the policy cover or elsewhere at the company's option *al*, identified with a CS letter code, alphabetically list the classifications applicable to general liability insurance, as well as to crime, commercial fire and allied lines, and multiple-lines insurance. The "Classification Table" consolidates the various classifications used in the previous manuals for these lines of insurance. The total number of classifications in the table therefore exceeds the number used in any one of the previous manuals. As a result, the table reduces the need for classification by analogy and encourages more uniform coding and rating. This section of the *CLM* is divided into two parts, the explanatory rules and the classifications listing.

**Explanatory Rules.** The explanatory rules provide an orientation to the "Classification Table." They include definitions, symbols, and abbreviations appearing in the table. These rules also describe the general content of the "Classification Table," outline its column headings, and explain the use of certain general symbols. For general liability coverage, the most important rules are those explaining the symbols used in the general liability columns and the definitions and abbreviations used in the classification descriptions.

***Symbols.*** The exposure base column in the "Classification Table" uses certain symbols to indicate the applicable basis of premium. These symbols are:

| | |
|---|---|
| a—area | p—payroll |
| c—total cost | s—gross sales |
| m—admissions | u—units |

All other premium bases are spelled out in the classifications listing (there is a letter *t* referring the reader to the classification notes). The definitions of these premium bases appear in the coverage rules of Division Six—General Liability in the *CLM* and they are explained later in this chapter. All exposures are expressed on a per thousand basis unless otherwise indicated.

The symbol "+" or "†" next to the exposure base in the "Classification Table" listing indicates that products and/or completed operations coverage is included within the rate for premises-operations coverage at no additional charge.

***Definitions and Abbreviations.*** The explanatory rules also define certain words or abbreviations that have the same meaning whenever they appear in a classification description. These words and abbreviations are defined below.

*Including.* If the classification description contains this word, the operations so designated shall not be assigned to a separate classification even though such operations are described by another classification or are conducted at a separate location.

*NOC.* This abbreviation means not otherwise classified. An NOC classification applies only if no other classification more specifically describes the insured's business.

*NPD.* This abbreviation means no payroll division. In other words, the payroll may not be divided with another classification. Either that particular classification applies solely, or it does not apply at all. However, a classification so restricted may be used for division of payroll according to the following provisions:

- It constitutes a separate and distinct enterprise having no connection with the operations covered by any of the classifications specified in the restrictions.
- An unqualified NPD restriction shall not be used for division of payroll with any other classification unless it has no connection with the operations covered by any other classification in the policy.

For classifications applicable to construction or erection operations, these two provisions apply only to the operations composing each separate job or location.

*Distributor.* A distributor is a merchant or middleman who sells products mainly for resale or business use and who chiefly sells to dealers or stores, other merchants, and industrial, institutional, and commercial users.

*Dealer or Store.* These terms include all merchants or mercantile establishments who are not distributors and who sell products directly to the consumer.

**Classifications Listing.** Exhibit 7-4 shows a sample page from the classifications listing. The "Description" column alphabetically lists the classifications that describe the insured's operations or line of business. The wording is chosen to reflect concisely the operational activities in a manner intelligible to most users of the manual. It uses terms common to retailing, wholesaling, manufacturing, servicing, contracting, or professional business. Classification descriptions avoid highly technical terminology, which might obscure the applications of the classification.

In many instances, the wording parallels that used in the workers compensation manual. Cross-referencing the classification sections of the two manuals sometimes makes it easier to assign an insured the proper classification.

The first column under the heading "General Liability" shows the code number for each classification. The Commercial Lines Policy and Rating Simplification Project assigned new code numbers unique to each classification. The same classification and code number applies to

**Exhibit 7-4**
Classification Table Listing*

| DESCRIPTION | Fire and Allied Lines | Multiple Line | | | Conts. BP Fire or CPP Rate Group | General Liability | | Crime | | | For Company Use |
|---|---|---|---|---|---|---|---|---|---|---|---|
| | Class Code | CPP PMA | BP Class Code | BP Rate No. | | Class Code | Premium Base | Class Code | Rate Group | Class Limit | |
| Carpentry - construction of residential property not exceeding three stories in height | (1) | (1) | | NA | 2 | 91340 (2) | p | | * | | |
| Carpentry | (1)(3) | (1) (3) | | NA | 2 | 91342 NOC | p | | * | | |
| Carpentry - interior | (1) | (1) | | NA | 2 | 91341 (4) | p | | * | | |
| Carpentry - shop only | 3959 | IP | | NA | 2 | 91343 (5) | P | | * | | |
| Carpet or Rug Mfg. | (6) | (6) | | NA | 4 | 51777 | s | 2300 | 4 | 7,500 | |
| Carpet, Rug, Furniture or Upholstery Cleaning - on customers' premises | (7) | C,S | | NA | 2 | 91405 | p† | | NA | | |
| Carpet, Rug or Upholstery Cleaning - shop only | (8) | (8) | | NA | 6 | 11007 | s† | 7210 | 4 | 7,500 | |
| Catalog or Premium Coupon Redemption Stores | 0567 | M | 73905 | 6 | 2 | 11020 | s | | * | | |
| Caterers | 0542 | S | | NA | 7 | 11039 (9) | s | 5810 | 6 | 7,500 | |
| Caulking Compounds, Putty or Similar Products Mfg. | 5000 | IP | | NA | 2 | 51790 | s | 5230 | 1 | 3,000 | |

**Notes:**

(1) Contractors equipment storage, use code 0567 and CPP PMA C.
Equipment in the open, use code 1190 and CPP PMA C.
Office, use code 0702 and CPP PMA C or O.
Vehicle Storage or repair, refer to "Automobile" classifications.

(2) This classification includes construction of private garages in connection with such residential property.

(3) Carpentry shop, use code 3959 and CPP PMA IP.

(4) This classification includes the installation of doors, floors, windows, cabinets and hardwood or parquet flooring.

This classification is not applicable to contractors engaged in any other carpentry operations at the same job or location.

(5) The following shall be separately classifed and rated:

- lumberyards
- building material dealers
- Home Improvement stores.

(6) Use code 2800 and CPP PMA IP for carpet or rug manufacturing. Carpet sales, use code 0520 and CPP PMA M.

(7) For storage of cleaning equipment and supplies, use code 0567.

(8) Refer to "Laundries and Dry Cleaning" classifications.

(9) This classification applies to risks serving food away from the insured's premises only. Concessionaires selling beverages or food at exhibitions, parks, shows, sports contests or theaters and store operations shall be separately classified and rated.

**Exhibit 7-5**
Exposure Base Conversions*

| Major Business Group | New Uniform Exposure Base (Prem/Ops + Prod/Comp Ops) | Old Exposure Base Prem/ Ops | Prod/Comp Ops |
|---|---|---|---|
| Mercantile | Gross Sales | Area | Gross Sales |
| Manufacturing | Gross Sales | Payroll | Gross Sales |
| Contracting/Service | Payroll | Payroll | Gross Sales |
| Buildings/Premises | | | |
| —Apartments | Units | Area | N/A† |
| —Hotels | Gross Sales | Units | Gross Sales |
| —Offices | Area | Area | N/A† |
| —Lessors | Area | Area | N/A† |
| Miscellaneous | Various | Various | Various |

†Not Applicable



both premises-operations and products-completed operations coverage. These code numbers are arranged to reflect the five major business groups defined in the new *CLM*. Thus, the first digit of a code number always indicates the business group into which the classification falls as follows:

| *Business Group* | *Code Number* |
|---|---|
| Mercantile | 10000-19999 |
| Manufacturing/Processing | 50000-59999 |
| Contracting/Servicing | 90000-99999 |
| Buildings/Premises | 60000-69999 |
| Miscellaneous | 40000-49999 |

The second column under the heading "General Liability" contains symbols identifying the premium applicable for each classification. A *p* in this column, for example, indicates that the premium base used with this classification is payroll. Exhibit 7-5 shows the premium base for each of the above major business groups. Although not the case for any of the classifications shown in Exhibit 7-4, a *t* in the premium base column would mean that the premium base is explained in a footnote to that classification.

## Classification Procedures

Division Six—General Liability of the *CLM* states the rules for assigning classifications to insureds with general liability policies. Rules 25 and 26 present the general concepts of classification assignment and define the general classification inclusions and exclusions. Rules 27, 28, 29, 31, and 32 describe the classification procedures for the five major business groups.

General liability classification procedures closely resemble the workers compensation classification procedures. In both cases, the objective is to group like operations into the same rating classification. It is the business that is classified, not individual employments, occupations, or operations within a business. The underwriter must thus distinguish between single and multiple business operations. The *CLM* Division Six—General Liability rules stipulate how this is to be done in a uniform and consistent manner.

**Single and Multiple Business Operation.** The first rule in general liability classification procedures is to assign the *single* classification that best describes the insured's operations. This rule applies whenever the insured's operations normally comprise one type of business. For example, a rubber tire manufacturer may conduct the following operations: tire casing manufacturing, tire manufacturing, packaging, storage warehouse, and shipping. In addition, there may also be a maintenance department, a security force, groundkeepers, and a cafeteria. Several operations have nothing to do with manufacturing tires. Nevertheless, the total operation should be classified as "Tire Mfg.—auto, bus or truck" (Code 59750).

If the insured conducts two or more separate and distinct business operations or types of businesses, the total exposure may be divided between appropriate classifications. The previous version of the *CLM* listed specific guidelines to follow for payroll-rated risks in determining whether an additional classification might apply. The new *CLM* (under the Simplification Project) does not provide any specific guidelines in the general classification assignment section. It does provide some general guidelines in the more specific rules for classifying each of the major business groups.

**Classification Scope.** General liability classifications are designed to encompass the operations common to the specific business described. Certain incidental operations can be expected in a business; others present a profoundly different exposure that must be separately rated. Rule 26 defines the normal inclusions and exclusions for classifications in general. (Classification wording and footnotes take precedence over any general or coverage rules.)

***Included Operations and Hazards.*** Certain incidental operations are included within the scope of all classifications. These operations must not be separately classified *unless* they are conducted as separate and distinct enterprises. These operations are listed below. There are qualifications and exceptions to some of these operations, so the underwriter should consult the manual for a complete and accurate explanation of incidental operations.

- Advertising signs
- Athletic games
- Booths, exhibits, and other displays of the insured's merchandise
- Elevators and escalators
- Electronic games located on the insured's premises
- Greenhouses
- Maintenance, repair, or alteration of insured's buildings or equipment
- Medical facilities operated by the insured for employees
- Parking areas operated in connection with the insured's business
- Pickup and delivery
- Printing or lithographing
- Restaurants and commissaries
- Sale of used or second-hand goods
- Social gatherings
- Swimming pools or other athletic facilities not commercially operated
- Vending machines
- Workshops and workyards

***Excluded Operations and Hazards.*** Unless the classification footnotes state otherwise, the operations listed below do *not* come within the scope of other classifications and must be separately classified.

- Amusement centers
- Amusement devices (other than electronic games located on the insured's premises) or amusement parks
- Draft and saddle animals
- Machinery or equipment rented to others
- New construction or demolition operations
- Sawmill operations
- Stevedoring, including talliers or checking clerks
- Swimming pools or other athletic facilities if commercially operated
- Vehicles or carts from which goods are sold

**Manufacturing and Processing.** As indicated in Exhibit 7-6, specific classification procedures differ depending on the business group involved. Rule 27 states the classification rules for manufacturing and processing operations. The rates to be used are those of the territory where the products as classified are produced or assembled or where the processing as classified takes place. The three important principles involved in *classifying* manufacturing and processing operations are (1) separately classifying each named insured, (2) classifying by final product, not by component part or interim process, and (3) separately classifying and rating retail operations of the manufacturer selling its own products.

***Classifying by Named Insured.*** Each named insured listed in the declarations or subsequently endorsed should be independently classified. Named insureds are generally separate legal entities, and as such they may sue other named insureds. According to the commercial general liability coverage form, coverage applies "as if each Named Insured were the only Named Insured." Each named insured must thus be separately classified for an appropriate premium to be computed.

***Classifying by Final Product.*** Rule 27 also requires that the manufacturing of component parts or interim processes conducted by the named insured *not* be separately classified and rated. The value of any transfers of component parts or interim processes within the operations of the same named insured should thus not be included within gross sales. This is true only if such parts or processes are incorporated into a final product produced by the named insured *and* such component parts are normally manufactured by or the interim processes are normally conducted by similar businesses in producing that type of product. Thus, in such cases it is the final product that is classified.

The proper classification is the one that best describes the *intended use* of the insured's products or operations. This is so because two products can be similarly constructed, yet because of the way one is used, it carries a significantly greater potential for loss than the other. For instance, assume that a manufacturer produces a range of paper filters, some intended for use in the pharmaceutical industry, and others intended for use in home coffee makers. Clearly, the failure of a filter in a pharmaceutical application has a much greater loss potential, say, resulting from the contamination of prescription drugs, than does the failure of a coffee filter. Classifying the final product by use in this case allows the insurer to charge a premium that most appropriately reflects the extent of the exposure, or, in other words, the loss potential as measured in dollars. This classification by intended use applies separately to each named insured. Divisions or departments of a single named insured are not separately classified even if they are all located

**Exhibit 7-6**
How To Classify a Risk*

1. Determine the insured's business occupation (from application).

2. Check classification:
—Inclusions
—Exclusions
—Specific Classification Footnotes to determine whether additional classifications are necessary.

3. For Manufacturing risks:

—Classify by final product/process, not by component part or interim process. (For example, if the insured makes parts for a motorcycle in separate plants, incorporating these parts into the motorcycle, classify as a motorcycle mfg., rather than as seats, engines, etc., mfg.)

—Separately classify each named insured. (Each insured is a separate entity and may be sued as such. If, however, the policy is amended to exclude inter-company suits, it is *not* necessary to separately classify each named insured and gross sales between named insureds should not be included.)

3. For Contracting risks:

—If one classification description covers the operation, use it.

—If there is more than one operation, determine whether these similar separate operations are customarily part of the overall operation; if not, classify separately. (For example, in dam construction, ditchdigging should not be classified separately if ditchdigging operations are commonly performed by dam construction contractors.)

—If no one classification fits, classify every separate operation within the contracting operation separately. (For example, in building construction, separately classify and rate each operation [carpentry, electrical, concrete construction, etc.])

3. For Mercantile risks:

—Classify by the type of goods sold.

—Determine whether insured is a dealer or distributor in accordance with the definition.

—For combined dealer/distributor operations, use classification of higher-rate operation unless separate records for each operation are kept.

3. For Building/Premises risks:

—If owned and completely occupied by insured, classify according to occupancy.

—If owned and partially occupied by insured, classify portion occupied by insured according to occupancy, and remainder as lessor's risk.

—If owned or sublet but not occupied by insured, classify under appropriate lessor's risk classification.

—If occupied but not owned by insured, classify according to occupancy.

*Copyright, Insurance Services Office, 1985. Reprinted with permission.

in different states and even if these are classifications that describe the final products of each of the divisions.

***Classifying the Retail Operations of a Manufacturer.*** If the named insured is a manufacturer that sells its products through its own retail operations, the retail operations should be classified and rated apart from the manufacturing operations. The retail operations would be classified and rated according to the rules for mercantile risks (Rule 29). The retail and the manufacturing exposures are different, and a premium should be collected for each. In such cases, the wholesale value of the goods transferred to the retail operation should be the amount included within gross sales.

***Multiple Classifications.*** Multiple classifications other than the retailing/manufacturing classification described above may also apply to a manufacturer provided the rules regarding classification by named insured and classification by final product are observed. Suppose, for example, that Acme Motorcycle Company has a subsidiary, Acme Engine Company, and that both entities are named insureds. Acme Engine Company not only supplies motorcycle engines to Acme Motorcycle Company, but also sells them to other manufacturers. In this case, two classifications apply to Acme Engine Company:

- Engines sold to others: "Engine or Turbine Mfg.—Not aircraft—NOC" (Code 52619)
- Engines sold to Acme Motorcycle Company: "Motorcycle, Moped or Motor Scooter Mfg." (Code 57202).

Code 52619 applied in addition to the motorcycle manufacturing class because the engines are considered final products when sold to outside businesses.

***Special Classification Inclusions and Exclusion.*** In addition to the classification inclusions and exclusions listed earlier, the following special classification inclusions and exclusion also apply to manufacturers and processors.

*Special Inclusions.* Special classification inclusions (that is, such operations should not be separately classified and rated) for manufacturers are as follows:

- *Manufacturing of containers* such as bags, barrels, bottles, boxes, cans, cartons, or packing cases unless sold to others, including other named insureds. Manufacturing containers for the insured's own products is considered incidental to the product manufacturing.

- *Installation, servicing, or repair of the named insured's products.* This special inclusion applies even when the installation or servicing does not normally prevail in this business. This inclusion is an important exception to the principle of separately classifying distinct operations. However, if a separately named insured listed on the policy does the installation and servicing or if products other than those manufactured by the insured are installed, separate classifications would apply.

*Special Exclusion.* The special classification exclusion (that is, such operations should be separately classified and rated) for manufacturers is *office operations* located away from the premises where the insured's manufacturing, processing, or assembling operations are conducted. Any location or premises operated by a manufacturer used solely for an office should be separately classified.

**Contracting or Servicing.** Rule 28 stipulates the procedures for classifying contracting or servicing risks. In general, if the risk has a single operation or a number of separate operations that normally prevail in the business described by a single classification, then the single manual classification that best describes the single enterprise applies. If these separate operations do not normally prevail in a business described by a single classification, each operation is separately classified and rated.

***Separate Classifications.*** Because most construction operations depend on or involve other related operations, they are, by nature, performed in physical proximity to one another and involve some interchange of labor. Even so, Rule 28 requires the insured's payroll to be divided among the separate classifications that apply at each job or location provided that the insured's payroll records reflect this division. The rates that are applicable in the territory where the job is located should be used.

However, any particular part of an operation that could be otherwise classified may not be separately classified if it is an integral part, which is normal and usual, of the total operation. For example, "Concrete Construction" (Code 91560) includes making, setting up, and taking down concrete forms. Therefore, a carpenter involved with the construction of forms would be classified under Code 91560, rather than a carpentry code.

Any operation for which separate payroll records are not maintained shall be assigned to the highest rated classification applicable to the job or location. The insured's records must show a breakdown in payroll among the applicable classifications; otherwise, all of the payroll must be assigned to the highest rated classification of operations to which the employee is exposed. The payroll division must be in terms of dollars and not hours. Estimates or percentage splits should not be used.

At a job site, there may be employees performing various functions related to the entire job. Such *miscellaneous employees* include job superintendents, timekeepers or watchmen, workers performing general cleanup or snow removal, and performing similar incidental tasks. Miscellaneous employees should be assigned to the classification carrying the largest amount of payroll at a job or location during the policy period. This is the classification with the largest payroll, not the one with the highest rate.

There is sometimes confusion between miscellaneous employees and labor interchange. *Labor interchange* refers to employees involved in work that falls into several classifications, but not the overall job. Their payroll is assigned to the highest rated classification if no breakdown is provided.

If an employee's work involves more than one classification with different exposure bases, the entire payroll of such employees should be assigned to the classification where payroll is the exposure base. For example, an employee might normally work at a plumbing supply store (mercantile risk). Under normal circumstances, the exposure base used to measure the store's exposure would be gross sales. However, if the employee's work also includes installation or repair activities not related to the goods sold from the store, it can be established that part of this work is of a contracting nature, which carries a different exposure base—payroll. While the store or shop operation could be separately classified, the installation classification will include the entire payroll of the above employee. If a construction or servicing operation has any incidental drafting employees who are exposed to any operative hazard of the business, their entire payroll should be assigned to the highest rated classification of the operations to which they are exposed.

***Special Classification Exclusions.*** In addition to the general classification exclusions, the following operations must be separately classified:

- *Blasting operations* performed by the insured should be separately classified as "Blasting Operations" (Code 91210).
- *Restaurant or commissary operations* in connection with construction, erection, lumbering, or mining operations.

***Subcontracted Work.*** Contractors often hire subcontractors to perform a portion of a project. When a subcontractor is hired to perform a *construction* operation, that operation must be separately classified. The presence of subcontractors on a construction site creates additional hazards. For this reason, the subcontractors must be separately classified and the appropriate premium developed. The rates that correspond to the "Contractor-subcontracted work" classification do not anticipate that coverage will be extended to the subcontractor. It only reflects the increase in the insured contractor's exposure. The subcontractors must still purchase their own CGL policy to cover losses for which they are held responsible.

The classification of subcontracted operations involved in construction depends upon two major factors, type of work performed and adequate insurance.

*Type of Work Performed.* If a subcontractor is adequately insured, the type of construction work the general contractor performs on any given project determines the classification. The possible classifications appear in the "Classification Table" under the heading "Contractors-subcontracted work." The basis of premium for these classifications is the total cost of the work.

*Adequate Insurance.* Each of the possible classifications referred to in the preceding paragraph carries the following important footnote:

> This classification applies to that portion of the operations performed by adequately insured subcontractors of the insured. Operations performed by subcontractors without adequate insurance shall be classified and rated under the specific classification description for each operation.[2]

There is a question as to exactly what "adequately insured subcontractor" means. The term has been interpreted in several ways including the following:

- The subcontractor carries limits of insurance equal to or greater than the limits of insurance of the contractor (probably the most widely used definition).
- The subcontractor carries limits of insurance at least equal to some amount, which is specified by each insurer.
- The subcontractor carries the limits as specified by the contractor.
- The subcontractor carries some combination of the above as specified by the contractor, but in no case less than a certain amount.

In view of both the confusion regarding the terminology and the fact that the *CLM* uses the term, an ad hoc committee of ISO addressed the problem. The committee agreed that any uniform definition would have the following problems:

- Difficult to develop
- Discriminatory against some subcontractors
- Intrusive to the operations of certain companies
- Not reflective of differences in exposures from one risk to another

In view of these conclusions, the committee decided not to establish a uniform definition of "adequately insured."[3] Underwriters should know what their company's interpretation of the term "adequately insured" is. In many cases, a substantial difference in premium could result from different interpretations. The definition used by the insurer should be explained to the insured at the beginning of the policy period.

When there is no insurance or it is not adequate, the subcontractor must be assigned to the specific classification that describes the operation performed. In other words, subcontractors with inadequate insurance are to be classified as though they were employees.

The *CLM* does not explicitly define what amount should be included for inadequately insured subcontractors assigned to the payroll-based classifications. In lieu of a specific company interpretation, the subcontractor rule in the NCCI workers compensation *Basic Manual* could be used.

**Mercantile.** Rule 29 describes specific procedures for classifying stores or other mercantile operations. Mercantile classifications are rated on a gross sales basis and use the rates applicable in the territory for each location of the insured's operations.

***Store Classifications.*** Stores vary considerably in the particular goods they carry. Some judgment may thus be necessary in applying the rules that *stores are to be assigned to the store classification that best fits the operation.*

When the insured is a combined dealer and distributor, it is assigned to the higher rated classification unless separate records for each type of operation are maintained. Assigning both a dealer and a distributor code requires that the insured's records clearly show a separation in the sales between the two operations. An estimate or percentage allocation should not be accepted.

***Special Classification Inclusion.*** Unless specified in a classification footnote, installing, servicing, and repairing merchandise sold by the insured need not be separately classified. For example, a carpet store usually installs the carpets it sells. A separate classification for carpet installation should *not* be added even though that classification exists. The installation of the carpet obviously creates some exposure for the insured for which the insurer desires some premium. The premium is generated in a somewhat roundabout way. The premium base for mercantile risks is gross sales. If a merchant does install, service, or repair its carpets, there is a cost involved. Most merchants will charge more for their carpet rather than absorb this additional cost. By charging more, gross sales are increased, thus increasing the premium.

**Building or Premises.** Rule 31 applies to offices, residences, or space leased to others. Classifying such premises depends on the ownership or occupancy of the building or premises since differences in ownership and uses of the property create differences in the exposure to loss.

***Classifications Rated on a Units Basis.*** Apartments, residential condominiums, and similar buildings are rated on a units basis. If the entire building is used for residential purposes, it is only necessary to find the single appropriate classification and to count the number of units. This is true regardless of whether the building or premises is owned, occupied, or operated by the insured or someone else. The portion of the premises rented to others that is not rated on a units basis must be separately classified and rated under one of the "lessor's risk only" classifications. If the owner of the building operates a business enterprise that is not residential and that business occupies a portion of the building not rated on a units basis, that portion of the premises must be separately rated and classified based on the operation being performed.

***Classifications Rated on an Area Basis.*** Some buildings or premises are rated on an area basis. Classification then depends on whether the insured owns the building and the extent to which the insured occupies the building.

*Owned, and Entirely Occupied, by the Insured.* If the insured owns and entirely occupies the building or premises, the nature of the occupancy determines the classification. For example, a building owned by a group of physicians and containing their offices only would be classified as "Medical Offices" (Code 66561).

*Owned, and Partially Occupied, by the Insured.* The classification for any portion of the premises occupied by the insured is based on that occupancy, as described above. If the insured occupies 90 percent or more of the premises, that classification applies to the entire premises. If the insured occupies less than 90 percent of the premises the remainder should be classified according to the appropriate "lessor's risk only" classifications. Thus, if the physicians in the previous example rent more than 10 percent of their building to an accountant, an additional classification "Building or Premises—bank or office—mercantile or manufacturing (lessor's risk only)" (Code 61211) applies.

*Owned or Sublet, but Not Occupied, by the Insured.* If the insured does not occupy the building, a "lessor's risk only" classification applies to the entire building or premises. Separate classifications apply depending on whether or not the insured is responsible for building maintenance. Thus, if the physicians moved out and rented their entire building to lawyers and accountants, the proper classification of their entire building would again be Code 61211 for the *physicians'* general liability insurance.

*Occupied, but Not Owned, by the Insured.* If the insured occupies, but does not own, the building or premises, the classification is based on the occupancy. Thus, if the group of physicians in the previous example rented space in an office building, the appropriate classification for their offices would be "Medical Offices" (Code 66561).

**Miscellaneous.** Rule 32 assists in determining the proper classification of an insured that does not clearly fall into a specific category. As with the other business groups, the classification that best describes the insured's operations should be used. The premium base for that classification is the one that will be used. The classification rules to be used with miscellaneous classifications depend on the premium base for the classification selected.

| *Premium Base* | *Classification Rule* |
|---|---|
| Gross sales | Rule 29—Mercantile risks |
| Payroll | Rule 28—Contracting or servicing risks |
| Area | Rule 31—Building or premises |
| Other (such as professional associations) | See the footnotes for the class for premium base and rating instructions |

## PREMIUM (EXPOSURE) BASES FOR GENERAL LIABILITY

One objective of the commercial lines simplification project was to establish a uniform exposure base and classification for both premises-operations and products-completed operations coverage. While initially more (or at least different) information may have to be gathered to classify and rate a risk with these coverages, the effect of the change should in the long run reduce the overall amount of information-gathering. For example, before the simplification project, the operations class may have been based on payroll, and the completed operations class (which may not necessarily have the same classification wording or code) may have been based on receipts. As a result of the project, there will be the same class and class code for both of these coverages. The new rating base will either be gross sales (which, for practical purposes, is synonymous with receipts) or payroll.

Another objective of the commercial lines simplification project was to employ inflation-sensitive exposure bases when practical. Such bases would measure the exposure in dollars so that a change in the value of the dollar would not require the insurer to adjust rates. Instead, the change in the value of the dollar would be built into the exposure base, and the premium would change accordingly. For example, a number of classes previously rated on the basis of area will now be rated on the basis of payroll or gross sales (both of which respond to inflation). Exhibit 7-5, shown earlier, illustrates the exposure base conversions involved in the new rating structure.

The importance of an inflation-sensitive rating base should not be overlooked, especially in this period of intense public attention to the cost of insurance. An inflation-sensitive rating base relieves at least some of the pressure for rate increases.

To illustrate, assume a risk is rated on the basis of area and has a building of 200,000 square feet. Since the rates are stated per 1,000 square feet, this risk has 200 exposure units. For simplicity's sake, assume a rate of $15. This risk would thus produce a premium of $3,000. This $3,000 in premium would remain constant year after year until the insurer requests a rate increase. The number of exposure units will not change.

Wages, however, are likely to increase each year because of inflation. Because wages enter into the cost of general liability claims (for example, the injured third party has to miss a month of work for which he or she expects to be reimbursed), the insurer's loss costs will increase. Because the exposure base, area, is not sensitive to inflation, premiums will not increase. As a result, the insurer finds its coverage for this classification to be underpriced. Assume that solely because of this increase in wages, the coverage is underpriced by 20 percent. Therefore, the insurer must request a rate increase from $15 to $18, making the total premium $3,600.

Assume, on the other hand, that the rating base for this risk is payroll, an inflation-sensitive base. If the insured has $200,000 in payroll, there are also 200 exposure units. A rate of $15 therefore produces the same initial premium of $3,000. This payroll figure does not remain constant from year to year. It increases with inflation just as the wages of the potential claimants increase from year to year. Thus, if wages in general are increasing, it is likely that the insured's payroll would have also increased. Ideally, it would have increased 20 percent to $240,000, and the premium would now be 240 exposure units times a rate of $15, or $3,600.

In both cases, the insured is now paying $3,600. In order to increase the premium in the first case, however, the insurer must file for a rate increase and get that approved. Assuming the full increase is granted, which is by no means a given, the insured sees his or her rate being increased by 20 percent. This is a possible cause for the insured to change insurers. In the second scenario, the insurer does not have to request a rate increase, and the insured sees the insurer charging the same rate. The only item responsible for the rate increase is the increase in the insured's payroll, a factor the insured is not likely to question. Although the result is the same in both cases, the increase in premium as described in the second scenario is much easier for insureds to understand and accept, especially if the insured has had no losses.

A more detailed discussion of premium bases is presented in the following seven sections. This discussion is based on the definition of premium bases and the exposure units for each as found in the *Commercial Lines Manual*, Division Six—General Liability, Rule 24.

## Admissions

A major potential source of liability facing theaters, stadiums, and owners of related operations open to the public is the possibility of harm to a spectator. This exposure is the same regardless of ticket price. Policies covering such operations may therefore be written with the premium based not on the cost of admissions, but on the number of admissions.

According to the *Commercial Lines Manual*, admissions means "the total number of persons, other than employees of the named insured, admitted to the event insured or to events conducted on the premises whether on paid admissions, tickets, complimentary tickets or passes." When admissions is used as a premium base, the manual shows the rates per 1,000 admissions.

Most theaters keep a ticket count as a check on dollar amounts received. Each ticket has a number on it, and the tickets are dispensed sequentially. As a result, the difference between the number on the first ticket sold on a given day and the number on the last ticket sold that day tells how many people were admitted to the theater. This number can be compared to cash receipts to verify the total cash sales for that day. Complimentary admissions must be added to the total number of admissions.

## Area

Manual rates apply per 1,000 square feet of area. Area is one of the oldest units used to measure public liability exposures for insurance purposes. This is probably because the physical existence of a building or property occupies a measurable space. It is difficult to dispute the reality of the property area; consequently, it has been one of the bulwarks of coverage and exposure determination.

The extent of some liability exposures depends on the size of the premises. For offices and lessors, the chances of a person slipping on a wet floor and sustaining an injury, for example, are increased when the floor space is larger. Thus, area provides a suitable premium base in such cases.

The *Commercial Lines Manual* defines area as "the total number of square feet of floor space at the insured premises." For entire buildings, the manual specifies that the area is determined "by multiplying the product of the horizontal dimensions of the outside of the outer building walls by the number of floors, including basements." However, it should exclude the area of (1) courts and mezzanine-type of floor openings and (2) portions of basements or floors where 50 percent or more of the area is used as a shop or as storage for building maintenance, for dwelling by building maintenance employees, or housing for heating units, power plants or air-conditioning equipment. The area of premises used for storage or for purposes other than public events should not be excluded from a computation of the exposure base. Nor should premises occupied by concessionaires be excluded. The method used to determine the area for the entire building is also used to determine the area occupied by tenants.

Loss control reports are often used to check the square footage reported on an application for coverage. The underwriter should know of any alterations to the insured's premises that may change the area. In addition, it is not always prudent to transfer the square footage from an expiring policy to a new policy. In addition to premises changes the insured may have made, there is the risk of carrying forward a typographical error made that may never have been discovered.

The illustration in Exhibit 7-7 shows a three-story building that may require a loss control representative to measure the area to verify the premium base. The first floor dimensions are 160 feet long by 80 feet wide—multiplying the horizontal dimension of one outside wall by that of the other outside wall, 160 feet × 80 feet = 12,800 square feet. Since there are three floors, the total for the building is 3 × 12,800 square feet = 38,400 square feet. The basement area houses the furnace and maintenance facilities and thus is not included in the computation. A light-well of open-court design pierces the top floor; it has an area of 1,600 square feet (40 feet × 40 feet). In compliance with the manual definition, the area of that open space court should be deducted from the total area. The total for the three floors is calculated as 38,400 square feet − 1,600 square feet = 36,800 square feet. Thus,

**Exhibit 7-7**
Illustration of Area Measurement

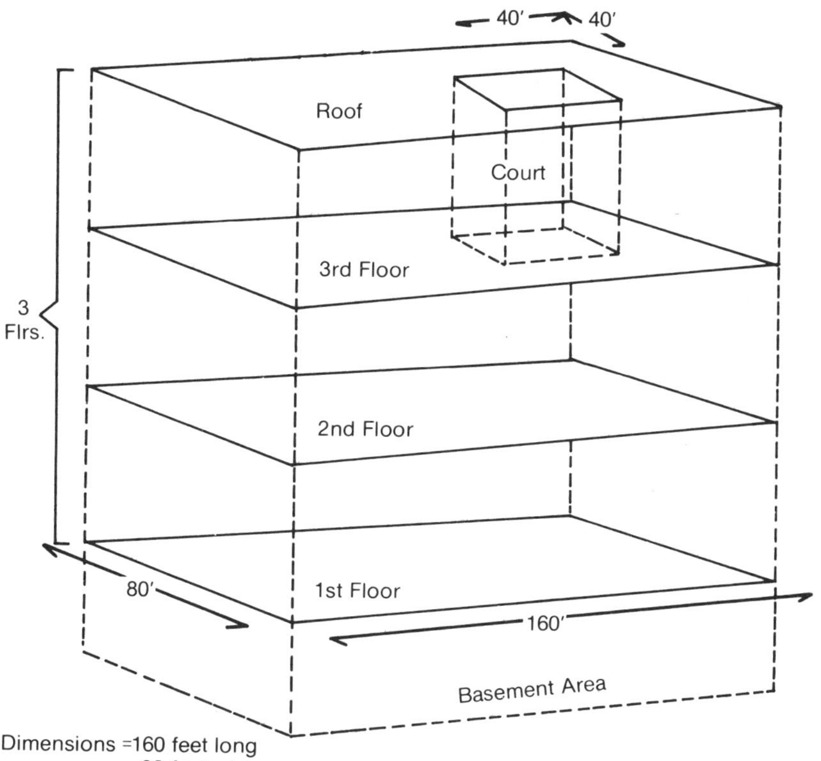


Dimensions =160 feet long
80 feet wide
Three stories tall with full basement
Open Court Light-Well = 1600 square feet
Basement area = 12,800 square feet

in this example the chargeable area for determining the amount of premium is 36,800 square feet.

## Each

On occasion, a more convenient measure than area may be the actual number of some commodity that is part of the insured's business. When such a measure is used, the classification footnotes in the *Commercial Lines Manual* indicate and define the unit. In these cases, rates may be stated per 100 tons, per 10,000 fillings, or per 1,000,000 gallons, to cite some commodity-related units.

In most cases, it is fairly easy to determine the proper number of units that should be used in computing the premium base, such as the number of members in a fraternal organization, for which the premium base is people. Other units for other premium bases may present more of a challenge. For example, premiums for camps are based on "each camper day." If the insured does not have adequate records to determine the number of camper days, camper days must be reconstructed from other records such as receipts or lot allocations. The premium auditor can help the underwriter when the premium base is difficult to determine.

## Gross Sales

When the exposure varies according to the volume of business, gross sales may be the best measure of the exposure and thus the best premium base. Sales usually reflect the exposure assumed under other coverages as well. Premises liability is partly a function of the premises area, but a store generally needs more area to increase its sales since the additional space allows it to carry more of a current product or to introduce additional products. Moreover, gross sales may be a better measure than area of the products exposure because it reflects the number of customers actually entering the store and purchasing products—and the more people who do so, the greater is the chance that someone will be accidentally injured. Rates are stated per $1,000 of gross sales.

The *Commercial Lines Manual* defines gross sales as the gross amount of money charged by the named insured, by the concessionaires of the named insured, or by others trading under the insured's name for the following:

- All goods or products, sold or distributed
- Operations performed during the policy period
- Rentals

In accounting terminology, gross sales includes the financial transaction occurring when a buyer and a seller agree on the sale of a product. In contrast, receipts is the cash received by the seller from the buyer. Receipts is rarely identical to gross sales because of deductions for returns and allowances, cash discounts for prompt payment, or uncollectible accounts.

**Inclusions.** The insured's sales accounts may show a reduction in profits from the sale of merchandise, but this should not necessarily be interpreted as a reduction in the liability exposure. The premium base should include the full sales price even if the insured does not collect the full amount. According to the *CLM,* the following items shall *not* be deducted from gross sales in determining liability premiums:

- Foreign exchange discounts
- Freight allowance to customers
- Total sales of consigned goods and warehouse receipts
- Trade or cash discounts
- Bad debts
- Repossession of items sold on installments (amount actually collected)

**Exclusions.** Items that may be excluded, or deducted, from gross sales include the following:

- Sales or excise taxes that are collected and submitted to a government division
- Credits for repossessed merchandise and products returned; allowances for damaged and spoiled goods
- Finance charges for items sold on installments
- Freight charges on sales if freight is charged as a separate item on customer's invoice
- Royalty income from patent rights or copyrights that are not product sales

**Foreign Sales.** According to the coverage form definition, *coverage territory* means the following:

a. The United States of America (including its territories and possessions), Puerto Rico and Canada;
b. International waters or airspace, provided the injury or damage does not occur in the course of travel or transportation to or from any place not included in a. above; or
c. All parts of the world if:
   (1) The injury or damage arises out of:
      (a) Goods or products made or sold by you in the territory described in a. above; or
      (b) The activities of a person whose home is in the territory described in a. above, but is away for a short time on your business; and
   (2) The insured's responsibility to pay damages is determined in a "suit" on the merits, in the territory described in a. above or in a settlement we agree to.

This definition eliminates the previous distinction between foreign and domestic sales by redefining coverage territory. All sales should thus be included in the premium base. Foreign exchange losses are not deductible from the sales and are to be included in determining the premium charged for products liability insurance.

Some insurance companies (and their policies) differ in their interpretation of whether or not foreign goods should be included in the exposure base. There are some specialty insurers who provide separate policies that cover only foreign sales. If this type of policy is used, it is probable that foreign sales will be excluded from the gross sales as the premium base for the primary (standard) policy. Underwriters should be certain about how their company interprets the definition of coverage territory as it relates to foreign sales.

**Intercompany Sales.** Insurance companies differ in their view of intercompany sales as related to gross sales. It is ISO's intent to include intercompany sales in gross sales. The commercial general liability policy does provide cross-liability coverage—coverage applies whether or not intercompany sales are shown as part of the premium base. However, this interpretation is not a hard-and-fast rule. In each insurance company, those responsible for developing the underwriting policy have the freedom to decide whether or not to include intercompany sales as part of the gross sales premium base. Some insurers feel that such transactions should be excluded from premium base computations. Other insurers feel that each entity on a policy should be separately rated and charged, including intercompany sales.

Intercompany sales is the exchange of goods between two or more separate legal entities who are named insureds on the same policy. Such sales are usually between a manufacturer or processor and its supplier(s). A manufacturer may require a specific item to complete its product. It may create a new manufacturer or absorb another manufacturer to produce this specific item. Both manufacturers may be shown as named insureds on the same policy. Sales volume of either manufacturer to entities *other than* those named on the policy as "named insureds" are obviously included for products coverage. It is the internal flow of goods that complicates the question of including the sales volume of these goods in gross sales.

Underwriters sometimes try to answer this question according to whether or not the goods exchanged on an intercompany basis are included in the products liability coverage. If coverage applies, it would seem logical to include intercompany sales in the premium base since the premium should reflect the coverage provided. However, answering this question becomes more difficult in light of the definition of the products-completed operations exposure, the category in which the product or operations generating intercompany sales would be included for coverage. The definition of the exposure assumes that liability is, in part, a function of the product having left the insured's premises or of the insured having completed work away from its premises. In intercompany sales, the product never really leaves the premises in the sense that premises as defined in the policy includes the premises of both named insureds, both companies in this case, even if those premises are geographically separate. Therefore, if liability depends on a product leaving the insured's premises, and the product cannot, by definition, leave the premises, then there can be no liability generated by this product. It follows that there is no need to purchase liability coverage for products sold on an intercompany basis. Therefore, if premium is a function of coverage, and coverage is not needed for intercompany sales, then such sales should not be included in the premium base.

The relationship between organizations engaged in intercompany sales should also be considered as a basis for answering the questions of whether or not to include intercompany sales in the gross sales premium base. This relationship can be used to argue for excluding intercompany sales from the gross sales premium base. For instance, corporations have the right to sue other corporations. However, wholly owned subsidiaries are not likely to sue (nor are they likely to be sued by) the parent company. In fact, the possibility of a lawsuit is even less if the parent company depends on the subsidiary to manufacture a component part used in equipment that the parent will sell to another organization. Because a lawsuit is highly unlikely, that is, because products liability may never be an issue between these two companies, there is no reason for the liability insurance of either organization to provide products liability coverage for goods sold on an intercompany basis. Therefore, if there is no need for the coverage, and if premium is a function of coverage, then intercompany sales should not be included in the gross sales premium base.

On the other hand, arguments for including intercompany sales hold that there may be claim situations between named insureds on the same policy. These situations and their assumed severity proceed from the *separation of insureds condition* which states that, except with respect to the limits of liability, the insurance applies "as if each Named Insured were the only Named Insured; and separately to each insured against whom claim is made or 'suit' is brought." Thus, each named insured should be treated as separate in *all* aspects if the policy provides for severability of interests. Under this clause, the opportunity is provided for each named insured to sue the other as if they were totally unrelated and insured by separate policies. The fact that such suits are not likely is irrelevant—what matters is that they are possible.

The possibility of intercompany suits indicates a need for the insurer to secure premium that reflects this possibility. The aforementioned separation of insureds condition argues for the inclusion of intercompany sales. Despite the fact that convincing arguments can be made for including or excluding intercompany sales, it should be recognized that under Rule 27 for the classification assignment and premium computation of manufacturing and processing risks, Rule 27.B.2.a specifically states that one should "include all sales of goods or products from one company to another including sales from one named insured to another." This leaves little room for interpretation.

In addition, there is an endorsement (CG 21 41) available from ISO that excludes coverage for intercompany *products liability* suits. This would imply that the coverage (and exposure) is otherwise there. The intercompany sales amount should thus be included in the premium base for both premises-operations and products-completed operations. If the exclusion endorsement is attached, the gross sales premium base for the premise-operations exposure would still include the intercompany sales figure since the endorsement applies only to products-completed operation suits. The products-completed operations premium base would differ in this case from the premises-operations premium base by an amount equal to intercompany sales.

## Payroll

Payroll serves as the premium base for contracting or servicing operations, for which it provides a good measure of the exposure. Payroll is also advantageous because it does not require additional, burdensome record keeping by the insured since such records are already required for other purposes. Payroll also reflects the degree of direct control over operations. Employees are involved in most of those activities that create potential liability.

Since payroll also serves as the premium base for workers compensation insurance, the underwriter's task is simplified if he or she writes workers compensation as well as liability insurance. *The definitions of payroll are now identical.* The liability inclusions are also identical to the workers compensation inclusions with the exception of the addition of payroll for mobile equipment operations, reference to executive officers, partners and individual insureds, and fees paid to employment agencies for temporary personnel. Exclusions are also identical except for the additional exclusions of standard exception classifications, aircraft pilots and co-pilots, and the separate classification of draftsmen.

**Inclusions.** The specific items included as payroll according to the *Commercial Lines Manual* are listed below.

- Commissions
- Bonuses

- Extra pay for overtime work (except as provided in Rule 24.E.4)
- Wages for holidays, vacations, or paid sick days
- Statutory insurance or pension plans
- Wages paid on a basis other than hours worked as for piecework or under incentive or profit-sharing plans
- Payments or allowances to employees for hand or power tools furnished by them
- Rental value of an apartment or house provided
- Value of lodging other than apartment or house
- Value of meals
- Value of certificates or merchandise
- Payroll of mobile equipment operators and their helpers whether or not the operators are designated or licensed to operate automobiles (This item is handled differently under workers compensation.)
- Payroll of executive officers, individual insureds, and copartners (This item is handled differently under workers compensation.)
- Fees paid to employment agencies for temporary personnel provided to the insured (This item is handled differently under workers compensation.)

**Exclusions.** According to the *Commercial Lines Manual,* payroll does *not* include the following items.

- Tips and other gratuities
- Voluntary payments by the insured on behalf of the employees to a group insurance or pension plan
- Rewards for invention or discovery
- Dismissal or severance payments except for time worked or accrued vacation
- Payroll of clerical office employees (This item is handled differently under workers compensation.)
- Payroll of salesmen, collectors, or messengers who work principally away from the insured's premises (This item is handled differently under workers compensation.)
- Payroll of drivers and their helpers if their principal duties are to work on or in connection with automobiles (This item is handled differently under workers compensation.)
- Payroll of aircraft pilots or co-pilots if their principal duties are to work on or in connection with aircraft in either capacity (This item is handled differently under workers compensation.)
- Payroll of draftsmen (This item is handled differently under workers compensation.)

**Estimating the Payroll.** In most cases for new business, the underwriter uses the payroll estimate provided by the insured as the estimated payroll to be shown on the policy. The underwriter should at least verify the accuracy of that estimate. The underwriter will usually ask to see the estimate on the expiring policy or perhaps on the most recent audit statement. It is unfortunate that the most recent complete year audit will be almost a year old because the audit for the expiring policy will not be conducted until after that policy has expired. By that time, the underwriter must have already made the decision regarding the reported estimated payroll amount.

If the insured's estimate seems low, the underwriter may issue the policy using that estimate but with the understanding that the underwriter will be given a copy of the final audit on the expiring policy. If that final audit seems to indicate that the insured's estimate is, in fact, low, the underwriter will endorse the current policy so that the insurer will receive a more adequate deposit premium. In addition, the underwriter will usually watch closely any interim audits as an additional check on the estimate.[4] The underwriter never wants to be in a position where the insured is purposely underestimating the exposure base in order to reduce the initial premium, providing a more favorable cash flow. Too often insurers find that the insured is unable to pay the large additional premium that is due when the final audit is completed.

### Total Cost

The *Commercial Lines Manual* defines total cost as a premium base as the total cost of all work let or sublet in connection with each specific project including the cost of all labor, materials, and equipment furnished, used, or delivered for use in the execution of the work; and all fees, bonuses or commissions made, paid, or due. The manual rates are stated per $1,000 of total cost.

### Units

This premium base is simply a count of exposures, such as apartment units. It is normally used with dwelling classifications. The manual defines a unit as a single room or group of rooms intended for occupancy as separate living quarters by a family, by a group of unrelated persons living together, or by a person living alone.

## PREMIUM DETERMINATION

As for other kinds of insurance, the premium for a commercial general liability policy is found by multiplying the applicable rate by the measured exposure. The premium computation, however, must also be adjusted for premium modifications and the application of minimum premiums. The new *CLM* contains a Premium Determination Rule, Rule 35, which gives step-by-step instructions for premium computation. Exhibit 7-8 summarizes the Premium Determination Rule. The first two steps in this process regarding determining the appropriate classification and premium base have already been described.

## Rates

Rates that have been filed and approved for use in a particular state may be found in the manual. These are the basic limits rates, which may need to be adjusted for coverage changes on a particular policy, increased limits, or deductibles.

**Basic Limits Rates.** Rates appear on the State Rate Pages opposite the identifying code numbers of the classifications. Next to the classification code numbers are the basic limits rates for general liability coverage. There are separate rate pages for claims-made and for occurrence coverage. Rates are shown for both premises-operations and products-completed operations. In some cases the premises-operations rates may be broken down by territory. A copy of a state rate page is shown in Exhibit 7-9.

The rates on the state rate pages apply to the premium base indicated for the classification in the "Classification Table." The premium base listed next to any particular classification in the "Classification Table" must be used.

If the symbol (a) appears on the rate pages instead of a specific rate, then that classification is *(a) rated.* This symbol means that such classifications are to be specially rated by the underwriter. These (a) rated classifications usually describe operations with unique characteristics or for which there is little statistical experience. The underwriter attempts to base rates for such unusual exposures on the experience of an analogous classification. The rate for a similar operation may be used, or another rate assigned, at the underwriter's discretion.

In some cases, ISO separately furnishes *guide (a) rates* for (a) rated classifications for use by underwriting executives. These are to serve only as a *guide* and are not treated as if they were manual rates. These guide (a) rates in conjunction with the experience of analogous entities or classifications may suggest appropriate rates or modifying factors related to the exposure, simplifying the determination of the applicable rate. In many cases the guide (a) rates are stated as a range of possible rates.

**Exhibit 7-8**
Rule 35: The Premium Determination Rule*

| | |
|---|---|
| A. Determine the applicable classification | —Determine the insured's business operation and find an appropriate classification. You will be using only one classification for both premises/operations and products/completed operations.<br>—Use the Classification Table to determine the code number.<br>—Check the classification footnotes to determine whether any operations need to be separately classified and rated. Multiple classifications may be necessary when footnotes indicate that certain operations need to be separately classified. |
| B. Determine the premium base applicable to the classification(s). Use the premium base column in the Classification Table. The same premium base applies to both premises/operations and products/completed operations. | |
| C. Select the basic limits rate(s) for the classification(s) from the appropriate State Rate Section for both premises/operations and products/completed operations. | —Determine the basic limits rate applicable to the classification(s) (either "occurrence" or "claims-made") for the appropriate territory. In other words, determine the policy version desired and then find the code.<br>—For manufacturing or processing risks, use the territory where the products as classified are produced or assembled, or where the processing as classified takes place.<br>—For contracting or servicing risks, use the territory where the job is located.<br>—If "claims-made" coverage is chosen, adjust the "mature" claims-made rate(s) by the factor for the appropriate year in "claims-made." Note that after four years, the factor is 1.00. |
| D. Adjust the basic limits rate(s) to reflect any coverages (other than deductibles). | —Adjust the rate(s) for any coverages deleted or restricted except those required by classification footnotes. There are probably more deletions in the new forms than previously because the new policies *include* coverages previously added by the broad form endorsements. |

—Adjust the rate(s) for any coverages being bought back—that is, those deleted by classification footnotes. Underwriters must consider the hazards of the particular risk in determining whether to provide the excluded coverage and, if so, the appropriate price. Example: medical payments for pupils in schools.

E. Adjust the resulting basic limits rate(s) by the appropriate increased limits factors and any other applicable rate modification(s). Then adjust for coverage written on a deductible basis according to Rule 15.

—Determine which Increased Limits Table applies. Use the indicator in the State Rate pages.

—Determine the appropriate increased limits factors (separately for each subline) for the limits selected. The increased limits factors are found in the Increased Limits Section of the manual or in the State Exceptions Section.

—If a deductible is purchased, determine the deductible discount. Subtract it from the appropriate increased limits factors. Note that this is a shortcut procedure. Since the deductible applies only to the basic limits rates, subtracting the discount from the increased limits factors gives the same result as performing the entire standard calculation.

—Apply any applicable experience and schedule rating modification (debit or credit).

—Multiply the basic limits rate(s) by the increased limits factors.

F. Multiply the number of units of exposure developed under the premium base for each classification by the corresponding adjusted rate(s) developed in Item E.

—For manufacturing risks, include gross sales from one named insured to another. The new rules reflect the possibility that named insureds under the same policy can sue each other because they are separate legal entities. The gross sales used to determine the exposure units are the wholesale value of the goods, unless separate records are kept.

Since manufacturers' retail operations are separately rated, include as gross sales of the manufacturer the wholesale value of goods transferred to his or her own retail operation.

If the policy is amended to *exclude* inter-company products suits (that is, one named insured suing another), the value of goods transferred from one named insured to another should *not* be included in determining the exposure for products/completed operations.

| | |
|---|---|
| G. Determine the application of any minimum premium. | —For contracting or servicing risks, use the entire payroll developed when rating a single operation. If more than one classification applies, however, divide the payroll for each distinct type of operation.<br>—For subject classifications, apply the Transition Program, if applicable.<br>—Determine the minimum premium(s) based on the increased limits assignment.<br>—Refer to the Countrywide Rates Section for the minimum premium table.<br>—Determine whether a special storekeepers minimum premium applies. |
| H. Determine any other additional premiums. | —If you identified more than one classification in Step A of this rule, repeat Steps B through G as many times as necessary to determine the premium for each classification. |
| I. Add the premium determined in Step F or G, whichever is greater, to the premium(s) determined in Step H to obtain the total policy premium. | |
| J. Charge the premium developed in Step I or the policywriting premium, whichever is greater. | —The policy writing premium is $100.00. This minimum is the least you can charge for a policy, which may include general liability and other coverage parts. |

If coverage has been on a claims-made basis for five years or less, the claims-made rate (referred to as the *mature claims-made rate*) must be adjusted by a factor found in the manual. This will be described subsequently in the text.

**Coverage Change Adjustments.** Since the new forms include coverages previously added by endorsement, insureds may be expected to more often refuse these now included coverages, which should then cause the premium to drop.

There may also be cases when the insured desires coverage for an exposure excluded in a classification footnote. Since the basic limits rates are strictly for coverage of the operations defined by the classification wording and footnotes, underwriters usually charge a higher rate when agreeing to provide broader coverage.

**Increased Limits.** Limits of liability may be increased or otherwise altered by endorsement. The endorsement may specify a particular job or location subject to these altered limits. In that case, the exposure should be considered as a separate entity. If the overall limits of liability for the policy are changed during the policy period, the two periods affected should be separated and shown as two separate coverage periods. This procedure helps to properly apply the higher rates that reflect the higher limits of liability. These rates are calculated using the increased limit tables provided in the *CLM.*

There are two sets of increased limit tables. For premises-operations coverage, Tables 1, 2, and 3 display the increased limits factor corresponding to various levels of aggregate and per-occurrence limits. Table 1 applies to the least hazardous operations, and Table 3, shown in Exhibit 7-10 applies to the most hazardous. Similarly, for products-completed operations, Tables A, B, and C show the increased limits factors. Table A applies to the least hazardous operations, and Table C to the most hazardous. The state rate pages indicate which table applies for each classification. Some of the increased limits factors shown in the manual are specifically stated to be guide (a) rates.

**Deductibles.** Deductibles can be valuable to the insurer by helping to eliminate small claims and encourage safety measures. They may also enable the insured to settle claims quickly, thus maintaining goodwill with customers and reducing premiums.

The philosophy regarding the use of deductibles varies from company to company. The underwriting approach to deductibles can also vary depending on whether the deductible is low or high or whether it applies to bodily injury or property damage liability.

Bodily injury liability deductibles are not considered to be a sound

**Exhibit 7-9**

*CLM* General Liability State Rate Page*

**CLAIMS-MADE**

Prem./Ops. (Subline Code 334)
Products (Subline Code 336)

**GEORGIA (10)**

| | | Prem./Ops. | Prem./Ops. | | | | Prem./Ops. | Prem./Ops. | |
|---|---|---|---|---|---|---|---|---|---|
| Code No. | Limit I.D. | Territory 002 | Territory 003 | Prod/ Comp Ops | Code No. | Limit I.D. | Territory 002 | Territory 003 | Prod/ Comp Ops |
| 11210 | 3– | 37.60 | 37.60 | – | 13205 | 2B | .33 | .33 | .224 |
| 11211 | 3– | 36.10 | 36.10 | – | 13314 | 1A | .021 | .027 | (a) |
| 11212 | 3– | 29.50 | 29.50 | – | 13350 | 1A | .196 | .238 | .32 |
| 11213 | 3– | 18.80 | 18.80 | – | 13410 | 3C | 1.03 | 1.03 | 2.42 |
| 11214 | 3– | 18.80 | 18.80 | – | 13411 | 3C | (a) | (a) | (a) |
| 11222 | 2– | .35 | .35 | – | 13412 | 3C | 1.47 | 1.47 | .69 |
| 11234 | 1A | .40 | .49 | .49 | 13453 | 2C | 1.05 | 1.05 | (a) |
| 11248 | 2B | .243 | .243 | (a) | 13454 | 2B | 1.37 | 1.37 | (a) |
| 11257 | 1A | .27 | .33 | .60 | 13455 | 2C | 1.37 | 1.37 | (a) |
| 11270 | 1– | 35.70 | 27.70 | – | 13505 | 1A | .40 | .49 | (a) |
| 11288 | 1B | .75 | .86 | 1.36 | 13590 | 1A | 2.24 | 2.24 | 1.57 |
| 12014 | 2B | .42 | .42 | 1.53 | 13621 | 3B | 1.03 | 1.03 | .82 |
| 12356 | 1A | .98 | 1.11 | .35 | 13670 | 2B | .031 | .039 | .059 |
| 12361 | 2B | .031 | .039 | .132 | 13671 | 1A | .54 | .61 | .218 |
| 12362 | 2B | .031 | .039 | (a) | 13715 | 2B | .041 | .051 | .68 |
| 12373 | 2B | .031 | .038 | .165 | 13716 | 1B | .42 | .52 | .64 |
| 12374 | 1C | .32 | .39 | .53 | 13759 | 1C | .33 | .41 | .61 |
| 12375 | 2C | .73 | .80 | .53 | 13930 | 2B | .031 | .039 | 1.70 |
| 12391 | 2B | .031 | .038 | .44 | 14068 | 1A | .031 | .039 | (a) |
| 12467 | 1A | .129 | .163 | (a) | 14101 | 1A | .40 | .49 | (a) |

| | | | | | | | | | |
|---|---|---|---|---|---|---|---|---|---|
| **12509** | 2B | 1.43 | 1.43 | (a) | **14279** | 2B | .75 | .75 | .44 |
| **12510** | 2B | 1.43 | 1.43 | (a) | **14401** | 1A | 1.01 | 1.14 | .73 |
| **12583** | 2B | .41 | .41 | (a) | **14405** | 2– | 1.35 | 1.35 | – |
| **12651** | 2B | 1.20 | 1.20 | 1.26 | **14527** | 2B | .031 | .039 | (a) |
| **12683** | 2B | .41 | .41 | (a) | **14655** | 1– | .093 | .114 | – |
| **12707** | 2B | .031 | .038 | 3.75 | **14731** | 1– | 7.18 | 5.75 | – |
| **12797** | 2A | .031 | .039 | (a) | **14732** | 1– | .225 | .28 | – |
| **12805** | 1A | .196 | .238 | .32 | **14733** | 2– | .30 | .38 | – |
| **12841** | 1– | .40 | .49 | – | **14734** | 1– | .82 | .61 | – |
| **12927** | 1– | .40 | .49 | – | **14855** | 1B | .50 | .50 | (a) |
| **13049** | 2A | .031 | .038 | .092 | **14913** | 1A | .56 | .69 | (a) |
| **13111** | 1A | .59 | .67 | .218 | **15060** | 3C | (a) | (a) | (a) |
| **13112** | 2A | .031 | .039 | .059 | **15061** | 3C | (a) | (a) | (a) |
| **13201** | 2B | 2.22 | 2.22 | .58 | **15062** | 2B | .93 | .93 | (a) |
| **13204** | 2B | 1.08 | 1.08 | .225 | **15063** | 3B | 1.22 | 1.22 | 2.67 |

Refer to the countrywide rate page and state exception pages for minimum and maximum conversion factors for classifications subject to the transition program.

**CLAIMS-MADE MULTIPLIERS**

Multiply the above rates by the following:

| **Year in Claims-Made** | **Premises/Operations** | **Premises/Operations** | **Prod/Comp Ops** |
|---|---|---|---|
| | Codes 50000-59999 90000-99999 | All Other | All Codes |
| 1 | .82 | .89 | .84 |
| 2 | .91 | .95 | .90 |
| 3 | .96 | .99 | .97 |
| 4 | .98 | 1.00 | .98 |
| 5 or more | 1.00 | 1.00 | 1.00 |

CG-R- 004 **5TH EDITION 07-88** □

**Exhibit 7-10**
Increased Limits Table*

SECTION IV
INCREASED LIMITS

**TABLE 3**

PREMISES/OPERATIONS†
(subline code 334)
TABLE 3
(POLICY LIMIT CODES ARE IN PARENTHESES)

| | Per Occurrence | | | | | | |
|---|---|---|---|---|---|---|---|
| **Aggregate** | **25** | **50** | **100** | **200** | **300** | **500** | **1000** |
| **50** | **1.00** (46) | **1.25** (51) | | | | | |
| **100** | **1.05** (48) | **1.33** (49) | **1.61** (55) | | | | |
| **200** | **1.09** (48) | **1.40** (51) | **1.72** (55) | **2.09** (60) | | | |
| **300** | **1.11** (48) | **1.43** (51) | **1.77** (52) | **2.17** (60) | **2.42** (66) | | |
| **500** | | **1.47** (51) | **1.83** (53) | **2.27** (57) | **2.54** (66) | 2.95 (67) | |
| **600** | | **1.48** (51) | **1.85** (55) | **2.30** (58) | **2.58** (64) | 3.00 (70) | |
| **1000** | | | **1.90** (54) | **2.38** (59) | **2.69** (66) | 3.16 (68) | 3.92 (71) |
| **1500** | | | | **2.44** (60) | **2.76** (66) | 3.27 (69) | 4.11 (73) |
| **2000** | | | | **2.48** (60) | **2.82** (66) | 3.34 (70) | 4.24 (73) |
| **2500** | | | | | **2.86** (66) | 3.40 (70) | 4.34 (73) |
| **3000** | | | | | **2.89** (66) | 3.44 (70) | 4.42 (72) |

Factors shown in **boldface** are manual factors; all others are guide (a) factors and must be referred to company before using.

†Limits are in thousands.

decision by many underwriters. The insurer would lose control of claims handling by allowing the insured to settle the claims in the deductible area. Additionally, claims tend to be reported late and, therefore, may develop into much larger losses. A deductible program also distorts claims frequency patterns so that the underwriter cannot properly evaluate the loss picture if all losses are not reported to the insurer. The insurer's claims expense determination may be distorted by inclusion of deductible programs with the remaining book of business.

A small deductible on property damage liability coverage is not as much of a problem since the losses are usually smaller in size. As a result, underwriters will consider writing property damage liability deductibles more often than bodily injury liability deductibles, even though by using a property damage deductible, the underwriter will have little knowledge of the frequency of small claims.

The underwriting philosophy regarding the use of high liability deductibles, for example, $10,000 and over, is often very different from that regarding low liability deductibles, for several reasons. The use of high deductibles is almost a form of "self-insurance." In addition, the underwriter does not lose control of claims since these programs are usually offered only with the insurer performing the claims service. The insured, therefore, reimburses the insurer on a regular basis for the losses in the deductible area paid by the insurer's claims department. Claims reserve practices are maintained by the insurer, who also gains complete knowledge of loss experience. Thus, the major disadvantages of a deductible program from the insurer's point of view are eliminated.

There are distinct advantages to a high deductible program for the insured. Obviously, since a substantial portion of the exposure is retained, there is a significant savings in premium. Since the insured only reimburses the insurer for claims that have been settled, the insured has the advantage of a better cash flow. The cash flow consideration has induced many manufacturers (particularly those with very hazardous products) to change their insurance to a high deductible program. Deductible discounts were at one time found in the ISO rate manual. However, in recent years they have been removed and discounts are now on an (a) rated basis. Deductible discounts apply only to the basic limits portion of the rate, and excess limits charges should be collected in full.

In high deductible programs, the underwriter often determines the credit to be allowed for the deductible. Generally, the underwriter prices the coverage for the deductible level and for the full limits of liability and charges the difference between these two amounts for the premium. In these high deductible programs the insurer will, as mentioned earlier, usually only offer the deductible if it is on a basis whereby the insurer handles and pays the claims and the insured reimburses the insurer for any claims within the deductible. This method of handling deductibles means that any reduction in rate must be a function of only the loss portion of the rate and that the expense portion would be the same as it would be for a policy with no deductibles.

## Individual Insured Rates

In pricing individual risks, the primary objective is deciding how that risk compares with the average risk anticipated by the manual classification. By being aware of the characteristics that make up the average risk anticipated by the classification, the underwriter can compare the characteristics of the individual risk with the average characteristics anticipated by the rate.

**Experience Rating.** Experience rating has been described as a plan that will

> ... vary the insured's rate based upon an actuarial consideration of the insured's actual incurred losses over a period in the past, usually three years ending one year before the effective date of the contract. A rather formal and relatively rigid formula is used which compares the insured's incurred losses with the provision for losses in the manual rates on the effective date of the modification, with increased credibility for the insured's experience as the size of the insured's premium increases.[5]

Experience rating is available to general liability risks that develop an annual basic limits manual premium of $3,000 or more for bodily injury and property damage liability exposures. The experience modification is usually determined from the latest available three years of experience incurred by the insured. In the event that experience for the full experience period is not available, at least one year of experience shall be used, and the experience period shall end at least six months prior to the rating, but generally one year is used.

Experience rating is an involved mathematical process. Companies use a computer to calculate experience modifications. In that case, the underwriter fills out a worksheet. The worksheet identifies the variables that the underwriter must verify for accuracy, if the experience rating is to be correct. Specifically, the underwriter has to determine the accuracy of the premium and incurred loss information.

**Schedule Rating.** Schedule rating is a technique that permits the underwriter more flexibility in determining the premium for any given risk. It is a process that recognizes the underwriter's business experience as well as his or her knowledge of a particular risk. The

**Exhibit 7-11**
Schedule Rating Table*

| | Range of Modifications Credit | | Debit |
|---|---|---|---|
| A. Location: | | | |
| 1. Exposure inside premises | 5% | to | 5% |
| 2. Exposure outside premises | 5 | to | 5 |
| B. Premises—condition, care | 10 | to | 10 |
| C. Equipment—type, condition, care | 10 | to | 10 |
| D. Classification peculiarities | 10 | to | 10 |
| E. Employees—selection, training, supervision, experience | 6 | to | 6 |
| F. Cooperation: | | | |
| 1. Medical facilities | 2 | to | 2 |
| 2. Safety program | 2 | to | 2 |

*Adapted with permission from "Commercial General Liability Experience and Schedule Rating Plan " (New York: Insurance Services Office, Inc., 1985, 1986), p. 8, 8-87 Ed.

resulting schedule debit or credit reflects the conditions that are expected to directly influence the occurrence of future losses for that risk. Since the conditions influencing losses are also reflected to some extent in the experience rating plan, schedule rating should be used to adjust only those factors not specifically considered and for those most recent changes in the insured's operation that may not be covered by the experience rating plan. Essentially, schedule rating debits or credits the premium by recognizing specific risk characteristics not reflected by previous rating plans. Schedule rating is more of an "art" and requires more underwriting judgment than experience rating. While experience rating is fairly objective and follows a set formula as identified above, in schedule rating, the assignment of debits and credits are more flexible and based on the underwriter's experience and judgment. Schedule rating is usually limited to those risks that produce a basic limits manual premium in excess of $1,000.

The characteristics that are evaluated for general liability schedule rating include location, premises, equipment, classification peculiarities, employees, and management cooperation as shown in Exhibit 7-11. No more than 25 percent schedule credit or debit can be supplied to a given risk.

The following checklist, provided by ISO, identifies some specific considerations when evaluating location as a characteristic of a risk. Similar questions are asked about the other characteristics shown in Exhibit 7-11.

A. *Location*

i. *Exposure inside premises*

What are the storage facilities?
Are floors slip-resistant?
Are trash containers provided?
What is total capacity?
What is the number of employees living on the premises?
Are stairways, laundry chutes and elevator shafts enclosed?
With what kind of material are they enclosed?
Are the *exits* lighted? How are they designated? How many from each floor?
Is the building sprinklered? How many extinguishers?
Is there a paid or volunteer fire department in the area?
What is the type of construction of the walls, floors and roof?
How old is the building?

ii. *Exposure outside premises*

Is the parking lot paved? Lighted?
Are the sidewalks in good repair? How many feet of "public" sidewalk? Do they clean ice and snow off sidewalks?
Is there a parking garage?[6]

The underwriter can apply schedule debits or credits to a risk to account for conditions known to exist under experience rating but not accounted for under that rating system. For example, there may be evidence of a catastrophic loss potential, which may not be adequately reflected in the experience modification, but which the underwriter wants to include through schedule rating.

If a particular risk has significantly upgraded the condition of its premises through renovation during the most recent year and the underwriter believes that those renovations will reduce the frequency of accidents within the premises, up to a 10 percent schedule credit could be applied. This reduction in hazard occasioned by the renovation would not be reflected in the experience rating plan for several years. Another risk, however, has always provided excellent training and supervision for its employees, and over the years its loss experience has been lower than average, a reflection of this condition. In this case, schedule rating may not be appropriate because the better-than-average conditions are reflected in the experience credit the firm has already received.

## Composite Rating

The composite rating approach simplifies the pricing of a package of coverages. The underwriter may agree to rate the policy on a premium base other than one specified in the manual. Any form or format of measurable base can be used as long as it is indicated on the policy. The premium developed under composite rating should be the same as it would be without composite rating. *Composite rating is used for administrative convenience and not for reasons of price reduction or increase.*

Problems may arise, however, with the exact definition of the premium base. The composite rating endorsement should precisely spell out what the premium basis is. Since there are no manual rules to follow, the composite rating base is left up to the underwriter to explain in that endorsement. The underwriter should strive to select a base that reflects the insured exposures and is convenient to measure.

Assume, for example, that the underwriter wishes to insure the M-T Barrel Company. The underwriter estimates the premium necessary to insure the exposure and defines the premium as a certain rate "per barrel." The M-T Barrel Company estimates sales of 10,000 barrels in the coming year. If the underwriter requires $20,000 in premium to grant coverage, the rate is specified as $2 per barrel. The policy is issued with a composite rating endorsement to this effect.

## SUMMARY

The line of insurance that probably receives the most public attention is general liability. General liability encompasses both the premises-operations and the products-completed operations exposures. Both are described in this chapter and the two that follow.

A major part of the underwriter's job focuses on the correct pricing of a risk. One of the first steps in properly pricing a risk is determining which classification should be used. This task should not be approached lightly. The incorrect classification of a risk has a much greater impact than might be expected. Many would simply say that the effect of the one incorrectly classified risk is payment of the wrong premium. Although this is not, by far, the only consequence, even it should not be ignored. First, by charging the incorrect premium, the underwriter has not followed the filed rating plan of the insurer. Second, the underwriter has in a sense practiced discrimination, which is prohibited by state rate regulatory laws. Still, the impact goes farther than this. The premium and loss data that is used to produce future rates is skewed by an incorrect classification. The future rates for the class that should have been assigned have not included this additional data, and the class that was improperly assigned would include the experience of a risk that should not have been included.

The remainder of the pricing process, including the proper determination of the number of exposure units according to the premium base definition and the actual premium determination, must also be carefully undertaken. Errors here create a result similar to that created by the misclassification of a risk. This chapter goes into great detail in these areas.

Underwriters should not take the attitude that determining the premium base is a job for the auditor; the proper classification, the job of the producer; the premium, the job for a rater (or the computer). The underwriter must know how to determine all three, regardless of the other people who might be primarily responsible for them. With regard to classification, it is not appropriate for the underwriter to wait for the final audit to see if the classifications shown on the application are correct. The proper classification should be determined at policy inception so that the insured knows what rate is being charged. Knowing the classification inclusions and exclusions alerts the underwriter to the need for an additional class or the need to delete a class shown by the producer on the application. Finally, the underwriter must know what makes up a rate and what factors change that rate in order to do a proper job of underwriting.

The next two chapters continue the discussion of underwriting general liability insurance. Chapter 8 will look at some of the major CGL policy provisions, claims-made coverage, and the underwriting of the premises-operations exposure. Chapter 9 will conclude the discussion with an examination of the products-completed operations exposure and the management of a book of general liability insurance.

# Chapter Notes

1. Adapted with permission from Donald S. Malecki, Ronald C. Horn, Eric A. Wiening, and James H. Donaldson, *Commercial Liability Risk Management and Insurance*, 2nd ed., vol. 1 (Malvern, PA: American Institute for Property and Liability Underwriters, Inc., 1986), p. 203.
2. *Commercial Lines Manual* (New York: Insurance Services Office, 1987), "Classification Table," note 3, p. CS-49 (2nd ed., January 1987).
3. Minutes of Insurance Services Office, General Liability Committee meeting, 24 September 1987.
4. When a policy is written on a monthly, quarterly, or semiannual reporting basis, the insured pays an initial deposit premium that is a certain percentage of the total estimated annual premium. This percentage varies with the reporting period selected. At each reporting interval, the insured submits the necessary payroll or gross sales figures for that period. This is called an interim report. For some very large insureds, the insurer may actually send out an auditor to gather these figures or to confirm that the figures submitted by the insured are accurate. However, in most cases, the interim report is simply a matter of the insured filling in the correct figures on a form supplied by the insurer.
5. C.A. Kulp and John W. Hall, *Casualty Insurance*, 4th ed. (New York: Ronald Press Co., 1968), p. 883.
6. "Schedule Rating," *Casualty Individual Risk Rating Plans—Workbook* (New York: Insurance Services Office, 1976), p. 32.



# CHAPTER 8

# Underwriting General Liability Insurance, II

Building on the discussion of the *CLM* and the simplified commercial lines policies presented in Chapter 7, this chapter on general liability insurance underwriting reviews the concept of general liability insurance and some of the more important CGL policy provisions. It goes on to explain the important concept of claims-made coverage. Although simple in concept, claims-made coverage becomes much more difficult to implement in practice. This discussion of the claims-made procedure should help those faced with underwriting this coverage.

The chapter then covers the underwriting of the premises-operations exposure; the underwriting of the products-completed operations exposure is discussed in Chapter 9, which shows that many of the factors considered in underwriting premises and operations are also considered in underwriting products liability coverage. (The factors presented in this chapter will not be repeated in the next.)

## GENERAL LIABILITY INSURANCE COVERAGE

One of the coverage parts that may be included in a commercial package policy is commercial general liability. As a result of the ownership of property, normal business operations, or the sale and distribution of products, an insured may be held liable for damages resulting from injuries to others or for damage to the property of others. General liability insurance responds to this exposure.

General liability insurance covers two major exposures—premises-operations and products-completed operations. The former exposure arises from the ownership, maintenance, or use of property and from operations in progress. The latter exposure arises when a product or operation is no longer in the insured's control, that is, when the product has been sold or the operation has been completed and turned over to a third party.

A simplified commercial general liability policy would include, in addition to the common policy conditions and common policy declarations, the commercial general liability declarations, one of two coverage forms, the broad form nuclear exclusion endorsement, and any other endorsements that may apply. This section examines each of these components.

The two coverage forms differ in that one provides coverage for *events that occur* within the policy period, known as an *occurrence form;* and the other provides coverage for events for which a *claim is made* during the policy period, known as a *claims-made form.* The differences between these two forms (and essentially the basis on which each provides coverage) are critical—they are described in the next major section of this chapter. Exhibit 8-1 illustrates the components of a monoline commercial general liability policy.

## Commercial General Liability Declarations

Like all other simplified policies, a commercial general liability policy includes not only the common policy declarations, but also a declarations page specific to the coverage. Exhibit 8-2 shows a sample commercial general liability declarations page. Like the common policy declarations, this page shows the policy number, the insured's name and address, and the policy period.

Both declarations pages must identify the named insured. The full legal name of the named insured must be stated on the declarations. If more than one firm of a group of related entities are to be insured, all must be named so that proper coverage is provided. It is very important to properly identify the named insured in the declarations since the way the name is shown will sometimes determine the coverage provided. As most underwriters have learned, any ambiguities in the policy are interpreted by courts in favor of the insured.

For a parent corporation that owns and controls its subsidiaries, the subsidiaries are also frequently shown as part of the named insured. While it may not be necessary to do this for wholly owned subsidiaries to be covered by the policy, many underwriters do so for identification and auditing purposes.

In some cases, there is insufficient space on the declarations to show the entire named insured. In this case, many underwriters will make enough of an entry to identify the named insured on the declarations and will then state, "See endorsement," on which the full name will be stated. When this is done, the underwriter must indicate

**Exhibit 8-1**
Commercial General Liability Policy*

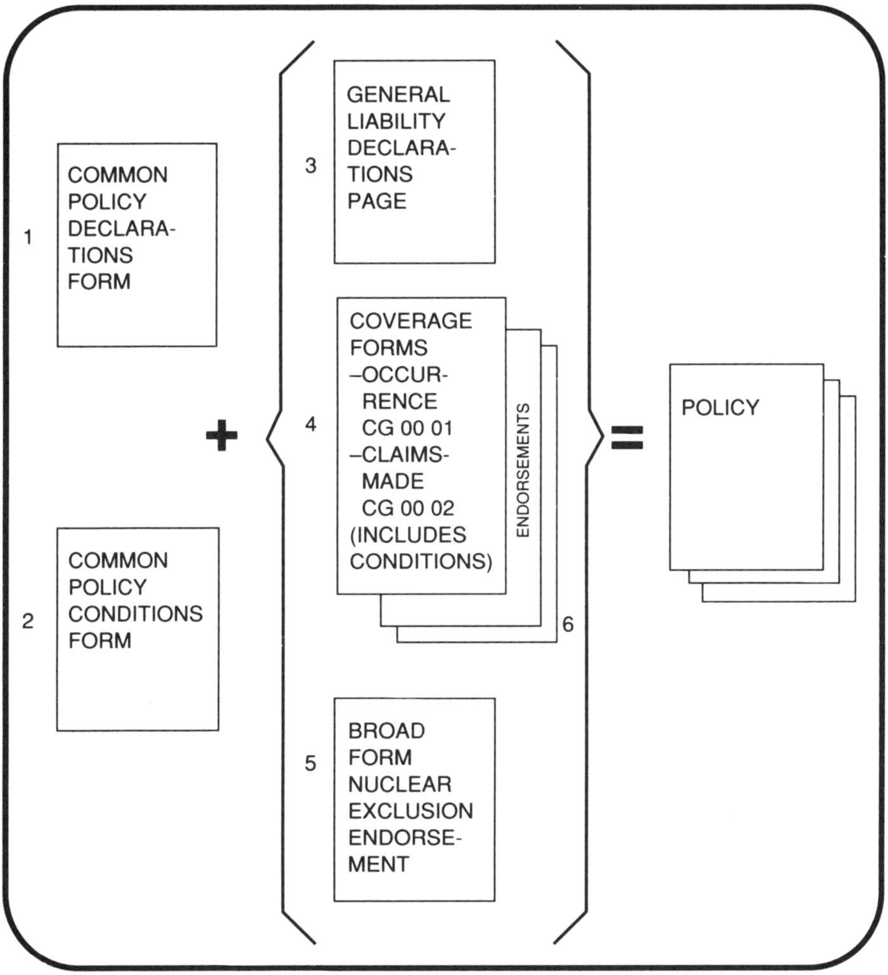


*Adapted with permission from *Workshop Leader's Guide,* ISO Commercial Lines Policy and Rating Simplification Project© Insurance Services Office, 1985, p. 52.

clearly on the endorsement that the entries are named insureds and not additional insureds to ensure that proper coverage is afforded. Unless the actual legal name contains abbreviations, abbreviations should be avoided when identifying the named insured.

In addition to all named insureds, the declarations page shows the applicable limits for general liability insurance. These limits are broken down into the following segments:

- A general aggregate limit applying to medical expense coverage as well as to Coverages A and B (except the products-completed operations coverage)—$50,000 basic limits.
- An aggregate limit applying to the products-completed operations coverage—$50,000 basic limits.
- A per person or organization limit for the personal and advertising injury coverages—$25,000 basic limits.
- An "each occurrence" limit applicable only to the bodily injury, property damage, and medical expense coverages—$25,000 basic limits.
- A fire damage coverage sublimit (subject to the each occurrence limit) for *any one fire*—$25,000 basic limits.
- A medical expense sublimit (subject to the each occurrence limit) applicable to *any one person*—$5,000 basic limits.

As a result of this setup, one accident or occurrence causing bodily injury could be subject to several of the above limits. Although it may be a bit confusing, the "each occurrence" limit is applicable to both the occurrence and the claims-made versions of the CGL. Regardless of whether coverage is "triggered" by the occurrence itself or by a claim in response to the occurrence, the policy would limit the amount paid because of that one occurrence to the "each occurrence" limit.

The addition of these aggregate limits to the simplified policy (especially the general aggregate) should reduce some of the problems under the old policy of an almost unlimited exposure for some coverages for which no aggregate existed. Manual rates base limits are now a combined single limit for both bodily injury and property damage.

The CGL declarations also provides space for the *retroactive date* (discussed subsequently). This would be applicable only when coverage is provided on a claims-made basis. It is of utmost importance that this section be completed properly. Failure to do so could subject the insurer to claims related to exposures that were not intended to be covered and for which a premium was not charged. Underwriters should work closely with policy typists and rating personnel to stress the importance of checking that this section is completed properly. Renewals should also be carefully monitored to see that the retroactive date shown is the one intended.

The declarations also provide information concerning the insured's business. The form of ownership is indicated by checking the appropriate box. A brief description of the business appears along with the location of all premises owned, rented, or occupied by the insured.

It is important that the form of ownership be correctly stated. The choices are (1) individual (sole proprietorship), (2) partnership, (3) joint

**Exhibit 8-2**
Commercial General Liability Declarations

Policy No. ____________

Company Name Area | Producer Name Area

Name Insured ____________

Mailing Address ____________

____________

Policy Period: From ____________ to ____________ at 12:01 A.M. Standard Time at your mailing address shown above.

In return for the payment of the premium, and subject to all the terms of this policy, we agree with you to provide the insurance as stated in this policy.

Limits of Insurance

| | | |
|---|---|---|
| General Aggregate Limit (Other than Products—Completed Operations) | $____ | |
| Products-Completed Operations Aggregate Limit | $____ | |
| Personal & Advertising Injury Limit | $____ | |
| Each Occurrence Limit | $____ | |
| Fire Damage Limit | $____ | Any One Fire |
| Medical Expense Limit | $____ | Any One Person |

Retroactive Date (CG 00 02 only)

Coverage A of this insurance does not apply to "bodily injury" or "property damage" which occurs before the Retroactive Date, if any, shown below

Retroactive Date: ____________
(Enter Date or "None" if no Retroactive Date applies.)

Form of Business:

☐ Individual ☐ Partnership

☐ Joint Venture ☐ Organization (Other than Partnership or Joint Venture)

Business Description: ____________

Location of All Premises You Own, Rent or Occupy:

____________

| Classification | Code No. | Premium Basis | Rate | Advance Premium | |
|---|---|---|---|---|---|
| | | | | PR/CO | All Other |
| | | | | $ | $ |

TOTAL ____________

Premium shown is payable: $____________ at inception.

Endorsements attached to this policy: IL 00 21 11 85—Broad Form Nuclear Exclusion

COUNTERSIGNED ____________ BY ____________
(Date) (Authorized Representative)

Note: Officers' facsimile signatures may be inserted here, on the policy cover or elsewhere at the company's option venture, or (4) organization other than a partnership or joint venture (which would be a corporation in most cases). The section of the policy titled "Who Is An Insured" answers that question based upon the form of business of the named insured as shown on the declarations. In those cases where there are multiple forms, this should be so noted, perhaps by endorsement. For multiple named insureds with multiple forms of ownership, it is often better to indicate the form of ownership directly after the name. For example, it might be best to show the named insured as Bonnie and Elan Baglini (a partnership) and Baglini Company (a corporation).

The advance premium calculation is shown in columns for the classification, code number, premium basis, rate, advance premium for products-completed operations, and advance premium for all other coverage. Finally, all of the endorsements attached to the policy are listed by number.

## Commercial General Liability Coverage Form

Both versions of the commercial general liability coverage form, the occurrence and claims-made forms, contain the essential scope of coverages formerly provided under the comprehensive general liability policy and the broad form endorsement. By consolidating these coverages, the new coverage forms replace the many forms once needed.

The occurrence version of the commercial general liability coverage form consists of five sections, and the claims-made version consists of six sections. The following explanation of those sections apply to both the occurrence and the claims-made version except as noted.

**Coverages.** In both versions, Section I describes the three kinds of coverage. Coverage A provides bodily injury and property damage liability coverage. It obligates the insurer to "pay those sums that the insured becomes legally obligated to pay as damages because of 'bodily injury' or 'property damage' to which this insurance applies." The two versions differ only in regard to the coverage *trigger* which is what must happen during the policy period for coverage to become available for particular instance of bodily injury or property damage. Under the occurrence form, the bodily injury or property damage itself must occur during the policy period. Under the claims-made form, the claim for damages must be made against the insured during the policy period.

Coverage B applies to personal and advertising injury liability arising as a function of the insured's business. It covers judgments against the insured for offenses, such as libel or slander, committed during the policy period.

Coverage C provides medical payments coverage. It covers certain medical expenses for injuries suffered on premises owned by the insured or suffered as a result of the insured's operations if the accident takes place during the policy period.

Thus, for Coverages B and C, the triggers are the same in both versions of the policy. *Only Coverage A is available on a claims-made basis.* These three coverages are described in more detail in a later section.

**Who Is An Insured.** Section II of the commercial general liability coverage form clarifies who is an insured under the policy. If the insured is identified in the declarations page as an individual, the owner of the business and the owner's spouse are insured, but only with respect to the conduct of that business. If the declarations indicate that the business is a partnership or joint venture, all of the members or partners and their spouses are also insured, but only with respect to the conduct of the business. If any other form of organization is designated, the entity is insured, the executive officers and directors are insured with respect to their duties, and the stockholders are insured with respect to their liability as stockholders. No partners or parties to joint ventures with the insured are covered unless the partnership or joint venture is shown as a named insured in the declarations.

The policy also insures employees acting within the scope of their employment, persons acting as the insured's real estate manager, and if the insured dies, temporary custodians of the insured's property and the legal representatives of the insured. Any person driving the insured's mobile equipment along a public highway with permission is insured, as is any person responsible for the conduct of the driver when no other insurance is available. Any newly acquired organization of the insured is also covered automatically for ninety days for any insured events occurring after the acquisition date.

**Limits of Insurance.** Section III stipulates the rules that fix the limits of insurance regardless of the number of insureds, claims, or claimants. The *general aggregate limit* is the maximum the insurer will pay, except for products and completed operations liability for which there is a separate aggregate limit.

Within those aggregate limits are certain sublimits. One limits the amount paid for damages to any one person or organization from personal or advertising injury. Another limits the total payments for damages and medical expenses for bodily injury and property damage arising out of any one occurrence. Within that maximum there are further sublimits on property damage per fire and medical expenses per person.

**Commercial General Liability Conditions.** In both versions, Section IV stipulates conditions regarding bankruptcy; the insured's duties in the event of an occurrence, claim, or suit; the right of legal action against the insurer; other insurance; premium audit; representations; separation of insureds; and the transfer of recovery rights against others to the insurer. In the claims-made version, the other insurance condition makes the policy excess over any applicable insurance not on a claims-made basis if no retroactive date is shown in the declarations or the other insurance continues in effect after the retroactive date. The conditions in both versions are otherwise identical.

**Extended Reporting Periods.** Section V in the claims-made version provides an extended reporting period to remedy possible coverage gaps. Coverage gaps can occur if the claims-made coverage is canceled or not renewed by either party, renewed or replaced by a claims-made policy with a later retroactive date, or replaced with an occurrence policy. If an accident causing bodily injury or property damage *occurs* before the end of the policy period, but the resulting claim is *first made* after the end of the policy period, it could fall into such a gap. Under certain circumstances, the extended reporting period will treat the claim as though it had been first made during the expiring policy period. Extended reporting periods are examined in more detail later.

**Definitions.** Section V of the occurrence version and Section VI of the claims-made version are identical. They define terms used in the policy. These terms are advertising injury, auto, bodily injury, coverage territory, impaired property, insured contract, loading or unloading, mobile equipment, occurrence, personal injury, products-completed operations hazard, property damage, suit, your product, and your work. Each of these terms has a special meaning when used in the policy.

## Three Coverages Under the New CGL

**Coverage A—Bodily Injury and Property Damage.** An insurer makes the same basic promise, paraphrased below, in the insuring agreement of the CGL coverage forms—both claims-made and occurrence:

> We will pay those sums that the insured becomes legally obligated to pay as damages because of "bodily injury" or "property damage" to which this insurance applies.... The "bodily injury" or "property damage" must be caused by an "occurrence." The "occurrence" must take place in the "policy territory."

In the first part of the insuring agreement, the phrase *to which this insurance applies* is noteworthy. An insurer does not have to fulfill its promise to pay damages if the claim or suit does not allege a "bodily injury" or "property damage," as those terms are defined, or if the claim or suit is otherwise excluded. Bodily injury is defined as "bodily injury, sickness or disease sustained by a person, including death resulting from any of these at any time." Property damage is defined as: (1) "Physical injury to tangible property, including all resulting loss of use of that property;" or (2) "Loss of use of tangible property that is not physically injured."

However, the insurer's duty to *defend* is broader than its duty to pay damages. Even if a suit is later found to be groundless, false, or fraudulent, the insurer must defend an insured whenever the plaintiff alleges facts that could conceivably fall within the coverage of the policy. In determining whether the insurer has a duty to defend, some courts have based their findings solely on the allegations expressed in the complaint or petition of the plaintiff, while other courts have looked beyond the allegations and considered the actual facts and/or the reasonable expectations of the plaintiff.

For coverage to apply under either form, the "bodily injury" or "property damage" must be caused by an "occurrence." Occurrence is defined in the forms to mean "an accident, including continuous or repeated exposure to substantially the same general harmful conditions." The term accident is not defined in the policy, but the intent is to provide coverage for any adverse condition that continues over a long period and eventually results in bodily injury or property damage, as well as a sudden event that immediately results in bodily injury or property damage.

**Coverage B—Advertising and Personal Injury Liability.** Both advertising and personal injury liability coverages, Coverage B of the CGL, are automatically included, unless they are excluded by endorsement.

***Scope of Coverage.*** The insuring agreement of advertising and personal injury coverage parallels the insuring agreement pertaining to bodily injury and property damage liability coverage. The insurer agrees to pay the sums that the insured becomes legally obligated to pay as damages because of "personal injury" or "advertising injury" (as those two terms are defined in the policy), as long as an exclusion or some other policy provision does not rule out coverage.

The CGL policy provides coverage for personal injury only if caused by an *offense* (1) committed in the coverage territory, (2) during the policy period, and (3) arising out of the conduct of the named insured's business, other than advertising, publishing, broadcasting, or telecasting done by or for the named insured. Publishers, broadcasters, and telecasters should have special coverage for personal injury.

Advertising liability is covered by the CGL—not as "personal injury," but as a separate item. Like personal injury, coverage for advertising liability is conditioned on an offense (1) committed in the coverage territory and (2) during the policy period, but only for injury arising in the course of advertising the named insured's goods, products, or services. This coverage is not intended for a firm that is in the advertising business. Rather, it is intended for the business that *buys* advertising in order to sell its own goods or products.

***Definitions.*** Of obvious importance in determining the scope of coverage are the definitions of advertising injury and personal injury.

*Advertising Injury.* The policy makes the following statement about advertising injury:

> "Advertising injury" means injury arising out of one or more of the following offenses:
> a. Oral or written publication of material that slanders or libels a person or organization or disparages a person's or organization's goods, products or services;
> b. Oral or written publication of material that violates a person's right of privacy;
> c. Misappropriation of advertising ideas or style of doing business; or
> d. Infringement of copyright, title or slogan.

While defamation is not specifically mentioned as an offense, it is a generic term that includes both libel and slander, and the terms defamation or defamation of character also refer to the nature of the injury when a public material is libelous or slanderous. Thus, if defamation is alleged without any specific mention of libel or slander, coverage should still apply.

In recent years, firms have been quite open in publicizing the presumed disadvantages of competitors' products or services. It seems likely that this practice could lead to an increase in claims of advertising injury. The allegation that the insured has made an untrue statement about a competitor's goods or services in order to influence the customer would qualify as disparagement, an offense listed under the definition.

*Personal Injury.* Personal injury is defined as follows:

> "Personal injury" means injury, other than "bodily injury," arising out of one or more of the following offenses:
> a. False arrest, detention or imprisonment;
> b. Malicious prosecution;
> c. Wrongful entry into, or eviction of a person from, a room, dwelling or premises that the person occupies;
> d. Oral or written publication of material that slanders or libels a person or organization or disparages a person's or organization's goods, products or services; or

e. Oral or written publication of material that violates a person's right of privacy.

In some insurance policies the term "personal injury" encompasses bodily injury and other offenses as well. In the CGL, "personal injury" is defined to mean *injury,* other than "bodily injury," arising out of one or more of the offenses listed above. "Bodily injury," as defined in the CGL, represents physical harm or impairment. The word *"injury"* is not defined in the policy, but can encompass any other wrong inflicted on another such as mental anguish, fright, humiliation, loss of reputation, and shock.

Such intentional torts as false arrest, detention, and malicious prosecution are offenses frequently alleged in claims against law enforcement agencies. However, it is not likely that Coverage B of the CGL will be written for such agencies, whether privately owned or part of municipal government, because an endorsement is available to exclude such exposures. Nonetheless, false arrest or malicious prosecution can easily be committed by citizens who are not law enforcement officials.

***Underwriting Personal Injury.*** Many underwriters believe the key to underwriting personal injury liability is avoiding adverse selection. Certain risks will be much more susceptible to personal injury claims than will others and those risks naturally will seek protection. The following is a list of classifications and the type of personal injury claims to which they seem to be primarily exposed.

| *Classification* | *Personal Injury Exposure* |
|---|---|
| Collection agencies | False arrest, invasion of privacy, libel, slander |
| Credit investigators | Invasion of privacy, libel, slander |
| Department stores | False arrest, invasion of privacy, libel, slander |
| Hotels, motels, large apartment buildings | Invasion of privacy, false arrest |
| Detective agencies | False arrest, invasion of privacy, libel, slander |
| Financial institutions | Libel, slander, invasion of privacy |
| Security, protective, or patrol agencies | False arrest |
| Municipalities | All types |

This list is not all-inclusive but highlights several classes that have significant personal injury exposures. Personal injury should not be just another coverage that is automatically provided. It can present significant exposure to loss and should be underwritten as carefully as any other coverage. Particular attention should be paid to the following:

- The nature of the operation in terms of the opportunity to infringe on the legal rights of others
- The background and loss experience of the risk
- Publications
- The existence of a security force
- The clientele of the risk (Is the store prone to shoplifters? Do the tenants pay their rent promptly?)
- The controversial nature, of principals or key employees

**Coverage C—Medical Payments.** Premises medical payments coverage was optional with former general liability policies, but is automatically included in the CGL. This coverage has its own trigger, the accident causing bodily injury.

The medical payments coverage under the CGL policy is not a form of liability insurance in a strict sense because negligence of the insured need not be established as a condition precedent to payment by the insurer. Medical payments are made if there is reason to believe that the resulting bodily injury would not have occurred had it not been for some condition on the insured premises or for operations conducted by the insured.

Specifically, payments are made for medical expenses incurred by members of the public who sustain injuries caused by an accident (1) on premises the named insured owns or rents; (2) on the ways next to such premises as described in (1); or (3) because of the named insured's operations (whether caused by the name insured or by other insureds on behalf of the named insured) in the coverage territory, and during the policy period. Another condition is that medical expenses must be incurred *and* reported to the insurer within one year of the date of accident. An accident that requires an injured person to undergo a series of treatments that extend beyond the period of one year would not be covered by medical payments. A claim for any injury that serious would likely be filed under bodily injury liability coverage.

Note that if the named insured does not have bodily injury liability coverage for the circumstances under which injury occurs, the named insured is not covered for the claimant's medical bills.

## Coverage Triggers

The term *trigger,* as commonly used with the occurrence and claims-made forms, can be defined as the basis on which coverage of the policy is activated. The gun analogy is fairly obvious—"pulling the trigger" sets off a response from the insurer; if coverage is not "triggered," there is no response. The only difference between the two CGL coverage forms is in the concepts surrounding the Coverage A trigger. The triggers of Coverages B and C are identical under both forms.

**Coverage A Triggers.** *The event that triggers coverage under the occurrence form is bodily injury or property damage that is sustained by a third party during the policy period.* Although a claim must be made before insurance coverage is made available, it does not matter when a claim is filed under the occurrence form. As long as a covered event occurs during the policy period, the insurer is obliged to respond on behalf of the insured—even if the claim is not presented until years after the event and years after the policy has expired. In other words, in an occurrence form for bodily injury and property damage, it is the event that triggers coverage.

On the other hand, *the coverage trigger in a claims-made form is the filing of the claim itself.* Coverage is invoked when the notice of claim is received and recorded by any insured or the insurer (whichever comes first). However, unlike the occurrence form, a claim under claims-made coverage must be made during the policy period. But because of some unique characteristics of the claims-made CGL form, such as the extended reporting period, the form under which coverage is triggered may have an expiration date that precedes the date of the claim. This condition is explained later in the chapter. At this point in the discussion, it is enough to remember that the time of the accident is not *as important* a factor under claims-made coverage as it is under occurrence coverage (the retroactive date does limit when the accident can have occurred). In fact, one of the reasons for the claims-made approach is to overcome the difficulty in determining the point in time at which an accident caused bodily injury or property damage. It is often easier to pinpoint the time at which the claim was made, especially if the accident does not occur at a point in time but over a period of time, such as the exposure to some toxic substances, for instance.

Apart from provisions relating to the Coverage A triggers, both CGL forms are identical. "Bodily injury" and "property damage" under both forms must be caused by an "occurrence," as these terms are defined in the forms. "Occurrence" means an accident, including continuous or repeated exposure to substantially the same general harmful conditions.

**Coverage B Trigger.** Up to this point, the claims-made policy and its special features has been discussed only in terms of Coverage A. Coverage B, for personal injury and advertising injury liability, is subject to an entirely different trigger. The trigger of Coverage B under *both* the occurrence and claims-made forms is "personal injury" or "advertising injury" caused by an *offense committed during the policy period* in the "coverage territory."

The coverage trigger is not that a *claim is made* involving personal injury or advertising injury. If an executive of Alpha Manufacturing Company were to say something untrue about someone else during 1990 CGL policy period, and a resulting suit for slander were to follow during that same year, there would be no question as to which policy provides coverage, since the injury and suit occur in the same policy period. But if the offense were committed in 1989 and the personal injury claim is not made until 1990, the 1989 policy for both kinds of forms would be triggered. It is not always easy to ascertain when an offense has been committed. This can be an especially troublesome problem with regard to malicious prosecution cases, because the courts are divided as to the time when the offense of this kind of personal injury is considered to have been committed.

**Coverage C Trigger.** Under both the occurrence and claims-made forms, medical payments coverage, Coverage C of the CGL forms, is triggered by an *accident that takes place* in the "coverage territory." The word *accident* is not defined in the policy but is commonly defined as an event that is both (1) accidental or unforeseen *and* (2) sudden or definite in time or place.

In any event, Coverage C is subject to a trigger that differs from those of Coverages A and B. Coverage C does *not* depend on when bodily injury occurs or when a claim is made. What triggers medical payments coverage is when the accident occurs.

## INSURANCE ON A CLAIMS-MADE BASIS

The term claims-made has been mentioned several times in the preceding discussion of coverage. Even though the claims-made form is used less frequently than had been expected, the reasons for the introduction of this coverage and how it operates are important to every liability underwriter. In some lines of insurance and for some types of risks, claims-made may be not only the preferable form to use, it may be the only form that insurers offer.

This section examines the reasons for introducing claims-made policies for use in general liability insurance. It also considers some important concepts related to the claims-made policy. Finally, it discusses how the claims-made form is being used in general liability insurance.

## Claims-Made Concepts

**Claims-Made Versus Occurrence.** General liability coverage has traditionally been provided on an occurrence basis. That is, the policy covers incidents causing bodily injury or property damage when the bodily injury or property damage "occur" during the policy period. In many cases, especially with the premises-operations exposure, it is obvious that some bodily injury or property damage has occurred that will give rise to a claim. For example, if an insured plumber accidentally starts a fire in a customer's house while sweating a copper pipe, or if the plumber accidentally hits a customer in the head with a length of pipe causing a cut requiring stitches (but with no long-term medical problems), it is likely that the property damage and bodily injury will give rise to a claim.

There are two important characteristics of these events. First, it is fairly obvious as to when the property damage and bodily injury occurred. Second, the claim for the damage or injury is likely to be made shortly after they occur. In fact, it is fairly likely that a lawsuit will not even be filed, and the claim will be settled out of court. Under an occurrence form of the CGL policy, the policy providing coverage at the time the property damage or bodily injury occurred is the policy that will respond to claims from such property damage or bodily injury. In fact, the claim in such cases will often be settled even before that policy period has expired. Pricing for such claims is also fairly easy since there are few incurred but not reported (IBNR) claims and few claims remain open for extended periods of time.

An insurance pricing problem arises when the two preceding characteristics are absent. For example, assume the plumber hits an infant instead of an adult in the head with the pipe. Also assume that in addition to the cut, there is some question as to whether there might be some permanent loss of vision or hearing since the infant is less able to withstand the impact and because at the present time, the infant is too young to conduct any detailed hearing and vision tests. In addition to the delay in even being able to determine if permanent damage occurred, another problem arises from the fact that minors have until they reach majority (and oftentimes the statutes of limitation begin to run only after they reach majority) to file a suit. Even though a minor's parents might sign a release, such release is not binding on the infant. Thus, there may be a lengthy delay from the time the plumber hit the child until the child files suit and then until the suit is settled. These two delays—from incident to claim and from claim to settlement—are collectively known as the *long-tail problem.* A claims-made policy only addresses the part of the tail from incident to claim. No policy can realistically address the settlement delay. If coverage was triggered by settlement of the claim, everyone involved would be using all sorts of tactics to speed up or delay settlement until the most favorable policy terms were in effect. Any current claims-made policy covers claims that are made during that policy period, not losses occurring during that policy period unless a claim is also made during that time.

This delay creates obvious pricing problems for the insurer providing coverage on an occurrence basis (assume for now the insurer has not changed). If there is a fifteen-year delay between the time the child is hit and the time the suit is finally settled, it is very difficult for an insurer to predict fifteen years into the future what the legal "climate" might be like and the likely amount of the final settlement. In addition, the impact of inflation is also impossible to accurately predict over such a long period. Yet, it is the reserves set up by the insurer for such claims that will determine what its future rates will be.

Additionally from the insured's standpoint, limits of liability that were adequate at the time the loss "occurred" will likely be inadequate when the claim is finally settled if there is a long tail. It is hard for a producer or an underwriter to predict in 1986 what juries might decide in the year 2001; yet in the above case of the plumber hitting the infant, that is how long a tail there was until the case was settled. Limits that were recommended in 1986 would probably be inadequate in 2001 (or the aggregate limits may have been reduced by previous claims). In addition, even if the producer could predict what might be adequate, it is likely that the underwriter might not be willing to provide such high limits, the insured could not afford such high limits, or the insured would not be willing to purchase such high limits even if he or she were offered them and could afford them.

Similarly, suppose this same plumber is hired to do some work for another customer. Without knowing it, the plumber fails to securely join two pipes behind a wall. Sometime over a two-year period, water begins to leak into the crawl space under the house and slowly begins to weaken the outside wall of the house. Eventually the outside wall collapses, causing severe structural damage to the home.

In this situation, there may be some question as to how long the pipes have been leaking. They may have started leaking the day after the work was done and have lasted for two years, or they may have only begun leaking a few months before the wall collapsed. If the plumber is found to be liable, he or she may have as many as three different policies that could respond to the loss. In addition, these policies might be with different insurers and with different limits of liability. Only those policies in effect when the damage "occurred" should respond to the loss. Until the claim is finally settled, the insurers involved would have a difficult time determining whether or not to establish reserves and, if so, for what amount. These decisions in the meantime would affect any rate changes that included these policy periods in the experience period.

These are the problems faced by many insurers and insureds today with regard to the asbestos problem, but with more complexity, dollars, and a much longer time period over which the injury "occurred." Many of the lawsuits arising from the asbestos exposure involve periods of up to thirty years, millions and millions of dollars, and multiple insurers and limits. Insurers who are held liable in 1990 under policies issued in the 1940s and 1950s have no opportunity to go back and collect additional premiums for these losses. In these cases, reserves were usually not set up until sometime in the 1980s, and therefore no rate changes until that time even reflected a reserve for possible asbestos losses.

While the examples given other than asbestos are fairly simple, they do serve to point out some of the possible problems with pricing under occurrence forms. Under a claims-made form, the policy in force at the time the claim is first made would respond to the claim. While a claims-made version will not solve all of the insurers' pricing problems, it should help at least reduce some of the problems described earlier and specifically help eliminate the problems with pricing for the IBNR-type claims. Using the asbestos problem as an example and assuming coverage had always been on a claims-made basis, insurers in 1940 would not have had to worry about claims that might arise in 1990 from policies issued in 1940. But insurers in 1990 still have to worry about claims made in 1990 (regardless of when the loss "occurred") that might not be settled until 1993.

**Retroactive Date.** When issuing a claims-made version of the CGL policy, a retroactive date must be entered on the CGL declarations form. It is expected that in many cases, this date will be the date that the insured first purchased claims-made coverage. Thereafter on renewals, the retroactive date would remain the date that the insured first purchased claims-made coverage and would not be moved forward with each successive renewal.

***Operation.*** If the insured first purchases a claims-made policy on 1 March 1986 after previously having occurrence policies, many insurers would use 1 March 1986 as the retroactive date on the new policy and all subsequent renewals. (Note that this is not required.) By using this date, the new policy and its renewals would not respond for any claims made during the policy period that arise from bodily injury or property damage occurring prior to 1 March 1986. Coverage for those losses would be provided by one of the previous occurrence forms.

Thus, the first claims-made policy in this example only provides coverage for bodily injury or property damage that occurs during the policy period *and* for which the claim is made during the policy period. This logically gives less coverage than an occurrence policy or a claims-made policy with no retroactive date. This "reduced" coverage is reflected in the rates. In fact, in this situation, the claims-made rates are reduced for the initial four years to reflect the reduction in coverage.

By keeping the retroactive date as 1 March 1986, there should be no claims denied on the basis of the retroactive date. For example, claims made during the 1990–1991 policy period would be covered under the 1 March 1990 policy, even if they arise from bodily injury or property damage occurring on 1 June 1986. All that is required is that the bodily injury or property damage occurs after the retroactive date shown on the declarations, which in this case was 1 March 1986.

If no retroactive date is shown, the underwriter enters the word "None" in the space for the retroactive date on the declarations page. The claims-made policy would then respond to any claims made during the policy period, regardless of when the bodily injury or property damage occurred. This situation also allows the same bodily injury or property damage to possibly be covered by both an occurrence and a claims-made policy.

Using the same policy as above with a 1 March 1986 inception but with no retroactive date, assume the insured is held liable for bodily injury that occurred in December 1985, the claim for which was filed in June 1986. The 1985–1986 occurrence policy responds since the bodily injury occurred during the policy period. The claims-made policy also responds since the claim was made during the policy period, regardless of when the bodily injury occurred (since there was no retroactive date). The claims-made policy applies because it states that it is considered to be excess over any other valid and collectible insurance (regardless of whether the other insurance is considered to be excess, primary, contingent, or on any other basis) that is effective prior to the beginning of the claims-made policy in question and that applies to bodily injury or property damage on other than a claims-made basis, if (1) there is no retroactive date shown or (2) the other insurance has a policy period that continues after the retroactive date which is shown. This latter portion would handle cases of overlapping occurrence and claims-made forms.

Two situations have been addressed—a policy using the first date of claims-made coverage as the retroactive date and retaining that date on renewals; and using no retroactive date. A third possibility is to advance the retroactive date at each renewal. In this case, the insured is charged the reduced "first year" claims-made rate each year, but the insured is also faced with the need to buy extended reporting period or "tail" coverage each year. (Tail coverage is described under the next heading.) This is because each renewal would respond only to bodily injury or property damage occurring during its policy period and for which the claim is made during the same period. Claims for bodily injury or property damage occurring during a previous policy period would not be covered. The only coverage the insured might have would be the extended reporting period coverage. Some of this extended coverage is provided automatically without additional charge. (This is described later.)

***Rule Limiting Advancement of Retroactive Date.*** To prevent insurers from routinely advancing the retroactive date with each renewal, a rule in the *CLM* imposes certain restrictions on advancing the retroactive date. Once the retroactive date is set for a claims-made policy, it can be advanced only with the consent of the first named insured *and* if the following are true:

- There is a change of insurance companies.
- There is a substantial change in the insured's operations that results in an increased exposure to loss.
- The insured fails to provide the insurer with information the insured knows or should know concerning the nature of the risk that would have been material to the insurer's acceptance of the risk, or the insured fails to provide information requested by the insurer.
- The insured requests the advance.

Under any of these conditions, the underwriter must get the *written* acknowledgment from the first named insured that the first named insured has been advised of the right to purchase tail coverage.

**Extended Reporting Periods (Tail Coverage).** To summarize the discussion up to this point, the following is required to trigger claims-made coverage:

1. Notice of a claim must be received and recorded during the policy period.
2. The notice must allege bodily injury or property damage that took place after the policy's retroactive date, if there is one.

When, for whatever reason, the insured's claims-made coverage with a certain insurer is stopped, it is possible that the insured will have an uninsured exposure. Any claims made after the expiration date of the last claims-made policy are not covered since the claim was simply not made during the policy period. To maintain continuity of coverage, thereby protecting against a situation where the injury or damage occurs after the retroactive date but a claim is not made until after the policy's expiration, the claims-made policy must include an extended reporting period (ERP), commonly referred to as a "tail."

While there are many variations of "tails" or extended reporting periods, they all have the same underlying function. When activated, the tail extends coverage of a claims-made policy to claims (1) first made after the expiration of the policy and (2) for bodily injury or property damage that occurred *before* the expiration of the policy, but *after* the retroactive date. The effect of tail coverage is to extend the time within which a claim can be made and still be eligible for coverage. Section V of the ISO claims-made CGL form describes the extended reporting periods and the situations in which they apply.

The extended reporting periods are designed to close, or at least reduce, certain gaps that are inherent in the use of a claims-made form. Thus, tail coverage may be necessary when the claims-made policy is:

1. Renewed or rewritten subject to an advanced retroactive date (either with the current insurer or a new insurer)
2. Replaced with an occurrence form
3. Canceled or not renewed *for any reason* either by the insured or insurer (even for nonpayment)
4. Subject to a "laser beam" endorsement (described later)

These conditions exemplify many possible combinations of coverage (or lack of coverage). If the insured switches insurers and the new insurer uses the same retroactive date as the old insurer, there should be no problem. However, if the new insurer advances the retroactive date to the inception date of the new policy (or the present insurer just advances the retroactive date), there is a coverage gap for claims made after the new policy inception date, but arising from bodily injury or property damage that occurred prior to the new policy's inception date. The new policy would not cover the claim since the bodily injury or property damage occurred prior to its retroactive date and the old policy would not cover the claim since it was made after the old policy period had ended.

***Basic Extended Reporting Period.*** Each claims-made policy protects against such gaps in coverage to some extent in that some extended coverage is provided automatically for no charge. This coverage is referred to as the *basic extended reporting period* on BERP. The first portion of the BERP is a five-year tail that extends five years after the end of the policy period and applies to claims resulting from occurrences reported to the insurer no later than sixty days after the end of the regular policy period. (Again, the occurrence has to have taken place during the policy period and after the retroactive date.) Some persons refer to this tail as the "five-year midi tail."

The second portion of the BERP is a "sixty-day mini tail" for "all other claims." Basically, this mini tail is for the incurred but not reported occurrences existing at the end of the policy period. Remember that the *five-year tail required that the occurrence be "reported" no later than sixty days after the end of the policy period.* The sixty-day tail does not have such a reporting requirement. It thus might cover a claim filed against the insured on the fifty-ninth day after the policy period expires and of which the insured was totally unaware. Thus, when the insured sends the claim to the insurer on the sixty-first day, it would be covered by the "sixty-day mini tail" portion of the BERP. Importantly, the BERP is *not* in effect after every claims-made policy expires, but only after the continuous pattern of claims-made coverage is interrupted. The BERP coverage does not apply if the insured has purchased other insurance that would apply to the claim (or would apply were it not for the new policy limits being exhausted).

***Supplemental Extended Reporting Period.*** The policy also offers the insured the option to purchase an unlimited *supplemental extended reporting period endorsement* (SERP) or "maxi tail" for an additional charge not to exceed 200 percent "of the annual premium for the coverage part to which the endorsement would be attached." This tail takes over where the BERP ends, but again, does not extend the policy period, only the time during which a claim can be made.

The named insured must request the unlimited tail in writing within sixty days of the end of the policy period and must pay the entire premium when due. Once the premium is paid, the endorsement cannot be canceled. The SERP, or unlimited tail coverage, is considered excess over any other valid and collectible insurance available to the insured and whose policy period begins or continues after the tail takes effect. Additionally, the SERP contains a separate set of general and products-completed operations aggregate limits for claims made under the SERP. These are equal to the aggregate limits shown on the declarations page at policy termination. The policy wording should prevent any possible attempts to have claims filed specifically under the SERP instead of the BERP in order to benefit from possibly higher aggregate limits (in cases where the original aggregate may have been partially or totally exhausted).

According to the policy provisions in Section V, the ERPs are provided for the following reasons:

1. The coverage is canceled or not renewed.
2. The coverage is renewed or replaced by the insurer with insurance that (i) has a retroactive date later than the one shown in the declarations page or (ii) does not apply to bodily injury or property damage on a claims-made basis.

***Pricing the Tail Coverage.*** Underwriters are faced with the task of pricing the unlimited tail coverage. The amount they can charge is limited only by the policy provision limiting the premium to 200 percent of the annual premium. Interestingly, the claims-made policy provides some guidance for the underwriter within the policy itself. In the provision mentioning the 200 percent limit, the policy provides that in pricing the tail coverage, the insurer can consider the following:

- Exposures
- Previous types of insurance and the amounts thereof
- Limits of insurance still available under the policy
- All other related factors

This provision was used to help reduce some of the fear on the part of producer and buyer organizations that insurers would, on a blanket basis, always charge the 200 percent maximum. Whether or not this procedure occurs, remains to be seen. If it does, some type of specialty tail market that will offer the coverage to the more desirable insureds at a reduced price will probably develop.

Underwriters should follow the suggestions of the policy while staying within company guidelines in pricing the coverage. For some insureds, there will be few claims falling within the tail coverage, and therefore, the coverage should probably be offered at a price much below the 200 percent maximum. For example, a policy covering an office exposure would most likely have very few claims after the policy period had expired, and thus, the tail coverage should be priced relatively low.

However, a manufacturer of medical equipment presents a much different exposure in that some bodily injury or property damage may have occurred for which a claim is yet to be filed. In this case, the tail coverage would be relatively expensive. The problem lies in trying to price all of the risks that fall between these two, and it is for those risks that underwriters must use their judgment, underwriting guidelines, and so on. The use of tables showing the loss development factors and the IBNR factors of various classes will be useful in trying to price the tail coverage.

It is important that underwriters make sure insureds and producers understand that the tail coverage extends the time during which the claim can be made, not the policy period itself. Essentially the policy says a claim filed during the tail coverage is considered to have been filed on the last day of the policy period. *The bodily injury or property damage must still have occurred before the expiration of the policy period and after the applicable retroactive date.* Coverage for bodily injury or property damage occurring after the policy period has expired has to be provided by some other policy.

**Laser Beam Endorsements.** There are several endorsements that are closely related to the retroactive date and its use. It was stated earlier that an insurer might "for whatever reason" move its retroactive date forward at each renewal. Initially, it might seem that one reason to do so would be to avoid the filing of a claim with regard to a certain event. By advancing the retroactive date before the claim is made, bodily injury or property damage occurring before the retroactive date is excluded. However, this argument cannot be supported since the insurer would be required by the policy to provide the BERP and offer the SERP, one of which would likely end up covering the particular event intended to be excluded. The laser beam endorsements allow the insurer more flexibility in controlling the retroactive date and the extent of exposure to be assumed. It might initially seem that these endorsements benefit only the insurer, but the following discussion shows how the entire set of endorsements work to the advantage of both the insurer and the insured.

An *exclusion of specific accident(s), products, work or location(s) endorsement* (sometimes referred to as the *laser beam endorsement*) for Coverage A can be used by the insurer at the inception of the policy or at renewal. An insurer may wish to attach such an endorsement to a policy at inception in order to issue the policy without a retroactive date or with an earlier retroactive date.

For example, assume the insured does not want a retroactive date on the policy, and the insurer would be willing to go along with this were it not for a particular product the insured has manufactured in the past and against which the insurer expects future claims. The insurer then issues the policy without a retroactive date, but the policy would be written to exclude claims arising out of that particular product. (This same situation might arise if the insured is changing insurers and wishes to keep the same retroactive date, but there have been some products that have caused losses in the past and are expected to continue to cause some losses.)

Similarly, at renewal date, the insurer may be aware of a particular location that is likely to cause a number of losses in the future. In order to limit its exposure, the insurer may wish to exclude that particular location at renewal through use of this endorsement. One way that an underwriter might be made aware of such a location is that the insured is required in the policy to notify the insurer "as soon as practicable of an 'occurrence' that may result in a claim." In the claims-made policy it is made clear that such notification still does not constitute a claim being "made" in the sense that it would not trigger coverage. A claim is considered to have been made when a notice of a claim is received and recorded by an insured or the insurer. The endorsement can also be used when an insured wants to retain a particular exposure.

If the endorsement is imposed at a renewal date, the insurer is required to amend *the expiring policy* with an endorsement titled *amendment of Section V—extended reporting periods for specific accident(s), products, work or location(s).* This endorsement provides that the insured is able to purchase the SERP or unlimited tail coverage for the specific work, locations, and so on, that are being excluded. The BERP also applies automatically. If the insured does elect to purchase the supplemental extended reporting period endorsement for the particular exposure, a special endorsement is issued to cover only those exposures.

It is likely that this set of endorsements will be widely used when claims-made coverage is provided. When used properly, they will be of benefit to both the insured and the insurer. The insured is likely to be able to continue coverage on most of the exposures, while by excluding those exposures not insurable in the standard market, the insurer is able to write those parts of an insured's operations that are desirable without having to decline or nonrenew the entire account because of one specific exposure.

**Claims-Made Versus Occurrence Premiums.** Claims-made CGL coverage premiums should be less than those for occurrence coverage. This reflects the average shorter time between policy inception and claim date, limited to a maximum of five years unless the insured requests and pays extra for the supplemental extended reporting period, versus the unlimited "tail" automatically provided, in effect, by all occurrence policies. During the first four years of claims-made coverage, an additional discount applies to claims-made policies because some claims will be covered by prior occurrence policies. In any case, occurrences prior to the retroactive date are not covered. This discount decreases each year because more claims will be covered as the claims-made policy matures if the retroactive date is not advanced. Also, policies with no retroactive date or one earlier than the inception date of the claims-made policy will cost more than those with a later date to reflect the extra coverage being provided for prior occurrences.

The premium determination discussion in Chapter 7 noted that there are separate sets of rates for claims-made and occurrence-based policies. The claims-made rates shown in the manual are referred to as *mature claims-made rates.* To give the above discount if coverage has been provided on a claims-made basis for less than five years, a factor of less than 1.00 must be applied to the mature claims-made rate. The factor for year 5 and subsequent years is 1.00.

Two points are noteworthy here:

1. The policyholder who changes from occurrence coverage to claims-made coverage may think he or she is continuing

equivalent coverage at a discount—particularly during the initial years of claims-made coverage when the additional discounts apply. In fact, the reduced premium does not reflect a bargain, but the fact that fewer claims are covered and there is no automatic unlimited "tail." The apparent savings may quickly vanish when "unlimited tail" coverage must be purchased for an additional premium.

2. Advancing the retroactive date reduces the premium that an insurer may charge according to rating manual rules. This gives the insurer an incentive for *not* advancing the retroactive date when a policy is renewed or replaced.

**Insured's Right to Obtain Claim and "Occurrence" Information.** Claims-made insurance can require insureds to make many decisions. In addition to the ever-present question of whether to continue coverage with the same insurer, claims-made insurance raises additional issues relating to the following:

- Advancement of retroactive dates with related premium adjustments
- Potential impact of "laser beam" endorsements
- Existence of reported occurrences that could give rise to a claim
- Existence of reported and recorded claims that are not yet settled
- Adequacy of "automatic tail" coverage of the basic extended reporting period
- Possible need to buy "unlimited tail" coverage under a supplemental extended reporting period as weighed against a potentially high premium
- The extent to which aggregate limits are impaired by occurrences or claims

Many, if not all, of these issues can best be resolved when the insured has current information on reported occurrences and on paid and reserved claims.

To ensure that a policyholder has access to current information, the claims-made CGL contains a provision titled "Your Right to Claim and Occurrence Information." If the insured elects to cancel or nonrenew the CGL, the insurer is obligated to provide such information no later than thirty days before the policy terminates. In other circumstances, the information must be provided if the first named insured requests it in writing within sixty days after the end of the policy period. The information must be provided no later than forty-five days after the request is received. Since a considerable amount of judgment is used in setting loss reserves, the CGL contains a disclaimer strongly stating that the reserves should not be regarded as ultimate settlement values and noting that the insurer makes no representations or warranties about the information, although it does exercise reasonable care in gathering the information for its own business purposes.

## Use of Claims-Made Form

**Reasons for Use.** As noted, the major reason for developing the claims-made form was to eliminate deficiencies of the occurrence form in its handling of long-tail exposures. With the claims-made policy, one and only one policy is intended to apply to a claim—the policy that is in force when the claim is first received and recorded. (An exception may occur if a supplemental tail on an expired policy overlaps with a new, current claims-made policy.) This condition is not like occurrence policies whose limits have been stacked because in the latter case, several policies have been deemed to apply to the same claim. Another reason for using the claims-made policy is that the loss experience attributable to any given policy is more readily determinable despite long-tail exposures, thereby making it possible for insurers to price insurance in a way that is more responsive to actual experience. Just how the mechanics of the claims-made policy vary from those of the occurrence form might best be understood with an illustration.

**Illustration.** Assume that Alpha Manufacturing Company had been covered continuously since 1975 under CGL policies written on an occurrence basis. At renewal on 1 January 1988 the insurer is willing to write only a claims-made policy with $500,000 aggregate limits and a retroactive date the same as the inception date of that first claims-made form. One year later, in 1989, the policy is renewed on a claims-made basis without changing the retroactive date. During this policy year of 1989, Alpha Manufacturing is confronted with a large product liability claim because of an occurrence during the 1988 policy period. The claim results in the payment of a $250,000 bodily injury liability judgment. As a result of this claim, Alpha Manufacturing Company's remaining products-completed operations aggregate limit is $250,000. Later in 1989 Alpha reports an "occurrence" to the insurance company related to a new product line. By the end of 1989, no claims have been made against Alpha Manufacturing because of that occurrence. As a safety measure against a possible large claim against it because of that reported 1989 occurrence, Alpha Manufacturing makes known to its insurer that it would like to increase its primary limits to $1 million when the 1990 renewal policy takes effect. Consider Alpha's reasoning here: If the insurance company renews the claims-made policy in 1990 and retains the 1988 retroactive date, Alpha Manufacturing Company will not have to worry about the reduced aggregate limit of the 1989 policy year because once that policy expires, it is the next policy that covers any claim that might be made stemming from the occurrence reported during the preceding year. And, if the insurer honors the request of the insured to increase the per occurrence and aggregate limits on renewal, Alpha Manufacturing will now have access to $1 million limits, if claim is made during 1990, as opposed to $250,000, if the claim were to be subject to the expiring policy's eroded aggregate limit.

***Insurance Company Options.*** The insurance company is not required to honor the insured's request; the insurer also has other options to protect its interests. Thus, the insurer can do the following:

1. Nonrenew the policy
2. Make the 1990 claims-made policy subject to the "laser-beam" endorsement
3. Make the 1990 claims-made policy subject to a later retroactive date, that is, move it from 1988 to 1990 (but this may be done only under certain circumstances that may not apply here)

If the insurer chooses to nonrenew the policy, it will still be obligated to pay up to $250,000 for claims made within the expiring policy's five-year tail period. Moreover, the insured will have the option of purchasing unlimited tail coverage with $500,000 aggregate limits that would apply if claim is made, say, six years after the nonrenewal.

If the insurer elects the second option and makes the 1990 claims-made policy subject to a laser beam endorsement excluding the problem product, the new claims-made policy would not provide coverage in two important areas. First, under the new 1990 policy, coverage would not be provided for any claim caused by the excluded product and arising out of an occurrence involving that product before the inception of the new policy. This would be true whether or not the claim resulted from the 1989 occurrence already reported or any other unknown occurrence related to the product. As explained in the next section, the expiring policy would be endorsed to provide some tail coverage for such claims. With the "laser" endorsement, the retroactive date of the 1990 policy could remain as originally set in 1988. This means that any claim made during 1990 because of an unknown occurrence involving bodily injury or property damage any time after the 1988 retroactive date, and not as a result of the excluded product, would be covered under the 1990 claims-made policy.

Second, coverage would not be provided during 1990 for any other claim made during that period alleging bodily injury or property damage *that occurred during that same 1990 policy period* as a result of the *product* that is specifically excluded by the "laser" endorsement. No tail coverage is available for these claims. The impact of choosing the second option is explained later in the section, "Another Potential Gap."

If the insurer were able to elect the third option and make the 1990 claims-made policy the subject of a later retroactive date, no claim during the 1990 policy period would be covered by the policy if it arose out of bodily injury or property damage that occurred before the 1990 retroactive date.

***Effect on Coverage.*** Any of the three preceding choices made by the insurer creates a situation that must be understood by the insured. If the retroactive date is advanced to the year 1990 or the laser endorsement is used instead, the 1989 expiring claims-made policy is subject to an *automatic* five-year tail that will apply only to claims arising out of the occurrence that was reported to the insurer during the 1988 claims-made policy year. As explained earlier, when the laser beam endorsement is attached by an insurer to its renewal policy, the insurer *is required* to attach an *Extended Reporting Period for Specific Accident(s), Products, Work or Location (s) Endorsement* to the expiring policy. This endorsement amends the expiring policy to provide sixty-day and five-year basic extended reporting periods for the specified exposure, and also gives the insured the right to purchase supplemental extended reporting period coverage (unlimited tail coverage) applicable only to the exposure excluded by the renewal policy.

Recall that the automatic tail does not increase the limits of the policy to which it applies. In this case, any claim made after the expiration of the 1989 claims-made policy involving the occurrence reported during that year would be subject to coverage but only to the extent of the aggregate limit that remains. In this illustration, the insured would have protection only to the extent of the remaining $250,000 aggregate limit. However, the supplemental extended reporting period coverage would provide $500,000 aggregate limits applicable to other unknown occurrences from that specific product during 1988 or 1989.

When the retroactive date is advanced but no laser beam exclusion is used, there is still another potential problem that requires the attention of the insured. Also not covered under the policy for the year 1990 are claims for bodily injury or property damage that took place prior to the 1990 retroactive date from an occurrence that was unknown to the insured before the expiration of the 1989 policy period and therefore not reported to the insurer. If there had been such an occurrence, the claim made during 1990 would not be covered because of the policy's retroactive date.

To close this gap, the insured should request in writing the unlimited tail immediately or some time within the sixty-day tail period following the expiration of the 1989 claims-made policy. Once this tail is purchased, the reporting period of the insured's expired 1989 claims-made policy is indefinitely extended for *any* claims for bodily injury or property damage that took place before the 1989 claims-made policy expired. In addition, the unlimited tail also provides a new set of aggregate limits corresponding in amount to the limits that applied to the expired policy to which the unlimited tail coverage endorsement is attached. However, this new set of aggregate limits applies only to claims stemming from occurrences that happened since 1 January 1988 and before the 1990 retroactive date and that were unknown to the insured and therefore unreported. The new aggregate limits cannot be used to pay for claims involving occurrences that were reported during an earlier period if the claim is made during the sixty-day tail period or during the automatic five-year tail period that follows it.

***Another Potential Gap.*** The laser beam endorsement in the second option above excludes all future claims involving the new product of Alpha Manufacturing Company. The insurer, in other words, may be willing to retain the earlier retroactive date of 1988 but only on the condition that the 1990 and subsequent policies be subject to the laser endorsement specifically excluding the problem product.

Excluding coverage is not an approach unique to claims-made coverage or even a novel approach. Insurers have long excluded coverage for specific exposures that are considered undesirable or uninsurable. Insureds must remember that even with the automatic tail coverage and the supplemental extended reporting period, there may still be a gap in coverage. In the case of Alpha Manufacturing Company, the automatic five-year tail applies only to occurrences reported to the insurer not later than sixty days after the expiration of the 1989 policy period. The purchase of the unlimited tail coverage of the SERP does provide protection to Alpha for claims made during a subsequent policy because of an occurrence during 1988 or 1989 of which Alpha was unaware. But suppose the product in question causes bodily injury and a resulting claim in 1990. The unlimited tail coverage of the expired 1989 claims-made policy will not apply since its purpose is to extend the reporting period of the 1989 policy, not to extend the period of coverage. In this case, Alpha Manufacturing Company would be without protection. Unless it obtains other products liability insurance specifically for the exposure excluded by the laser endorsement, Alpha Manufacturing Company would retain future losses. This is no different from any other type of insurance where a particular exposure might be excluded.

Many other situations could be used to illustrate the mechanics of the claims-made policy. However, the preceding discussion should provide a basic understanding of the claims-made policy and its retroactive date, tail coverages, and laser endorsements that may be applied to specific situations that may develop.

**Extent of Use.** Although the claims-made form was never intended to be used for every type of risk, it is probably written for even fewer risks than many expected when it was introduced. This is because most insureds do not want claims-made coverage and in most instances can find at least one insurer willing to offer occurrence coverage. It is typical that only when a risk is unable to find occurrence coverage is the claims-made policy used.

It is likely that the use of claims-made policies will fluctuate somewhat with the underwriting profit cycle. However, because of the problems associated with switching back and forth between occurrence and claims-made forms, it is not likely that this fluctuation will be especially significant. At some point, it is possible that many insureds of a certain type or class will be written on a claims-made basis because of the nature of the exposure they present. However, it is difficult to speculate when that might occur. Despite the limited use of the claims-made form, underwriters should be familiar with the coverage and where it might be appropriate.

## PREMISES-OPERATIONS UNDERWRITING

Having reviewed some of the more important general liability policy provisions, the discussion will now focus on the underwriting of the premises-operations exposure under the general liability policy. This portion of the chapter will look first at those policy provisions of the CGL that pertain to the premises-operations exposure and especially those provisions that are different under the new CGL. Following that, the various types of information needed and the factors to consider for underwriting the premises-operations exposure are presented. Many sources of information have already been described in Chapter 3, and this section will build on that discussion. Additionally, note that much of this information is also applicable to underwriting the products-completed operations exposure (described in the next chapter).

### CGL Policy Provisions Related to the Premises-Operations Exposure

The entire CGL policy will not be described in this section. Only those provisions that have changed significantly from the previous version of the policy and that significantly affect the underwriting process and decisions, or those often subject to misinterpretation, will be described.

**Explosion, Collapse, and Underground.** Under the previous version of the CGL policy, the explosion, collapse, and underground (XCU) exposure was excluded unless specifically included by endorsement. Under the new CGL policy, the reverse is true except for a very few special classes. That is, most classes *include* the XCU exposure in the rate, and if the underwriter wants to exclude the exposure, an endorsement must be issued.

The XCU exposure relates to property damage and usually exists for risks engaged in construction involving digging or blasting. In some cases, firms with manufacturing processes using highly flammable or volatile substances, such as paint solvents, will also have the XCU exposure.

Because of its severity potential, this exposure must be underwritten carefully. Just because the rate now includes the exposure, underwriters should not assume that XCU is not a possible problem. To the contrary, XCU should now be underwritten much as all other exposures are underwritten. That is, the rate assumes an "average" XCU exposure, and if the particular risk being underwritten has a better- or worse-than-average exposure, then the risk should be considered more or less desirable than average, respectively, all other things equal.

The qualifications of blasters and the experience of equipment operators are important considerations, as is the proximity of the operations to property that may be damaged. For example, an excavator digging a trench in a rural field presents a less severe exposure than the same operations conducted on a downtown street. However, the portion of the rate reflecting the underground exposure will likely be the same for both operations.

**Pollution.** Another part of the new CGL policy that has also been controversial (and that was actually added after the introduction of the new program and its submission to some commissioners) is the exclusion of virtually all pollution liability coverage under the policy. Initially, ISO planned to reword the old exclusion, but still provide "sudden and accidental" coverage while excluding "gradual" pollution coverage. However many insurers wished to see a total exclusion.

One of the primary reasons for the total exclusion was that many courts were determining that the old CGL policy provided complete pollution coverage despite the gradual pollution exclusion. In some cases, the courts held the terms "sudden and accidental" to be ambiguous and therefore to be interpreted in favor of the insured. In others, if the damage was accidental from the insured's standpoint, the courts have held that the pollution was accidental and therefore covered (essentially ignoring the sudden part of the requirement).

Regardless of how the courts determined that there was total coverage, insurers were not very confident that the wording in the new policy would preclude the same result. They therefore pressed for a (hopefully) clear, total exclusion of pollution. ISO did subsequently introduce a total pollution exclusion.

When this total exclusion was announced, the market for gradual pollution coverage was close to nonexistent. Producers were therefore very alarmed with ISO intentions and encouraged ISO to go back to the old wording. Some regulators were also concerned as to whether there would be any market for gradual or sudden and accidental pollution coverage (even though ISO has proposed an endorsement that can be added to the CGL policy for an additional premium to provide "sudden and accidental" pollution coverage) and were considering this before approving the new forms. Many states did approve the total exclusion, but it will be years before anyone will know if it performs as intended.

**Liquor Liability Exclusion.** The so-called *liquor liability exclusion* applies to firms in the business of manufacturing, distributing, selling, serving, or furnishing alcoholic beverages. The exclusion excludes bodily injury and property damage coverage for claims in which any insured may be held liable for the following actions:

1. Causing or contributing to the intoxication of any person
2. Furnishing alcoholic beverages to a person under legal drinking age, or to a person under the influence of alcohol
3. Violating any statute, ordinance, or regulation relating to the sale, gift, distribution, or use of alcoholic beverages

The laws mentioned in (3) above, which apply in varying degrees in many states, are sometimes referred to as *dram shop acts* or *alcoholic beverage control acts.* While the application and scope of these laws vary by state, their general purpose is to give a person, when injured by an intoxicated adult or by a minor who is served alcoholic beverages, a right of action against the dispenser of the beverages. In some states, the common law creates liability even when a statute may or may not apply. In any event, a seller of alcoholic beverages confronted with a liquor liability suit does not have any protection under an unendorsed commercial general liability policy.

It is not always easy to determine whether an organization is "in the business of" selling, serving, or furnishing alcoholic beverages. For example, would a nonprofit organization that sells liquor without profit motive be considered "in the business"? How about an organization that conducts a special event where alcoholic beverages are sold? Would the fact that the organization requires a license be the determinant? These are all important questions that must be answered before any coverage is to be expected by exception to the exclusion. For example, if the insured is not considered to be *in the business,* then by inference the insured could be considered a *host* and covered by exception to the exclusion. This "coverage" is sometimes referred to as *host liquor liability coverage.*

Note finally that the liquor liability exclusion does not apply to the owner or lessee of premises used by others for liquor businesses. The owner or lessee therefore would be protected by the CGL policy for any claim or suit alleging that had the owner or lessee been more careful in the selection of tenant (vendor), the injury might not have occurred.

**General Property Damage Exclusion.** Because of its length and nature, this exclusion will first be stated and then discussed section by section. The policy does not cover property damage to the following:

(1) Property you own, rent, or occupy;
(2) Premises you sell, give away or abandon, if the "property damage" arises out of any part of those premises;
(3) Property loaned to you;
(4) Personal property in your care, custody or control;
(5) That particular part of real property on which you or any contractors or subcontractors working directly or indirectly on your behalf are performing operations, if the "property damage" arises out of those operations; or
(6) That particular part of any property that must be restored, repaired or replaced because "your work" was incorrectly performed on it.

Paragraph (2) of this exclusion does not apply if the premises are "your work" and were never occupied, rented or held for rental by you.

Paragraphs (3), (4), (5) and (6) of this exclusion do not apply to liability assumed under a sidetrack agreement.

Paragraph (6) of this exclusion does not apply to "property damage" included in the "products-completed operations hazard."

***Exclusion of Insured's Property.*** Paragraph (1) of the general property damage exclusion precludes any protection for damage to real or personal *property* that is owned, rented, or occupied by the insured. This exclusion allows the insurer to avoid paying for damage to property that should and normally would be covered by some form of first-party property insurance. Because the CGL policy automatically includes a certain amount of fire legal liability coverage, explained later, the only exception to this exclusion is liability for fire damage to real property rented to a named insured.

***Exclusion of Alienated Premises.*** Paragraph (2) of the general property damage exclusion is commonly referred to as the *alienated premises exclusion.* (Earlier policies used the word "alienated," but the new policy does not.) This exclusion is designed to preclude coverage for liability for property damage to premises sold by a firm that is negligent in not informing the purchaser about premises defects when the property damage arises out of and is confined to the sold premises. The following are examples:

- A firm sells its building that is known to have an electrical defect, and the seller, because of an oversight, does not make the defect known to the purchaser. The latent defect causes a fire that damages the building.
- The insured created a structural defect in the building by making modifications to the building or by overloading the floors beyond their load-bearing capacity.

In either case, the policy is not designed to cover the property damage resulting from any dangerous condition that should have been corrected by the seller before the sale or communicated to the purchaser.

However, it can be inferred from this exclusion that coverage does apply to bodily injury emanating from defective, sold premises, as well as to property damage to other than the sold premises created by the sold premises. If the electrical fire in the first example were to spread to an adjoining building, the seller would have protection, provided coverage was not precluded by other policy provisions.

***Exclusion of Personal Property in the Named Insured's Care, Custody, or Control.*** This exclusion, referred to as the *care, custody, or control exclusion,* is designed to preclude any coverage for damage to *personal* property that could have been prevented through the exercise of care or that is better handled by insuring the exposure under some form of property or inland marine insurance. Paragraph 3 is similar, but it applies to any property (not just personal property) that is loaned to the insured. In both cases, other insurance is more appropriate.

Note, however, that there is an exception to the property damage exclusion under paragraphs (3) and (4), affecting also paragraphs (5) and (6) to be discussed subsequently, concerning liability assumed under a *sidetrack agreement.* This exception means that the CGL policy provides a business with protection for any liability stemming from the use of a sidetrack spur, as well as protection for any liability because of damage to the sidetrack spur itself.

***Exclusion of Property on Which Work Is Being Performed or Was Performed.*** Paragraphs (5) and (6) of the general property damage exclusion address property damage liability exposures that are deemed to be uninsurable under the CGL policy. The exclusions apply to losses taking place while operations are in progress by or on behalf of the named insured and losses arising from the insured's incorrectly performed work. Following damage to real property while operations are in progress, the liability coverage that may apply must be inferred from the exclusions in paragraphs (5) and (6). These two exclusions relate to the care, custody, or control exclusion just described. The care, custody, or control exclusion applies only to personal property. Paragraph (5) applies to real property, and paragraph (6) applies to any property. Paragraphs (5) and (6) clarify that the exclusion for damage applies to a particular part of the property in question, not all property in the area.

Thus, under paragraph (5), there is *no coverage* for property damage to that particular part of *real* property on which operations are being performed by the named insured or on behalf of the named insured by any contractor or subcontractor, if the property damage arises out of those operations being performed. The key words are "that particular part." No coverage applies to that particular part of the real property that is damaged while work is being performed on it. But, by inference, *coverage does apply* for damage to other parts of the real property, on which work was performed by or on behalf of the named insured, resulting from that particular part of the work on which operations are being performed at the time of the occurrence.

For example assume that a developer hires a general contractor to construct condominiums. While employees of the general contractor are positioning one of the beams, it slips, falls, and bends so that it is no longer usable. When it falls, it also damages other steel beams that had already been erected. Both the developer and the general contractor would be protected for damage to the real property, the other steel beams, that was damaged by the beam that fell because operations were not being performed on those other beams at the time of the accident. However, no coverage would apply for damage to the fallen beam because it was the particular part on which operations were being performed. As another example, assume that in the course of making repairs, a plumber mistakenly bursts a water heater, and the water from that heater results in damaged walls and floors. The damage to the walls and floors is not excluded. Only the damage to the water heater is excluded.

Damage to work involving separate, identifiable parts should not present problems. But when work is being performed on a unit whose parts are more "connected" with each other, such as a machine or a switchboard, it may be difficult to determine the particular part from which damage arises. Not covered is property damage to that particular part of any property that has to be restored, repaired or replaced because work or operations performed by or on behalf of the named insured (your work) was incorrectly performed on it.

This exclusion does not necessarily mean that property must be physically damaged, but only that the work is performed so improperly that it has to be redone. The painter who uses the wrong shade of paint, the plumber who places pipes in areas not designated in the work plans, and the elevator installer who installs a unit that does not perform properly following its installation would have no coverage because of paragraph (6). In each case, the insured will undo or repair the faulty work at its own expense.

However, paragraph (6) of the exclusion does not apply to property damage within the products-completed operations hazard. This means that paragraph (6) applies only to losses while operations are in progress. Once the operation has been completed according to the criteria established by the definition of the "products-completed operations hazard," paragraph (6) cannot be used by the insurer as a basis for denying a claim. But the property damage may still be excluded by virtue of exclusion (1) concerning damage to the named insured's work as explained in the next chapter.

**Contractual Liability Coverage/Exclusion.** The CGL policy contains a contractual liability exclusion that precludes coverage for liability assumed by the insured under any contract or agreement—except as otherwise provided for by the policy. Coverage for many of the exposures that are excluded can be purchased either through other policies or by attachment of a coverage form to the CGL policy.

Despite the contractual liability exclusion, the CGL provides protection for business firms and other organizations to whom the legal liability of others has been transferred under many contracts or agreements. In a sense, it might be more appropriate to refer to the CGL's contractual liability coverage instead of the exclusion since so much coverage is still provided.

To determine the scope and nature of contractual liability exposures covered, it is necessary to examine the contractual liability exclusion. This exclusion states that no coverage applies for bodily injury or property damage for which the insured is obligated to pay damages by reason of the insured's assumption of liability under any contract or agreement—with two exceptions. The exclusion does not apply to liability for damages (1) assumed under an "insured contract" or (2) that the insured would have in the absence of the contract or agreement. Liability for all other instances of contractual agreement is intended to be excluded.

***Insured Contracts.*** Whether a contractual liability exposure is covered depends partly on the meaning of the term "insured contract," which is defined in both forms to mean: (1) a lease of premises; (2) a sidetrack agreement; (3) an easement or license agreement in connection with vehicle or pedestrian private railroad crossings at grade; (4) any other easement agreement, except in connection with construction or demolition operations on or within 50 feet of a railroad; (5) an agreement required by a municipality, except an agreement required in connection with work for a municipality; (6) an elevator maintenance agreement; or (7) that part of any other contract or agreement concerning the named insured's business under which the named insured assumes the tort liability of another to pay damages because of bodily injury or property damage to a third person or organization. Tort liability is defined by the policy to mean "a liability that would be imposed by law in the absence of any contract or agreement."

***Liability in Absence of a Contract.*** As noted, there are only two exceptions to the exclusion for liability assumed under a contract or agreement:

1. When the assumption of liability takes place under an "insured contract"
2. When the liability would have prevailed at law despite the contractual assumption of liability

To illustrate the second exception, consider Arrow Builders, a construction firm, hired to construct a manufacturing plant for Quiver Manufacturing. Arrow agrees to hold harmless and indemnify Quiver for bodily injury or property damage sustained by any person because of the acts or omissions of Arrow. During the course of construction, an employee of Arrow's subcontractor is injured because Arrow allegedly failed to provide proper safeguards. The injured employee files suit not only against Arrow, but also against Quiver based on the failure of both parties to warn the employee of any unsafe conditions and to remove the hazards. It ultimately is determined that Quiver is free from any fault. Assuming no other policy exclusion is applicable, Arrow's CGL policy should respond to the claim because Arrow would have been liable at law because of negligence even in the absence of its contractual assumption. The contract had nothing to do with Arrow's liability to the injured employee.

Going one step further, suppose Arrow, the builder, agrees to hold harmless and indemnify Quiver, the plant owner, in every instance except when any injury or damage as alleged is due solely to Quiver's negligence. If in the foregoing example Quiver were to be held partially liable for failure to warn the injured employee of a hazardous premises condition, Arrow's CGL policy should respond here as long as the liability of the plant owner would be imposed by law. In this case, Quiver's portion of the claim would be attributable to liability assumed under an "insured contract"; Arrow's portion would be attributable to liability in the absence of contract.

***A Word of Caution.*** The two parties to a contract that transfers liability from one party to the other are often under the mistaken impression that the entire assumption of liability by the one party, as agreed upon in the contract, is covered by insurance—especially when contractual liability coverage is listed on a certificate of insurance. However, as pointed out earlier, certain types of assumption of liability are beyond the scope of the contractual liability coverage automatically provided by the CGL policy. Furthermore, the assumption of liability provisions of some contracts have been declared void under the applicable statutes of some states. And, even in absence of statute, a court of law may hold the terms of a contract to be in violation of public policy. In such instances, despite the contract, the transferor has not in effect transferred the exposure.

**Mobile Equipment.** The new definition of mobile equipment has already been covered in the chapter on commercial auto underwriting. The general liability underwriter must know what mobile equipment is owned and operated by the applicant. The use of mobile equipment is one of the leading causes of claims under the general liability coverage. Mobile equipment will also give an underwriter an indication of the type of work the insured intends to perform. The underwriter can often compare the classifications shown on the application with a list of mobile equipment (perhaps obtained through a loss control report) to determine if the classifications are correct.

## Application Information

The application as a source of underwriting information was described in Chapter 3. In this section, those portions of the application related to the premises-operations exposure are examined. First examined is the general information found on the application that is helpful to the underwriting of the premises-operations exposure, followed by an explanation of the importance of the premium adjustment period and the timeliness of the loss information shown on the application.

**General Information.** Most liability applications include general questions about the applicant. For example, it is important to know if the premises are owned by the applicant and leased to others, if they are owned and occupied by the applicant, or if they are owned by someone else and occupied by the applicant. Occupancy and ownership by the applicant directly affect the degree of care owed the public and how the location will be classified and rated. Some insurers use special hazard questionnaires for special occupancies or types or risks in addition to the application.

Sometimes questions about the existence of extrahazardous structures, such as gymnasiums and grandstands, are asked. Many applications also require information about off-premises exposures such as advertising signs, vending machines or other equipment, animals, conventions or exhibitions, sponsored athletic or other events, boats, docks, or piers. It is not likely that the applicant will remember to mention these items, so questions need to be asked.

To provide the underwriter with general information needed to underwrite the risk, the application asks questions regarding the following major areas of concern to the general liability underwriter.

- Insured's financial status, character, and related information (covered in Chapter 3)
- Quality of the work force
    - Training
    - Experience
    - Turnover
    - Ages
- Equipment, tools, and materials
    - Condition
    - Age
    - Appropriateness/suitability for type of work
    - Suppliers
- Work quality
    - Reputation of insured regarding quality of work
    - Complaints about work
    - Losses
- Overall physical condition/hazards of premises and operations
    - Cleanliness of premises/operations
    - Neatness (no litter, empty boxes, used materials)
    - Condition of premises (clear aisles, well-maintained sidewalks)

Again, many of these factors are also relevant to products-completed operations underwriting. They will not be repeated in that discussion. Any characteristic of a risk that implies an inferior work force or lack of concern about losses or safety on the part of management affects any coverage provided even if all the other factors considered for that coverage give little or no indication of a problem.

**Premium Adjustment Period.** If the policy is written on an auditable basis, the premium base should not be underestimated, and the financial capacity of the insured to pay any additional premium should be ensured. A reduced deposit premium is allowed when the applicant requests monthly or quarterly audits or installment payments. A lower initial deposit or installment premium, however, results in fewer investment dollars to offset losses and expenses. The value of the insured's premium payment request must be assessed against the potential cash flow losses to the insurer. An inadequate premium exposure base should never be used as a means of financing the policy or insured.

Any substantial fluctuations in the premium base (either actual or estimated) must be explained to the underwriter. A significant increase or decrease in the premium base or stable figures in a period of inflation may also be indicators of financial difficulties or a significant change in operations. The change in operations may be the elimination of an undesirable operation or the acquisition of a different operation. It must be determined if the pattern of change can be anticipated in the future and if the insurer wishes to provide coverage in the event of such a change. For policies of sufficient size it is common to obtain independent verification of operations and classifications by obtaining an inspection, a credit report, or financial statements.

**Timeliness of Loss Information.** The underwriter must be sure that the loss information shown on the application is the most recent "valuation" of that information. (This issue was briefly addressed in Chapter 3.) If the loss information submitted with the application is a computerized loss run generated by the previous insurer, it is usually simply a matter of looking for the "run date" to see the date at which the losses were valued. If the losses are simply a handwritten list based upon what the previous insurer has furnished the applicant, the underwriter may want some confirmation of those figures.

Much of what the underwriter does at this point, however, depends on the size of the risk and the reported loss experience. If the risk is a small painting contractor who reports only one small property damage loss paid two years ago, the underwriter is likely to accept what the applicant reports. If the applicant is a very large contractor with an extensive listing of losses, both closed and reserved, the underwriter may want more than a listing supplied by the applicant because too often the reserves are changed or the claims paid and the applicant is not informed.[1] Only with the most recent, comprehensive listing of losses from the previous insurer can the underwriter be sure that his or her evaluation of the risk is based on the most accurate information.

Even after the risk is written, the underwriter may sometimes want to go back to the previous insurer and get updated loss information. One reason for doing so is when the risk is subject to experience rating; another reason is if there is some question at the renewal date as to whether or not to continue providing coverage. The underwriter requests updated loss information to see if additional losses have been reported (under an occurrence policy) or if reserves have changed. Although experience rating has factors to apply to losses to bring them up to present dollar values, these factors should be applied to the most accurate and recent estimate of the losses. Additional reported losses may indicate a recent problem with one of the insured's products or operations. Such a problem would be of concern to the present underwriter if that product or operation has not been changed since the time of the loss.

## Industry Guides

*Best's Underwriting Guide (BUG)* and Best's *Loss Control Engineering Manual* were both described in Chapter 3. These publications can give the underwriter a good idea of what to expect with regard to a certain type of risk.

The industry guides can be of tremendous value to an underwriter when he or she is faced with a new type of risk. This may happen if the underwriter has moved to an area of the country in which certain types of risks not found in the underwriter's previous area are located. For instance, few underwriters in Florida are faced with writing general liability coverage for snow ski facilities. In addition, these guides can also remind the underwriter to ask certain questions of the insured or the loss control representative. The disadvantage of industry guides is that they do not provide any information on a specific risk. A loss control or inspection report must provide that information.

Exhibit 8-3 is a reprint of a portion of the *BUG* report on casinos. Only those portions relating to the overall risk and to liability coverage are reprinted. Although casinos are legal in only two states, it is possible that other states will approve them, and an underwriter may be asked to provide coverage. Some insurers also provide coverage to offshore casinos.

## Inspection Reports

As mentioned above, specific information about a risk must usually be obtained from an inspection or loss control report. The underwriter can use the report as a basis for requesting specific areas or operations to be examined in detail or specific questions regarding the insured's

## Exhibit 8-3
Excerpt from *Best's Underwriting Guide*

Best's Underwriting Guide

**sic code** 7011 Hotels and Motels
7993 Coin Operated Amusement Devices
7999 Amusement and Recreation Services, NEC

# Casinos

| Line | Best's Hazard Index | Underwriting Comments |
|---|---|---|
| Automobile Liability | 4 | |
| Automobile Physical Damage | — | |
| General Liability | 7 | Large crowds/dim lighting. |
| Product Liability — Completed Operations | 1 | |
| Environmental Impairment Liability | — | |
| Professional Liability | — | |
| Liquor Liability | 9 | Monitoring patrons' consumption difficult. |
| Workers' Compensation | 3 | |
| Crime | 2 | Extensive security measures employed. |
| Fire and E.C. | 7 | Excludes hotels. |
| Business Interruption | 7 | Relocation difficult. |
| Inland Marine | 4 | Valuable Papers and Records coverage essential. |

Low 1-3, Medium 4-6, High 7-9, Very High 10

### Related Classifications

Bars, Taverns, Cocktail Lounges, Nightclubs and Discotheques

Hotels, Motels and Conference Centers

Theatres

### Special Exposures

Extensive electrical wiring

Large amount of cash on premises

Large crowds

Moral hazard/undesirable associates

Serving alcohol

**RISK DESCRIPTION**

This classification includes all buildings and rooms in which legalized gambling takes place. A typical casino will include slot machines and a variety of gaming tables including Blackjack, Craps, Roulette, and Baccarat. The majority of these operations are located in and associated with large, luxurious hotels. Others may be located on cruise ships. This write-up will examine only the hazards involved with casinos. For more information on hotels see Hotels, Motels and Conference Centers.

Casino gambling is legal in 38 countries around the world. Within the United States it is legal only in the states of Nevada and New Jersey. Nevada was the first to adopt gambling in 1931; it was not until 45 years later, in 1976, that New Jersey allowed this type of activity, but only in Atlantic City. There also are a number of casinos operating in Puerto Rico and the U.S. Virgin Islands.

The size of a casino may differ from place to place. In Nevada, for example, the size of an operation will vary from the smallest ones with one or two table games and a limited number of slot machines to ones larger than football fields which contain hundreds of games and thousands of slot machines. The industry in New Jersey, on the other hand, consists of 11 large casinos all very similar in size and methods of operation.

Casino gaming is an industry that is considered to be only marginally accepted by many people in the United States. Therefore, in order to gain public support, the casino industry must operate under strict regulations. There are two general phases involved in gaming regulations. The first is entry licensing. In Nevada the licensing focuses on those operating the business and key employees. New Jersey's licensing is much broader. Original licensing includes all casino employees, all hotel/casino employees and all industries that support or supply goods and services to the casinos.

10/89

The second phase of regulation involves ongoing control and regulation. In Nevada there are three organizations responsible for licensing, setting and enforcing rules and regulations, and reviewing casinos' internal accounting procedures. The three agencies are the Gaming Policy Committee, the Gaming Commission, and the Gaming Control Board. New Jersey has two bodies, the Casino Control Commission and the Division of Gaming Enforcement, involved in regulating this industry.

Casinos on cruise ships and on Caribbean islands also have regulations to follow. On cruise ships at sea, the regulations the casino must follow are established by the cruise line themselves. On the islands, regulations may be established by organizations much like the Department of Gaming of Tourism in Puerto Rico.

Casino gaming is an emerging industry. With the legalization of casinos in New Jersey, the visibility of the industry has expanded greatly. Continued growth, however, is not guaranteed. In order for the industry to continue growing, widespread legalization of casinos must take place, which in turn depends on the social acceptance of the legitimacy of casino gaming.

## MATERIALS AND EQUIPMENT

Slot machines, blackjack tables, baccarat tables, crap tables, roulette wheels.
Gaming equipment including chips, coins and plaques.
Drop boxes and slot cash storage boxes.
Bill changing machines, booths.
Computers.
Surveillance systems including cameras and two-way mirrors.
Furniture, stools.
Elevators, escalators.
Kitchen, restaurant, bar and office equipment and supplies.
Cleaning compounds and equipment.
Cars, shuttle busses, vans.

---

### Automobile Liability

The insured may own passenger cars or limousines to transport guests to and from airports, bus and train stations and other facilities in the area. If the casino is based in a hotel, this service may be operated — and insured — by the hotel rather than the casino. In addition, many larger casinos will operate shuttle busses which transport employees from a general parking area to the facility. Vans, trucks and station wagons are frequently used for running errands and picking up supplies.

The underwriter should ascertain the type, number, age and condition of all vehicles. What is the quality of vehicle maintenance? Does the insured do any in-house maintenance work on vehicles? What training and experience do mechanics have? How is the company-owned fleet garaged and protected?

Many insureds will have arrangements with independent bus companies to provide daily transportation to their facility. The arrangements can include providing bus riders with "free" coins for slot machines and discount coupons for meals. These packages usually are advertised under the casino's name. Although the insured does not own the busses they may be named in a suit. Check all contracts to determine the liability assumed by the insured. For more information see Bus Charter Services.

### General Liability

The constant flow of huge crowds of people throughout a casino creates a potentially severe hazard. The underwriter should determine the average daily number of visitors to the premises as well as the peak number allowed in the facility at one time. Most casinos have multiple entrances with little or no control over ingress.

The potential for extensive loss must be reduced through the efforts of both facility management and the insurer. What measures does the insured take to control the crowds? What is the size of their security force? Are employees trained in crowd control?

Has the insured hired a qualified individual to assess the facility's liability potential? Fire or building collapse present the greatest chance of large-scale losses. Serious losses also may ensue from panic situations resulting from small fires or other disturbances.

With large crowds usually present it is very important for the insured to have an adequate number of exits. Because of the dim lighting and the vast amount of space in most casinos, visitors may have trouble finding the exits. What is the quality of lighting in the insured's building? Are all exits well-lit and easily accessible? Are signs posted throughout the casino indicating where the exits are? The underwriter should be aware that some casinos, especially those in New Jersey, may be filled with senior citizens who will have a more difficult time escaping the building in the case of a fire or other emergency.

Claims will be filed with more frequency for slight injuries arising from slips and falls on the premises than for severe injuries. Crowding, pushing and excitement around the gaming tables add to this exposure. The dim lighting also will contribute to tripping and falling accidents. The underwriter should carefully examine the physical layout of the insured's facilities. Many casinos will have aisles of slot machines close together in a small area. Are these aisles wide enough for passage, particularly when customers are playing the machines? Does the insured post signs instructing customers to keep canes, purses and other obstacles out of the aisles? Does the insured provide space near the machines where such materials can be stored? The underwriter should be aware of the fact that many people passing by machines may be looking for a machine to play or may be watching others play and not paying attention to where they are going; this may lead to accidents.

Are staircases, escalators and elevators kept in good repair? Elevator and escalator maintenance and inspection are usually performed by outside firms; their programs and contracts should be reviewed. Is there an emergency power source for the continuing function of elevators during a power failure? A daily mechanical check of elevators and escalators by the insured's maintenance employees is a positive underwriting sign. A record should be kept of inspection dates, breakdowns and repairs.

What is the condition of the stools used by customers at the playing tables? Stools should have backs to reduce the risk of customers falling over backwards. Movable stools may be easily tipped over, increasing the chance of injury.

What are the insured's hours of operation? Most casinos will be open long into the early morning hours. Individuals walking around the casino may be tired or under the influence of alcohol, which will increase the chance of an accident taking place. (See also Liquor Liability.)

Determine the number, type and condition of slot machines. Are machines properly balanced and secured to the ground? Although remote, the possibility of an unbalanced machine tipping over and falling on a patron does exist. How often are machines inspected to make sure the lever is firmly attached to the body of the machine? Ineffectively grounded machines present a shock hazard.

Personal Injury Liability cases may arise with the use of inadequately trained or overzealous security personnel. If security guards or other employees attempt to detain a suspected wrongdoer or make unfounded accusations, a claim charging false arrest, wrongful detention, malicious prosecution, slander, or invasion of privacy may result. Determine if the insured hires their own security or hires them from an agency. Are background checks conducted before hiring? What training and experience is required? Are management personnel consulted before alleged wrongdoers are confronted? What percentage of alleged wrongdoers are spotted by management or non-security personnel?

**Product Liability and Completed Operations**

A Product Liability exposure exists because the insured will be involved in selling beverages to customers. Losses may arise from foreign objects in drinks. However, since most drinks will be poured straight from a bottle, the chances of something being wrong with them is minimal. Accidents or injuries arising out of the serving of alcohol will be covered under Liquor Liability.

**Liquor Liability**

Most casinos will include lounges and will serve alcoholic beverages to their patrons. The insured and all employees must be aware of the consequences of serving alcoholic beverages to minors and obviously intoxicated persons. For more information on the hazards of serving alcoholic beverages see Bars, Taverns, Cocktail Lounges, Nightclubs and Discotheques.

In addition to the basic exposures present in a bar, there are some hazards which are unique to casinos. In a recent pretrial ruling in a New Jersey court, a federal judge held that casinos should fall under dram shop laws which hold taverns responsible for injuries caused by their intoxicated patrons. The ruling also held that the casino in question could be held liable for money lost by a drunk gambler who was served alcohol by the casino.

Another characteristic of casinos which is clearly related to and affected by this court decision is the policy many casinos have of serving gamblers free drinks as long as they are playing. The underwriter should check the insured's guidelines relating to this practice. Is there a set limit to the amount of drinks — free or purchased — that can be given to one customer? If so, how is the amount registered? In a casino it is very difficult to keep track of the number of drinks a customer has because there are many waitresses walking the floor and serving drinks and patrons may move between gaming tables. Therefore, it is likely that more than one person will serve a patron drinks. Do the employees monitoring the players and dealers to ensure that all gaming rules and regulations are followed also check for signs of inebriation? Have employees serving drinks been given any training or guidelines for assessing inebriation?

**Workers' Compensation**

Exposures are slight. Employees who work at the playing tables may be exposed to repetitive motion injuries (i.e., from dealing cards for blackjack). The underwriter should determine what precautions are taken by the insured to protect their employees from such injuries as tendinitis, bursitis and inflammations of the shoulder or elbow. Workers also may develop medical problems with their legs and feet because they are spending long hours on their feet. Are employees encouraged to wear comfortable shoes? Frequent breaks are a positive underwriting sign. Determine the average number of years employees work at the same job. A lengthy stay in one job will increase the chances that repetitive motion injuries will occur.

Waitresses serving customers on the playing floor may suffer arm, shoulder and back problems as a result of carrying heavy trays. Is any training given dealing with the proper way to carry a tray to prevent such problems? Does the insured have any procedures that limit the order size or the number of customers a waitress can serve at one time? Cuts from picking up broken drinking glasses are a possibility.

Good housekeeping is important to reduce the potential for employee injuries from slips and falls. Do employees have ample space to move about in their work area? What is the condition of the floor and floor coverings?

Employees who lift and move heavy coin bags may sustain back injuries. Proper lifting techniques should be taught to all involved in this type of work. Are pre-employment physical examinations — with emphasis on back problems — standard practice?

Employees who work in cash/token/voucher exchange booths may be subject to severe injury during a robbery attempt. What security measures does the insured have to prevent such an occurrence? In addition to the presence of security guards, most casinos will have bars over the openings in the booths to protect the cashiers. Are workers instructed in how to respond to such a situation? Likewise, employees on the gaming floor may suffer injuries from assaults from disappointed patrons who have lost large sums of money. What training is given to employees dealing with the treatment of angry and disappointed customers? Does the gaming table design provide protection and easy escape? How quickly can dealers summon assistance?

Does the casino hire workers to clean the premises? Do cleaning crew members ever move slot machines, gaming tables or other pieces of furniture? If so, they may be subject to back injuries. What cleaning compounds are used? Refer to Janitorial Services for more information.

Workers who take shuttle busses from parking areas to the casino may be exposed to vehicular accidents.

Employees who work on casinos on cruise ships will be covered under the Longshoremen's and Harbor Workers' Compensation Act.

**Crime**

Although the exposure is large, the chance of loss will be minimal because of the extensive security precautions taken by each casino. It is nearly impossible for someone to walk out of a casino with stolen money or property. Most casinos will have security personnel stationed at or near every exit as well as some walking the gaming floor. Determine the number of guards employed by the insured. What training are these guards given in regards to detecting criminal behavior and actions to take to prevent it? In addition to guards, surveillance cameras and two-way mirrors are used to keep a close watch on all activities taking place on the floor of the casino.

Although there is a huge amount of cash on hand, it does not present a big chance of loss because of the way it is carefully handled. Each step of the money-handling process is outlined in detail in the regulations governing the casinos. In New Jersey, for example, these regulations can be found under the New Jersey Administrative Codes, Chapter 19.45 — Accounting and Internal Controls. This chapter describes in detail such things as the procedure for opening tables for gaming, the procedure for accepting cash at gaming tables, and the procedure for transporting drop boxes to and from gaming tables, as well as many other important accounting practices. The underwriter should obtain a copy of regulations pertaining to the insured's operation and determine if they are followed closely.

Cashier booths, where large sums of money may be kept, usually are protected with bars and are heavily guarded.

Fidelity losses are possible. It should be noted, however, that employee dishonesty is unlikely because gaming floor employees are watched not only by patrons, guards and surveillance cameras, but also by pit bosses (the person who stands behind the tables and supervises all activities on them). Any conspiracy with a patron to obtain money is unlikely because the employees rotate tables and at each table there is normally at least one other employee present in addition to the pit boss.

Areas which may be vulnerable to fidelity losses include cash/token/voucher exchange booths and the accounting office. All accounting procedures should be investigated carefully and reviewed periodically. How often are audits performed? Are unscheduled outside audits ever made? What are the average and maximum amounts of daily receipts? How often is money transferred to an on-premises safe and/or to a bank. Determine what precautions the insured takes when transporting money.

Pre-employment checks must be made on all hirees (including machine repair personnel), and all references should be contacted. It is unlikely that a casino will hire anyone with a criminal record, but if one does it should be noted by the underwriter. Such individuals should be excluded from fidelity coverage.

### Fire and E.C.

Fires most likely will be electrical in origin. Casinos are filled with flashing signs and glittering displays designed to attract the customers' attention and create an ambiance. Such displays require an enormous amount of electrical wiring. Frayed or exposed wiring, faulty wiring, overloaded circuits, wrong-size electrical fuses and inadequate extension cords are all possible ignition sources. The underwriter should carefully examine the insured's electrical system. Is proper circuit protection provided to prevent overloading? Is all electrical equipment UL-listed? How often is the wiring inspected? The use of temporary wiring should be strictly prohibited, and all switches, panel boxes and receptacles must be adequately covered. Who maintains or repairs electrical systems? What are their qualifications?

The presence of kitchen facilities in or near the casino also will increase the chance that a fire may start and spread to the casino. A physical inspection of the cooking facilities will reveal potential hazards. Stoves and deep-fat fryers must have fixed fire suppression systems and exhaust hoods. Prevention of grease buildup is extremely important. How often are stoves and ranges cleaned? Is debris allowed to accumulate? For more information on cooking hazards see Restaurants and Fast Food Restaurants.

What is the insured's policy on smoking? If smoking is permitted at gaming tables, ashtrays should be readily available and should be emptied regularly. Are floor personnel instructed to keep an eye out for smoldering cigarette or cigar butts that have fallen to the floor? Fire-retardant fabric carpeting is a positive underwriting sign.

The fire load is increased with the presence of alcohol. Liquor bottles may explode during a fire, and the spilled liquor will add to the fire. Determine how much liquor is on the premises and where it is stored. Flammable wall and table coverings, as well as paper playing cards, will also increase the load.

Is the casino protected by smoke alarms and an automatic sprinkler system? Strategically located fire extinguishers also must be provided. Are employees trained in the proper operation of such equipment? Since most larger casinos are located in hotels, the underwriter should examine the fire detection and suppression systems used in the hotel. For a more complete discussion on the fire hazards in hotels see Hotels, Motels and Conference Centers.

The possibility of moral hazard must be taken into consideration. Determine the location of the establishment, the clientele and the insured's reputation. Competition from nearby casinos may pose a financial threat to the insured. Compare current figures to those of the past five years. If the insured also owns a range of other businesses, the underwriter should asses the insured's overall financial status.

### Business Interruption

Materials and equipment can be replaced rather easily. However, the location of the casino will have a big effect on the writing of this coverage. Most casinos will be located in a specific, limited area where they are surrounded by other casinos and related businesses. Finding suitable replacement quarters within the same high business area may be difficult. Repairing or rebuilding on site may be the only alternative. Determine the length of time it will take to repair or rebuild the structure.

Casinos located in hotels (as most are) will be affected by any loss suffered by the hotel. A small fire which closes the hotel may not force the casino to close, but it may cause potential guests to avoid the establishment. Patrons may find other casinos that they prefer and the insured's business may be affected after repairs to the hotel have been completed. To what extent is the casino dependent on the hotel?

Depending on the regulations of the state where the casino is located, relicensing of the establishment or employees may be necessary and could delay the resumption of operations.

### Inland Marine

Slot machines and all gaming tables are covered under this policy. The underwriter should determine how much eq pment the insured has on its premises and the value of each piece. Perils affecting the equipment — other than fire — are few and will not be widespread. Slot machines, if not balanced or anchored, may tip over. Irate patrons may attempt to damage individual tables or machines.

Large, expensive outdoor signs are subject to damage from wind and vandalism. Rooftop signs must be secured properly to the building structure. Freestanding signs must be structurally sound, anchored to the ground, and out of the way of all traffic patterns. All signs and outside lighting should be constructed of metal or other non-combustible materials.

Computers play a very important part in a casino's operation. Many casinos will use computers not only for accounting procedures but also to record such variables as a player's preferred games, the time spent at each game, and their betting habits. With this much computer use it is essential for the insured to have EDP coverage.

Does the insured have a coat-check facility on the premises? If so, a Bailee Liability exposure exists. If coverage is to be written, determine if effective procedures have been developed to decrease the possibility of returning an expensive garment to someone other than the rightful owner.

Accounts Receivable coverage should be included. Valuable Papers and Records coverage also is desirable, especially for documents relating to accounting procedures and compliance with casino operation regulations. Records of accounts should be kept in UL-listed, fire-resistive safes, and a duplicate set should be stored safely off the premises.

Additional coverage may be necessary for costumes and equipment used by entertainers performing in the lounge of the casino. This coverage will apply to the belongings of entertainers with an independent contractor status if the equipment is left in the "care, custody and control" of the insured at any time. For more information see Bars, Taverns, Cocktail Lounges, Nightclubs and Discotheques.

**A physical survey, an evaluation of security programs, a review of a financial report, and a careful analysis of the laws and regulations affecting the insured's operation (including the serving of alcohol) are necessary to underwrite this classification.**

## Underwriter's Check List

Is the insured in compliance with the laws and regulations affecting casino operation (including the serving of alcohol)?

Does the insured own passenger cars or limousines used to transport customers to and from airports, bus and train stations and other facilities in the area? What is the age and experience of all drivers?

Does the insured operate shuttle busses for employees?

Does the insured have arrangements with bus companies to provide daily transportation to their facility?

What measures does the insured take to control the crowds?

What is the size of the security force? What training and experience is required of the guards? Are any guards armed?

What is the quality of lighting in the insured's building?

Are all exits well-lit and easily accessible?

Are aisles between slot machines wide enough for passage?

Are staircases, escalators and elevators kept in good repair?

Do stools at playing tables have backs to reduce the risk of customers falling over backwards?

Are slot machines properly balanced and secured to the ground?

Is there a set limit of drinks — free or purchased — that can be given to one customer? If so, how is the amount registered?

Have employees serving drinks been given any training or guidelines for assessing inebriation?

What precautions are taken by the insured to protect their employees from repetitive motion injuries such as tendinitis, bursitis and inflammations of the shoulder or elbow?

Are employees permitted to take frequent breaks?

Are waitresses given any training dealing with the proper way to carry a tray to prevent arm, shoulder and back problems?

Are workers instructed in how to respond to a robbery or an assault by a disappointed patron?

What kind of security/surveillance system does the insured employ to protect their premises?

What training do security guards have in detecting criminal behavior and actions to take to prevent it?

How often are audits performed? Are unscheduled outside audits ever made?

What are the average and maximum amounts of daily receipts?

Are pre-employment checks made on all hirees?

Is all electrical equipment UL-listed? How often is the wiring inspected?

What is the insured's policy on smoking within the casino?

Is the casino protected by smoke alarms and an automatic sprinkler system?

How long will it take for the insured to repair or rebuild the structure?

How much equipment does the insured have on its premises? What is the value of each piece?

Are records of accounts kept in UL-listed, fire-resistive safes, and a duplicate set stored off the premises?

Does the insured have a coat-check facility on the premises?

operations or products to be answered. Much of the information listed earlier under the application is confirmed by the inspection. In other cases, the inspection supplements the information on the application. Exhibit 3-2 shows a sample inspection report with a general liability/workers compensation supplement. Note that the areas investigated on the supplement include (1) the operations, (2) personnel, (3) management controls, and (4) physical conditions, hazards, and controls. Insurers may organize the report differently depending on the factors they consider to be most important. Most will have a section regarding the machinery, equipment, and materials used (this is most likely included under item (4) in the preceding list). Information regarding losses as well as an overall description of operations is usually included in the general section of the loss control or inspection report.

Exhibit 8-4 is another sample loss control report. This report covers information on general liability, fire, and business interruption coverage. It uses a short-answer format rather than a fill-in-the-blank or check-the-blocks format. Notice that under the general liability section, the loss control representative picked up on the fact that the insured sponsors a Little League team. Because of advertising on the uniforms, actions by the team could create a liability exposure. Few underwriters would think to ask about, and few insureds would think to mention, this kind of information. A photograph of the insured building and a diagram of the building and surrounding area were also attached to the report, but they are not reproduced in the exhibit.

When loss control representatives make the physical inspection, they frequently submit loss control recommendations to the insured. Most of the time the recommendations are intended to correct physical hazards found in the operation or premises. While these recommendations are helpful, they are not intended to be a substitute for a full loss control program.

## Specialized Reports

In addition to the information regarding the premises and operations of the applicant, more specialized reports are required of certain risks. Each insurer has rules about when a specific report must be used. A more specialized report is frequently required particularly when there is a large loss potential. Exhibit 8-5 illustrates the concern of the general liability underwriter with high-rise buildings. This exhibit is a supplement to the basic application. It includes an evaluation of building construction, furnishings and occupancy, and fire protection. A review of the exhibit shows that a major concern is features that affect the life safety of the occupants. In order to properly underwrite the life

**Exhibit 8-4**
Loss Control Report

## IIA INSURANCE COMPANY

LOSS CONTROL/ENGINEERING — NARRATIVE REPORT

Survey Date 8/21/X4 Location ZIP Code 19355

| Account | Policy Number | Loss Control Representative |
|---|---|---|
| EBA Grinding Corp. | ABC 587-20-1658 | L.C.Spellman |

| Location Surveyed | Agent/Broker and Code No. |
|---|---|
| 720 Providence Road,Malvern,MS 19355 | Yourtown Ins. 39-11375 |

Person Contacted ahnd Position
Elliott Arnold, Owner

Person to Receive Recommendations, Address, ZIP Code
As above

| Type of Report | Type of Business |
|---|---|
| Original | Machine Shop |

SURVEY SUMMARY:

This is a limited production job machine shop specializing in tool modification and manufacturing cutting tools and equipment used by the medical/ health industry. Both common and special hazards are adequately controlled. Public and private protection features are adequate. Neighborhood is an average suburban town with fair facilities. Exposures are none. Building condition is average. Business interruption exposure is light. Management attitude and reaction was above average. The owner of this business, Mr. Elliot Arnold, was contacted and provided a very in-depth description of operations. Mr. Arnold appears to maintain a very positive attitude and was very cooperative. No recommendations were developed.

NATURE OF BUSINESS:

Business is split between servicing the medical/health industry and refurbishing metal tool cutting equipment and accessories. The medical/health business accounts for about 40% of annual gross sales, with the remaining 60% from the modification tool process. Medical/health tools are the dies and taps used for reconstructive surgery which involves bone reconstruction or reinforcement. These tools, dies and taps are very high quality stainless steel items which are manufactured by precision machinists. The machinery and equipment are typical to a precision tool and die shop, utilizing laths,grinders, buffing and sanding machinery. The equipment is state of the art and computer numerically controlled. These operations are limited production items with sales directly to hospitals and physicians. The tool modification process is a recutting,edging, and tipping operation, utilizing th same specialized equipment. In addition to the typical machine shop equipment, the modification process will sometimes require Tig welding and conventional and acetylene welding operations. Finished products are not inventoried. They are shipped to customers by contract carriers, mostly by United Parcel Service.

EBA GRINDING CORP
720 Providence Road
Malvern, MS 19355

L.C. Spellman
587-20-1658
8/21/X4



They are currently operating with eight full-time employees, five days per week from 7:00 AM to 3:30 PM.

Business activity is reported as normal with continued profitable business anticipated.

Loss history has been clear.

## SPECIAL HAZARDS:

### HAZARDOUS CHEMICALS:

Cutting and lubricating oils are purchased in 55 gallon metal drums from local petrochemical supplier. The drums are stored in the upright position and dispensed from ordinary pumping arrangements. Housekeeping around the drum area is excellent with good control over spillage.

### DUST REDUCING OPERATIONS:

The polishing and sanding equipment is connected to an internal dust collection system with cyclone and bag filter system. Control over dust adequate.

### SPONTANEOUS IGNITION:

Oily waste rags are thrown into ordinary trash receptacles which are emptied each night. The trash receptacles are emptied into an outside metal dumpster which is located over 25 feet away from the southern wall.

### WELDING AND CUTTING:

Tig, electric resistance, and oxygen and acetylene operations are connected on well-arranged steel board benches located on concrete flooring. Welding operations are adequately arranged and protected.

### HEAT TREATING:

None conducted on premises. All stainless steel which is primarily used for manufacturing the medical/health equipment is sent off premises for heat treating purposes.

## COMMON HAZARDS:

### HEAT:

The shop area is heated by suspended gas-fired unit heaters with adequate venting arrangements with good clearances. The office is heated with a combination air conditioning and heating unit which is roof-mounted.

### ELECTRIC:

Wiring is mostly metal conduit with drop cords provided to machinery from overhead bus system. Overcurrent protection is adequate by circuit breakers.

### SMOKING:

Controlled in essential areas. Smoking in most manufacturing areas does not present a significant problem due to the low continuity of combustibles and concrete floor. No carelessly discarded smoking material is noted. In areas where smoking is permitted, adequate ash receptacles are provided.

EBA GRINDING CORP
720 Providence Road
Malvern, MS 19355

L.C. Spellman
587-20-1658
8/21/X4

3

**HOUSEKEEPING:**
Both inside and outside areas are well maintained.

**PROTECTION**

**PRIVATE:**
By an adequate supply of well maintained portable fire extinguishers..

**PUBLIC:**
Fire department is paid and located within three miles. Accessibility is excellent by well maintained public roadways. Water supply was not determined; however, risk is located on a major roadway with heavy industry. Water supply is mot likely adequate by 8" - 10" public water mains.

**CONSTRUCTION:**
No unusual construction features noted. The office area is partially separated from the manufacturing area by an 8" hollow concrete block wall with unprotected openings. Interior finish in the office area is wood panelling and suspended ceiling system of noncombustible ceiling tiles. No insulation seen.

**BUSINESS INTERRUPTION:**
No process bottlenecks noted. The computer numerically controlled machinery is used for production machining of the tools used in the medical/health industry. This machinery is expensive; however, readily replaceable and all operations on these machines can be performed by the manually controlled equipment with redundancy throughout.

**LIABILITY:**

**OPERATIONS:**
No unusual features. Independent contractors are not customarily used; however, the importance of obtaining certificates of insurance was discussed and the idea well received by Mr. Arnold. Mr. Arnold does support a local Little League baseball team. His support is strictly financial and was not sure about the advertisement that might be on any team uniforms.

**EXTERIOR:**
No unusual features.

**INTERIOR:**
Public exposure is limited to office areas which are adequately lighted and two exits provided.

EBA GRINDING CORP
720 Providence Road
Malvern, MS 19355

L.C. Spellman
587-20-1658
8/21/X4

4

PRODUCTS:

This is a job shop operation which works with customers specifications and blueprints. Engineering performed by insured is limited to consultative type remarks. The final print is provided by his customers and is not prepared by insured. This is a limited production shop with a very rigid quality controlled program associated with the health/medical industry. All products are quality controlled in process and there is a 100% quality control check on all finished products prior to shipping. The quality control records are well maintained and kept on premises. Quality control equipment is state of the art and tests are all well documented. Raw materials are provided with certificates from metallurgical laboratories which insure purity of material. However, insured sends a sample piece of all shipments to be heat treated to insure technical content of the metallurgical report. Reportedly, stainless steel will only take a proper heat treat if purity is as specified.

RECOMMENDATIONS:

None.

Signed ______________________

safety exposures connected with high rises and similar risks, liability underwriters must understand property underwriting and exposures.

## Extent of Exposure to the Public

General liability insurance has as its basis the exposure of the public and the public's property to the hazards of the insured's business or operations. The public includes customers, representatives of suppliers, anyone else associated with the business, and the general public. While all businesses have this liability exposure, the extent of the exposure can vary widely. The underwriter will want to know if the exposure is common for the classification and how much variation in the exposure is likely.

Some differences in the extent of exposure may be a result of location, type of business, time in business, or a combination of the three. For example, a store with a good reputation and steady business is more likely to attract customers than a new store or one that is on the decline. The increase in customer traffic increases the exposure. Location may create a similar increase in traffic and thus, in the extent

**Exhibit 8-5**
High Rise Survey Supplement

**To be fully completed and attached to Property Checklist if the building is either:**
**(a) more than 80 feet or 8 stories above ground level; or**
**(b) higher than local fire department apparatus can reach.**

**High rise structures and structures with abnormal evacuation problems require more in-depth detail for proper underwriting analysis. The categories given above indicate only a need for additional information and should not be construed as standards:**

**If earthquake or windstorm exposures exist, also refer to guides and checklists for these exposures.**

**Name of Account** ______________________________

**1.0 BUILDING CONSTRUCTION**

1.1 Frame: ☐ Reinforced concrete, ☐ Structural steel (☐unprotected ☐ protected by ____________; hourly rating _____ Hrs. Fireproofing workmanship is ☐ Satisfactory ☐ Missing or Removed (describe where ______________________________)).

(Note: The true high rise does not have bearing walls but has a skeleton frame to which is attached enclosing or curtain walls. The frame is normally of reinforced concrete or structural steel. The steel frame may be protected by sprayed-on material or encased in concrete.)

1.2 Insulation: ☐ Yes ☐ No. If yes, ☐ Combustible ☐ Non-combustible ☐ Toxic ☐ Non-toxic. If combustible, spray-on foam, rigid foam boards, panels, etc. give details on material, where located and if protected by any thermal barrier. Also, give thermal barrier material, name of manufacturer, thickness and workmanship.

1.3 Interior Partitions and Ceilings: All non-combustible ☐ Yes ☐ No. If no, describe combustible construction and the approximate percentage for each floor.

1.4 Floor Openings (includes electrical service, plumbing and other pipe, heating and air conditioning ducts, telephone wire and conduit, stairways, elevator shafts, laundry or rubbish chutes, mail conveyors, space between outside wall and floor, etc): All protected against passage of smoke, heat and flame? ☐ Yes ☐ No. If no, describe deficiencies in detail:

1.5 Air Conditioning, Heating and Other Air Moving Systems: Serve more than one floor? ☐ Yes ☐ No. If yes, describe how the system can be isolated by floor levels to prevent spread of heat, smoke or flame; if dampers, are they smoke or heat actuated; pressurized stairways:

1.6 Smoke Removal Means: ☐ Yes ☐ No. If yes, describe how floors can be ventilated to remove smoke, i.e., reverse fans on air conditioning system, windows that can be opened, etc.

1.7 Automatic Fire Doors: Installed where needed? ☐ Yes ☐ No. (consider smoke, towers, stairwells, elevator shafts, mail conveyor shafts, dumb waiter or trash shafts, boiler rooms, storage rooms or closets, etc.)

1.8 Elevator Shaftway Doors: Listed? ☐ Yes ☐ No. Fit closely enough to be useful as smoke barriers? ☐ Yes ☐ No. (Note: Doors should be listed for Class B openings and installed to cover the opening tightly to limit the spread of smoke, heat or fire to other floors. This can best be determined from inside shaft with doors closed observing light entrance. The clearance between the door and the wall shall not exceed 3/8 in., and between the door and sill, 3/4 in. and lap opening at sides and top at least 4 inches.)

1.9 Elevator Electrical Circuitry: Wiring for interlocks in conduit or otherwise reasonably protected from excessive heat or flame? ☐ Yes ☐ No.

1.10 Call Buttons: Electronic or touch sensitive ☐ Yes ☐ No. (touch sensitive call buttons have been responsible for calling elevators to a fire floor, and if car occupied, subjected occupants to the fire when doors opened and held open by electric eye. These buttons can be operated by heat, smoke, flames and other conditions present during a fire).

1.11 Elevator Override Switch: Are elevator lobbies provided smoke detectors or manual override switch to recall all elevators directly to the ground floor?

☐ Yes ☐ No.

1.12 Are special "Fireman Switches" provided any elevators to prevent their being called to fire floor when used by firemen? ☐ Yes ☐ No.

**2.0 FURNISHINGS AND OCCUPANCY:**

2.1 Carpet: Approximate percentage ___%. Flame or smoke rated ☐ Yes ☐ No. ☐ Unknown. Rating if known: ______ Flame spread ______ Smoke developed. (Recommended not to exceed 75 flame spread or 100 smoke dev. in corridors and noncombustible for exists.)

2.2 Drapes and Curtains: Flame proofed or inherently noncombustible ☐ Yes ☐ No.

2.3 Furnishings: Do any tenants introduce any highly combustible material or large accumulations of combustibles? ☐ Yes ☐ No. (consider shops or stores, restaurants, computer print outs, reference libraries, drawing racks, overstuffed chairs, with foam padding, stock storage rooms, etc.)

2.4 Hazards of Construction: Not completed or not fully occupied ☐ Yes ☐ No. If yes, describe any construction hazards to be encountered including future tenant arrangements:

**3.0 PROTECTION**

3.1 Sprinklers throughout ☐ Yes ☐ No. Partial sprinkler protection☐ Yes ☐ No. If partial, describe areas protected:

3.2 Standpipe system in stairway for fire department use ☐ Yes ☐ No. Are there small hose systems on the floor for occupant use ☐ Yes ☐ No.

3.3 Emergency Plan: Written? ☐ Yes ☐ No. (If yes, attach to this report). Does it include floor wardens, fire safety director, drills with tenants and fire department. ☐ Yes ☐ No. Are emergency drills held? ☐ Yes ☐ No. How often ________.

3.4 Emergency Alarm and/or Communication Systems: Effective to all parts of the building ☐ Yes ☐ No. If yes, describe alarm and procedure:

3.5 Emergency Power Equipment: ☐ Generator ☐ Switchover to alternate power line ☐ None (a) is equipment located and powered to be reliably free of disruption during an emergency? ☐ Yes ☐ No. (b) where is equipment located? ____________________: (c) tested on regular basis? ☐ Yes ☐ No. (d) Is switchover ☐ automatic; ☐ manual. (e) Specify which equipment is emergency powered: consider no. of elevators, fire pumps, exit lights, etc.):

3.6 Fire Department: Response time under most adverse traffic or weather conditions ____ Min. Alarm transmitted by ☐ telephone ☐ pull box ☐ other ______________.

3.7 Deficient Fire Equipment: Is this the reason, per criteria, for use of this supplement? ☐ Yes ☐ No. Describe any deficiency:

3.8 Are all protective devices (standpipes, fire pumps, sprinklers, detection and alarm systems, emergency venting, etc.) tested at sufficient frequent intervals. ☐ Yes ☐ No.

**4.0 COMMENTS: Consider the following points and comment accordingly:**

4.1 Can any trouble spot within the structure by evacuated promptly and safely, either vertically or horizontally? ☐ Yes ☐ No.

4.2 How susceptible is the structure and contents to damage from smoke, heat, flame, or water? ☐ High ☐ Moderate ☐ Light.

4.3 Does the structure conform to the Life Safety Code, NFPA 101, or a similar local code? ☐ Yes ☐ No. Describe if no:

of exposure. A downtown TV store may open up a new branch in a suburban shopping mall. A mall usually has several well-known large stores which attract traffic to other smaller stores in the mall. The people are in the mall to shop and are much more likely to enter the television store premises than would pedestrians on city streets. In addition, because of differences in store hours and customers' shopping habits, malls are likely to have a greater percentage of their customers present at nights or on weekends. Even if the total number of customers was average for the class, the mall TV store would have a relatively high concentration of customers at certain hours. The fire exposure also increases in extent because the setup of a mall and more customer traffic make it less likely that customers will be able to successfully exit the premises. In contrast, the extent of most weather-related exposures would decrease for a store located in a mall because the quality of mall maintenance usually helps to eliminate such premises hazards as icy walkways or sidewalks. Each risk must be underwritten individually so that the exposure can be evaluated.

Nevertheless, a concentration of people does not necessarily indicate excessive exposure. What may create an underwriting problem for the TV store would not do so for a theater. The rate for the store may be inadequate, while the rate for the theater may be sufficient because it anticipates concentrations of people.

Consideration must also be given to the legal status of persons likely to be on the premises. What is the insured's legal duty to these persons and what standards of care are expected? The insured must demonstrate behavior that is consistent with the standard of care required. A comparison must be made between the duties owed by the insured and an average risk in the same classification. If they are the same there is usually no problem, but if they vary, the underwriter must account for the difference. For example, a retail store with mostly adult customers may need to exercise reasonable care, but a toy store attracting a large number of children may need to exercise additional care. This clientele and the related degree of care owed are an indication that the liability exposure of a toy store is greater in extent than that of a retail store. For a review of these legal concepts, refer to Chapter 2.

While bodily injury is usually given the primary consideration in underwriting, often due to the higher limits written for the bodily injury coverage, potential property damage losses cannot be ignored. Property damage losses include claims not only for the value of the damaged property but also for the loss of use thereof.

## Physical Hazards

Many physical hazards, such as those that induce slips and falls, are common to many premises, although there may be wide variation in the degree of hazard. Other physical hazards such as chemicals, dust, and explosives exist only in certain types of businesses.

Many types of accidents likely to occur within a building (slipping, falling, tears, cuts, and burns) are really the result of conditions or hazards that may be present on the premises. The causes of the injuries are what is important to the underwriter. The underwriter tries to determine what hazards or conditions increase the likelihood of injury or damage for which the owner or lessor of the premises will be held liable. Some of the more common hazards are uneven stairs, tears in carpets, inadequate lighting, congestion, poor housekeeping, and defective heating or electrical equipment. Other hazards such as the presence of sharp objects, flammable liquids, explosives, toxic or infectious gases, and welding equipment, would usually be found only on premises at which specific operations are located. The potential number of hazards at various premises is almost unlimited.

Risks whose exposures principally arise from the interior of the premises may also have numerous exterior exposures to loss. Injuries can be caused outside the building by broken sidewalks, icy sidewalks, parking lots in poor condition, falling signs, building collapse, or playground equipment, swimming pools, and other attractive nuisances. Mobile equipment could cause injury inside or outside the building depending on the type and use of the equipment.

Generally, businesses with heavy premises exposures like apartment houses and office buildings have minimal operations exposures. Businesses with small premises exposures, such as service businesses and contractors, have substantial operations exposures. An electrical contractor is likely to have a premises, but it may be little more than a desk and telephone, or it could be a store and shop where electrical fixtures are sold and repaired. The desk-and-telephone contractor has little premises exposure and a greater operations exposure as a result of installation and repair work. The electrical contractor who has a sales and repair operation on the premises has both a premises and an operations exposure.

There tends to be greater variation in the hazards related to the operations exposure. Each service or contracting risk will use different tools. Some will have heavy machinery or mobile equipment; some will use flammables and blowtorches; some will rent or lease equipment; and some will blast, excavate, or erect. The builders of both single, ranch-style residences and high-rise apartments do similar work, use similar tools, and create attractive nuisances at construction sites;

however, the similarity ends there. The high-risk building contractor works with steel girders, land leveling equipment, deep excavations, and hoists, often in heavily populated areas. The variation in hazard as a result of these differences is great.

In addition to the bodily injury exposure of premises-type risks, the underwriter must also consider the physical hazards that can cause property damage losses. Torn or stained clothing and damage to vehicles in parking lots are the most common property damage losses, but pollution has one of the greatest potentials for severe losses. If a factory accident releases waste into a stream, sewer system, or the air, an enormous amount of property damage could result.

Risks of the operations-type generally have a greater potential for causing property damage losses than premises-type risks. A plumber can damage the customer's house with equipment or solvents, cause water damage, and possibly cause fire damage from the use of welding equipment. Leased equipment can damage a customer's property if not kept in good repair or if misused by the customer. Use of heavy equipment is likely to cause serious property damage, but the major sources of property damage losses would be fire, collapse, water damage, and in some cases, pollution.

**Premises—An Example.** What is the potential for bodily injury or property damage liability? Are there conditions that will produce injury or damage? In order to answer these questions, the underwriter must systematically consider every possible aspect of the premises or operation that could produce a loss. A department store as an example may help to illustrate this process. This store is a downtown store of brick construction built approximately forty years ago. It occupies one square block and is eight stories high.

This is principally a premises-type risk with some incidental operations exposures. There is a large public exposure, as many people are present when the store is open. The public would include customers and delivery and service personnel, all of whom would be business invitees. Therefore, a high degree of care is owed these people by the owner of the store.

What bodily injury hazards exist in this department store? Common hazards such as uneven stairs, congested aisles, loose wires, worn floors, and poor lighting can cause people to trip and fall. Even well-maintained department stores have premises hazards that are simply a function of normal department-store construction—elevators, escalators, and revolving doors, however safely constructed or operated, can cause people to slip or trip and fall.

The toy department and "kiddies' playrooms" are special attractive nuisances. Children are often allowed in these areas, with little or no adult supervision. The ways in which the children could injure themselves in these playrooms are unlimited. Other areas of the stores could also be considered attractive nuisances and must be evaluated by the underwriter in addition to the playrooms. (Pools and fountains are good examples.) There is usually a great deal of breakable glass in showcases and exterior doors of a department store. Sidewalks and parking lots, especially if they are not well maintained, create external premises exposures.

Most of the losses caused by these hazards tend to occur frequently and are not likely to be severe.

Many department stores have cooking demonstrations to show new products. If the cooking unit is portable and heated by propane, there is an exposure arising out of the possibility of explosion as a result of such equipment. Adding to this hazard is the possibility that the persons using the equipment may be unskilled in its safe and proper use. If a propane tank were to explode, injuries would likely result not only from the explosion but also from the ensuing fire. Exhibit 8-6 shows a sample loss experience record for a department store.

As seen in Exhibit 8-6, typical department store hazards result in a large number of injuries from falls, some of which could result in severe losses. Fire, however, is usually the primary cause of severe loss in a department store.

For most department stores, the property damage exposures are not as great as the bodily injury exposures, but they cannot be ignored. The frequent slips and falls often will involve minor property damage claims for damaged clothing. If there is a parking lot, there is also the possibility of auto damage. Department stores that provide services such as equipment installation and repair have, in addition to a premises exposure, an operations exposure that increases the potential for property damage.

What characteristics of the department store in Exhibit 8-6 make it better or worse than other department stores? From the experience shown in Exhibit 8-6, it can be seen that this store has a proportionally high frequency of falls that occur on level surfaces and a significant frequency of falls on stairs. The underwriter must determine what is causing the falls and not just assume that this frequency is typical for all department stores. (If statistics from the industry on accidents are available, it would be extremely helpful to compare them with this loss data in seeing how this store compares to the "average.") Are the falls on level floors due to the type of floor, torn carpets, slippery surfaces, or poor condition? Do they occur principally in the aisles or entrances and exits? Do the falls from stairs or other elevations occur principally on the stairs or on the escalators or elevators? Are the stairways well lighted? Do the elevators stop even with the floors? Do the escalators

**Exhibit 8-6**
Department Store Loss Experience

| Accident Type | Number of Accidents | Percent of Total Accidents | Percent of Total Costs |
|---|---|---|---|
| False arrest—slander | 65 | 6.1% | 19.2% |
| Bodily reaction | 28 | 2.6 | 0.2 |
| Caught in, under, between | 43 | 4.0 | 0.1 |
| Caustics, chemicals, etc. | 12 | 1.1 | 0.2 |
| Electrical current | 2 | 0.2 | — |
| Temperature extremes (burns) | 1 | 0.1 | — |
| Falls—stairs, elevations | 157 | 14.7 | 8.7 |
| Falls—level surfaces | 309 | 28.9 | 41.0 |
| Overexertion—strains | 2 | 0.2 | — |
| Product defect | 23 | 2.1 | 1.0 |
| Rubbed, bruised | 59 | 5.5 | 0.6 |
| Struck against objects | 176 | 16.4 | 7.9 |
| Struck by object | 183 | 17.1 | 16.5 |
| Motorized equipment | 5 | 0.5 | 4.6 |
| Data unavailable | 5 | 0.5 | — |
| Total | 1,070 | 100.0% | 100.0% |

move too quickly, or are they or the landings in poor condition? After the hazard has been identified, it must be reduced or eliminated—a subject which will be discussed in the next section of this chapter.

The department store has had a substantial frequency of "struck by object" and "struck against object" accidents. Are these accidents caused by narrow or congested aisles, poor housekeeping, or stockroom personnel pushing carts? Whatever the hazard, the underwriter must determine if it can be controlled—otherwise, the frequency of claims can be expected to continue.

Also important is evaluating the hazards that can create severe losses. Fire is one of the most frequent causes of severe bodily injury losses for a department store. Thus, it must be determined if there are premises hazards that increase the probability of a fire. Are paints or other flammable liquids sold in the store? If so, in what part of the store are they sold and are any extinguishers or protective devices present? What is the construction of the building and is it in good condition? Is there automatic sprinkler equipment? Are there adequate exits? Have the employees been instructed in the procedure for handling customers if a fire occurs? Are aisles congested or exits blocked or inaccessible?

**Exhibit 8-7**
Summary of Liability Claims by Type of Accident—Television Sales, Installation, and Repair Store

| Type of Accidents | Number of Claims | Cost | Percent of Claims | Percent of Costs |
|---|---|---|---|---|
| Falls | 8 | $34,092 | 20% | 49% |
| Struck by | 2 | 1,850 | 5 | 3 |
| Electric shock | 1 | — | 2 | — |
| Property damage by service personnel | 20 | 13,737 | 49 | 20 |
| Damage to a vehicle | 7 | 849 | 17 | 1 |
| Smoke damage | 1 | 15,500 | 2 | 22 |
| Miscellaneous or unknown | 2 | 3,700 | 5 | 5 |
| Total | 41 | $69,728 | 100% | 100% |

Are there fire alarms or a procedure for notifying the fire department? Do the elevators have heat-sensitive call buttons?

**Operations—An Example.** Consider a firm that sells, repairs, and installs television sets. The primary exposure for this business is the possibility of loss arising out of operations conducted in the homes of customers. Bodily injury losses could result from the use of soldering irons or electricity and from service personnel carelessly leaving tools where customers can trip over them. Generally, however, the underwriter would not expect a high frequency of bodily injury claims from a television sales and repair business. It might be expected that such a business would generate a high frequency of property damage losses. The very same tools and use of electricity that cause the bodily injury losses can also cause property damage losses.

For example, Exhibit 8-7 shows the losses of a firm selling, repairing, and installing television sets. For each type of loss, the number of claims and total cost of claims are shown. Each type of loss is then evaluated with respect to what percentage of the total number of claims and the total cost of all claims this type of accident represents.

The frequency and severity of property damage losses depend primarily on the nature of the operations of the particular business. If most of the repairing (that is, soldering and electrical work) is done at the shop rather than the customers' homes, the frequency of loss should be reduced. On the other hand, a key factor in evaluating loss severity is the quality of workmanship. Are the repair and installation personnel well trained? How long have they been performing their jobs? How much supervision do they get?

Based on the number of property damage losses shown in Exhibit 8-7, it is likely that the work is being performed in a careless manner. This would lead the underwriter to expect that future losses related to the work of service personnel would occur. Since the majority of these losses occur at the job site, the underwriter must evaluate whether or not the loss frequency can be controlled—perhaps by performing more repair work at the shop rather than in the customers' homes.

This kind of operations exposure can also create severe as well as frequent losses. In addition, frequent losses increase the likelihood of random severe losses. A given hazard may produce widely different levels of loss severity. For example, a hazard that helps to create a fire can result in smoke damage or in the destruction of an entire structure, depending on when the fire is extinguished.

**Unexpected Physical Hazards.** There is an additional and rather unpredictable factor the underwriter must consider in reviewing a risk for general liability insurance. The risk may have exposures to loss that are not characteristic of the class as a whole, thus presenting an unexpected increase in the chance of loss. Therefore, it is important for the underwriter to identify for a particular risk any hazards that are not characteristic of that class of business, and that would increase the liability exposures beyond what would typically be expected for that class. These hazards could evolve from an incidental operation, "one shot deals," gradual diversification of operations, or assumption of operations not contemplated when the risk was originally classified.

It has been mentioned that some department stores provide special services that add operations exposures to a normally premises-only type business. Many stores also have an auto service area, a grocery section, or a restaurant. Department stores or any business can sponsor sporting events either as a promotional activity or for the benefit of employees. Such activities are not inherent in the operation of the business and therefore, any related hazard is relatively unexpected; yet such activities could significantly increase the likelihood of a liability loss.

Exposures in the television repair business can also deviate from the norm. The owner could negotiate a special service contract with a motel or hotel chain to install and service their TV sets. This may mean hiring extra employees without having the benefit of training them completely or burdening the regular employees with rush jobs, which may result in carelessness or lower quality workmanship. It could also involve rebuilding or rewiring work. The television operation could also expand into performing other types of electrical work, such as rewiring homes. Would the employees have the ability and expertise to perform such tasks? Peak seasons, demonstrations, exhibits, and hiring subcontractors are other conditions that might create unexpected hazards that could increase the liability exposure of department stores and TV repair businesses beyond the scope of their particular class.

## Subcontracted Work

Chapter 7 described the manual rules regarding subcontractors. If the subcontractors are adequately insured, a set of nine subcontracted work classifications applies to the insured's coverage for the work of subcontractors. If the insurance is inadequate, the subcontractor is classified and rated as if the work is being done by employees. The problems related to defining adequate insurance were described in that discussion.

Even if properly rated, the work of subcontractors is still a factor to consider in premises-operations underwriting. The most desirable circumstances for an underwriter would be a subcontractor with its own insurance. In this case, only a small charge is made on the insured's policy to cover those few circumstances when the insured may be held liable for the work of the subcontractor. The underwriter should ideally try to determine in advance the subcontractors the insured will use on a particular project and gain some underwriting information about them. In reality, this is very difficult since the subcontractor is not the one applying for insurance and may be hesitant (or unwilling) to supply information to an insurer with which it has no insurance.

If the subcontractor has no insurance, it should be treated as an employee of the insured, and the underwriter should gather the same kind of information that would be gathered in that case. Nevertheless, there is still the problem of getting the subcontractor to provide information because it is not the subcontractor who is applying for insurance. However, since the insured is providing coverage for the subcontractor, the insured may be able to persuade the subcontractor to provide some information.

The biggest problem with any subcontractor used by "your insured" is that the insured may not know at the outset of the policy term exactly which subcontractors will or will not be used. If this is so, it would be impossible to underwrite all subcontractors. No underwriter or insurer is going to request the insured to notify the insurer each time a new subcontractor is hired. Nor is it expected at those times that the underwriter will be given time to examine the subcontractor.

The underwriter must underwrite the insured much as the reinsurance underwriter underwrites the primary insurer's underwriters and not every individual risk. If the insured is acceptable, has a good reputation, and shows pride in his or her work, then it is likely the insured is going to be selective in hiring subcontractors. If the insured values his or her reputation, the insured will only hire well-qualified subcontractors (regardless of whether or not they have their own insurance). In practice, if the insured is a large enough and reputable enough contractor, many (if not most) of the subcontractors hired probably have their own coverage. If the underwriter is satisfied that this is the case, then the premium that will be charged should be commensurate with the exposure to loss.

## SUMMARY

This chapter on general liability insurance reviewed some of the more important CGL policy provisions.

For a complete discussion of the coverage, readers should refer to the program in general insurance, the CPCU program, or other sources.

Next, the chapter examined claims-made and occurrence policies. Even if the underwriter is not writing any claims-made coverage, he or she should be able to understand the differences between claims-made and occurrence coverage and should be prepared to underwrite risks on a claims-made basis. It is likely that the use of claims-made policies will increase over the years and all underwriters should be ready to respond to this trend. It is important to remember that although the underwriter must be familiar with the operation of retroactive dates, tail coverage, and laser beam endorsements, these are simply the mechanics of providing claims-made coverage that is suitable for the insured and the insurer. The actual factors that should be considered in determining the desirability of a risk, as well as in classifying and rating a risk, are the same in claims-made and occurrence policies. The form of coverage agreed on by the underwriter and insured has no impact on the losses the insured will suffer. The form simply determines which policies and which insurers are responsible for paying for these losses. Claims-made policies were introduced for pricing reasons. To the extent that pricing is a part of underwriting, claims-made policies influence underwriting. There are some risks that are unacceptable under an occurrence form, but acceptable under a claims-made form. This is true only because the insurer believes that under the claims-made policy, it can better determine the extent of the exposure it has assumed and adequately price that exposure. The organization applying for insurance has not changed.

This chapter concluded with a discussion of many of the factors considered in the underwriting of the premises-operations exposure. Many of the factors in that discussion also apply to products-completed operations underwriting, as discussed in the next chapter. That chapter concludes the discussion of underwriting general liability insurance. Also included is a detailed discussion of the law as it relates to products. The following chapter ends with a description of some of the pricing problems in products liability insurance. When reading that section, the student should think about which of the delays discussed are addressed by the claims-made policy.

# Chapter Note

1. A closed loss refers to an incident for which a claim has been made and paid and for which the insurer expects no further claims or payments. For example, the insured damaged the claimant's roof, the insurer paid $750 to have it repaired, and no further claims or payments are expected to arise out of that incident. A reserved loss is one for which payments may or may not have been made, but for which the insurer expects to make payments in the future. For example, the insured may have caused bodily injury to a third party and even though the insurer has paid for that third party's medical bills to date, the insurer expects to have to pay additional amounts in order to "close" the claim.

# CHAPTER 9

# Underwriting General Liability Insurance, III

This chapter concludes the discussion of underwriting general liability insurance. Most of the chapter is devoted to products-completed operations coverage. Many of the "problems" of the general liability line of insurance can be traced to the products exposure. This is especially true of the pricing problems.

Much of the underwriting of products liability coverage involves the law as it applies to the applicant's product. This chapter examines the law and other factors related to products liability underwriting. The problems in pricing products liability coverage are also briefly presented.

The chapter concludes with some illustrations of how the general liability line of insurance is managed. It is impossible in a few pages to present what takes most people many years to understand. A book or chapter cannot make anyone an underwriting manager. This chapter can, however, help the reader understand some of the factors considered at the higher levels of underwriting management and the options at those levels for handling underwriting problems.

## PRODUCTS LIABILITY LAW

Chapter 2 described most of the legal concepts needed to understand and to underwrite liability insurance. The discussion of the law as it applies to products liability was purposely reserved for this chapter. Many of the terms used here are the same as those used in Chapter 2. The reader should refer to that chapter for a more detailed discussion of those terms.

The field of products liability is one of the most rapidly changing, fastest growing areas of tort law. While most of this section is focused on products liability, the discussion is applicable to both products and completed operations. In fact, many of the problems discussed are actually related to completed operations exposures. These coverages are usually sold as one—primarily because they address exposures that are a function of accidents or damage caused by a defect in "finished work" that is away from the insured's premises and for which the insured has essentially relinquished control. The finished work can be a product made by the insured (the basis of the products liability exposure) or some service or operation performed by the insured (the basis of the completed operations exposure). Manufacturers and retailers would have the products liability exposure; contractors and repair organizations would have a completed operations exposure.

The liability underwriter must attempt to keep current, not only with court decisions and with new laws, but also with changes in the manufacturing and sales operations of insureds. Many insurance authorities have come to believe that the products liability situation has placed such a heavy burden on many private organizations that product liability laws will have to change if these organizations are to continue to exist. Evidently, the only safe prediction concerning products liability is that safety requirements are certain to change. Of course, the law on which past products liability cases were based is relevant, but the consumer demand for safety and perfection is bringing rapid changes that the commercial liability underwriter dare not ignore.

## Sources of Products Liability

Liability for the sale, manufacture, and distribution of products can arise from breach of warranty, the tort of negligence, fraud, strict liability, and breach of contract.

**Breach of Warranty.** Breach of warranty actions can be based on either express or implied warranties. An *express warranty* is a promise or a guarantee regarding the product's quality or performance and is part of the basis for the sale of the product. Where the buyer bases a purchase on a statement of the sales person or on a statement printed on the product or its container with a reasonable assumption that the product will be as stated, an express warranty exists. The manufacturer or the seller has made a statement about the product, and the buyer is entitled to rely on that statement.

The express warranty need not be in writing or in any specific form (for example, the seller does not have to state, "I warrant. . . ."). It is only necessary that a fact be stated and that the fact become a part or term of the transaction. The seller's own opinion, identified as such, regarding the value of the product does not create a warranty. The express warranty can be made before or after the sale.

An *implied warranty* is an obligation imposed by courts on a seller to warrant or guarantee certain facts about a product. This obligation arises out of the transaction between the buyer and the seller and is implied without any specific agreement between the parties. The two major types of implied warranties which have a bearing on insurance are (1) warranty that the goods are merchantable and (2) warranty of fitness for a particular purpose.

The *implied warranty of merchantability* warrants that the product is safe and reasonably fit for the purpose or purposes for which the product is normally intended. This implied warranty only applies to merchants, not to "nonmerchants," who deal in, but are not as knowledgeable about, the kind of goods being sold. For example, a person buying a lawnmower relies on the implied warranty that the mower is reasonably fit for mowing lawns. If the mower loses its blades when cutting grass and injury or damage results, the injured person may sue on the basis of breach of the implied warranty of merchantability. Most breach of warranty cases are based on a breach of the implied warranty of merchantability.[1]

The *implied warranty of fitness for a particular purpose* comes into play when the buyer relies on the knowledge of the seller in selecting a particular product for a particular purpose. If a seller sells a product knowing the purposes for which it is purchased, the seller is understood to warrant it to be reasonably fit for the purpose for which it was bought. For example, a person might mention to the salesperson in a garden shop that he is looking for a poison to kill the bugs in his vegetable garden, and the salesperson might hand the customer a certain poison. In this situation, there is an implied warranty that the poison selected will be fit for that particular purpose. This implied warranty would be applicable regardless if the salesperson knows, but fails to mention, that the product should not be used on any type of plant that will bear an edible fruit or vegetable. If the customer's family members become ill after eating the vegetables from the garden containing this poison, the customer could sue based upon the implied warranty of fitness for a particular purpose. Unlike the merchantability warranty, this warranty is not restricted to "merchants." However, in practice, it is usually only the merchant seller who has such skill and knowledge that would cause the implied warranty to be invoked (that is, the casual seller would not be viewed as being so skilled and knowledgeable that the buyer should rely on the seller in determining whether a product is fit for a particular purpose).

Every product sold is expected to meet all express and implied warranties. The failure of a product to meet warranties can result in products liability claims if bodily injury or property damage is the result. The products liability underwriter must search for express warranties, either in advertising or in sales presentations, and he or she must carefully consider the warranties implied when a product is offered for sale. In asserting a claim for damages arising from a breach of warranty, the injured party does not have to prove negligence on the part of the seller or the manufacturer. However, the injured party must establish that he or she gave the seller notice of the breach within a reasonable time after discovery of the breach.

**Negligence.** Negligence is another one of the grounds on which products liability claims are brought. Negligence can find its way into many different steps in the production process, including the manufacture or inspection of the product as well as the instructions or warnings accompanying the product. Regardless of the source of negligence, the result is a defect in the product.

A defective product is one that operates improperly or does not operate at all as the result of improper manufacture or handling. A tire company might manufacture thousands of excellent auto tires, but one with a defective sidewall could blow out and cause serious injury and property damage. A plaintiff could bring suit based on the fact that the manufacturer was negligent in the manufacturing of that particular tire, the tire was defective, and the defect caused harm.

Negligence involving improper inspection can also be the basis of a products liability suit. Many manufacturing firms do not inspect every product produced; instead a sample (10 or 20 percent, for example) is inspected on the assumption that the quality of the sample will correspond with the quality of all products produced. Such a procedure is probably adequate when the product is an item like a paper clip where the risk is low. But the manufacturer of more dangerous items should probably inspect each item coming off the assembly line. A company that sells furnaces, for example, should be aware of the potential for loss of life and property from a defective furnace and should carefully inspect each one. Failure to do so might be grounds for a negligence action. Retailers can also be sued for negligence for failing to inspect or for improperly inspecting certain kinds of products with suspected defects if those products cause damage as the result of the defect. Car dealers would likely face this exposure.

The design of a product has much to do with its effectiveness and its safety. Manufacturers can be found liable for negligence when products are improperly engineered or designed. The manufacturers of rotary lawnmowers added a safety shield at the rear of the blade housing after it was shown that the original design of such mowers allowed the user to pull the mower back over his or her feet.

Lawnmowers are now designed to stop if the operator does not depress a certain bar or lever. In this way the blades of a mower left on but unattended will not continue to move.

Some products are dangerous if used improperly, no matter how well they were manufactured, handled, inspected, or designed. Machinery can cause bodily injury, electrical appliances can electrocute their users, and cleaning liquids can poison children. Where the nature of the product is such that it cannot be made completely safe, adequate warnings of the danger are necessary. Where the operation of the product is difficult or confusing, adequate and easy-to-understand instructions must be given. Containers of dangerous liquids or medicine must clearly be indicated as such and should be kept from the reach of children. They should also include instructions as to what to do if swallowed. Electrical appliances often carry warnings that only qualified repairpersons should attempt repair. Obviously, any printed warnings must be clear and if foreign markets are involved, in a language that the consumer can understand. In some cases, failure to give proper warnings or instructions may also be a violation of a statute. Retailers, especially, should try to be sure that the customers understand these warnings since they have direct contact with the customer.

**Fraud.** Persons who are defrauded by a seller or a manufacturer who knowingly makes false or misleading statements, or has reckless disregard for the truth of the statements, will generally be able to recover in tort for any harm or damages as a result of such statements.

**Strict Liability.**[2] In 1963, the Supreme Court of California, in *Greenman* v. *Yuba Power Products, Inc.,*[3] ushered in the new era of strict liability. That case involved an injury to the plaintiff caused by a piece of wood that flew out of a lathe. The lathe manufacturer was held strictly liable on the grounds that inadequately set screws were used to hold the lathe parts together so that normal vibrations let the wood fly out, and further that there were better ways of fastening the machine together that would have prevented the accident. The crux of the decision is contained in the following statement by the court:

> A manufacturer is *strictly liable in tort* when an article he places on the market, knowing that it is to be used without inspection for defects, proves to have a defect that causes injury to a human being [emphasis added].

This doctrine has now been adopted in some form in almost every state. It has been incorporated into the Restatement of Torts as Section 402A reading as follows:

(1) One who sells any product in a defective condition and unreasonably dangerous to the user or consumer, or to his property, is subject to liability for physical harm thereby caused to the ultimate user or consumer, or to his property, if,
   (a) The seller is engaged in the business of selling such a product; and
   (b) It is expected to and does reach the user or consumer without substantial change in the condition in which it is sold.

(2) The rule stated in Section (1) applies although
   (a) The seller has exercised all possible care in the preparation and sale of his product; and
   (b) The user or consumer has not bought the product from or entered into any contractual agreement with the seller.

***Elements of a Strict Liability Action.*** Most modern product liability actions are brought both in negligence and strict liability. It is important to understand the difference between the two. Negligence is still the basic cause of action in product suits because strict liability does not apply in many cases. In a negligence case, the plaintiff must prove that the manufacturer was not reasonably prudent in the design or manufacture of the article that caused the injury. It focuses on the manufacturer's conduct, that is, how conscientious he or she is. Under strict liability, the focus is on the product itself, and whether it was, in fact, unsafe. The manufacturer could have used the utmost care in making the article, but if it was unsafe, there may still be liability under the doctrine of strict liability. A strict liability action generally requires that the plaintiff prove three elements:

1. The product was defective when it left the custody or control of the manufacturer or supplier.
2. The defective condition made the product unreasonably dangerous. Unreasonably dangerous means that the article is dangerous to an extent beyond that which would be contemplated by the ordinary user who has common knowledge about the article. (This element is not required by all courts.)
3. The defective product was the proximate cause of the plaintiff's injury.

The key word in these three elements is "defective." A product may be defective in three ways. These ways closely parallel the ways in which negligence was defined in the sense that both "negligence" and "defects" are introduced at the same points in the production process and that the latter is often interpreted to be a result of the former. In fact, the determination of "defectiveness" as part of a strict liability claim would be based heavily on past decisions on what was considered defective even though those decisions involved a determination of negligence.

1. *Defective due to faulty manufacture or assembly* means that the product is not in the condition that was intended by the manufacturer.
2. *Defective in design* means that the product is built exactly as intended, but the design is alleged to be faulty, thereby producing injury. The defendant is charged with liability because of a design fault incorporated into all products of the same kind and not just one particular item that injured the plaintiff.
3. *Failure to give warning* means that the product is defective neither in manufacture nor design but has some inherent danger about which the manufacturer has failed to give proper warning.

*Defect in Manufacture.* Defects in manufacture usually involve errors in putting a product together or the use of faulty materials. This is the simplest grounds for strict liability because if the object is improperly manufactured or assembled, a defect is proved by that fact alone. The question of whether it is unreasonably dangerous is not an issue because the fact that it caused injury demonstrates that it was dangerous.

The plaintiff must prove that the product was defective when it left the defendant's possession. A product is not considered defective in connection with a given defendant if it was in a safe condition when it left the defendant's possession and subsequent events made it unsafe at the time of use. This problem of a superseding or intervening cause is a major area of product liability law, and space does not permit a full analysis. It is safe to say that at the very least, courts have been reluctant to permit manufacturers to escape liability for defects found to exist after a product has been used or even altered.

*Defect in Design.* Design errors or defects introduce a different set of problems, and in this area there is the greatest divergence among the various courts. In a strict liability case based on design, the article was properly manufactured or assembled and the alleged defective condition is in the design of the article. The Restatement requirement that the article be "unreasonably dangerous" is particularly applicable to the design situation. As mentioned, "unreasonably dangerous" means that the article is dangerous to an extent beyond that which would be contemplated by the ordinary user with common knowledge about its characteristics. The principal effect of this requirement is that if the condition is open and obvious, the article is not unreasonably dangerous and there is no strict liability. The courts of at least five or six states have rejected the "unreasonably dangerous" requirement and treat design defects as manufacturing defects.

Many design defect cases arise out of an alleged failure to install safety devices, or the installation of allegedly defective devices. In such cases the manufacturer is held strictly liable only if the alleged failure made the product unreasonably dangerous in normal use. Common situations include lack of guards, or installation of defective guards, on machines such as punch presses, metal shears, or pizza dough rollers. Litigation in the area of auto design is becoming common. It has focused on the placement of the gasoline tank, the steering wheel, and other components that have caused injury following a collision. Originally courts took the position that a collision was not a "normal use" of an auto and manufacturers were not required to design their product in anticipation of such an abnormal use. However, many later decisions support the belief that collisions are part of common use and a manufacturer should foresee that its product might be involved in one and take reasonable steps to avoid injury to the occupants.

Cases involving design defects raise collateral problems. It is possible that the safety device or construction method was unknown at the time the article was made but has subsequently been developed. Most courts adhere to the rule that the state of the art at the time of construction governs, but some courts do not follow this rule. The mere fact that the article was designed in accordance with federal standards or accepted industry standards or practices does not in and of itself constitute a defense if other adequate safeguards actually were available.

The extent to which the pendulum has swung is illustrated by a 1981 case in which the U.S. Supreme Court refused to review a state supreme court decision. In this case the jury decided that the manufacturer had built a defective automobile, based on an implied warranty that the vehicle was crashworthy and would withstand the damage that occurred when the plaintiff's car struck a steel pole which penetrated the car and injured the plaintiff. The car met all federal safety standards. The court of appeals noted that this created a "troubling public policy dilemma—namely, that under existing federal law individual juries in the various states are permitted, in effect, to establish national automobile safety standards." On the other hand, there are cases that hold that compliance with federal safety regulations by an aircraft manufacturer would preclude any strict liability claim for an alleged defect in design.

*Failure to Give Warning.* Many products, such as drugs, are essential and yet incapable of being made completely safe. Such products are not defective or unreasonably dangerous if they are properly made and properly used. Improper preparation is similar to a manufacturing defect and gives no problem. However, usage raises the issue of the adequacy of directions and warnings as to the proper application of the product, possible side effects, and so forth.

A warning is required when a product has a potential for danger that is not generally known to the public, or if known, is one that the user would not readily expect. The seller must know of the condition or should have known of the condition and danger. Failure to give adequate warning under such conditions renders the product defective for the purpose of strict liability. When a warning is given, the seller may reasonably assume that it will be followed and that a product bearing an adequate warning is not defective or unreasonably dangerous.

The test of whether there is a duty to warn with respect to drugs is whether the hazard is foreseeable by a person using ordinary care, taking into consideration the appreciable number of persons that might use the product. Thus, allergic reaction to drugs frequently falls outside the strict liability area because it is not foreseeable by the manufacturer. In the case of prescription drugs, the general rule is that the warning need be given only to the physician. As in other strict liability situations, compliance with governmental requirements for directions for use or warnings as to side effects is not always enough to escape liability.

In nondrug cases the element of foreseeability is not as controversial. Thus, manufacturers have been held liable for failure to warn that a certain type of hammer would become brittle with use and thus be more susceptible to chipping, or for failure to warn that a car tire would fail if more than six passengers were carried in a nine passenger station wagon.

***Persons Liable.*** Under the Restatement rule, strict liability is applicable to a person who engages in the business of selling a product. All courts appear to agree that this embraces the manufacturer, including the manufacturer of a defective component, unless it is altered by the assembler of the final product. A majority of courts also apply the doctrine of strict liability to distributors and wholesalers. Most courts also hold retailers strictly liable. It does not apply to persons who make an occasional sale.

There is a tendency to expand the meaning of salespeople to include bailors and lessors. Thus, the lessor of an auto with defective brakes can be held strictly liable. Most jurisdictions that accept this expanded definition appear to recognize a distinction between a lessor or bailor engaged in a regular leasing business, such as a rental car agency, and those who lease on an irregular basis. At least one state has extended the doctrine to persons using products in a service business, such as a beauty parlor.

One significant extension of the doctrine of strict liability in many jurisdictions has been to builders and contractors. Courts have reasoned that the rationale underlying the application of the strict liability rule to defective product manufacturers is equally applicable to builders and contractors. Thus contractors have been held strictly liable for the installation of a faulty hot water heater that caused a fire; a defective heating system that had to be replaced; and even for failure to properly compact dirt in a filled lot on which a house was later built.

***Persons Protected.*** Originally, the concept of strict liability was to permit the injured buyer of a defective article to recover from the manufacturer without having to specifically prove negligence, or to enable that buyer to circumvent contractual liability defenses such as lack of privity of contract, warranty disclaimer, or failure to promptly notify the manufacturer of a breach of warranty. The courts had little trouble eliminating the privity requirement because changes in distribution methods resulted in very few manufacturers selling directly to the ultimate buyer. However, the early cases required that the plaintiff be the ultimate buyer of the product in order to sue on the basis of strict liability. Once the product went past the ultimate buyer, there arose some diversity in the decisions. It is important to differentiate between the ultimate buyer and the ultimate user or consumer. The latter includes many additional parties such as a person who received the article as a gift. The Restatement rule extends protection to the ultimate user or consumer, which includes the ultimate buyer. However, the rule states nothing about nonusers such as bystanders or other strangers injured by the defective product. The majority of courts have ruled that at least regarding actions against sellers, any nonuser may assert strict liability. For example, a person injured by the explosion of a companion's defective shotgun may assert strict liability. A special situation arises where a person riding in one vehicle is injured when struck by another vehicle and the accident arises out of a defect in the other vehicle. Most courts will allow the injured party to assert strict liability against the manufacturer of the other vehicle, but a few will not.

**Breach of Contract.** A person who has a contract with a seller or manufacturer can sue for damages resulting from a breach of that contract. This is not a tort action and is generally not insurable, so it is not discussed here.

## Defenses to Products Liability Claims

The defense against any products liability claim usually attempts to disprove that the product was defectively manufactured or designed, that the warnings about the safe use of the product were inadequate, or that there was a warranty with the product. The defenses against a defect and inadequate warnings would apply equally to negligence claims. If this line of defense is successful, the insured would not be found negligent, or strictly liable, or in breach of a warranty.

If the insured is held to be negligent, strictly liable, or to have breached a warranty, there are few available defenses. First, any of the defenses described in Chapter 2 that apply to the tort of negligence could be used as a defense against a products liability claim alleging negligence. Second, if a manufacturer is found to be strictly liable for certain injuries or damage, there is generally only one real defense, which is a meshing of the contributory negligence and assumption of risk defenses. However, some claims based on a breach of warranty may be successfully defended on the basis of a disclaimer. Finally, in certain situations the existence of a middleman and the allergy or sensitivity of the injured person to a product may be used as defenses.

**Contributory Negligence/Assumption of Risk.** As mentioned, the only defense to a strict liability action is a limited form of contributory negligence and/or assumption of risk. In applying this defense, most courts distinguish between so-called "active" and "passive" negligence. *Passive negligence* is the failure to discover a defect in the product or to guard against a defect. Most courts hold that passive negligence will not bar recovery.

*Active negligence* (often used interchangeably with assumption of risk) applies when the injured person knows of the danger existing due to the defect but voluntarily and unreasonably proceeds to use the product. For example, a worker who, knowing the caustic properties of a certain batch of concrete, puts his bare hands into it anyway would be denied recovery. The burden of proving that the plaintiff had knowledge of the defect or danger is on the defendant.

Closely akin to active negligence is *misuse or abnormal use of a product*. For example, the failure to follow directions on the container or the attempt to open a glass container by tapping it against a sink constitute sufficient misuse or abnormal use to deny recovery. In these cases the burden is on the plaintiff to disprove misuse or abnormal use. This is because the liability of the defendant is based on the product being defective, and the plaintiff must therefore prove that it was being used in a proper and foreseeable manner in order to establish the defect.

**Disclaimer.** Although it is not frequently done except with used goods or factory seconds, it is possible to sell goods on an "as is" basis. The seller may disclaim any responsibility for defects in the goods and injuries or damages resulting therefrom. Some courts have held such disclaimers to be invalid for personal injuries but have supported them for property damage losses. Some courts also refuse to uphold any disclaimer of liability for negligence or for a statutory duty. The courts have usually insisted that the facts show that the buyer was aware of the disclaimer and took the product with a full realization of the consequences of the disclaimer. Thus, they have not upheld disclaimers of which the buyer was unaware, or where the buyer bought the product and later discovered notice of the manufacturer's disclaimer in the package. The rationale behind these decisions is that since the buyer never assented to such terms, he or she is not bound by them.[4] Disclaimers are usually applicable only to warranty liability and are not to strict liability, fraud, or negligence cases. Also, disclaimers usually only apply to liability to the buyer and not to third parties.[5]

**Existence of a Middleman.** Products liability cases often raise the issue of the actions of a middleman who distributes or sells a manufacturer's products. The central question in this issue is do those actions (or omissions) relieve the manufacturer of liability? If the middleman's acts or omissions are the cause of the product defect and if such acts or omissions were not foreseeable by the manufacturer, generally the manufacturer will not be held negligently liable. Similarly, if the manufacturer believes or has reason to believe that the middleman is to take steps to remove or prevent an otherwise foreseeable defect or danger, the manufacturer will not be held negligently liable for such defect. However, if the manufacturer is held to be strictly liable for such defect, the liability of the manufacturer would not be relieved by the existence of a middleman even if the middleman is to perform the final inspection of the product.

**Allergy and Susceptibility.** Few products have been produced to which at least one person is not allergic. The manufacturer or seller of cosmetics and similar products is not required to know the allergies of every potential customer.

If a product is safe for normal use but there are a few persons allergic to the product, a manufacturer or seller will usually have no duty to alter the product because of those few persons. Even if there is an ingredient in the product to which a number of persons are allergic, the product will not be considered defective if adequate warnings are given.

A manufacturer can be held liable for failure to warn adequately on the basis of negligence, strict liability, and breach of express and implied warranties. In determining negligence, several factors must be considered. Probably the most important is the number of persons susceptible or allergic to the product relative to the number of products sold or used.

What is considered a substantial number or percentage of users such that warnings should be given? The courts have varied on the answer. One in five million,[6] three in 500 million,[7] and one in 1,000[8] have been held to be a percentage of allergic persons so small that a warning is not required. In one case, the court held that a warning is necessary when one in 50 million people is allergic to the product. To some extent, this decision was based on how serious the injury might be.[9] The trend is toward requiring warnings in more cases (that is, when the percentage of those people allergic to the product is small).

Other factors to consider in the decision to require a warning include seriousness of the possible injury, whether the manufacturer knew or should have known of the possible allergic reactions, and the difficulty in including a warning on the product.

If strict liability requires the manufacturer or seller to include a warning about allergic reactions, the injured plaintiff must still show that he or she is "a member of an appreciable class of potentially allergic users."[10]

## PRODUCTS LIABILITY AND COMPLETED OPERATIONS UNDERWRITING

The challenge in underwriting products liability comes partly from the evolution from the concept of negligence to strict liability in some areas of products liability. Strict liability clearly directs the underwriting emphasis toward the product itself as the basis of products liability underwriting. As in premises-operations underwriting, the underwriter is concerned with the potential exposure of the public to products hazards and the relative seriousness of those hazards. Although many factors can affect the products exposure, if the product by its nature is not inherently hazardous, there is significantly reduced exposure to loss. To illustrate, consider two products: a power lawn mower and a pillow. It is apparent that the lawn mower is a much more hazardous product due to the inherent characteristics which increase the likelihood of loss. Determining the inherent hazards of the product is therefore the first and most important step in underwriting a product. This would be followed by an analysis of the exposure of the public to these product hazards.

Before describing the inherent hazards and other product-related factors the underwriter considers, this section examines products-completed operations coverage. Again, all the policy provisions are not discussed. Only those provisions that have changed significantly from the previous version of the policy, have significant underwriting implications, or are often misinterpreted are addressed.

## Products-Completed Operations Coverage

Products-completed operations coverage is provided as part of the commercial general liability policy. The distinction between the two is not important since they come as a "package," but it is important to understand how each is defined. The policy defines products-completed operations hazard as a single term, but then defines "your product" and "your work" separately. The preceding discussion of the new CGL coverage concentrated on aspects applicable to premises-operations and products-completed operations underwriting. This section considers some more details of the CGL coverage applicable to only products-completed operations and the underwriting implications of those details.

The more important distinction is that between products-completed operations and premises-operations since there are separate aggregate limits (the products-completed operations aggregate limits and general aggregate limits, respectively) applying to each under a commercial general liability (CGL) policy. It is possible for these limits to be different. (Under previous forms, it was possible that there was no aggregate at all for the premises-operations exposure.)

The products-completed operations hazard has two parts. The first deals with products and the second, more extensive part, deals with completed operations. They will be discussed separately here.

**Products Hazard.** The products hazard includes all bodily injury and property damage arising out of "your product" occurring (1) away from premises owned or rented by the named insured and (2) after the product is in the physical possession of someone other than the named insured.

Both of these conditions must be met. For example, if a person purchases the named insured's product but is injured on the named insured's owned premises, the injury is treated as a premises-operations claim. There are certain classifications within the manual that are shown as including products-completed operations. In many cases, the reason for this is that the exposure is minimal. Regardless of the reason, the policy states that losses otherwise meeting the two preceding criteria will not be considered a part of the products hazard.

Additionally, certain classes require an endorsement altering the definition of the products hazard. An example is the restaurant classification, which removes the requirement that the loss occur away from the named insured premises. Other similar classes where the product is customarily consumed or used on the named insured's premises require the same endorsement.

Important to the determination of what is included in the products hazard is the definition of "your product." This definition includes goods or products (other than real property) manufactured, sold, handled, distributed, or disposed of by (1) the named insured; (2) others trading under the named insured's name; and (3) a person or organization whose assets or business have been acquired by the named insured. Containers (other than vehicles) are also included within the definition. Vending machines are not included. Finally, the definition "includes warranties or representations made at any time with respect to the fitness, quality, durability or performance" of the products or containers as described above.

**Completed Operations Hazard.** The completed operations hazard includes all bodily injury and property damage arising out of "your work" (as defined) (1) occurring away from premises owned or rented by the named insured and (2) after the work has been completed or abandoned. As might be expected, it is the second part of the definition that requires further explanation and is usually the subject of debate. If the work is not completed or abandoned, the loss falls under the premises-operations coverage. Each type of loss is subject to a different set of aggregate limits.

To resolve the question of when an operation is deemed complete, the definition of the completed operations hazard lists three time periods, and it specifies that the work is deemed to be complete at the earliest of the three following times:

1. When all of the work called for in the named insured's contract has been completed
2. When all of the work to be done at the site has been completed if the named insured's contract calls for work at more than one site
3. When that part of the work done at a job site has been put to its intended use by any person or organization other than another contractor or subcontractor working on the same project

Work that may only need service, maintenance, correction, repair, or replacement, but otherwise is complete, is treated as completed.

The definition of "your work" is similar to that of "your product." It includes work or operations performed by the named insured or others on the named insured's behalf as well as the materials, parts, or equipment furnished in connection therewith. Additionally, warranties or representations made at any time with respect to the fitness, quality, durability, or performance of this work or operations is included.

**Exclusions.** Many of the court cases involving products-completed operations coverage result disputes about the interpretation of the exclusions related to this coverage. It is imperative that the underwriter (and insured) understand what is not insured by products-completed operations coverage. This section examines some of the more difficult-to-understand exclusions.

***Exclusion of Damage to the Named Insured's Product.*** No coverage applies for "property damage" to "your product" arising out of it or any part of it, whether the product is physically damaged or is merely rendered useless. This exclusion (k) prevents an insurer from having to pay for the repair or replacement of a product that is incorrectly designed or defectively produced. Two aspects of this exclusion deserve emphasis.

1. When damage arises out of a portion of a product and such damage makes the remaining part of the product useless, the exclusion applies to the whole product—not just to that part from which the damage arises.
2. Damage to a product arising from it or any part of it is also excluded, whether the underlying cause is attributable to the work of a manufacturer, an assembler, or a supplier of any component.

For purposes of illustration, assume Alpha Manufacturing Company is under contract to produce electric generators that Baker Manufacturing Company uses with its steam turbines. One of Alpha's electric generators is defective. It burns out and causes damage (physical injury or loss of use) to the steam turbine while in the possession of a utility company.

- Baker Company would be without liability protection under its CGL for damage confined to the electric generator and to the turbine because both are considered to be Baker Company's products. (While Baker Company may initially be responsible for repairing or replacing the electric generator or the entire unit, depending on the resulting loss to the product, it has a right of recourse against Alpha Company whose defective component is the proximate cause of loss.)
- Alpha Company has responsibility for the costs of repairing or replacing its defective component, without benefit of insurance, because that component is considered to be its product.
- On the other hand, products liability coverage of Alpha Company's CGL policy should respond for the payment of damage to Baker Company's steam turbine since that turbine is not Alpha Company's product; that is, the turbine was not manufactured, sold, handled, distributed, or disposed of by Alpha Company.

If physical injury to the generator and to the steam turbine were sudden and accidental, the situation would change:

- Baker Company would at least have protection under its product liability insurance (for loss of use of other undamaged tangible property sustained by the utility company) under the exception to the so-called *failure to perform exclusion* (m), which is described later. Adjustments between the insurers of Alpha and Baker Companies would then be required depending on the proximate cause of that loss. But damage to the product itself is still excluded from insurance coverage.

Suppose, however, that Alpha's defective component were to make the entire turbine inoperable. In other words, the electric generator does not burn out and the turbine does not break down, but the entire unit simply does not work.

- Baker Company, again, would have no coverage for its own product because of the exclusion of damage (including loss of use) to the named insured's product. It would also have no liability protection for loss of use of the utility company's undamaged tangible property because of the failure to perform exclusion.
- Alpha Company will more than likely have to assume the costs of repairing or replacing its defective component because that component is considered to be its product and, therefore, is excluded under its products liability coverage. It will also have to assume those costs representing loss of use of undamaged tangible property of the utility company for two reasons: (1) the loss was caused by its product and (2) such loss is not covered under the failure to perform exclusion.

While damage to the named insured's product is excluded regardless of whether the products are made by one entity or by several, coverage does apply to bodily injury and to other property damage, including loss of use of any tangible property arising out of those products. So, for example, if the defective steam turbine were to damage other property of the utility company, that damage and any loss of use of such property stemming from that damage is covered under Baker Company's CGL.

While the above illustrations deal with situations involving component products that are clearly distinguishable, many losses are much more complicated. For example, finding the exact source of food poisoning can be extremely difficult and costly, particularly if the product comprises many ingredients from several sources. Bodily injury by food poisoning is covered, of course, if it ultimately is determined that the product contained botulism or some harmful foreign substance. But the insured's loss of use of the product is not covered, nor are the costs of withdrawing the food product from the market and destroying it (the latter costs are not covered due to the so-called "sistership" exclusion discussed hereafter). Yet, determining which ingredient is responsible for this kind of loss is sometimes difficult, if not impossible. Every entity involved may be required to pay a portion of the damages, even though one entity alone may have caused the loss.

***Exclusion of Property Damage to the Named Insured's Work.*** The property damage to "your work" exclusion (l), also referred to as the *injury to work performed exclusion,* is designed to prevent an insurer from having to pay for replacing, repairing, or otherwise redoing faulty work of the named insured. Under exclusion (l), no coverage applies for liability because of "property damage," (that is, physical injury to tangible property, including all resulting loss of use of that property, and loss of use of tangible property that is not physically injured) to "your work" arising out of it or any part of it and included in the "products-completed operations hazard." The term "your work" is defined to mean (a) work or operations performed by you or on your behalf and (b) materials, parts, or equipment furnished in connection with such work or operations. "Your work" includes warranties or representations made at any time with respect to the fitness, quality, durability, or performance of the items in (a) and (b) above. However, the exclusion of "your work" does *not* apply if the damaged work or the work out of which the damage arises was performed on behalf of the named insured by a subcontractor.

Two points are important:

1. This exclusion *applies only to the "products-completed operations hazard;"* it does not exclude coverage for property damage liability that occurs while operations are in progress. Recall that paragraph (5) of the general property damage exclusion dealing with damage to property being worked on will control the extent to which coverage may or may not apply when operations are in progress.
2. This exclusion does not apply if the damaged work or the work out of which the damage arises was performed by a subcontractor on behalf of the named insured. By inference, *damage to all work performed by the named insured is excluded* (unless it arises out of a subcontractor's work), as well as damage to all materials, parts and equipment furnished in connection with such work as performed solely by the named insured. The net effect is to exclude the particular part of any work that causes

damage, as well as any portion of the work performed that is adversely affected by that damage.

The following illustration should help to clarify just how all-encompassing this second exclusion actually is.

*Work Performed by Named Insured—Excluded.* Assume a contracting firm was hired to build a one-family dwelling on a concrete slab. Part of its work involved placing pipes for steam heat on impacted soil and pouring concrete over them in constructing the slab. Because a coupling on one of the pipes was not tightened, steam eventually escaped, condensed, and caused leakage into the dwelling. The contracting firm was required not only to tear up a large portion of the slab and retrieve and replace the loose coupling, but also to replace the concrete slab. All costs incurred by that contracting firm in performing that work would be excluded. The damage to "your work" exclusion (l) precludes coverage for property damage to "your work," that is, work or operations performed by the named insured or on the named insured's behalf (installing the piping and constructing the concrete slab) when damages arise out of the work or any part of it, or out of materials, parts, or equipment furnished in connection with such work (for example, a defective coupling). The only coverage the contracting firm may have is for property damage to the dwelling owner's carpeting by water leakage, provided the carpeting was not supplied and installed by that contracting firm. (As for the defective coupling and the damages caused by it, the contracting firm's only recourse would be against the distributor or manufacturer of that coupling.)

Suppose the condensation remains undetected and the water eventually causes the ground to sink, the slab to crack, and the dwelling to tip to the point that it becomes uninhabitable. The contracting firm is required to raze and rebuild the dwelling. The exclusion in question will preclude coverage for all damages, including loss of use of the dwelling, for two reasons:

1. The entire dwelling is considered to be work performed by that contracting firm, and physical injury or destruction to work performed is excluded (even if the underlying cause of loss is a defective coupling).
2. Loss of use of the dwelling by its owner is not covered, since the definition of property damage includes all resulting loss of use of that property. When damage to property is covered, any resulting loss of use is also covered; but, when damage to property is excluded, any resulting loss of use is also excluded.

*Work Performed on Behalf of Named Insured—Not Excluded.* Assume now that the general contracting firm did not perform any of the work on the dwelling but, instead, subcontracted all of its work out to another firm. If the general contractor were to be sued for the resulting damages or were to become liable for damage to work performed on its behalf by the subcontractor, this exclusion should *not* apply to the general contractor. To repeat, this exclusion does not apply if the damaged work or the work out of which damage arises was performed on behalf of the named insured. It is important that the ramifications of this exclusion be fully understood because the financial consequences can be overwhelming.

***Impaired Property/Property Not Physically Injured Exclusion.*** The policy definition of property damage includes loss of use of tangible property that is not physically injured. Exclusion (m) places some limits on this coverage. The exclusion reads as follows:

> "Property damage" to "impaired property" or property that has not been physically injured, arising out of:
> (1) A defect, deficiency, inadequacy or dangerous condition in "your product" or "your work," or
> (2) A delay or failure by you or anyone acting on your behalf to perform a contract or agreement in accordance with its terms.
> This exclusion does not apply to the loss of use of other property arising out of sudden and accidental physical injury to "your product" or "your work" after it has been put to its intended use.

To understand this exclusion, the reader must understand the policy definition of impaired property.

> "Impaired property" means tangible property, other than "your product" or "your work," that cannot be used or is less useful because:
> a. It incorporates "your product" or "your work" that is known or thought to be defective, deficient, inadequate or dangerous; or
> b. You have failed to fulfill the terms of a contract or agreement;
>
> if such property can be restored to use by:
> a. The repair, replacement, adjustment or removal of "your product" or "your work;" or
> b. Your fulfilling the terms of the contract or agreement.

This exclusion can be illustrated in several ways. For example, assume the insured makes a boiler that is a part of a steam turbine used by a manufacturer. If for some reason the boiler is defective and the steam turbine therefore cannot produce its expected power, then the manufacturer may suffer reduced output and lower revenues. That is, the turbine is less useful as a result of a defect in the insured's product. If the problem can be corrected by replacing or repairing the boiler (see the second a. in the definition of impaired property), then the turbine is considered "impaired property," and the resulting loss of revenues is excluded.

As another example, assume the insured manufactures compressors that are sold to an air conditioning manufacturer. If the manufacturer discovers just before shipping the air conditioners to its stores that the compressor does not produce the necessary amount of pressure due to a defect, it is possible that the entire air conditioning sales season may go by before the compressors can be replaced. The resulting loss of revenues would be excluded.

Remember, however, that if the boiler or compressors were to explode after being put to use, causing no damage to the turbine or air conditioners but rendering them unusable, the loss of revenues or other losses arising from the shutdown would be covered (see the exception to the exclusion). For example, the loss of air conditioning may cause a building owner to lose some rents. Such loss would be covered.

The exclusion also applies when an insured does not fulfill its contractual obligations. An example is the general contractor who agrees to complete construction of an office building within a certain period. The general contractor fails to complete the contract, and the building owner has to return rental payments it collected in anticipation of the grand opening. Here, it is not because of a defect, deficiency, inadequacy, or dangerous condition to the contractor's product or work that the loss is excluded. Instead, it is excluded because of the delay or failure of the named insured to fulfill a contractual obligation.

Referring to the air conditioning example, assume the manufacturer of the compressors failed to deliver the compressors by the time stated in the contract and in time for the manufacturer of the air conditioners to assemble them for the summer sales season. In this case, the problem is not a defect, but again, a failure to fulfill the terms of a contract. The property (air conditioners) could have been "restored to use" if the insured compressor manufacturer had fulfilled the contract terms. As a result, the air conditioners would be considered "impaired property," and the loss of sales revenues would be excluded.

***Sistership Liability (Recall) Exclusion.*** "Sistership liability" is terminology used by the aircraft liability insurers to signify the liability for damages that usually follows the withdrawal, inspection, repair, replacement or loss of use of aircraft because of known or suspected defects. When one aircraft, for example, has a suspected defective condition because of its design or production error, all the aircraft of the same manufacturer—all sisterships—also are grounded until they are fully inspected. Sistership liability in insurance is used to refer to all kinds of products that must be withdrawn from the market or from use when a like product is known or suspected to be defective.

The so-called "sistership" liability exclusion can be thought of as an exclusion of product "recall" losses. It precludes coverage for the costs incurred by an insured for the loss of use, withdrawal, recall, inspection, repair, replacement, adjustment, removal or disposal of the named insured's product, work, or impaired property when the product, work, or impaired property is withdrawn or recalled from the market or from use because of a known or suspected defect, deficiency, inadequacy, or dangerous condition in the product.

*Duty To Withdraw.* Note, finally, that if an entity does not take steps to withdraw its products from the market or from use following a series of similar losses to its product, it may be without future protection for its liability to others. This is because the CGL excludes bodily injury or property damage expected or intended from the standpoint of the insured.

*Applicability to Completed Operations.* The sistership liability exclusion also applies to work of the named insured or work performed on its behalf in the same way that it applies to products. The potential exposures involving the withdrawal of materials, parts, or equipment can be costly, particularly when they already form a part of the completed work. Examples include removing defective concrete blocks that already form a part of a building, removing defective wall paneling, and retrieving defective couplings on piping even if it involves tearing up concrete.

## Information to Consider in Underwriting Products Coverage

The quantity of information needed by the underwriter varies with the nature of the product. Much of the information presented earlier in the text regarding premises-operations underwriting also applies to underwriting products coverage. The business of the applicant, limits of liability, and the size and scope of the business are important in underwriting both types of coverage. As in underwriting premises-operations liability, the first source of information for products underwriting is the application. However, most applications have a section (or the insurer has a separate questionnaire) that requires information about products liability exposures. Exhibit 9-1 shows the information requested by one insurer for the products exposure.

In addition to the application, other information must be considered by the underwriter in order to get a complete picture of the applicant's exposures. Some of this information supplements what is shown on the application and some of it verifies what is shown.

**Inherent Hazards.** In products liability underwriting, the nature of the product, and more specifically, its inherent hazards, are one of the most important pieces of information on which the underwriter

**Exhibit 9-1**
Products Liability Questionnaire

IF PRODUCTS LIABILITY INSURANCE IS DESIRED, PLEASE COMPLETE THE FOLLOWING (IF APPLICANT IS CONTRACTOR, COMPLETE COMPLETED OPERATIONS SECTION INSTEAD):

1. Please list below all products that applicant manufactures or handles

| NAME AND DESCRIPITON | MFR OR DISTR. | YEARS ON MARKET | EXPEC-TED LIFE | INTER-NAL USE | PRIN. COMPON-ENT | HOW SOLD BULK | HOW SOLD PKGE. | ANNUAL SALES VALUE | ANNUAL SALES UNITS |
|---|---|---|---|---|---|---|---|---|---|
| | | | | | | | | | |
| | | | | | | | | | |
| | | | | | | | | | |

2. Totals for past 3 years: Value ________ Units ________________
3. Does applicant manufacture a price ☐ or quality ☐ product?
4. Which of the above products bears applicant's name, label, or serial number?
________________________________
5. Describe any other products applicant has manufactured or sold within the past five years. ________________
6. Describe any new products applicant may place on market soon
________________________________
7. Which of applicant's products are sold for further processing?
________________________________
8. Which of applicant's products have been sold for further processing?
________________________________
9. Which of applicant's products have been tested by Underwriters Laboratories or other recognized testing bureau? ________________
10. Brief description of method of inspecting products for quality or purity before being shipped ________________
11. Percent of service or installation to total operations ________ %

12. Does applicant make express warranties regarding the quality, safety, or performance of your products? ________ If yes, please attach samples of warranties.
13. Which products are sold outside the U.S.? ________________
14. Which products use foreign components? ________________
15. Which products are demonstrated? ________________
16. Which products are sold to or used in the aircraft and space industry?
________________________________
17. Which products have been recalled, discontinued, or changed in the last five years? ________________
18. Are any products of others sold or repackaged under the applicant's label? If so, list these. ________________
________________________________
19. Which products are sold under others' labels? ________________
________________________________
20. Does any named insured sell to another Named Insured? ________ If so, give details. ________ ________

Please attach copies of literature, brochures, labels, warnings, hold harmless agreements, and so on.

bases the evaluation. If the hazards are minimal, as in a pillow, the underwriting evaluation is made simpler.

What information does the underwriter need to develop in order to evaluate the hazards of the product? In addition to an adequate description of the product, several factors must be considered. Is it designed to be safe and can it be used safely if directions are followed? Poisons or noxious chemicals are good examples of such products. Are understandable directions provided? Is the product such that it is difficult to use properly? Can the product be misused? A power lawn mower is an example of a product that would be considered relatively hazardous based on these questions.

How serious will the resulting injury or damage be if the product fails? In other words, can it cause loss of a limb, death, or serious disease? Will its failure cause a breakdown in a chain of events or interrupt business? Will it be used in a dangerous activity, such as a parachute? If the product is a component part, into what final product will it be assembled? Airplane crashes have been caused by the failure of products as simple as a nut or bolt. If a product is particularly complicated to make, the chance of error in its manufacture is enhanced and therefore the chance of malfunction or failure is more likely. The underwriter must receive satisfactory answers to these questions in order to determine the characteristics that are likely to affect the loss frequency and severity of particular products. *Best's Underwriting Guide (BUG)* is helpful to the underwriter in evaluating the inherent hazards of product. Many answers to these kinds of questions can be found in the guide.

**Sales Materials/Advertising.** Sales materials such as brochures and specifications are underwriting tools unique to products underwriting. In addition to pictures of the various products made by the manufacturer, they provide valuable information regarding the materials from which the product is made, the uses of the product, the ultimate consumer, warranties and guarantees, and often quality control. Although these sales materials are produced by the manufacturer to enhance the sale of the product, they still provide the underwriter with factual information about the products and possible exposure to loss. Despite the value of advertising, it can create a liability exposure if it makes promises that are not kept or if it improperly describes a product. Advertising also creates the general liability exposures to libel; slander; defamation; infringement of copyright, title, or slogan; and so on. Any history of claims or suits for liability in these areas, even if the suits were not successful, should be investigated. The involvement of legal counsel in the drafting or review of advertising would be considered as a positive factor by the underwriter.

**Technical Manuals.** Many manufacturers produce technical or instructional manuals for employees or customers. The manuals provide information regarding the nature of the product, how it is to be used safely, possible malfunctions and how they can be avoided or breakdowns fixed, and the expected life of the product. These manuals can also provide details on design, testing procedures, and quality control. In addition, such manuals may give detailed information on how to assemble and use the product. This can be an important underwriting consideration for highly technical or complicated products.

**Packaging.** How the product is packaged is an underwriting consideration. Good packaging can reduce losses because it protects the product from damage so that it is able to operate and function as intended. Poor packaging can increase losses by not protecting the product, which may be used by someone who does not know that a safety feature on the product has been damaged to the point where it is ineffective. Packaging may also contain warnings, and instructions for use, assembly, and maintenance. If the packaging is such that it can be damaged and the warnings become unreadable, it is possible that an injury or property damage could result. Too often, something as simple as the retailer covering up an important message on the packaging by a price sticker can lead to a claim. Important messages should be inside the package as well as outside to avoid such a situation.

Any labels to the package should be so applied that they will not easily come off or become unreadable due to handling. The language should be clear and the print legible. If the product requires assembly, each part or bag of parts should be clearly labeled. There should be no question in the consumer's mind as to which part goes where. The labels should also be placed where they will do the most good. For example, a warning label should be placed directly on the product and not on the packaging, which will likely be disposed of as soon as the product is opened.

Finally, the packaging itself can create a loss. An example is the plastic bag containing pillows, which otherwise would be an inherently safe product. If proper warnings about disposing of the bag are not given, it is possible that a child will place the bag over his or her head as part of a game and be suffocated. Other packaging may have sharp edges or contain nails that could lead to injury. The loss control department would be extremely helpful in examining the packaging used and making recommendations regarding the safest way to package the product. If the insured complies with these recommendations, the underwriter would look favorably on this action.

**Instructions.** More important than ever are instructions for use provided with new products. Too many instructions in handling the product are directed at an expert. Instructions should be easy for all customers to read. Adequate warnings regarding the consequences of the product's misuse must be provided. Oral instructions or warnings usually are not adequate. The underwriter should see the message that goes to the consumer to determine the adequacy of the instructions and warnings and whether or not they will stand up in a legal action against the insured.

**Warranties.** Warranties or guarantees[11] can provide information about the type and nature of the product, how it is expected to perform, and for how long. A warranty is of concern to the underwriter not only as a source of product information, but also because it could tend to overstate the capability of the product. Too often a manufacturer offers a "lifetime guarantee" when the product can be realistically expected to last only five to ten years. Or the manufacturer warrants that the product is "safe on any surface" when it is not. If a formal warranty states what the product will do, but the product fails to perform as stated and thus causes bodily injury or property damage, the manufacturer will probably be held liable for the injury or damage. The underwriter should take note of a history of claims based on warranty misstatements.

The underwriter should notice whether or not manufacturers and retailers are careful in their warranties and guarantees. Such warranties and guarantees should be realistic in what is promised and should always be reviewed by legal counsel. This is not to say that if a manufacturer believes its product will last ten years, it should "play it safe" and say it will only last five years. The underwriter will view positively the manufacturer who states under what conditions, use, maintenance, and so on the product can be expected to last ten years. If a manufacturer is negligent in producing a product, it is going to be held liable regardless of what the warranty or guarantee says. What the manufacturer does not want is to properly and safely produce a product, but then incur claims simply because the warranty or guarantee was poorly worded.

**Loss Control.** Loss control is an important underwriting consideration primarily because efforts in this area directly affect the frequency and severity of losses that the insurer must indemnify. In evaluating loss control for products liability, the underwriter would examine efforts by the insured and by the insurer.

***Efforts by the Insured.*** Products liability loss control by the insured requires a series of pre-sale and post-sale loss controls, as shown in Exhibit 9-2. To begin with, the product designers must be safety conscious and test their concepts of design and safety with customer-use tests. Reliable raw materials and suppliers must be specified, and adequate product standards must be drafted. Marketers must be certain that warranties and instructions for use, as well as promises of product performance, do not invite misuse, and that responsible distribution channels are selected. Manufacturing risks must adhere rigidly to established production and quality control procedures. Additionally, after the product is in the customers' hands, satisfactory servicing procedures, effective complaint handling, and customer usage analysis can help reduce product liability claims.

Focusing on these critical points in a loss control system, the insured should have an overall loss control plan in effect. In evaluating a loss control program, the first step for the underwriter is to determine what degree of control is necessary and second, if these controls are being used. Not every insured needs a highly sophisticated loss control program. The extent and nature of the controls depends on the hazardous characteristics of the product.

Loss control must be supported by management. This idea has already been discussed, but it is primary to the successful underwriting of products liability insurance. The insurance loss control representative (LCR) cannot achieve success with a risk that does not recognize this principle. Control programs can become meaningless without management support. The development of a corporate product safety policy statement is often a sign that management is concerned with and supports safety efforts.

***Loss Control Reports by the Insurer.*** The value of the insurance company's loss control reports was stressed earlier in this text. Many underwriters do not require loss control reports in the process of underwriting premises-operations exposures. However, they are prevalent in the products liability field because the exposure has recently grown tremendously.

The general loss control report usually contains several questions related to products liability. Many questions relate to the insured's loss control efforts. Depending on the product, these questions frequently elicit enough information for the underwriter to make a decision. In underwriting more hazardous products, many insurance companies have developed special inspection forms designed to elicit more detailed information. Such a form for manufacturers might include the following questions:

**Exhibit 9-2**
Product Loss Control Checkpoints*

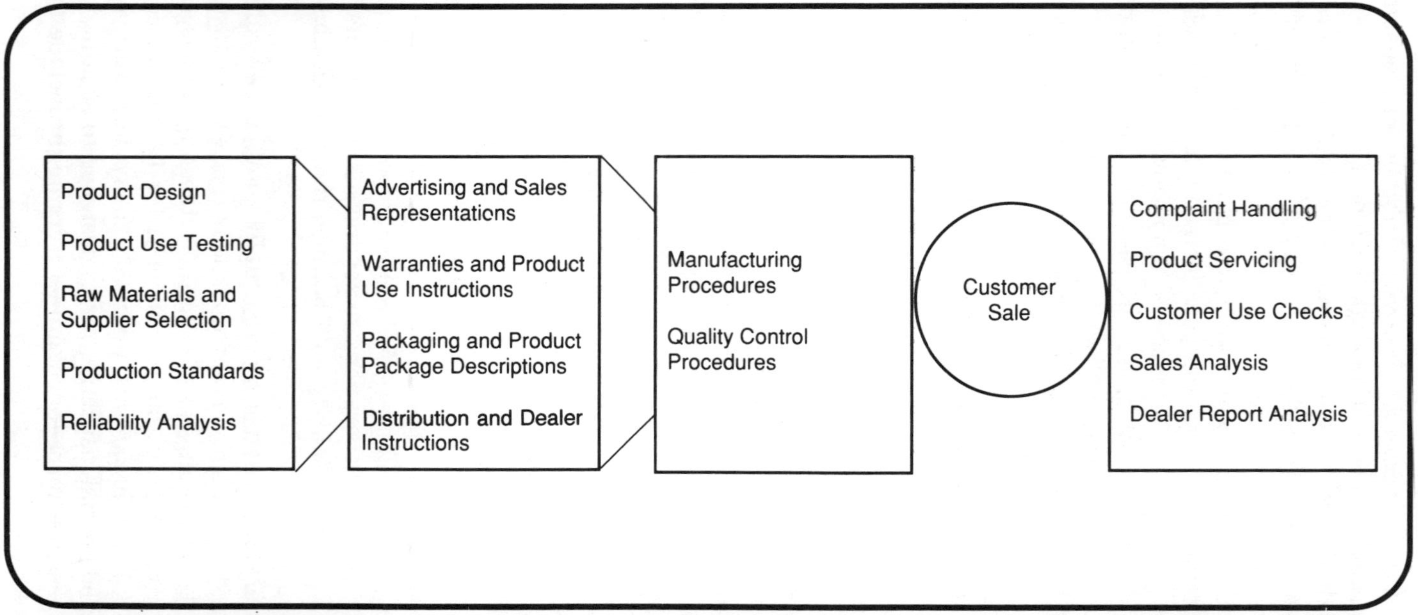


* Adapted with permission from *The Product-Safety Function: Organization and Operations* (New York: The Conference Board, Inc., 1979), p. 4.

1. What are the products manufactured and/or distributed by the risk, including any private label products?
2. What are the typical applications for these products?
3. How can these products cause injury or property damage through failure or misuse?
4. What types of quality control procedures are employed? Include description of incoming, in-process, and finished product inspection.
5. Are any products labeled by a recognized testing lab such as Underwriters Laboratories? With what industry standards do the products comply?
6. What types of labels, warnings, or precautionary statements are provided on the product?
7. What instructional materials or manuals are provided with the product to inform the user of the proper use and maintenance of the product?
8. Is there a formal product safety program in operation?
9. What types of engineering procedures does the firm utilize to anticipate potential product safety problems?
10. What type of testing is performed during the design and development of the products?
11. What types of safety features, devices, or precautionary markings are designed into the product as a result of the engineering procedures in (9) above?
12. How are the products distributed?
13. What types of records are kept of design test, quality control inspections, sales, customer complaints, and product failure reports and analyses?
14. What previous claims and types of corrective action or product changes have been implemented due to these claims?

Many of these questions simply elaborate on those that were shown on the questionnaire in Exhibit 9-1. Other specialized engineering reports have been developed for food products, retailers, and component manufacturers. The exposures to loss and methods of loss control vary so widely among these types of products that highly specialized inspections have become a necessity.

**Complaint Handling System.** Almost every insured should have some formal method for following up on complaints and other product-related incidents. This is especially true for insureds with a products liability exposure. If there is a possibility that a product is causing a problem, the manufacturer (and insurer) would want to know as soon as possible in order to take steps to prevent further injuries or damage. However, the complaint handling system should not be limited to products that have already caused injury or damage. The "near-miss" incident is also important since there may not be a "miss" the next time. One estimate based on a study of almost two million accidents concluded that for every 600 incidents at work with no visible injury or damage, there were 60 property damage accidents, 10 accidents with minor injuries, and one serious or disabling injury.[12] While these were not cases of products liability, the same idea applies. A manufacturer must investigate every complaint or incident even if injury or damage does not occur.

A complaint handling system should include the following components:

- A copy of each written complaint, or a memo describing each complaint received by phone
- A complete description of the product in each case by generic and trade name, model number, date of manufacture, and so on
- The date that each safety complaint was received and the date of the firm's initial response, as well as a copy of that response
- Copies of all correspondence from the complainant, or his or her representatives, on the alleged product injury
- A complete description of the injuries occurring, if any, as a result of the alleged product failure
- A record of lawsuits and claims filed
- A record of the final response and actions taken
- Copies of any notices to the press, customers, or regulatory agencies concerning each product-safety incident[13]

**Quality Control.** Quality control is an important focus of products liability underwriting. It essentially is a formal program established by a manufacturer at all levels of production to ensure that the product will perform efficiently and safely. As such, quality control identifies problems before they cause injury or damage.

The checkpoints for quality include design, inspection, testing, record keeping, complaint review, claims review, and advertising. Quality control is the responsibility of the manufacturer and is probably the best weapon against products losses. The extent of a quality control program is a function of the product. The underwriter must evaluate the particular program in relation to the product. For example, the lawn mower manufacturer needs a very complete quality control program—one involving every point on the above list. The pillow manufacturer, however, requires a less complex program. In the case of the former, the underwriter must determine, as elaborate as the quality control program may be, whether or not it is sufficient.

There are many questions that should be addressed by a quality control program. For instance, is the lawn mower designed by engineers, to particular specifications, and with safety in mind? Does it meet applicable governmental safety standards? A product that operates efficiently is not necessarily safe. Is the lawn mower designed so that it cannot be started when fingers or feet are exposed to the blades? Are there guards that prevent objects from flying out at the operator or any person standing in the area? Is each new model tested and every lawn mower inspected before it leaves the plant? Are inspection and testing performed by qualified technicians or engineers? Are the materials in the lawn mower capable of withstanding normal, or even abnormal, usage? Does the manufacturer specify the material strength requirements to its suppliers and does it test to be sure these requirements are consistently met? Some manufacturers or even underwriters may ask why the manufacturer should spend money to inspect the parts it receives from its suppliers. If the component is held to be the faulty part that caused an injury, the manufacturer of the component should be the one to be held liable. While this is partly true, it is still possible that the manufacturer that used the component in its product would also be held liable for not inspecting the component. In either case, there will be substantial defense costs involved.

**Record Keeping.** Record keeping is important information to consider in underwriting products coverage. The type of records necessary depends on the function of the business; that is, whether the business manufactures the whole product, assembles it from components manufactured by others, or merely sells the product. In the first case, records must be kept of suppliers of raw materials. In the second case, records must be kept of the suppliers' parts. Serial numbers help identify the batch and/or date of production. Sources of materials or components are documented by demanding identifying records from suppliers. Records of batches sent to distributors, stores, or other marketing agents help to identify and trace the life history of the product. This identification and documentation is necessary to produce evidence for defense purposes. If a person is injured by the malfunction of a lawn mower, he or she will submit a claim to the manufacturer whose name and location is on the label on the lawn mower. The manufacturer of the lawn mower will probably be held liable under the doctrine of strict liability, and its insurance company will probably pay the loss. If there were no records or documentation, the lawn mower manufacturer and its insurer would have no other possible recourse. With records, however, the manufacturer may be able to offer evidence that traces the malfunction to another source, such as a component part, the metal frame, or an ordinary bolt manufactured by another party. Records may also prove that the distributor or seller had altered the lawn mower deliberately or accidentally, and the malfunction is traceable to that alteration. It is, therefore, important (especially when insuring a manufacturer) for the underwriter to make sure the insured keeps sufficient records that can be used for evidence in defending a claim. Defense coverage is very important in all liability insurance but is especially necessary for products liability. A good defense backed by good evidence can reduce or eliminate the cost of the claim itself.

Record keeping is also an important element in product recalls. With proper record keeping, a manufacturer or distributor can trace faulty products, where they were sent, and possibly the name of the purchaser of the product. For many products it is impossible (and in some cases, unnecessary) to keep track of every purchaser. For others, it is essential so that the person can be notified if there is a problem. The manufacturer cannot rely on the purchaser to send in the warranty or product registration card. Therefore, the manufacturer should encourage the retailer to gather the necessary information at the point of sale.

The ability of a manufacturer to identify and recall faulty products is important to the underwriter because it will likely reduce the number of claims resulting from the faulty product. A manufacturer with inadequate records may spend much time and money trying unsuccessfully to locate all products of a certain type, not knowing exactly which of the products is faulty.

For example, a washing machine manufacturer may be faced with a number of suits for fire damage resulting from faulty wiring in the machines. Assuming the damage can be traced to a certain component, a manufacturer with good record keeping could likely (1) identify which washing machines contain that component, (2) know where those machines were distributed, and (3) have a list of the names of the vast majority of persons that own those machines. These persons can be contacted so that their machines can be immediately repaired. The manufacturer would probably make some form of notice in newspapers and magazines and try to locate those machines for which it does not have the name of the purchaser. With adequate records, the manufacturer would only have a small percentage of the total number of faulty machines for whom the owner would be unknown.

If the manufacturer in this same case had poor record keeping, a recall would be much more difficult. The manufacturer would not be able to identify those machines with a faulty component. Thus, all machines (or at least a larger number than in the previous example) would have to be recalled. In addition, without the names of the purchasers, the manufacturer would have to search its records of retailers hoping to find the purchasers. Because of the additional time required to identify and locate the machines, additional injuries or damage could occur that could have been prevented with proper record keeping.

**Product Line Changes.** In addition to current products, discontinued products and plans for future products must also be considered by the underwriter. This is true primarily because most products liability coverage is written on an occurrence basis. Since the coverage therefore responds according to when the injury occurred, the underwriter must consider which products no longer manufactured remain in use and their potential for causing loss. Coverage written on a claims-made basis applies to any claims made during the policy period. The primary limitation is that the injury-causing incident must have occurred after the retroactive date. Thus, discontinued products can be a problem for claims-made coverage, too.

The exposure to loss as a result of products still in use but no longer manufactured is faced largely by manufacturers of durable equipment. For example, when a product is manufactured, it may be completely safe, containing the necessary electrical grounding, mechanical safeguards, and other safety equipment. With time, however, the product may become dangerous as a result of misuse, modification, or lack of maintenance. Nonetheless, if the equipment finally fails and someone is injured, the original manufacturer is often the target of a products liability suit. Despite the fact that the product originally met safety standards, the changes that may have caused a failure are both out of the manufacturer's control and not always considered when suit is brought. A survey by the National Machine Tool Builders Association found that one out of seven liability lawsuits against mechanical power press builders involved machines that were over forty years old. In one out of four cases, the machine was over thirty years old; and, in almost half the cases, the machines were over twenty years old. A majority of the machines had been resold and modified and maintained at less than optimum levels of safety and technical proficiency.

It is particularly important to determine whether the products that are no longer produced were discontinued for marketing reasons, low quality, or too many defects. The latter two reasons should immediately cause the underwriter to be concerned.

Another problem created by discontinued, but still used, products is that in some cases, the underwriter may not have made a premium charge for them although it is possible to do so. Consider for example, a manufacturer of very safe widgets that have a very low products liability insurance rate. If an insurer begins providing occurrence-basis products liability insurance for this manufacturer, it is possible that the premiums developed are rather small due to the low products rate for these widgets. If the underwriter is unaware of the fact that this same manufacturer produced very dangerous widgets up until five years ago and that many of these discontinued widgets are still in use, it is likely that no premium charge will have been made for the dangerous widgets. If one of the discontinued widgets causes a loss during the policy period, the current insurer will have to respond to the loss without the benefit of ever having charged a premium for them.

In addition to products that have been discontinued, new products must also be considered by the underwriter. The products section of the application usually inquires about the insured's plans for new products. It is fortunate that in the majority of cases, the new products are similar to current ones, and that the same level of care goes into both. In addition, the new products will be picked up at audit, and an appropriate premium charge will be made. It is very possible, however, that the insurer does not want to write the new products or that they are perhaps excluded by the insurer's reinsurance treaties.

In addition, it may be that the insured has acquired another firm that produces these products, and the production quality of the new firm is not as good as that of the insured. If there is a substantial difference in product quality, the acceptability of the risk from an underwriting standpoint may change.

**Mergers.** Another consideration is whether the firm frequently merges with or acquires other firms. In these situations, the newly formed organization acquires not only the assets, but often the liabilities of the previously separate organizations. Consider Firm A, which has a very low products liability exposure and does not manufacture widgets. Consider also Firm B, which has a very large products liability exposure for its widgets. When Firm A acquires Firm B, Firm A ceases the production of widgets. An underwriter who examines Firm A shortly after the acquisition would not know that there is still an existing products liability exposure because of the widgets originally manufactured by Firm B that are still on the market unless he or she asked about previous products and operations of both firms. Even if the underwriter was aware of the widgets, current gross sales (the premium base for products liability insurance) would not reflect the former sales of the widgets or the current exposure presented by the widgets.

Management and operations may also change with a merger. If two manufacturers of the same product merge, it is likely that only one of the firms will direct the manufacture of that product. If the management teams of those two firms differ greatly in their quality control, safety features they consider important, and so on, the underwriter would want to know which of the two management teams would be the one to continue. It would be an advantage if the underwriter has been providing coverage for the firm that cares about quality and safety, and the management team of that firm takes over. If a team that is not quality conscious takes over, the underwriter must seriously consider the desirability of writing the coverage.

**Channels of Distribution.** Channels of distribution are the roads to the market. Even when a fine and innovative product is developed, buyers must be found and the product must be delivered. In analyzing marketing methods and to assess potential liability, the underwriter must determine the applicant's position in the channel of distribution.

If the applicant is a manufacturer, products liability is of paramount importance. If the applicant is a common carrier transporting motor freight, auto liability and legal liability for damage to cargo in transit are the major loss exposures. If the applicant is a wholesaler, there are products liability exposures; but these are usually of lesser importance than the products exposure of a manufacturer. The wholesale firm usually has an auto exposure when it delivers its products to retailers. The retailer's major liability exposures come from the operation of the business premises, but it also has exposures to products liability and to auto liability if it makes deliveries. The type of retailer is also important to the underwriter. Retailing can range from a small shop in a mall to a large mail order company. Each presents a different exposure in terms of injury to the public. From manufacturers to retailers, the applicant's position in the channel of distribution has a significant impact on the underwriting analysis because each position presents different exposures and different degrees of the same exposures.

**The Ultimate Consumer.** Another important underwriting consideration is the consumer who will ultimately use the product. A high degree of care is required of those that manufacture or market products specifically designed for children. The doctrine of strict liability may apply in these situations. The federal government has established standards regarding the flammability of children's clothing, primarily in response to a number of fatal burn cases among infants a few years ago. The manufacturer needs to foresee who the consumer will be. The hazards need to be controlled so that the ultimate consumer can use the product safely.

An additional consideration is whether the product will be used in industry or by the general public. Generally, industrial products are used by fewer people, thus reducing the number of people exposed to the injury-producing event; but if the product is a component that becomes a part of a hazardous product or one capable of producing a catastrophic loss, that industrial product would have a greater loss potential than many products for use by the general public. Products for underwriting purposes are not easily categorized, making class underwriting not very useful.

In evaluating the exposure created by the ultimate consumer of the product, the underwriter should consider how complicated the product is to use. Some manufacturers have been held liable where the product was misused. The manufacturer must therefore be sure not only that there are instructions on how *to use* the product but also on how *not to use* the product. Does the manufacturer provide adequate instructions, warnings, and labels? If they are provided, will the average person be able to use the product without injury, or does it require the technical knowledge or ability of an expert? The loss potential of a complicated electrical apparatus, therefore, can be greatly reduced if operated by an expert technician and even more so if it operates by itself. However, the insured will not always know that the machine should be operated by an expert. Clear, understandable instructions are a necessary part of any product that is chemical, mechanical, or electrical in nature regardless of who the consumer is.

**Age-Adjusted Frequency-Severity Index (AFSI).** Using the data collected through the National Electronic Injuries Surveillance System (NEISS), the Consumer Products Safety Commission has developed an index of consumer products associated with a high frequency and severity of injuries. The index represents a relative ranking of products associated with injuries in terms of age-adjusted injury frequency and severity. The AFSI is calculated by multiplying the national estimate of the numbers of injuries treated in hospital emergency rooms among those age fifteen and over for a product category by the estimated mean severity of these injuries. For injuries suffered by children age fourteen and under, the calculations were multiplied by 2.5. The fifteen product categories with the highest index for one year are listed in Exhibit 9-3. Some product numbers in the table are followed by an asterisk. These numbers represent grouped products and the number listed in the NEISS product code for a typical product in the group.

The underwriter is not likely to turn to this information when a certain risk is submitted. In many cases, the person who underwrites specific risks (unlike underwriting management) does not even have access to this information. More likely, underwriting management reviews information such as this when setting up the guidelines for underwriters to follow. For example, if based on the AFSI an insurer considers bicycles too dangerous a product to insure, the underwriting guidelines may list bicycle manufacturing as an unacceptable type of

**Exhibit 9-3**
The Age-Adjusted Frequency-Severity Index (AFSI)—1977*

| Rank | Product Number | Product Description | AFSI |
|---|---|---|---|
| 1 | 1202 | Bicycles and bicycle equipment, including add-on features (baskets, horns, non-standard seats, handlebars) | 40,608 |
| 2 | 1842 | Stairs (including folding stairs), steps, ramps, landings | 23,506 |
| 3 | 1211 | Football, activity, related equipment and apparel | 13,682 |
| 4 | 1204 | Baseball, activity, related equipment and apparel | 12,908 |
| 5 | 1241 | Swings, slides, seesaws and playground equipment | 12,498 |
| 6 | 1401 | Power lawnmowers and unspecified lawnmowers | 12,002 |
| 7 | 1308 | Skates, skateboards and scooters | 11,111 |
| 8 | 1231 | Swimming, swimming pools and related equipment | 11,070 |
| 9 | 0645 | Non-glass table and unspecified tables | 10,989 |
| 10 | 0601 | Beds, including springs, frames, bunk beds and unspecified beds (excluding mattresses or box springs, water beds, sofa beds, infant beds and special beds) | 9,735 |
| 11 | 0602 | Chairs, sofas and sofa beds | 8,300 |
| 12 | 1205 | Basketball, activity and related equipment | 7,848 |
| 13 | 1807 | Floors and flooring materials | 7,392 |
| 14 | 1819 | Nails, carpet tacks and screws, thumbtacks | 6,286 |
| 15 | 1815 | Architectural glass, including glass doors | 6,286 |

* Adapted from *Consumer Product Hazard Index* (Washington, DC: Consumer Product Safety Commission, 1978), p. 11.

risk. The underwriter would base a decision on this conclusion instead of reviewing the AFSI.

## Completed Operations Underwriting

Completed operations is characterized from an underwriting standpoint by a very wide range of possible hazards. Activities that generate completed operations hazards, and thus, face the completed operations exposure may include bridge, road, and building construction, the distribution of electricity and the installation of plumbing, heating, and electrical systems in buildings, setting up machinery and process equipment in industrial plants, as well as maintaining and servicing these operations.

There are relatively few completed operations classifications as compared with products liability classifications. One reason for this is the lack of a sufficient number of claims. Another reason is that completed operations exposures are often included within the products exposure or premises and operations exposure. Some premises and operations classifications such as photographers, printers, and swimming pool installers include the completed operations hazard within the classification and rate. In these cases, ISO has included the completed operations losses with operations in promulgating the rate.

As in the case of the other general liability sublines, it is important to classify the completed operations exposure correctly. If the classification does not specifically state that completed operations are included in the rate, a separate classification must be shown.

Businesses that perform services generally have an operations rather than a premises exposure. It follows that such businesses are likely to have completed operations exposures. The activities or operations, particularly those performed off-premises, which could cause a loss are the basis of operations underwriting. Thus, the manner in which the job is performed is important to the underwriter in evaluating the exposure to loss. Quality of workmanship and equipment, supervision of employees, technical skill, reputation, and years of experience are all factors which help the underwriter evaluate the operations exposure. If any of these qualities are lacking to any significant degree, the underwriter would conclude that the loss potential arising out of the operations has been increased. These same risk characteristics are important in evaluating the completed operations exposure. For example, faulty workmanship is likely to cause a loss while the work is being performed, but it will also increase the potential of loss occurring after the work is completed.

A TV repairperson who has careless work habits or lacks technical knowledge could damage the customer's premises and even cause a fire. The same result, stemming from the same cause, could happen after the repairperson finishes the work and leaves the premises. The resulting damage or injury would fall within the scope of the completed operations exposure. The underwriter, however, must evaluate to what degree the overall liability exposure is increased because of the completed operations exposure. Lack of technical knowledge or faulty workmanship is likely to increase loss frequency to a comparable degree for both the operations and completed operations hazard. While the nature of the operation affects the severity of the operations and completed operations exposures, hazards to be considered may not be at all comparable. A contractor building high-rise apartments is an example. While constructing the building, workers can cause extensive property damage from fire, collapse, or water, as well as bodily injury from falling objects, operation of equipment, and use of construction materials and tools. Consider, however, the extent of loss possible after the apartment building is completed. After the apartments are inhabited, fire or collapse could cause even more serious injuries and damages. If the cause could be traced to the faulty workmanship of the contractor, the insurer who underwrote the completed operations exposure would be responsible for the loss. In this particular case, the characteristics affecting loss frequency are greatly reduced once the building is completed, but the loss severity potential is greatly increased due to the nature of the business and operation. At the other extreme, a piano tuner could cause damage to the customer's property while in the process of performing the work, but it is extremely unlikely that injury or damage will occur after the work is completed. Logically, piano tuning is an operations classification in which the completed operations exposure is included in the rate.

In evaluating an applicant for completed operations coverage, the underwriter must determine the likelihood and severity of potential losses by evaluating the nature of the applicant's business. The completed operations exposure may be considerably different from the operations exposure for a class, just as the exposure to loss as a result of the operations hazard varies from one risk to another within a class.

## Pricing Problems in Products Liability Insurance

Pricing products liability insurance can present unique problems or the same problems that are found in other lines where they are less severe. First, as in other lines of insurance, there is concern about the credibility of the loss data within each class. As the number of products-completed operations classes increases to keep pace with the growing number of products sold, the credibility of premium and loss data within each class decreases. Many products and completed operations classes are on an (a) rated basis—that is, there is no rate published by the rating organization.

The problem of adequately charging for discontinued products that are still in use was briefly discussed earlier. If a product has been discontinued altogether but is still in use, it is possible that the present insurer is receiving no premium for the exposure to possible losses from such products (gross sales, upon which the premium is based, is zero for that product). If the sales volume of the product has fallen significantly, the insurer is receiving some premium, but not one that is commensurate with the exposure that is a function of higher past sales.

The situation can be reversed, and the insurer can be receiving a premium greater than the exposure really is. For example, if the insured introduces a product in year 1 and produces it during year 1 and year 2, the insurer during these two years will receive premium dollars based on the sales volume during that period. Assume that the product is such that any losses resulting from the product will not likely occur until four years after the product is sold. If the insured, for whatever reason, switches insurers after year 2, the insurer during year 1 and year 2 will have received premium dollars for very little exposure. It is the next insurer that would have to respond to losses from these products.

A similar pricing problem arises regarding the equity of the premium when gross sales is used as a premium base. Assume Manufacturer A and Manufacturer B produce identical widgets. The retail cost per widget is $100. Manufacturer A realizes that there is a potential loss-causing problem with the widget and spends $12.50 per widget to include a safety mechanism that corrects the problem. Manufacturer A raises the price of its widget by only $10 (to remain somewhat competitive) to cover at least part of the costs of the safety feature. Unless schedule rating is used to recognize this price increase, Manufacturer A will have a premium base that is 10 percent greater than Manufacture B and will pay approximately 10 percent more in premium (assuming the number of widgets sold is the same for both manufacturers) despite the fact that Manufacturer A is producing a safer product.

The *long-tail problem* is probably the most recognized problem in pricing products liability coverage. (It is a problem, but less of one, for premises-operations coverage.) The tail refers to the delay between the time the product is produced or sold and the time the claims are settled. This delay can be broken down into three parts. First, and the part that is most related to products liability insurance, is the delay from the time the product is produced until the time it causes bodily injury or property damage. For some products with life expectancies of twenty, thirty, and forty years, this can be a significant problem.

This delay is a problem because it is very difficult to price coverage for a product that may cause losses so far into the future. This is because there is no way to look thirty or forty years into the future to see what juries might be like, what the laws will say, what the standards will be for determining what a safe product is, how people might use (or misuse) the product, and so on. Many safety features common today were probably never even thought of in the 1950s. And yet, jurors are aware of those safety features and will find it difficult not to ignore the fact that the product is produced more safely today than it was in the 1950s, regardless of possible instructions to the contrary from the judge.

Second, there can be a delay between the time the loss-causing incident occurs and the time the claim is actually filed. For products coverage, this is not a great problem in most cases except for pharmaceutical products for which disastrous results may not be known for years.

The third delay in the long-tail problem is that from the time a claim is filed until it is finally settled. This delay is present in almost all lines of liability insurance. Discovery proceedings, finding witnesses, reviewing production records, and settlement negotiations take time. Cases that cannot be settled out of court will usually take even longer because of the crowded dockets in most courts.

## MANAGING A BOOK OF BUSINESS

In addition to underwriting individual risks, underwriting management must continuously underwrite the "book" of business. Book refers to all risks with something in common. It may be the book of all risks located in a certain state. It may be the book of all general liability risks, and so on.

This task must be done continuously because risks change, laws change, and so on. Even if (and this is a big "if") all underwriters follow all underwriting guidelines perfectly, these changes may cause an insurer to lose money. In addition, it is possible that the guidelines are not correct. Therefore, underwriting management must monitor the decisions of underwriters not only on a risk-by-risk basis, but also at the book of business level.

### Managing a Book of General Liability Insurance

How does an underwriting manager for the book of general liability insurance "manage" that book? One logical way is to examine the loss ratio and see if it is acceptable. Regretfully, this process is much more complex than simply calling up the overall loss ratio on a computer terminal. First, the manager must decide which loss ratio to use (that is, exactly how the loss ratio should be defined). The manager must next determine if he or she wants more than just an overall loss ratio. How should it be broken down, if at all?

Consider the following scenario. Because an analysis of the loss ratio in general liability insurance indicated a rising loss ratio overall, the underwriting manager asked for a loss ratio breakdown by major business grouping. This information indicated that the loss ratio problem was confined to the contractors classifications. At this point, the manager could have (1) tightened the guidelines for the acceptability of contractors as a group, (2) issued guidelines discouraging the use of schedule credits for this group, (3) attempted to get a rate increase for this class of businesses, or (4) investigated further. Exhibit 9-4 shows what further investigation might have revealed. A breakdown of the contractors pinpointed that the greatest problem was with the general contractor classes. Given the favorable loss ratio for plumbers, it is good that the manager did not immediately try to discourage the writing of all contractors. Plumbing contractors apparently are a very desirable class of risks. With this information in hand, the underwriting manager was able to implement some form of controls or to establish guidelines on underwriting the general contractors only.

A second method of managing a book of business of any type is to examine the pricing of the risks in the book. For example, are underwriters giving too many scheduled credits relative to the number of scheduled debits given? Are too many risks being written at other than manual rates? What is the status of rate increase filings in the various states? The solution to any pricing problem depends on the information developed from such questions.

One other way to examine underwriting results is to break out each of the coverages. For example, separate premises-operations from products-completed operations based on the differences between the two. In addition, other coverages under the commercial general liability policy could be isolated.

For example, if an underwriting manager sees a problem with the overall products liability loss ratio, just the products book of business could be analyzed. Products can also be broken down according to certain business classes or industries as shown for general liability (including products-completed operations) in Exhibit 9-4. Exhibit 9-5 shows a similar breakdown of products liability only. The breakdown can also be based on any of a number of other factors as long as the premium and loss information is broken down in that way.

Exhibit 9-6 shows a breakdown of products liability insurance

**Exhibit 9-4**
Classification Premium/Loss Analysis by Type of Contractor

| General Contractors | Earned Premium | Total Incurred Losses | Loss Ratio |
|---|---|---|---|
| 1/1/X1 to 1/1/X2 | $ 192,136 | $ 69,260 | 36.0 |
| 1/1/X2 to 1/1/X3 | 248,551 | 176,944 | 71.2 |
| 1/1/X3 to 1/1/X4 | 388,566 | 402,359 | 103.5 |
| 1/1/X4 to 1/1/X5 | 613,260 | 490,975 | 80.1 |
| 1/1/X5 to 1/1/X6 | 608,593 | 1,054,281 | 173.2 |
| Total | $2,051,593 | $2,193,819 | 107.0 |
| **Electrical Contractors** | | | |
| 1/1/X1 to 1/1/X2 | $ 59,766 | $ 12,700 | 21.2 |
| 1/1/X2 to 1/1/X3 | 149,993 | 232,378 | 154.9 |
| 1/1/X3 to 1/1/X4 | 212,363 | 80,575 | 37.9 |
| 1/1/X4 to 1/1/X5 | 195,307 | 207,801 | 106.4 |
| 1/1/X5 to 1/1/X6 | 283,000 | 177,367 | 62.7 |
| Total | $900,429 | $710,821 | 78.9 |
| **Plumbing Contractors** | | | |
| 1/1/X1 to 1/1/X2 | $ 15,610 | $ 5,067 | 33.4 |
| 1/1/X2 to 1/1/X3 | 49,536 | 10,144 | 20.4 |
| 1/1/X3 to 1/1/X4 | 56,000 | 11,144 | 19.9 |
| 1/1/X4 to 1/1/X5 | 66,000 | 47,973 | 62.7 |
| 1/1/X5 to 1/1/X6 | 71,000 | 0 | 0.0 |
| Total | $257,696 | $74,298 | 28.8 |

according to the way in which the insurance was rated. The use of (a) and guide (a) rates is more prevalent in products liability insurance. Therefore, a breakdown according to how the insurance is rated is likely to give more credible results than a similar breakdown for premises-operations only. Note that this exhibit also breaks down the results by bodily injury and property damage. The exhibit would lead a manager to take corrective action in the area of other than guide (a)-rated bodily injury liability insurance and the bodily injury rates for composite-rated risks. Because composite rating is supposed to be premium neutral (that is, not changing the premium that otherwise would have been charged), there is some problem in the use of

**Exhibit 9-5**
Products Loss Ratios by Industry

| Industry | Rating Method | Loss Ratio |
|---|---|---|
| Total manufacturing | — | 86.9 |
| Food and beverages | Manual | 35.4 |
| Textiles and clothing | Manual | 130.1 |
| Furniture and wood products | Manual | 68.6 |
| Ladders | (a) | 105.7 |
| Metal goods | (a) | 55.2 |
| Machinery | (a) | 105.4 |
| Chemicals and paints | (a) | 362.2 |
| Rubber and plastic goods | (a) | 48.5 |
| Glass, brick, stone, and clay | Manual | 438.2 |
| All other | — | 52.0 |
| Contracting | — | 42.8 |
| Retail and wholesale trade | — | 38.4 |
| Restaurants | — | 22.4 |

**Exhibit 9-6**
Policy-Year Results—Products Liability

| | Premium | Losses | Loss Ratio |
|---|---|---|---|
| Products BI—Manual rated | $19,439,155 | $10,782,993 | 55.5% |
| Products PD—All classes | 43,296,782 | 18,594,108 | 42.9 |
| Products BI—Guide (a) | 11,438,219 | 7,837,870 | 68.5 |
| Products BI—Other (a) rated | 43,048,645 | 53,896,579 | 125.2 |
| Total | $117,222,801 | $91,111,550 | 77.7% |
| Composite rated risks—BI | $153,197,926 | $175,167,776 | 114.3% |
| Composite rated risks—PD | 66,608,381 | 53,365,223 | 80.1 |
| Total | $219,806,307 | $228,532,999 | 104.0% |

composite rating since the loss ratio in that area is almost 30 percent higher.

Exhibit 9-7 shows a different way to break down the products liability results—by geographical region for a two-year period. Assuming the insurer's underwriting offices are broken down in a similar

**Exhibit 9-7**
Products Liability Results by Geographical Region

| Division | Earned Premium | | Calendar-Year Loss Ratio | |
|---|---|---|---|---|
| | 19X1 | 19X0 | 19X1 | 19X0 |
| Total—All Divisions | $19,400,000 | $15,835,000 | 63% | 102% |
| Midwest | 2,459,000 | 2,224,000 | 76 | 196 |
| Chicago | 910,000 | 1,869,000 | 125 | 115 |
| New York | 1,931,000 | 1,488,000 | 90 | 21 |
| Eastern | 2,964,000 | 1,951,000 | 25 | 76 |
| Northeast | 3,773,000 | 3,481,000 | 57 | 132 |
| Southeast | 1,619,000 | 1,540,000 | 54 | 36 |
| South-Central | 1,722,000 | 858,000 | 57 | 87 |
| West | 2,728,000 | 2,006,000 | 79 | 76 |
| Canada | 177,000 | 163,000 | 109 | 70 |

fashion, the management can concentrate on certain regional or branch offices with the highest loss ratios.

## What To Do About Unfavorable Results

If an underwriting manager has found that the problem lies with a certain coverage for certain classes of business, how does he or she respond? This depends not only on the problem but on other factors as well. The term given to the overall response is usually *reunderwriting.* However, this term can be a bit confusing since it encompasses so much. Reunderwriting generally refers to the insurer's efforts to correct any problems with a given book of business. Reunderwriting might involve pricing, acceptability guidelines, coverages, marketing, and so on. Reunderwriting also often involves a review of every policy already on the books to see that each meets the new guidelines or standards. This review may be done all at once or as each policy comes up for renewal.

**Pricing.** Raising the rates is one response to correcting a book of business. However, the manager must consider the likelihood of a rate increase being approved, the impact of the increase in rates on marketing efforts, and the length of time before the rate increase would affect the unfavorable loss ratio.

Pricing means more than raising rates. It can include the application of schedule credits and debits and the use of various rating plans (composite rating, for example). Pricing can also include raising deductibles (this might also be considered a coverage change). Pricing is also a change away from allowing risks to be written on a deposit premium basis with periodic reporting to collecting the entire annual premium at policy inception.

**Change in Guidelines.** Underwriting management might decide that the best alternative is to alter the underwriting guidelines. This might involve changing the status of certain classes from acceptable to marginally acceptable or not acceptable—or vice versa.

Guidelines for the pricing areas just mentioned might also be changed. Underwriters may be discouraged from using, or prohibited from using, any (a) rates without home office approval.

The limits to each underwriter's authority may also be changed. Binding authority of certain agents may be curtailed. Prior approval of a person at a particular level may be required on risks with certain characteristics. Finally, appropriate information may be required before a certain type of risk can be written. For example, if the loss data indicates a problem with self-serve gas stations, a closer review of claims files may indicate that the problem is one of allowing a person pumping gas to lock the handle in an on position, thereby freeing him or her to check the oil and wash the windows. A change in the underwriting guideline may be to list as unacceptable any risk with such handles.

**Reinsurance.** A careful review of losses may indicate that the problem is one that can be solved through reinsurance. A review over a five-year period may show that there are wide fluctuations in loss ratios but that the overall experience for five years has been acceptable. In this case, reinsurance may be the way to smooth out these fluctuations. This alternative probably has the least impact on other departments or people.

**Nonrenewal/Cancellation.** Although nonrenewal or cancellation is not a very popular alternative, it may be the only solution in some cases for risks of a certain type. This alternative should be one of the last considered because it is drastic. The insurer should also be sure that it is an option to begin with. It is becoming more and more difficult to cancel or nonrenew a policy simply because the class involved has become undesirable. In some states, the reasons for which an insurer may cancel or nonrenew are spelled out in the law. Cancellation and nonrenewal also have a direct impact on marketing. They affect not only specific risks in question, but also the entire relationship between the insurer and the producer.

**Termination of the Producer.** If the review of the results shows that the problem lies not with any particular type of risk or rating method, but instead with one or two producers, it is possible that the insurer will want to cancel its agreement with that producer or at least sharply curtail what it accepts from that producer. This decision should never be made without consideration of the other business the producer gives to the insurer. Although the general liability results may be bad, general liability may be only a small percentage of the producer's overall premium volume, and the results of every other line may be favorable.

**Withdrawal.** The final alternative that should be considered is the withdrawal from the territory or the market altogether for that line of business. This is a very serious business decision that affects every department. Many insurance regulators resist an insurer's attempt to pull out of one line of insurance while continuing to write all other lines. The regulator usually requires that the insurer must pull out of all lines or none, but the emphasis is on inducing the insurer to stay.

## Caveats

As mentioned, many changes to correct a book of business affect departments other than underwriting. An increase in prices or a change in the insurer's policy toward deposit premiums directly affects the marketing department. This might also affect the investments and premium audit departments. Underwriting management should be sure that each affected department is contacted before the implementation of the change and that the impact on all departments has been considered.

After making the change, the underwriting manager must monitor the changes to see if they have produced the desired results. If the rates are increased, the results must be monitored to see that the loss ratios improve as the rate change is implemented.

Similarly, when the underwriting manager reviews the results of his or her company, that manager must be aware of any changes that have already taken place that would affect the analysis. For instance, the loss ratio of widget manufacturers may be poor over the past three years, but the manager must consider that all widget manufacturers were required as of six months ago to begin using a certain safety feature, the lack of which was the cause for 85 percent of the widget products liability claims. Any decision to raise rates based on loss experience or to change the desirability guidelines for such manufacturers would be inappropriate at this time. Examining loss data over several years will show at which point(s) experience changed.

Also of concern is the credibility of the results analyzed. If the breakdown of results is too fine, the premium and loss data within each grouping may be too small to be statistically credible. In such a situation, decisions based on this data would be inappropriate.

## SUMMARY

This chapter concludes the discussion of underwriting general liability insurance. General liability is a difficult line to underwrite and to understand. It is not like property insurance for which the underwriter at year end can look back and see whether or not the risks accepted had a loss. In general liability, many losses will not show up on the books for years to come. This is especially true in the products liability area.

Before considering the additional factors that apply to the underwriting of products liability insurance, the text examines the law as it applies to products. At times it may seem that no product is safe. However, a careful review of the product and the applicant's efforts to make the product safe allow the underwriter to select those manufacturers that are most likely to produce a profit in the long run.

Some of the problems associated with pricing products liability insurance are considered next in the chapter. Several of these problems also apply to general liability insurance, and some are part of the reason for the introduction of the claims-made policy. Pricing and other underwriting problems do not deter insurers from writing this line of business. What they do is encourage underwriting management to develop appropriate underwriting guidelines based on the experience of the insurer over many years. The job of the individual underwriter is to follow those guidelines and know the types of risks the insurer prefers to write and those that it prefers to avoid.

General liability insurance can be one of the most interesting lines of insurance to underwrite. The factors to consider are numerous, and the limits to which the underwriter can bind the insurer are quite large. Underwriting management is highly confident in the general liability underwriter's judgment and ability to follow guidelines in evaluating applicants. Chapters 7, 8, and 9 have presented the factors to consider and the impact of those factors. It is true that the risks covered in these chapters are going to suffer some losses and that some of these losses will be quite large. However, the underwriter should not let one loss on one risk deter him or her from continuing to follow the insurer's underwriting guidelines. These guidelines are based on underwriting management's review of the entire book of business over a number of years. The underwriter's book of business is much too small to have any statistical credibility.

# Chapter Notes


1. Donald S. Malecki, James H. Donaldson, and Ronald C. Horn, *Commercial Liability Risk Management and Insurance*, vol. I (Malvern, PA: American Institute for Property and Liability Underwriters, 1978), p. 165.
2. This section is adopted with permission from James J. Lorimer, Harry F. Perlet, Jr., Frederick G. Kempin, Jr., and Frederick R. Hodosh, *The Legal Environment of Insurance*, vol. II, 2nd ed. (Malvern, PA: The American Institute for Property and Liability Underwriters, 1981), pp. 191-197.
3. Greenman v. Yuba Power Products, Inc., 59 Cal. 2d 57-1963.
4. James H. Donaldson, *Casualty Claim Practice*, 3rd ed. (Homewood, IL: Richard D. Irwin, 1976), p. 287.
5. Henningsen v. Bloomfield Motors, 32 N.J. 358, 161 A. 2d 69 (1960).
6. Bonowski v. Revlon, Inc., 251 Iowa 141, 100 N.W. 2d 5 (1959).
7. Merrill v. Beaute Vues Corp., 235 F. 2d 893 (10th Cir. 1956).
8. Bennett v. Pilot Prods. Co. Inc., 120 Utah 474, 235 P. 2d 525 (1951).
9. Brown v. Roux Distrib. Co., 312 S.W. 2d 758 (Mo. 1958).
10. Dix W. Noel and Jerry J. Phillips, *Products Liability in a Nutshell* (St. Paul: West Publishing Company, 1974), p. 189.
11. These terms are synonymous. In casual usage, persons may usually refer to something as a warranty if the agreement is written or as a guarantee if it is oral, but the effect of the agreement and its underwriting implications are the same.
12. H.W. Heinrich, Dan Peterson, and Nestor Roos, *Industrial Accident Prevention*, 5th ed. (New York: McGraw Hill Book Company, 1980), pp. 63-64.
13. *The Product-Safety Function: Organization and Operations* (New York: The Conference Board, 1979), p. 58.

# CHAPTER 10

# Principles of Workers Compensation Insurance

This chapter and the two that follow examine workers compensation insurance. This chapter focuses on workers compensation laws and the insurance coverage to respond to those laws. Chapters 11 and 12 discuss the underwriting of workers compensation as well as the pricing and classification of workers compensation risks.

Workers compensation is a major line of insurance in the United States. It represents about 14 percent of all property and liability insurance premium income, second only to auto insurance. The loss experience in this line is closely related to the prevailing economic and political environment. There are several factors involved in this line over which the underwriter and insurer have little or no control, not the least of which are the coverage and benefits provided. However, the ability to recognize and understand the factors that *can* be controlled increases the underwriter's effectiveness.

## WORKERS COMPENSATION LAWS

The need for workers compensation coverage arises from an employee's right to compensation from the employer for a job-related injury. Early in the twentieth century, the common law rights of injured employees were significantly modified by state workers compensation laws.

Suits brought by workers against employers were a by-product of the Industrial Revolution. English common law provided that an employer did owe certain legal duties to employees. These were gradually clarified to include the following:

1. A place of work reasonably safe for the purpose intended
2. Machinery, tools, materials, and appliances reasonably safe in relation to the work to be done
3. Fellow servants reasonably fit, competent, and sober
4. Adequate rules enforced for the safe conduct of the business
5. Reasonably suitable and sufficient warning of dangers of which the employer is aware and of which the worker is excusably ignorant

The failure to fulfill these duties constituted employer negligence, and an employee could recover damages for injury that was a consequence of this negligence.

The employers, however, had several effective defenses against employee suits. First, they had the same *contributory negligence* defense as that used in other liability actions. If the worker could be shown to have caused (in whole or in part) his or her own injury, recovery of damages was not permitted. Second, if it could be shown that the relevant hazard was inherent in the employment, it was held that the employee *assumed the risk* of injury. The assumption of risk defense required proof that the employee knew about the hazard and voluntarily continued to work. Often, the mere acceptance of the job implied that the assumption of risk defense could be used. Third, employers could not be held responsible for injury to workers caused by a *reasonably fit fellow servant.* These three common-law defenses—*contributory negligence, assumption of the risk,* and the *fellow servant rule*—made it very difficult for an employee to collect damages for job-related injuries. Although some employees collected large amounts of money, the vast majority of workers collected nothing.

In 1909, the state of New York created, by statute, a commission on employers liability—the Wainwright Commission. The commission criticized the prevailing treatment of industrial accidents on the following grounds:

1. Compensation to injured employees was insufficient in most cases.
2. Most of the cost of employers liability was consumed by wasteful prosecution of lawsuits.
3. Even where compensation was adequate, court delays placed a severe strain on family finances.
4. Employers liability suits generated antagonism between employer and employee.

In response to such criticisms, states enacted workers compensation laws. Workers compensation is a social/economic trade-off. The employee gives up the right to sue the employer (in most cases), and the liability of the employer is limited to the benefits defined by statute. Many refer to workers compensation as the first "no-fault" system.

Workers compensation laws ideally function as follows:

- Provide sure, prompt, and reasonable income and medical benefits to work-accident victims, or income benefits to their dependents, regardless of fault.
- Provide a single remedy for, and reduce court delays, costs, and workloads arising out of personal injury litigation.
- Relieve public and private charities of financial drains—incident to uncompensated industrial accidents.
- Eliminate payment of fees to lawyers and witnesses as well as time-consuming trials and appeals.
- Encourage maximum employer interest in safety and rehabilitation through an appropriate experience-rating mechanism.
- Promote frank study of causes of accidents (rather than concealment of fault)—reducing preventable accidents and human suffering.[1]

Workers compensation laws vary from state to state. The largest differences from state to state are in the benefits provided by the laws and in the employments covered. While the underwriter uses the same process in evaluating each workers compensation risk regardless of state, the exposure varies with the benefits mandated by the state, administration, and the costs of medical care.

## Types of Law

Compensation laws are elective or compulsory. Under an *elective law,* employers may accept or reject the workers compensation act and its benefits for their employees, but if they do so, they become subject to employers liability suits and typically lose the three common law defenses. Generally, if the employee elects not to be covered by the workers compensation law, the employer retains the defenses. As a practical matter, the effect has been to make most laws compulsory. A *compulsory law* requires each employer within its scope to accept the provisions of the law and provide for the benefits specified.[2] As of 1 January 1989, only three workers compensation laws were elective, those of New Jersey, South Carolina, and Texas.[3]

## Coverage of Employees

One of the objectives of workers compensation laws has been that coverage should be as broad as possible. Coverage in this context means the number of employments subject to the state workers compensation law. However, for numerous historical, political, economic, and administrative reasons, all employments are not covered by workers compensation. Many persons now believe that most of these reasons are no longer valid and that a national goal should be the coverage of all employments under workers compensation laws. Almost 90 percent of all wage and salary employees are covered by workers compensation.[4]

**Exceptions.** Although practically all public and private employments are subject to workers compensation statutes, there are exceptions. These exceptions are more prevalent for public than for private employments. Two primary types of exceptions are used: (1) numerical exemptions and (2) excepted or excluded employments.

***Numerical Exemptions.*** The majority of states with compulsory workers compensation laws require all employers of one or more employees to provide workers compensation benefits to those employees. Approximately a dozen states with compulsory workers compensation laws, however, exempt from the compulsory provisions of the workers compensation statute employers who have less than a stipulated number of employees. The most common numerical exemption from the workers compensation requirements is for employers with less than three employees. In some states, employers with four and five employees are exempt. The drafters of the initial workers compensation laws most likely included these exemptions because they did not want to burden the small employer either with having to provide workers compensation benefits or with the administrative problems of implementing workers compensation laws. Today, however, the trend is toward the elimination of all numerical exemptions based on the premise that employees in a small firm are often those least able to protect themselves and least likely to have other benefits available to them in the event of a work-related injury.

***Excepted Employments.*** The workers compensation law of every state contains an exception, other than a numerical exception, in regard to coverage. This exception is for types of employment that do not fall within the compulsory aspects of the law. The most common exceptions to compulsory coverage for all employees are casual labor, domestic workers (sometimes called domestic servants), and agricultural employees. In most states, employments that are excepted from the law can be voluntarily brought under the law. In most of these cases, the employer simply elects to provide coverage. In a few states, the employees must agree to be covered.

If an employer does not want to bring (or for some reason cannot bring) the employee within the workers compensation *law,* it is possible for the employer to purchase insurance coverage that provides the same *benefits* as would have been provided under the law. The *voluntary compensation and employers liability coverage endorsement* (WC 00 03 11) is used for this purpose. Under the endorsement, the employee is *not* brought under the workers compensation law. He or she is only provided the benefits specified by the law. This endorsement is described in more detail later in this chapter.

The Vermont workers compensation law as of 1 January 1989, for example, is compulsory for all private employments. However, exceptions to this law include casual and domestic employees, amateur athletes, and farm labor whose employer's payroll is under $2,000 per year. The law also specifically states that exempted farmers and employers of domestics may nevertheless elect coverage and that circus and carnival employees must be covered. Corporate officers are allowed to reject coverage for themselves. Sole proprietors and partners may elect coverage for themselves.[5] The following are exceptions in other states:

- Real estate brokers and salespersons paid by commission only
- Workers and volunteers for charitable or religious organizations
- Participants in car pools to and from work
- Commercial fishermen
- Actors, except employees of motion picture producers
- Railroad workers covered by federal law
- Inmates
- Clergy
- Amateur athletes[6]

In the event of a negligence action by a noncovered worker, the employer retains the common law defenses. The employer can further protect itself from potential loss due to a successful suit and the costs of defense associated with the suit through employers liability coverage. This coverage is automatically provided in the standard workers compensation and employers liability insurance policy. If an employer has no covered employees, and hence no workers compensation policy, it is possible to purchase a separate employers liability policy.

*Casual Labor (Employee).* Casual labor refers to individuals hired to perform temporary odd jobs. If they are not likely to earn enough to require income tax withholding, their names probably do not appear on the payroll. Even so, they may still be covered by workers compensation depending on the state and the nature of the work.

The workers compensation laws of many states exclude casual labor. The rationale for doing so stems from the possible moral hazard involved. Since casual employment is brief and irregular, there is a much greater likelihood of unwarranted claims and malingering recoveries. The exclusion removes an obstacle that might otherwise prevent an employer from hiring casual labor.[7]

Some statutes define casual labor; others do not. While the precise definition varies from state to state, casual labor is generally held to be irregular, unpredictable, sporadic, and brief in nature. For example, a sixteen-year-old boy who was allowed to work for brief periods whenever he pleased was found to be a casual employee not covered by workers compensation.[8] Many state statutes, however, also require that the labor be outside the employer's regular business to be considered casual. Thus, a day laborer hired for one day to help at a construction site is a temporary employee of the contractor. In most states, such a day laborer would not be excluded from workers compensation coverage because the labor is a part of the employer's regular business and therefore not casual. Washing dishes in a restaurant, washing windows of a store, mowing lawns, or cleaning the premises may all be occasional, part-time jobs; but the need for all of these services can be anticipated as part of the regular business. Thus, these jobs would not be casual labor.

It is very difficult to give a "generic" example of a casual employee since each state's law is different. In addition, the final determination rests with the courts in interpreting the law of the state in question. Any example of a casual employee would have to be based on an actual case, and all the facts would have to be repeated in this discussion in order to make the example valid. One must remember that the courts and administrative bodies making the determination are often trying to find for coverage so that the injured person is compensated. For that reason, there are very few cases where a person has been held to be a casual employee. In view of the relatively few cases where a person has been held to be a casual employee and in view of the costs involved in litigating questions about casual employees, some states have specifically removed the casual employee exception.

A few state laws also add a time or monetary limitation to the definition of casual labor. In Iowa, for example, casual workers earning $200 or more per quarter are covered by the workers compensation law.[9]

Since relatively few cases meet the conditions of casual labor, underwriters must be alert for occasional or temporary employees working for the insured even though they do not appear on the payroll.

*Domestic Workers.* Domestic workers are employees engaged exclusively in household work—cooks, housekeepers, laundry workers, maids, butlers, companions, nurses, baby sitters, chauffeurs, or gardeners. Domestic workers are considered as such only if they are employed by an individual or a husband and wife. They cannot be employed by a business or other organization. A person performing domestic services such as those mentioned above and employed by an organization would be considered a miscellaneous employee.

For many purposes, domestic workers are treated differently from other employees. No federal income tax withholding is required in most cases. If domestic workers receive more than $50 in a calendar quarter, however, they are covered for social security and minimum wage purposes. In that case, overtime regulations also apply, except for sleep-in domestics. In many states, the workers compensation statutes specifically exclude domestics. Some others, such as California and Connecticut, consider them eligible for benefits only if they work a certain minimum number of hours per week. Other states exclude certain types of domestics, as in Alaska where part-time baby sitters and cleaning persons are excluded. Some states now allow workers compensation coverage for domestic workers to be included in homeowners policies.

Normally, an underwriter need not worry about household employees. When an agency provides baby sitters, housekeepers, or other domestic workers, however, there is the possibility of an employer-employee relationship between the agency and the domestic worker. An agency that supplies baby sitters, for example, may be a source of regular employment. A person on the agency's list of baby sitters may be sent to several different homes in the course of a month. Each client pays the standard agency rate directly to the baby sitter. The baby sitter then turns over to the agency a designated proportion as a service fee. Under this arrangement, the agency is not an employer for FICA, unemployment, or income tax withholding purposes.[10] The baby sitter is considered self-employed and subject to self-employment taxes.

For workers compensation and liability insurance purposes, however, the baby sitter may be considered an employee of the agency. A liability policy surely would define who is covered. For a workers compensation policy, the underwriter may have to judge whether the agency provides substantial employment for domestic workers as an integral part of its business. If so, a domestic worker could be considered an employee of the agency by the relative nature of the work test. An agency making a business of providing baby-sitting services would more reasonably be expected to incur a workers compensation obligation than the private individuals who are its clients.

*Agricultural Employees.* Another group of workers sometimes presenting problems to underwriters includes those who work on farms. The workers compensation laws of approximately thirty states either exclude or limit coverage for agricultural employees. For example, agricultural employees may be covered only if they use machinery or power equipment. Other states exempt employers from the requirements of the law if they have less than a specific number of employees. The Iowa workers compensation statute does not cover farms with less than a stipulated amount of farm labor payroll during the prior year.

Whether individuals are considered agricultural employees and thus exempt may depend on whether the employer is an agricultural or industrial enterprise. Agriculture means growing food by tilling the soil, cultivating orchards, or raising livestock. Sometimes, however, agricultural activities may be only one stage in a food processing operation. In that case, the enterprise uses the work methods and accounting procedures of an industrial operation, and is thus not exempt from providing coverage for its employee.[11] Even an enterprise that only produces food may become more of a factory than a farm by intensive specialization. For example, when chickens are hatched, nurtured, and butchered within a single building, the operation hardly meets the conventional definition of agriculture.

A farmer may also lose the agricultural exemption by engaging in other businesses besides farming. When a farmer ground grain for others as well as himself, the court ruled that the helper operating the grinder was not an agricultural employee.[12] If a farmer hires workers to help clear the land of trees, the work is agricultural even when the farmer sells the timber. The same activities on land not used for farming, however, constitute a lumbering business, and the agricultural employment exemption does not apply.[13] When farm workers engage in other activities, such as repairing farm machinery or fixing a fence, they are still agricultural employees as long as the other jobs are a routine part of running a farm. In the same way, workers covered by the workers compensation law, such as a carpenter repairing a barn, do not lose that status merely by temporarily working on a farm.[14] As in other cases, the underwriter needs to examine the nature of the work and the relationship between the employer and the employee in an analysis of agricultural employments.

**State of Employment.** When a worker's occupation takes him or her temporarily into another state, questions frequently arise as to which state's workers compensation law applies. Most state laws have *extraterritoriality provisions* that provide coverage to employees temporarily employed in another state. Determining which state's law applies depends on the provisions of the particular laws in question and typically requires consideration of the circumstances of the case, including the place and nature of employment, where the employee was hired, the state in which the employee was intended to work, how long the employee has been away from the state in question, the employee's state of residence, and the employer's state of domicile. This problem is complicated because of the multiplicity of state laws, and different coverage and benefit provisions in the various states. For example, a truck driver might live in Massachusetts, go to work for a trucking firm in Texas, and drive through all of the states as part of employment. If the driver is injured in the state of Pennsylvania, under which act would benefits be payable? A growing trend is to permit a compensation claim to be filed in the state where the injury occurred, where the employment was principally located, or where the employee was hired. From an underwriting standpoint, this amounts to allowing the employee to select the state with the most liberal benefits. Therefore, the underwriter must consider the scope of the employment and the possible state laws under which an employee might elect coverage.

## WORKERS COMPENSATION BENEFITS

As explained later in more detail, workers compensation coverage does not have limits in the usual sense of the word. Simply, the policy says that it will pay all that the workers compensation law says it has to pay. Instead of using the expression "coverage provided," the expression "benefits provided" is usually used since the policy is paying the benefits required by law. This section examines those benefits and what an employee must do to receive them.

### Requirements for Benefits

Workers compensation laws provide broad benefits to persons suffering work-related injuries and diseases. There are certain requirements that must be met in order for a person to collect these benefits, and these requirements can vary by state. In general, for an injury or disease to be compensable under a workers compensation statute, the employee must notify the employer of the injury or disease, there must be an impairment that is caused by a covered injury or disease, and the injury or disease must be work-related.

**Notice of Injury or Disease.** For an injury or disease to be covered, the injured employee must give notice to the employer of the occurrence of the injury or disease. Most state workers compensation statutes provide that notice must be given within a certain period of time (three years is common). The notice requirement is intended to limit coverage to truly work-related incidents (that is, if the notice is given promptly, any question as to the origin of the impairment can be answered). This requirement is often liberally interpreted, however. Failure of the employee to give notice of injury is usually excused if the employer knew of the occurrence of the accident, or if the failure to give notice did not prejudice the employer's rights. Failure to give prompt notice has been excused when the employee feared it might result in termination of his services.[15] Once the employer knows about the injury, a filing known as the *first report of injury* must be made with the state administrative agency overseeing workers compensation.

**Impairment.** For benefits to be provided, there must be an impairment (which can be temporary or permanent and partial or total) or death. An impairment is a purely medical condition resulting from any anatomic or functional abnormality or loss. An impairment is not the same as a disability since a *disability* is not necessarily a purely medical condition. An employee is disabled when the ability to work in gainful activity is reduced by the impairment. The extent of the disability may depend on the impairment and also on nonmedical factors such as the worker's age and education.[16]

**Covered Injury or Disease.** The impairment must be caused by a covered injury or disease. A traditional test of a covered injury is whether it is caused by an accident. For an injury to be accidental, it must occur at a certain point in time, usually interpreted to be a sudden event. It must also be unexpected. This definition has been broadly interpreted. For example, suddenness can be associated with either the cause or the effect of an injury. An employee engaged in heavy lifting may strain his or her back over a period of time, but if this action culminates in severe back pain at a definite point in time, the effect of the injury is considered sudden and therefore compensable. A similar theory of suddenness supports the compensability of heart attack cases in some jurisdictions. Physical injury resulting from mental stimuli, such as stress, may be compensable. A more difficult, yet compensable, situation exists for mental injury related to mental stimuli, such as the case of a secretary in New York who suffered extreme depression and was unable to work for six months after discovering her boss' suicide.[17]

There are some limited employer defenses against injury claims, such as intoxication. However, most statutes provide the intoxication must be the sole cause of injury or death if it is to be used as a defense. In a New York case, an employee was killed in an automobile accident. Evidence was advanced that he had been drunk, yet recovery was allowed because intoxication was only a contributing case, speeding and reckless driving being the other factors.[18] Another defense is willful injury or suicide. Again, however, the employer must prove that the injury or death was self-inflicted. This means proving intention, which is difficult to do in any case.

Although compensation laws originally had no specific provisions for occupational diseases, all states now recognize their compensability. Coverage and interpretation, however, vary considerably from state to state. In general, an *occupational disease* is a function of the employment. Most occupational diseases become evident during employment or soon after the exposure to injurious conditions, although for some exposures, the disease may be latent. As a consequence, many states now provide extended periods of time for the discovery of these slowly developing diseases. Special cases to consider in relation to what is covered are cumulative injuries where there is already an existing disability.

***Cumulative Injury.*** The concept of cumulative injury or *cumulative trauma* has been formally accepted in California and Michigan and informally accepted in other jurisdictions. Cumulative injuries typically arise from a series of minor mental or physical stresses and strains related to the employment that occur over a period of time, the combined effect of which causes disability or the need for medical treatment.

The major problem associated with determining compensability of these injuries is distinguishing between conditions brought on by the normal aging process or those to which the general public is subject and those that are truly job-related. In addition to the problem of how much of the disability is occupationally caused, determination of financial responsibility is another concern. The California Supreme Court ruled "the only moment when such an injury could be visualized as taking compensation form is the date of last exposure when the cumulative effect causes disability."

The following two examples give an idea of the types of cumulative injury claims. A fifty-eight-year-old civil engineer employed by the same employer for twenty-eight years commits suicide. His widow files for death benefits claiming continuous trauma in the form of emotional stress and physical strain due to overwork and uncertainty about his job's future.

In another example, a middle management employee has a sex change operation from male to female. Returning to the same employment, she is subjected to continuous kidding and teasing by fellow employees for wearing skirts, high heel shoes, and cosmetics. This allegedly results in a nervous breakdown. From an underwriting perspective, such developments can have a significant impact on the workers compensation system by imposing an incalculable financial responsibility on employers and insurers for an exposure to loss that is difficult, if not impossible, to evaluate.

***Second Injury Funds.*** One important goal of workers compensation is to get the injured employee back on the job. However, it has long been recognized that employers are hesitant to hire previously disabled workers. For example, if an employee with only one eye is hired and then loses that eye as a result of an occupational injury, the employer would be required to pay permanent total benefits rather than the usual permanent partial benefits.

Second injury funds have been established to deal with this problem and thus to encourage employers to hire disabled workers. They also more equitably allocate the costs of providing benefits to such employees. In the example, if the employee should lose the remaining eye, the current employer would be responsible for permanent partial benefits for the loss of one eye. The additional benefit to the employee would be paid by the second injury fund. Some second injury funds require the employer to be aware of pre-existing impairments before hiring the employee. If the employer is not aware of the condition, the second injury fund will not be responsible for the additional payment. The underwriter therefore needs to know about the hiring practices of the employer—whether physician examinations are required—and if the employer registers such impairments. The second injury fund is funded in various ways including, but not limited to, premium taxes, surplus state funds, and assessments against insurers and employers.

**Work Related.** In order to be compensable, the injury or disease must be work related.[19] That is, (1) it must occur as a consequence of a hazard that is peculiar to the employment (not one to which the general public is exposed), and (2) it must occur while the employee is at his or her usual place of work during the usual work hours and while the employee is doing the task for which he or she was hired. These requirements have often been paraphrased, "arising out of and in (during) the course (scope) of employment."

While these requirements may appear to be rather strict, they have been liberally interpreted in order to provide coverage to injured employees. For example, if an employee's chair were to collapse as he or she was sitting, the resulting injuries would be compensable because they are considered to have arisen out of a hazard peculiar to the employment because the employment requires the employee to be at the desk.

Additionally, the usual place of work has been interpreted to include more than just the employer's office, plant, or job site if the location is often frequented by employees during the course of work. An employee who regularly takes the deposit to the bank would likely be covered if injured in the bank. In addition, the employee is covered while entering and exiting the place of employment. This applies not only to the employer's immediate premises but also to the premises of the building in which the employer is located, regardless of the owner of the building. If an employee is injured in a parking lot provided by the employer for the use of employees, the employee is considered to be on premises. Bathroom facilities are also considered on premises, and injuries suffered while using these facilities are considered to have arisen out of the employment. However, once an employee is off the employer's premises, the injuries are no longer considered to have occurred on the employer's premises and therefore may not necessarily be considered work related.

Ordinarily, if the employee works primarily at one location, the time spent traveling to and from the work location is not considered to be work related. Thus, the accidents occurring while en route to and from work are not compensable.

Two exceptions to this are when the employer provides the transportation and when the employee travels as part of his or her job. If the employer provides a bus or private car for the employee to use to travel to and from work, injuries suffered from the time the employee enters the car until the time the employee leaves the car are considered to be work related. If the employee uses a car as part of the job, any injuries related to the use of the car are considered to be work related. However, if the employee deviates substantially from the normal course of travel for personal purposes, the employee is considered to be outside the scope of employment. Injuries occurring during that time are therefore not considered work related, so they are not compensable.

The same conditions apply to the use of a company car. If an employee is using the company car on company business, injuries arising therefrom are compensable because they are considered work related. If the employer requires that the employee take the car home in the evenings, injuries occurring when returning home or when driving to work the next morning are considered to be work related.

If an employer provides a lunchroom, employees can eat food brought from home or food supplied by the employer. If the employee is injured as a result of the food brought to work (for example, swallows a chicken bone), the resulting injury is not work related. It might just as well have occurred off premises. However, if the employee becomes ill after eating contaminated food supplied by the employer, the injury is considered to be work related.

If the employer furnishes an employee accommodations, and an injury arises out of a personal act of the employee, it most likely would not be considered work related. For example, in *Pisko* v. *Mintz,* 262 N.Y. 176, a janitor was required to sleep on premises and was burned by a fire caused by careless smoking in bed on the part of the janitor. It was held that the injury did not arise out of the employment; hence, compensation was denied. However, it is usually held that if the injury did not arise out of a personal act, it would be considered to be work related. In the example above, the injuries would most likely be considered work related if the fire had been caused by an explosion in a room next to the employee.

It has also been ruled that if an employer requires an employee to reside in a dangerous area, any accidental injury arising therefrom is compensable, regardless of whether or not the employee was at work at the time. In *Lewis* v. *Knappen Tippetts Eng. Co.*, 304 NY 461, an engineer assigned to work in Israel by a New York firm was shot and killed by Arabs while he was on a sightseeing trip. Compensation was awarded to his widow.

In other cases, as when the employee is in a remote area and the employer has provided adequate recreational facilities, compensation has been denied when the employee is injured while participating in recreational activities at a facility other than that provided by the employer. The reasoning was that nonemployer-sponsored recreational "jaunts" were not considered within the scope of employment.[20]

Like injuries, diseases are compensable only if they are work related. The disease must have been caused by a feature of the job common to all such jobs, such as a baker's contact with high heat, which causes dermatitis.[21] Not all diseases that develop in the course of work are truly "occupational." In general, there must be a causal relationship between the occupation and the disease for compensation to be provided.

## Benefits Provided

Workers compensation laws impose strict liability on employers to provide the benefits required by law. In exchange for benefits, the employees give up their right to sue the employer for both economic and noneconomic losses. Therefore, workers compensation insurance strives to substantially indemnify the employee for medical expenses and loss of earnings that result from occupational injury or disease. Benefits vary from state to state, but generally include medical, disability (indemnity), death, and rehabilitation.

**Medical Benefits.** The workers compensation law in all states provides unlimited medical expense benefits. This would include medical, hospital, and surgical expenses, and other related medical expenses including the cost for physical therapy and prosthetic devices. From an underwriting standpoint, most occupational injuries are minor and require only the payment of medical expenses not involving weekly indemnity or rehabilitation costs. However, the rate of inflation for medical expenses will continue to escalate the cost of this benefit. These benefits account for about one-third of total workers compensation costs.[22]

**Disability Income (Indemnity) Benefits.** Disability income benefits are intended to compensate an injured employee for wage loss. Unlike medical benefits, there is a deductible in the form of a waiting period before disability income benefits begin. This waiting period varies from two to seven days depending upon the state. If the disability continues for a specified number of days, most laws provide for retroactive payment of benefits to the date of injury.

Most disability cases involve *temporary total disability.* This means that the employee is totally disabled and unable to work as a result of the injury but is expected to recover from the injury and return to work. *Permanent total disability* means that the seriousness of the employee's injury is such that the employee is regarded as totally and permanently unable to perform gainful employment. The weekly benefit for both types of total disability is expressed as a percentage of the employee's average weekly pretax wage at the time of disability. In most states this percentage is 66 ⅔ percent.

Since these benefits are received tax free, it is possible that if the percentage were too high, the incentive for rehabilitation might be weakened. In fact, the take-home pay could be higher after the disability than before if the percentage were too high. Thus, there is a need to limit the percentage of the worker's weekly wage that will be paid in the case of disability. The weekly benefit is limited by maximum and minimum amounts, which vary widely from state to state. The maximum and minimum amounts are determined in various ways by the states, but a method growing in popularity is fixing the limits at a percentage of the state's average weekly wage (SAWW). In this way, the maximums and minimums will vary with the state's average weekly wage rather than remaining a fixed amount until an amendment is made to the law. In at least forty states, the maximum is automatically adjusted annually.[23] Additionally, some states impose time limits and aggregate amount limits on total disability benefits. The time limits tend to be longer and the aggregate limits higher for permanent total disability cases than for temporary total disability.

Whereas total disability means that the employee is unable to return to work (at least for some significant period of time), *partial disability* means that the employee is able to return to work but can only perform part of his or her usual functions. *Temporary partial disability* means that the condition is not permanent and the employee is not expected to have any permanent impairment from the injury. A broken leg is a good example of temporary partial disability for a truck driver. This employee may be able to return to work with a broken leg, but he or she may be assigned to duties other than driving until the leg has healed. *Permanent partial disability* means that the employee has sustained a permanent impairment that interferes with his or her usual tasks. The loss of a leg for a truck driver would be an example of this type of disability.

There are two types of benefits for partial disabilities—scheduled and a percentage of wages (nonscheduled). *Scheduled benefits* (or *scheduled injuries*) are for the loss, or loss of use of, specific body members. This usually includes arms, hands, fingers, legs, feet, toes, as well as sight and hearing. Which finger or toe is affected is usually specified. The resulting permanent handicap is assumed to result in a long-term wage loss. As a result, these benefits are payable without regard to actual wage loss. In most jurisdictions, the amount payable is a specific number of weeks of benefits. The weekly benefit amount is the same as for a temporary total disability. A maximum amount is also specified in the law. There is great variation in the laws in compensation for scheduled injuries. The maximum amount for an injury in one state can be ten times greater than the maximum amount in another state for the same injury.[24] In most states, the scheduled benefits for an injury are in addition to any other temporary disability benefits payable during the healing period.

In the majority of states, there is a combination of (1) specified benefits for certain scheduled permanent partial injuries and (2) a percent of wages-type benefit for nonscheduled permanent partial and temporary partial injuries. Some states, however, have no scheduled injuries and state all partial disability benefits as a percentage of wages. The *percent of wages benefit* for partial disabilities is similar to that for total disability in that the benefit is stated as a percent of wages subject to some maximum and minimum amount. For partial disabilities, however, the percentage or the maximum is based on the degree of impairment and the actual loss of earnings (that is, the difference in wages earned before and after the injury).

The trend, if there is one, is away from scheduled type benefits. There is greater emphasis on basing benefits on the actual drop in earnings as a result of the injury. This change is a result of the fact that the loss of a finger has different effects on different occupations. A typist's earning capacity would be impacted more by the loss of the baby finger than would that of a truck driver.

**Death Benefits.** Death benefits include a flat benefit for burial expense and partial replacement of the worker's former weekly wage. The burial expense allowance varies among the states and is expressed as a flat amount or as a multiple of the state's average weekly wage. The percentage of wage loss varies by state and depends primarily on the number and type of dependents. Some states provide a maximum benefit in the form of a maximum amount or maximum time period for benefits. These maximum death benefits are generally paid to the spouse until remarriage and to dependent children up to a specified age. In some states the spouse may get a lump sum payment (for example, two years of benefits) at remarriage.

**Rehabilitation Benefits.** The rehabilitation of injured workers was an early goal of the workers compensation system. Therefore, every state law includes some rehabilitation benefits. The primary rehabilitation benefit is the payment of expenses for complete medical treatment and medical rehabilitation. However, vocational rehabilitation may also be required. Most workers compensation laws today provide a maintenance allowance to injured workers during rehabilitation, which is in addition to other compensation benefits, but the allowance is usually limited. Additional rehabilitation benefits are available from state agencies. Because there is an economic incentive for the insurer to return the injured person to work, many insurers have provided rehabilitation services extending beyond the requirements of the law.

## Benefit Administration

Because of the compulsory and social nature of workers compensation, the state supervises the payment of benefits to ensure compliance with the spirit and letter of the law. Most states have a workers compensation board or industrial commission with responsibility to administer the law. Three states still exclusively employ the courts instead of a specific administrative agency to administer claims. The injured worker notifies the employer of the injury, and the employer submits the injury report to the producer or insurer, which then transmits the report to the administrative agency. If the claim is not contested by the employer, the injured employee and the employer's insurer agree upon a settlement. This agreement must be in compliance with the workers compensation law and is subject to review by the workers compensation agency. Other states use a direct-payment system, which does not require an agreement before benefits commence. Under this system, benefits are paid immediately, and the administrative agency reviews the amounts paid to determine compliance with the law.

If the claim is contested by the employer, most states require a hearing by an officer of the administrative agency. The decision of the hearing officer may be appealed to the workers compensation board or commission and then to the appropriate court.

# METHODS OF MEETING THE EMPLOYER'S OBLIGATION

Because workers compensation laws are intended to protect injured employees, the requirements imposed by these laws are designed to ensure that an injured employee will receive the benefits to which he or she is entitled. Employers to whom the workers compensation law applies are therefore required to prove that the benefits will, in fact, be provided.

States require that the employer secure the payment of the benefits, which can be done in the following ways:

- Provide financial and administrative capacity to retain ("self-insure") the risk of compensation benefits
- Purchase coverage through the state fund
- Obtain voluntary private insurance (a workers compensation and employers liability insurance policy) from an insurance company licensed to transact business in the particular state
- Purchase similar insurance through the assigned risk plan

The state law specifies which of these four (or which combination) the employer can select to meet its obligation under the workers compensation statute.

## "Self-Insurance" (Retention)

Employers can "self-insure," or retain, the workers compensation benefits in all but three states—North Dakota, Texas (with the exception of state and political subdivisions), and Wyoming. For the employer who wishes to retain the exposure, a surety bond or cash and securities must be provided to the workers compensation agency to guarantee the security of benefit payments. Most states also require evidence of the ability to administer benefits. Retention has traditionally been practical only for large employers, although the number of employers electing to retain the risk has significantly increased in recent years. The availability of catastrophe reinsurance has had a positive effect on increasing the number of employers electing to retain the workers compensation exposure. In addition, the majority of states allow *group self-insurance*—that is, several employers (usually too small to retain their own exposure) can join together for the purpose of "self-insuring" the workers compensation exposure.

## State Funds

Six states (Nevada, North Dakota, Ohio, Washington, West Virginia, and Wyoming) have what are known as monopolistic state funds. Thirteen states have what are known as competitive state funds. A state fund is essentially a state-operated insurance company. Employers purchase compensation insurance from the fund much as they would from a private insurer. In a *monopolistic state fund,* the employer cannot purchase insurance from a private insurer—private insurers are not allowed to sell workers compensation insurance in the state. Insurance must be purchased from the state fund. In Nevada, Ohio, Washington, and West Virginia, the employer does have the alternative of "self-insuring" the exposure.

In a *competitive state fund,* the employer can purchase insurance from a private insurer or from the state fund. In all thirteen of these states with this type of fund the employer can also "self-insure" the exposure.

A common reason for the establishment of monopolistic state funds is that workers compensation is a compulsory social program in which there should be significant state involvement and in which no private profit should be permitted. Those who support state funds cite the advantages that coverage can be provided at a lower cost, that the benefits are more secure, and that coverage is available to everyone who needs it. These advantages have not necessarily been shown to exist.

## Voluntary Private Insurance

In thirty states, the employer can purchase insurance from a private insurance company or "self-insure" the exposure. (State funds are not available.) Texas is not one of these states because it prohibits self-insurance. The policy used to provide coverage is the standard workers compensation and employers liability policy, which incorporates the state's workers compensation law. As a result, the policy from state to state is uniform because the same policy can be used in all states, with the appropriate state being listed on the information page. This includes that state's workers compensation law as part of the policy. Exhibit 10-1 presents a summary of the methods used to secure workers compensation benefits as of 1 January 1989.

## Assigned Risk Plans

A business cannot always obtain voluntary private insurance because it may not meet the established underwriting criteria of

**Exhibit 10-1**
Methods Used to Secure Workers Compensation Benefits—1 January 1989*

| Insurance from Private Insurer | Monopolistic State Fund | Monopolistic State Fund or Self-Insurance | Insurance from Private Insurer, Competitive State Fund or Self-Insurance | Insurance from Private Insurer or Self-Insurance |
|---|---|---|---|---|
| TX | ND, WY | NV, OH, WA, WV | AZ, CA, CO, ID, MD, MI, MN, MT, NY, OK, OR, PA, UT | AK, AL, AR, CT, DE, FL, GA, HI, IL, IN, IA, KS, KY, LA, ME, MA, MS, MO, NE, NH, NJ, NM, NC, RI, SC, SD, TN, VT, VA, WI |

*Adapted with permission from *Analysis of Workers Compensation Laws*, 1989 edition, U.S. Chamber of Commerce.

insurance companies. This condition, in combination with the compulsory nature of workers compensation insurance in most states, could literally force such an organization out of business. For this reason, assigned risk plans were developed to make workers compensation insurance available to all employers. An employer who has been rejected by private insurers may apply to the plan and obtain coverage.

In general, under an assigned risk plan, an employer who applies to the plan is "assigned" to one of the insurers that provides workers compensation insurance in that state. The National Council on Compensation Insurance administers what is known as the *National Workers Compensation Reinsurance Pool.* This pool is a voluntary association of insurers. Each insurer member does not receive an assignment from the assigned risk plan, but one or more of the member companies acts as a servicing insurer and receives a fee for providing policyholder services such as premium collection, loss control, claims adjustment, and premium auditing. This fee generally ranges from 24 to 30 percent of premium. The premiums and losses of a business assigned to these member servicing insurers are pooled. The premiums and losses are then allocated by state to all members of the pool in proportion to each member's workers compensation premium volume. The pool operates in approximately thirty states and provides some coverages in nine other states. In addition, the National Council on Compensation Insurance manages the statutory pool in two states. In some states, the state fund serves as the assigned risk plan.

## NEGLIGENCE LIABILITY OF EMPLOYERS

It is generally held by the courts that if the compensation law fails to give a remedy, employees may seek damages through the tort law. Therefore, in addition to the liability arising from an employer's responsibility to the employee under the compensation law of the jurisdiction, the employer has another potential source of liability arising out of occupational injuries that do not come within the compensation law. The workers compensation *and employers liability* insurance policy responds to the negligence liability exposures of an employer. The exact coverage is examined later in this chapter. The following employers liability hazards are generally recognized.[25]

1. Exempt employment. The employee is not eligible for workers compensation benefits because the employment, such as farm labor or domestic work, does not come within the compensation law.
2. Numerical exemption. The employer hires fewer than the minimum number of employees specified in the state workers compensation law.
3. Noncompensable injury or disease. A disease may not be considered an occupational disease and hence does not come within the scope of a compensation law and may subject the employer to suit. Certain types of injuries may also not be covered, such as nonaccidental injuries and those occurring during intoxication.
4. Illegal employment. An illegally employed minor, or his or her parents, may be entitled to sue in some jurisdictions in lieu of compensation benefits.
5. The employer may have failed to secure benefits as provided by the law. In some cases, the employee would then be permitted to sue the employer for resulting occupational injuries.
6. An employee's spouse may seek damages for loss of the employee's services as a result of occupational injury.
7. Third-party actions (sometimes referred to as *third-party-over actions*). A third party who has been sued by an employee for injuries arising out of the employee's work may in turn sue the employer claiming the employer's contributory negligence. All states do not allow such suits, however. These actions are described in more detail later in this chapter when the coverage is examined.

## RATING BUREAUS FOR WORKERS COMPENSATION INSURANCE

Most states require insurers to belong to the approved rating organization in order to write workers compensation and employers liability insurance in that state. These rating bureaus are the organizations that gather statistics for workers compensation in all states where private insurers are authorized to underwrite this coverage. The bureau files with supervisory authorities the manual for classifications, rules, rates, rating plans, and policy forms on behalf of its members. Although in many states rating laws encouraging open competition have eliminated the uniform application of rates, rating bureaus continue to have an important role in the administration of workers compensation insurance.

The bureaus employ actuaries and statisticians who compile loss experience statistics from insurers, promulgate rates, and develop experience and retrospective rating plans. The underwriting committee of the bureau establishes classifications and determines the rules and procedures for the administration of the rating system.

This administration of rates includes establishing classifications for insureds within the state. While the bureau for a particular jurisdiction has the authority to assign classifications, it actually inspects and classifies only a small percentage of the insureds in its territory. Its definitions and procedures, however, apply uniformly to all insurers guaranteeing that the workers compensation insurance system functions equitably for all insureds.

Rate filings include policy and endorsement forms. The policy and endorsements are highly standardized, and the same policy form is used in all states where private workers compensation insurance is permitted. The present workers compensation and employers liability insurance policy was adopted in 1984 by the National Council on Compensation Insurance (hereafter referred to as NCCI or National Council). The National Council serves as the filing agency for insurers in most states and prepares standard forms and endorsements. Uniform coverage implies the application of uniform rules and procedures in conjunction with such coverage. The manual for workers compensation and employers liability insurance also becomes a part of the rate filing in the state and provides a uniform set of underwriting regulations. The manual used by the National Council (and referenced in this text) is the *Basic Manual for Workers Compensation and Employers Liability Insurance* (referred to hereafter as the *Basic Manual*).

## National Council on Compensation Insurance

The National Council is the preeminent influence in the administration of workers compensation insurance. It is an unincorporated association of companies writing workers compensation insurance. In more than half the states and the District of Columbia, the National Council is the licensed rating bureau operating under the laws of the state. Other states have independent bureaus that rely on actuarial and statistical services provided by the National Council or that closely follow the methods of the National Council. Even in the states with monopolistic state funds for workers compensation insurance, the National Council may provide advisory services.

By means of the *Unit Statistical Plan* the member companies provide the National Council with remuneration, premium, and loss information for each insured. By studying the statistical trends developing in each jurisdiction for which it is the licensed ratemaking organization, the National Council determines when rate revisions are necessary. Some revisions result from amendments to the state's workers compensation law changing the benefits provided to injured employees. Other revisions are occasionally needed to keep pace with inflation. Still others may be prompted by technological or social developments significantly altering the loss experience for a particular rating classification. In any case, the rate revisions are to provide insurers with sufficient premium income to pay all workers compensation claims and expenses. When revisions are necessary in a particular state, the National Council or appropriate rating organization often files the necessary data with the insurance department. The rate filing may be accepted or rejected, or a smaller increase may be granted. In many states once new rates are approved, they are in force as of the announced effective date and must be used by all insurance companies. In other states the bureau filing may be a model from which individual insurers are permitted, or even required, to deviate. It is also possible for the National Council to provide only pure premium data to which insurers must add expense data in their individual rate filings.

The National Council underwriting department continually reviews classification problems. With the benefit of its extensive research information, the underwriting department can resolve difficult classification problems regarding individual insureds. As changes occur within an industry, this department is also able to study the situation and recommend the proper classification procedure. If necessary, it can establish a new classification for a unique new industry group, which, if approved by the underwriting committee, can then be filed for approval by the state insurance department.

The National Council also monitors social, economic, and regulatory trends to analyze the potential impact on the workers compensation system. Through activities in these areas, the National Council can undertake research and advise other organizations where warranted.

Because the credibility of actuarial studies depends on consistency in classification assignments as well as accuracy in obtaining remuneration, premium, and loss data, underwriters, premium auditors, and the National Council need to work closely together. National Council advisory opinions can be very helpful to underwriters and premium auditors in answering difficult classification questions.

## Independent Bureaus

Several states have independent rating bureaus for workers compensation insurance. Some of these use the services of the National Council. Others make their own rates and issue their own rules and manuals. In Texas the State Board of Insurance promulgates rates on the basis of statistics gathered by the National Council. In all of these states, however, the procedures generally resemble those of the National Council. While underwriters must, of course, be thoroughly familiar with the various state exceptions, the essential principles of premium determination and classification apply in independent bureau states just as they do in National Council states.

The independent bureaus consist of insurance companies that write workers compensation insurance in the state. They are controlled by a governing committee of representatives elected by the member companies. Most bureaus, in addition to the governing committee, have a classification and rates committee and an actuarial and statistics committee. The actuarial committee reviews the statistical information compiled by the bureau staff and makes rate recommendations to the classification and rates committee for rate filings. After its review and consideration, the rates committee instructs the bureau staff to make appropriate rate filings with the state regulatory body responsible for approving workers compensation insurance rates.

Rating bureaus have broad authority for the administration of workers compensation insurance. According to its manual, for example, the New York Compensation Insurance Rating Board "is empowered to determine, revise or modify the classifications or rates applicable to any individual risk. Every policy insuring a risk for which the classifications or rates have been established by the board shall be written in accordance with such classifications and rates."[26] Thus, if the rating board finds that any policy has not been rated or classified according to its rules, it has the authority to order immediate correction. While insurers may appeal bureau decisions, and often do so successfully, the rating bureau has the final authority.

## THE WORKERS COMPENSATION AND EMPLOYERS LIABILITY INSURANCE POLICY

The 1984 edition of the standard workers compensation and employers liability insurance policy simplifies the language of the standard form. Like the policy form that had been in use since 1954, it is designed to provide complete coverage for employee injuries except for specific exclusions. The policy combines blanket coverage for obligations imposed by the state workers compensation law and broad coverage for other employers' liability. This broad coverage and the additional flexibility provided by endorsements spare policyholders the necessity of revising the insurance program every time a new location is established or some other change in the business occurs.

An interesting feature of this policy is that it contains uniform provisions, even though workers compensation benefits vary by jurisdiction. It is possible to use the same policy for basic coverages in various states without endorsements because the compensation laws of states, not the policy provisions, control the conditions of coverage. The workers compensation laws are specifically incorporated into the policy contract by the reference in the policy. Thus, an underwriter analyzing the coverage and benefits provided must read the applicable statutes as well as the policy. The use of the standard policy by all insurers, together with uniform underwriting rules, also enables rating bureaus to calculate sound rates.

### Information Page (WC 00 00 01)

A complete workers compensation policy consists of an information page, a standard provisions workers compensation and employers liability insurance policy form (WC 00 00 00), and any necessary endorsements.[27] Exhibit 10-2 shows the information page, which lists the specific information about the insured that is needed to form a contract and to determine the earned premium. This information includes the following:

- Whom the insurance company is insuring
- What period the policy covers
- Coverage provided
- States covered
- Maximum amounts that will be paid under employers liability
- Classifications, premium basis, and rates to be used

**Exhibit 10-2**
Information Page*

**WORKERS COMPENSATION AND EMPLOYERS LIABILITY INSURANCE POLICY** **WC 00 00 01A**

**Original Printing** Issued May 1, 1988 **Standard**

**INFORMATION PAGE**

Insurer:

**POLICY NO.**

1. The Insured: ___ Individual ___ Partnership
   Mailing address: ___ Corporation or ______________
   Other workplaces not shown above:

2. The policy period is from ______________ to ______________ at the insured's mailing address.

3. A. Workers Compensation Insurance: Part One of the policy applies to the Workers Compensation Law of the states listed here:

   B. Employers Liability Insurance: Part Two of the policy applies to work in each state listed in Item 3.A. The limits of our liability under Part Two are:
   Bodily Injury by Accident $______ each accident
   Bodily Injury by Disease $______ policy limit
   Bodily Injury by Disease $______ each employee

   C. Other States Insurance: Part Three of the policy applies to the states, if any, listed here:

D. This policy includes these endorsements and schedules:

4. The premium for this policy will be determined by our Manuals of Rules, Classifications, Rates and Rating Plans. All information required below is subject to verification and change by audit.

| Classifications | Code No. | Premium Basis Total Estimated Annual Remuneration | Rate Per $100 of Remuneration | Estimated Annual Premium |
|---|---|---|---|---|

Total Estimated Annual Premium $

Minimum Premium $

Expense Constant $

Countersigned by: ______________________

- Estimated annual premium to be charged

Underwriters should carefully complete the information page since much of the identifying information found on it is essential for the proper coverage to be provided.

Before Item 1, at the top of the information page, the name of the insurer and the policy number assigned by that insurer are shown. The insured's previous policy number (if with the same insurer) may also be shown here. The word "new" indicates that this is an insured who is new to this insurer. This space above Item 1 is also where the insured's interstate or intrastate risk identification number is usually shown. This number must be shown somewhere on the information page.

All insurers use their own systems for numbering policies. Policy numbers yield much information about the policy. Many policy numbers include indicators of the issuing office, the kind of coverage, the year of expiration, and the policyholder's account number.

**Item 1.** This item gives essential information about the insured including the following:

- Name and mailing address,
- The type of legal entity, whether an individual, partnership, corporation, or other, and
- Work places located elsewhere from insured's mailing address.

Also included in Item 1 are any additional identifying numbers such as the insured's federal employer's identification number for each entity included on the policy and identifying numbers that might be required by a certain state. In some cases these numbers might be shown only on the bureau's copy of the policy.

**Item 2.** Item 2 shows the period of coverage of the policy. The effective date *and hour* as well as the expiration date *and hour* are shown. Policy coverage begins and ends at 12:01 A.M. at the address of the insured given in Item 1. Since this time is standard within the industry for workers compensation policies, there can be no argument about which policy covers an injury if an accident occurs on a day when a policy from one company expires and the policy of another company takes over. Injuries from accidents occurring before 12:01 A.M. of the date of expiration would be covered by the expiring policy, and injuries occurring later would be covered by the new policy. Some insurers preprint the 12:01 A.M. on their information page.

**Item 3.** This item summarizes the coverage provided by the policy.

***Workers Compensation Insurance.*** This section of the information page indicates the states in which workers compensation coverage applies. Benefits required by the workers compensation law of the state or states shown in Item 3.A will be paid in the event of an injury to an employee. Thus, all states in which the insured conducts operations *and* in which the insurer is licensed to provide coverage should be listed in this space.

***Employers Liability Insurance.*** Item 3.B shows the limits of liability under employers liability coverage for bodily injury by accident and bodily injury by disease. The standard limits of liability are $100,000 for *each accident* for bodily injury by accident; $100,000 for *each employee* for bodily injury by disease; and $500,000 as a *policy limit* for bodily injury by disease. These limits are often abbreviated as $100/100/500.

***Other States Insurance.*** An entry in this space indicates that workers compensation coverage will be automatically extended to the additional states listed if the insured expands operations. States may be shown in Item 3.C by name or by a designation such as "all others except...." States listed in Item 3.A, monopolistic state fund states, and states where the insurer will not provide coverage (for example, a state where the insurer is not licensed) should *not* be included. Thus, the designation "all states except states listed in Item 3.A" would not be correct since that would imply that coverage is provided for the monopolistic state fund states. If an underwriter learns that the insured has operations in a state listed in Item 3.C, the state should be removed from Item 3.C and added to Item 3.A if the company agrees to continue the coverage.

***Endorsements and Schedules.*** All endorsements and schedules attached to the policy at inception are listed in this section. This subpart is the only one that may appear elsewhere on the information page.

**Item 4.** The information needed to calculate the estimated policy premium appears in Item 4. It includes the data identified in the following nine headings.

***Classifications.*** This section gives a description of the classification(s) assigned to the insured's business. This description is taken exactly from the appropriate workers compensation manual unless it is necessary to use an analogous classification to describe the operation. The abbreviated classification description (indicated by bold print capital letters in the manual) may be used.

***Classification Code Number.*** The four-digit code number corresponds to the classification description found in the manual unless it is necessary to use an analogous classification to describe the operation.

***Premium Basis—Total Estimated Annual Remuneration.*** This column contains the insured's estimate of what the payroll will be for the period covered by the policy. The estimated payrolls are shown beside their respective classifications.

***Rates.*** This column contains the rates applicable to the various classifications in the Classifications column. A different rate applies for each classification. The rate must be the one shown in the manual rate pages for the state or states covered by the policy unless an approved independent filing or rate deviation applies. Usually the rate is per $100 of remuneration.

***Estimated Annual Premium.*** This column contains the estimated premium determined by multiplying the estimated remuneration by the rates for each classification.

***Minimum Premium.*** The minimum premium is the lowest amount for which the policy will be issued. The minimum premium is usually established by the appropriate bureau. Each classification carries its own minimum premium, which is listed with rates in the state manual rate pages. Minimum premiums do not necessarily exist, however, in states allowing competitive rating.

***Total Estimated Annual Premium.*** Total estimated annual premium is the total of the individual estimated premiums shown in the column above it or on appropriate attached schedules. This total appears on all policies.

***Expense Constant.*** The expense constant is a charge that applies to every workers compensation policy. It is shown in the state rate pages. It covers expenses such as policy issuance, recording, and auditing costs. These expenses are common to all workers compensation policies regardless of the premium size. The expense constant is included in the minimum premium for each classification.

***Additional Information Shown in Item 4.*** In addition to the preceding items, there is information that may be shown (in some cases, which are noted below, the information *must* be shown) in Item 4. If the risk is subject to experience rating, the *experience rating modification factor* must be shown. If schedule rating is approved, the *schedule rating information* must be shown. If a *premium discount* applies, that may be shown in Item 4.

If the insured pays less than the total estimated annual premium at inception, the amount paid is referred to as the *deposit premium* and it may be shown in Item 4. Adjustments are then made at a later date.

Deposit premiums were originally required to be no less than 25 percent of the estimated annual premium. As the rate of inflation increased and as policyholders became more efficient cash managers, insurers faced competitive pressures to reduce this requirement. Insurers yielded to this pressure, and the deposit premium requirement was reduced to 1/12 and lower. In addition, under some cash flow arrangements, insurers have spread the payment of the annual premium over a much longer period. Under some of these plans the insurer will bill the policyholder in the first year for the expense and profit/contingency portion of the premium as well as the cost of losses paid in the first year. From that point, the insurer bills the policyholder for the losses paid (plus expenses) as they are paid.

Policies are sometimes written on an interim adjustment basis. In such cases the insurer might perform an audit or require the insured to report actual remuneration at the necessary monthly, quarterly, or semiannual intervals. The insurer then bills the insured based on the premium developed from this remuneration. A final billing is sent after the final audit is made following policy expiration. Item 4 may indicate the *premium adjustment intervals* that will be used. These interim adjustments were originally geared primarily to policyholders who had seasonal fluctuations in their operations and wanted billings to match the cycle of their operations. In times of high inflation, more and more insureds requested interim billings in order to avoid paying the entire premium at the inception of the policy.

Item 4 may also include taxes, past experience, cancellation of similar insurance, place and date of policy issuance, producer's name, countersignature information, and other related information. In some states some of this information may be required to be shown.

## Standard Provisions Workers Compensation and Employers Liability Insurance Policy Form (WC 00 00 00)

While the information page shows specific information about the insured, the standard provisions policy form contains the general terms of the policy contract. Although the coverage it provides differs only in minor ways from the 1954 version of the standard workmen's compensation and employers liability policy, the 1984 standard policy form uses simplified wording and completely rearranges the material. This rearrangement places all related provisions together in the same part, even though some provisions are repeated as a result. Exhibit 10-3 is the standard provisions policy form.

The standard provisions policy form includes a General Section and six parts. Part One, Part Two, and Part Three describe three types of coverage: workers compensation, employers liability, and other states insurance, respectively. The insured's duties in the event of a loss appear in Part Four. Part Five contains all the provisions relating to premium determination. Part Six lists the five conditions of the policy.

**General Section.** The General Section explains the nature of the policy and defines important terms.

**Exhibit 10-3**
Standard Policy Form*

**WORKERS COMPENSATION AND EMPLOYERS LIABILITY INSURANCE POLICY** **WC 00 00 00**

**Original Printing** Effective April 1, 1984 **Standard**

**WORKERS COMPENSATION AND EMPLOYERS LIABILITY INSURANCE POLICY**

In return for the payment of the premium and subject to all terms of this policy, we agree with you as follows.

**GENERAL SECTION**

A. **The Policy**

This policy includes at its effective date the Information Page and all endorsements and schedules listed there. It is a contract of insurance between you (the employer named in item 1 of the Information Page) and us (the insurer named on the Information Page). The only agreements relating to this insurance are stated in this policy. The terms of this policy may not be changed or waived except by endorsement issued by us to be part of this policy.

B. **Who Is Insured**

You are insured if you are an employer named in item 1 of the Information Page. If that

C. **Workers Compensation Law**

Workers Compensation Law means the workers or workmen's compensation law and occupational disease law of each state or territory named in item 3.A. of the Information Page. It includes any amendments to that law which are in effect during the policy period. It does not include the provisions of any law that provide nonoccupational disability benefits.

D. **State**

State means any state of the United States of America, and the District of Columbia.

E. **Locations**

This policy covers all of your workplaces listed

employer is a partnership, and if you are one of its partners, you are insured, but only in your capacity as an employer of the partnership's employees.

in items 1 or 4 of the Information Page; and it covers all other workplaces in item 3.A. states unless you have other insurance or are self-insured for such workplaces.

## PART ONE - WORKERS COMPENSATION INSURANCE

### A. How This Insurance Applies

This workers compensation insurance applies to bodily injury by accident or bodily injury by disease. Bodily injury includes resulting death.

1. Bodily injury by accident must occur during the policy period.
2. Bodily injury by disease must be caused or aggravated by the conditions of your employment. The employee's last day of last exposure to the conditions causing or aggravating such bodily injury by disease must occur during the policy period.

### B. We Will Pay

We will pay promptly when due the benefits required of you by the workers compensation law.

### C. We Will Defend

We have the right and duty to defend at our expense any claim, proceeding or suit against you for benefits payable by this insurance. We have the right to investigate and settle these claims, proceedings or suits.

We have no duty to defend a claim, proceeding or suit that is not covered by this insurance.

### D. We Will Also Pay

We will also pay these costs, in addition to other amounts payable under this insurance, as part of any claim, proceeding or suit we defend:

1. reasonable expenses incurred at our request, but not loss of earnings;
2. premiums for bonds to release attachments and for appeal bonds in bond amounts up to the amount payable under this insurance;
3. litigation costs taxed against you;
4. interest on a judgment as required by law until we offer the amount due under this insurance; and
5. expenses we incur.

E. **Other Insurance**

We will not pay more than our share of benefits and costs covered by this insurance and other insurance or self-insurance. Subject to any limits of liability that may apply, all shares will be equal until the loss is paid. If any insurance or self-insurance is exhausted, the shares of all remaining insurance will be equal until the loss is paid.

F. **Payments You Must Make**

You are responsible for any payments in excess of the benefits regularly provided by the workers compensation law including those required because:

1. of your serious and willful misconduct;
2. you knowingly employ an employee in violation of law;
3. you fail to comply with a health or safety law or regulation; or
4. you discharge, coerce or otherwise discriminate against any employee in violation of the workers compensation law.

If we make any payments in excess of the

H. **Statutory Provisions**

These statements apply where they are required by law.

1. As between an injured worker and us, we have notice of the injury when you have notice.
2. Your default or the bankruptcy or insolvency of you or your estate will not relieve us of our duties under this insurance after an injury occurs.
3. We are directly and primarily liable to any person entitled to the benefits payable by this insurance. Those persons may enforce our duties; so may an agency authorized by law. Enforcement may be against us or against you and us.
4. Jurisdiction over you is jurisdiction over us for purposes of the workers compensation law. We are bound by decisions against you under that law, subject to the provisions of this policy that are not in conflict with that law.
5. This insurance conforms to the parts of the workers compensation law that apply to:

benefits regularly provided by the workers compensation law on your behalf, you will reimburse us promptly.

G. **Recovery From Others**

We have your rights, and the rights of persons entitled to the benefits of this insurance, to recover our payments from anyone liable for the injury. You will do everything necessary to protect those rights for us and to help us enforce them.

a. benefits payable by this insurance;

b. special taxes, payments into security or other special funds, and assessments payable by us under that law.

6. Terms of this insurance that conflict with the workers compensation law are changed by this statement to conform to that law.

Nothing in these paragraphs relieves you of your duties under this policy.

## PART TWO - EMPLOYERS LIABILITY INSURANCE

A. **How This Insurance Applies**

This employers liability insurance applies to bodily injury by accident or bodily injury by disease. Bodily injury includes resulting death.

1. The bodily injury must arise out of and in the course of the injured employee's employment by you.
2. The employment must be necessary or incidental to your work in a state or territory listed in item 3.A. of the Information Page.
3. Bodily injury by accident must occur during the policy period.
4. Bodily injury by disease must be caused or aggravated by the conditions of your employment. The employee's last day of last exposure to the conditions causing or aggravating such bodily injury by disease must occur during the policy period.
5. If you are sued, the original suit and any related legal actions for damages for bodily injury by accident or by disease must be brought in the United States of America, its territories or possessions, or Canada.

**WORKERS COMPENSATION AND EMPLOYERS LIABILITY INSURANCE POLICY** **WC 00 00 00**

**Original Printing** Effective April 1, 1984 **Standard**

B. **We Will Pay**

We will pay all sums you legally must pay as damages because of bodily injury to your employees, provided the bodily injury is covered by this Employers Liability Insurance.

The damages we will pay, where recovery is permitted by law, include damages:

1. for which you are liable to a third party by reason of a claim or suit against you by that third party to recover the damages claimed against such third party as a result of injury to your employee;
2. for care and loss of services; and
3. for consequential bodily injury to a spouse, child, parent, brother or sister of the injured employee;

provided that these damages are the direct consequence of bodily injury that arises out of and in the course of the injured employee's employment by you; and

4. because of bodily injury to your employee that arises out of and in the course of employment, claimed against you in a capacity other than as employer.

7. damages arising out of the discharge of, coercion of, or discrimination against any employee in violation of law.

D. **We Will Defend**

We have the right and duty to defend, at our expense, any claim, proceeding or suit against you for damages payable by this insurance. We have the right to investigate and settle these claims, proceedings and suits.

We have no duty to defend a claim, proceeding or suit that is not covered by this insurance. We have no duty to defend or continue defending after we have paid our applicable limit of liability under this insurance.

E. **We Will Also Pay**

We will also pay these costs, in addition to other amounts payable under this insurance, as part of any claim, proceeding, or suit we defend:

1. reasonable expenses incurred at our request; but not loss of earnings;
2. premiums for bonds to release attachments and for appeal bonds in bond amounts up to the limit of our liability under this insurance;

C. **Exclusions**

This insurance does not cover:

1. liability assumed under a contract. This exclusion does not apply to a warranty that your work will be done in a workmanlike manner;
2. punitive or exemplary damages because of bodily injury to an employee employed in violation of law;
3. bodily injury to an employee while employed in violation of law with your actual knowledge or the actual knowledge of any of your executive officers;
4. any obligation imposed by a workers compensation, occupational disease, unemployment compensation, or disability benefits law, or any similar law;
5. bodily injury intentionally caused or aggravated by you;
6. bodily injury occurring outside the United States of America, its territories or possessions, and Canada. This exclusion does not apply to bodily injury to a citizen or resident of the United States of America or Canada who is temporarily outside these countries;

3. litigation costs taxed against you;
4. interest on a judgment as required by law until we offer the amount due under this insurance; and
5. expenses we incur.

F. **Other Insurance**

We will not pay more than our share of damages and costs covered by this insurance and other insurance or self-insurance. Subject to any limits of liability that apply, all shares will be equal until the loss is paid. If any insurance or self-insurance is exhausted, the shares of all remaining insurance and self-insurance will be equal until the loss is paid.

G. **Limits of Liability**

Our liability to pay for damages is limited. Our limits of liability are shown in item 3.B. of the Information Page. They apply as explained below.

1. Bodily Injury by Accident. The limit shown for "bodily injury by accident-each accident" is the most we will pay for all damages covered by this insurance because of bodily injury to one or more employees in any one accident.

A disease is not bodily injury by accident unless it results directly from bodily injury by accident.

2. Bodily Injury by Disease. The limit shown for "bodily injury by disease-policy limit" is the most we will pay for all damages covered by this insurance and arising out of bodily injury by disease, regardless of the number of employees who sustain bodily injury by disease. The limit shown for "bodily injury by disease-each employee" is the most we will pay for all damages because of bodily injury by disease to any one employee.

Bodily injury by disease does not include disease that results directly from a bodily injury by accident.

3. We will not pay any claims for damages after we have paid the applicable limit of our liability under this insurance.

H. **Recovery From Others**

We have your rights to recover our payment from anyone liable for an injury covered by this insurance. You will do everything necessary to protect those rights for us and to help us enforce them.

I. **Actions Against Us**

There will be no right of action against us under this insurance unless:

1. You have complied with all the terms of this policy; and
2. The amount you owe has been determined with our consent or by actual trial and final judgment.

This insurance does not give anyone the right to add us as a defendant in an action against you to determine your liability.

## PART THREE - OTHER STATES INSURANCE

A. **How This Insurance Applies**

1. This other states insurance applies only if

3. We will reimburse you for the benefits required by the workers compensation law of

one or more states are shown in item 3.C. of the Information Page.

2. If you begin work in any one of those states and are not insured or are not self-insured for such work, the policy will apply as though that state were listed in item 3.A. of the Information Page.

that state if we are not permitted to pay the benefits directly to persons entitled to them.

B. **Notice**

Tell us at once if you begin work in any state listed in item 3.C. of the Information Page.

## PART FOUR - YOUR DUTIES IF INJURY OCCURS

Tell us at once if injury occurs that may be covered by this policy. Your other duties are listed here.

1. Provide for immediate medical and other services required by the workers compensation law.
2. Give us or our agent the names and addresses of the injured persons and of witnesses, and other information we may need.
3. Promptly give us all notices, demands and legal papers related to the injury, claim, proceeding or suit.
4. Cooperate with us and assist us, as we may request, in the investigation, settlement or defense of any claim, proceeding or suit.
5. Do nothing after an injury occurs that would interfere with our right to recover from others.
6. Do not voluntarily make payments, assume obligations or incur expenses, except at your own cost.

## PART FIVE - PREMIUM

A. **Our Manuals**

All premium for this policy will be determined by our manuals of rules, rates, rating plans and classifications. We may change our manuals and apply the changes to this policy if authorized by law or a governmental agency regulating this insurance.

B. **Classifications**

Item 4 of the Information Page shows the rate and premium basis for certain business or work classifications. These classifications were assigned based on an estimate of the exposures you would have during the policy period. If your actual exposures are not properly described by those classifications, we will assign proper classifications, rates and premium basis by endorsement to this policy.

C. **Remuneration**

Premium for each work classification is determined by multiplying a rate times a premium basis. Remuneration is the most common premium basis. This premium basis includes payroll and all other remuneration paid or payable during the policy period for the services of:

1. all your officers and employees engaged in work covered by this policy; and
2. all other persons engaged in work that could make us liable under Part One (Workers Compensation Insurance) of this policy. If you do not have payroll records for these persons, the contract price for their services and materials may be used as the premium basis. This paragraph 2 will not ap-

the business and work covered by this policy. If the final premium is more than the premium you paid to us, you must pay us the balance. If it is less, we will refund the balance to you. The final premium will not be less than the highest minimum premium for the classifications covered by this policy.

If this policy is canceled, final premium will be determined in the following way unless our manuals provide otherwise.

1. If we cancel, final premium will be calculated pro rata based on the time this policy was in force. Final premium will not be less than the pro rata share of the minimum premium.
2. If you cancel, final premium will be more than pro rata; it will be based on the time this policy was in force, and increased by our short rate cancelation table and procedure. Final premium will not be less than the minimum premium.

F. **Records**

You will keep records of information needed to

ply if you give us proof that the employers of these persons lawfully secured their workers compensation obligations.

D. **Premium Payments**

You will pay all premium when due. You will pay the premium even if part or all of a workers compensation law is not valid.

E. **Final Premium**

The premium shown on the Information Page, schedules, and endorsements is an estimate. The final premium will be determined after this policy ends by using the actual, not the estimated, premium basis and the proper classifications and rates that lawfully apply to compute premium. You will provide us with copies of those records when we ask for them.

G. **Audit**

You will let us examine and audit all your records that relate to this policy. These records include ledgers, journals, registers, vouchers, contracts, tax reports, payroll and disbursement records, and programs for storing and retrieving data. We may conduct the audits during regular business hours during the policy period and within three years after the policy period ends. Information developed by audit will be used to determine final premium. Insurance rate service organizations have the same rights we have under this provision.

## PART SIX · CONDITIONS

A. **Inspection**

We have the right, but are not obliged to inspect your workplaces at any time. Our inspections are not safety inspections. They relate only to the insurability of the workplaces and the premiums to be charged. We may give you reports on the conditions we find. We may also recommend changes. While they may help reduce losses, we do not undertake to perform the duty of any person to provide for the health or safety of your employees or the public. We do not warrant that your workplaces are safe or healthful or that they comply with laws, regulations, codes or standards. Insurance rate service organizations have the same rights we have under this provision.

B. **Long Term Policy**

If the policy period is longer than one year and sixteen days, all provisions of this policy will apply as though a new policy were issued on each annual anniversary that this policy is in force.

WC 00 00 00 **WORKERS COMPENSATION AND EMPLOYERS LIABILITY INSURANCE POLICY**

**Standard** Effective April 1, 1984 **Original Printing**

C. **Transfer of Your Rights and Duties**

Your rights or duties under this policy may not be transferred without our written consent.

If you die and we receive notice within thirty days after your death, we will cover your legal representative as insured.

D. **Cancelation**

1. You may cancel this policy. You must mail or deliver advance written notice to us stating when the cancelation is to take effect.
2. We may cancel this policy. We must mail or deliver to you not less than ten days advance written notice stating when the cancelation is to take effect. Mailing that notice to you at your mailing address shown in item 1 of the Information Page will be sufficient to prove notice.
3. The policy period will end on the day and hour stated in the cancelation notice.
4. Any of these provisions that conflicts with a law that controls the cancelation of the insurance in this policy is changed by this statement to comply with that law.

E. **Sole Representative**

The insured first named in item 1 of the Information Page will act on behalf of all insureds to change this policy, receive return premium, and give or receive notice of cancelation.



*Reprinted with permission from the National Council on Compensation Insurance.

***The Policy.*** The first paragraph explains that the policy is a contract and that the parties are "you" (the insured) and "us" (the insurer). The complete contract consists of the standard provisions policy form, the information page, and all endorsements and schedules listed on the information page. Any changes in the terms of the policy must be by endorsement issued by the insurer.

***Who Is Insured.*** This paragraph identifies the named insureds under the policy. The insured is the employer named in Item 1 of the information page. The policy explicitly states that if that employer is a partnership, coverage applies to the partners only in their capacity as employer of that partnership's employees. Thus, if one of the partners is also involved in an enterprise other than that named in the policy, and that enterprise also has employees, there must be a separate workers compensation policy or self-insurance plan.

***Workers Compensation Law.*** Paragraph C of the General Section defines workers compensation law to mean "the workers or workmen's compensation law and occupational disease law of each state or territory named in Item 3.A of the information page." Any amendments in effect during the policy period are included, but any provisions of a statute that relate to nonoccupational disability benefits are not included within this definition. This definition is limited to state laws. The United States Longshore and Harbor Workers Compensation Act or other federal laws are not included.

***State.*** According to Paragraph D, the term "state" means any of the fifty states and the District of Columbia. Thus, territories are not included, and coverage applies in a United States territory only when Item 3.A of the information page explicitly names that territory.

***Locations.*** Covered locations are defined to include all workplaces listed in Items 1 or 4 of the information page and all of the insured's workplaces in states listed in Item 3.A unless other insurance or self-insurance applies. Workplaces covered by other insurance or self-insurance should be excluded by endorsement. This approach protects the policyholder in that an oversight in arranging the coverage would leave the insured with too much coverage rather than too little.

**Part One—Workers Compensation Insurance.** The coverage provided by Part One obligates the insurer to pay all benefits required of the insured by the workers compensation law. The policy provides automatic statewide coverage under the workers compensation law or occupational disease law of any state listed in Item 3.A of the information page. The employer automatically receives complete protection under that state's workers compensation law for all locations, operations, and employees within the scope of that designated state law even if they were not stated in the declarations, were undisclosed to the insurer, or were unanticipated at the inception of the policy. Thus, the coverages provided and any ensuing claims for such operations will be covered even if the premium for the additional operations has not yet been paid. The one exception involves those operations of the employer otherwise insured or specifically excluded by endorsement.

This coverage pays the benefits of any designated state without territorial limitation beyond that imposed by the compensation law itself. For example, the Indiana Workers Compensation Act, like many others, is extraterritorial; that is, it covers injuries sustained within Indiana and elsewhere without restriction as long as it is an Indiana employee who is involved. Thus, an Indiana employee injured in the course of employment in Georgia would be covered for Indiana benefits. The policy would provide the Indiana benefits even though Georgia was not listed on the policy. Most states limit this protection to employees temporarily outside the state.

Nearly every workers compensation law contains a provision that makes the principal employer liable for workers compensation benefits for employees of a contractor or subcontractor who performs work for the principal and does not insure its employees under the workers compensation act. Since the insurer assumes all of the insured's liability under a designated workers compensation law, it would have to pay compensation benefits to the employee of an uninsured contractors or subcontractors.

Each paragraph in Part One emphasizes the major concepts involved in this coverage.

***How This Insurance Applies.*** The coverage applies to bodily injury by accident and disease. Bodily injury includes resulting death. The accident must occur during the policy period; the last day of last exposure to disease in the employment of the insured must occur during the policy period. The bodily injury by disease must be caused or aggravated by the conditions of employment. These stipulations clarify which policy applies when injuries arise out of and in the course of employment by more than one employer. This method is required by law in many states.

***We Will Pay.*** The insurer will pay "the benefits required" by the workers compensation law. This term is broad enough to include both compensation and medical benefits. The policy shows no dollar limit for these benefits since any applicable limits would be those delineated by the law itself.

***We Will Defend.*** This paragraph establishes the insurer's right and duty to defend claims covered by the policy, and it disclaims any duty to defend a claim not covered.

***We Will Also Pay.*** The insurer also agrees to pay additional costs, such as the expense of investigating a claim and litigation costs, that are listed.

***Other Insurance.*** This insurance, other insurance, and self-insurance contribute by equal shares to a loss covered by this insurance.

***Payments You Must Make.*** The workers compensation laws of a number of states include special provisions relating to illegal employment. Such illegal employment usually consists of the employment of minors in hazardous occupations, often involving the use of power machinery. When an illegally employed person is injured in the course of employment, some states provide for additional compensation or for double or triple benefits. Similarly, the law may impose such penalties in cases of discrimination or violations of health and safety laws. This paragraph provides that the insured will reimburse the insurer for any such *excess* benefits required under a workers compensation law because of (1) willful misconduct, (2) illegal employment, (3) failure to comply with health and safety laws and regulations, and (4) discrimination against employees claiming workers compensation benefits.

***Recovery from Others.*** The usual subrogation rights allowed by law are reaffirmed in this paragraph. When the insurer pays compensation or employers liability benefits on behalf of an insured, any right of recovery the insured or the injured employee may have against a third party becomes the right of the insurer. The insurer may then attempt to recover from the responsible third party. Any recovery in excess of actual payments and expenses will usually go to the injured employee.

***Statutory Provisions.*** This paragraph incorporates legal requirements making workers compensation coverage the direct obligation of the insuring company to any injured employee or, in the event of death, to the employee's dependents. Since the contract is made primarily for the benefit of employees and their dependents, they have a direct right of action against the insurance company and are, in effect, insureds under the policy much as if specifically named.

For the protection of the employee, a notice to the employer of an injury is presumed to be notice to the insurance company, insofar as any obligation rests upon the injured party, and the knowledge of the employer is held to be the knowledge of the insurer. In addition, a default by the employer in the payment of the premium after an accident will not jeopardize the position of the employee. Failure to give the company the notice required by the policy does not deprive the employee of the right to compensation; nor does debt, insolvency, bankruptcy, legal incapacity, or inability of the employer deprive the employee of that right. The placing of the employer's business in the hands of an executive, receiver, trustee, assignee, or other person does not in any way affect the insurer's responsibility to the insured's employees. The insurer is bound by all the findings or judgments rendered against the employer. All workers compensation laws covered by the policy become a part of the contract just as if they were written into the policy, and employees have the rights to compensation defined by those laws. If there is any conflict between the policy and the applicable workers compensation law, the policy terms change to conform to the law. Thus, the policy is automatically amended when there are changes in the law.

There are no exclusions in Part One. The exclusion of domestic, farm, or agricultural employments in the 1954 policy conflicted with the law of some states. The 1984 policy automatically provides coverage for these employments and excludes it by endorsement when necessary.

**Part Two—Employers Liability Insurance.** Part Two of the policy covers employers for their legal liability to an employee for injury arising out of and in the course of employment and not covered under the workers compensation law. While the coverage of the compensation laws is extensive, it is possible that the employer could have some legal responsibility to injured employees not addressed by workers compensation laws. For example, casual laborers might not be eligible for workers compensation benefits, but they may hold the employer liable for job-related injuries. Whereas benefits under Part One are paid without regard to fault, workers not entitled to the protection of the workers compensation law must prove the employer's liability for an injury to collect any damages. Under Part Two the insurer protects employers against suits brought by employees who have alleged that they sustained injury or contracted disease as a result of the employers' negligence.

***How This Insurance Applies.*** Coverage applies to bodily injury by accident and by disease. As in Part One and the remainder of the policy (including endorsements), bodily injury includes resulting death. The bodily injury must arise out of and in the course of employment. As in Part One, the accident must occur during the policy period, and bodily injury by disease must be caused or aggravated by employment conditions. The last day of last exposure to the injurious conditions must occur during the policy period. Coverage applies only to employment necessary or incidental to operations in states listed in Item 3.A of the information page. Suits for damages must be brought in the United States, its territories or possessions, or Canada.

***We Will Pay.*** This paragraph obligates the insurer to pay damages for bodily injury to an employee of the insured. These damages include, but are not limited to, third-party-over claims, care and loss of services, consequential injuries, and dual capacity claims.

*Third-party-over claims* have become more frequent in recent years, particularly with respect to products liability. The impetus for such claims is an employee who is injured by the negligence of another third party. In addition to the workers compensation benefits, the injured employee may sue the third party for damages. However, the third party may then contend that the accident was caused by some negligence of the employer and sue the employer on the grounds of this negligence. For example, a contractor's employee is digging a ditch to connect utility lines, and the employee's pick cracks the gas main. The gas company is notified to come and repair the leak but is slow in responding. As a result, gas concentrates, explodes, and one of the employees is injured. The employee sues the gas company, claiming it was negligent, and receives a $100,000 judgment. The gas company, in turn, sues the contractor for the $100,000 plus expenses by establishing that the contractor's negligence allowed the employee to break the gas main, thus causing the accident. The resulting loss would be covered by the contractor's employers liability coverage subject to the limits of liability.

*Care and loss of services* includes loss of consortium. *Consortium* is a husband's or wife's exclusive right to the services of the spouse and to his or her society, companionship, and conjugal affection. Loss of consortium is regarded as actionable in many states, and the spouses of injured employees have often been successful in winning substantial damages from employers in cases of this kind.

Consequential injury and dual capacity claims are recent developments in the common law. A claim for *consequential injury* occurs if a member of the worker's family suffers bodily injury solely because the worker is injured. For example, the children of an injured employee may visit their parent in the hospital. As a result of seeing how seriously injured their parent is, the children may actually become physically ill.

In some states, claims against employers have been allowed under the theory or doctrine of *dual capacity.* According to this doctrine, the workers compensation law (in trying to be the exclusive remedy for work-related accidents) only excludes suits against employers in their capacity as an employer. If the employer is also the manufacturer of the product that caused the injury, the employee can collect workers compensation benefits and the employer/manufacturer can then be sued by the employee in its capacity as a manufacturer. Some employers are also the landowner and may be sued as a landowner by the employee even if the employee has already collected under workers compensation for the work-related injury.

***Exclusions.*** Part Two contains seven exclusions, which prevent overlapping coverage with other forms of insurance and eliminate coverage not intended by the insurer.

1. Liability assumed under a contract with a third party is excluded since it is more appropriately covered by a general liability policy.
2. Punitive or exemplary damages for injury or death of any illegally employed person are excluded.
3. Employers liability coverage is also excluded for employees employed in violation of the law with the knowledge of the insured or any executive officers of the insured.
4. Since Part Two coverage is broad in scope, it should not be applied to any exposure that is appropriately treated within Part One. The two coverages are separated by providing that Part Two excludes any obligation imposed by a workers compensation, occupational disease, unemployment compensation, or disability benefits law or any similar law. For example, X, a manufacturer whose main plant is in Illinois, sells a machine to an Ohio firm and agrees to install the machine in the Ohio plant. X sends a crew from Illinois to make the installation and also employs a number of Ohio workers to assist. However, X fails to obtain workers compensation coverage from the monopolistic Ohio state fund. One of the Ohio workers sustains injury, and the Ohio Industrial Commission orders X to pay benefits required by the Ohio Workers Compensation Act. In this case the law of the state of Ohio would be considered to be a workers compensation or occupational disease law, and there would therefore be no coverage under Part Two of the policy. Since Ohio is a monopolistic state, the insured would also not have Part One coverage under the policy. Even with other states insurance, coverage would not extend to the monopolistic state.
5. Intentional bodily injury is excluded.
6. Coverage is restricted to the United States, its territories or possessions, and Canada (except for citizens and residents of the United States or Canada who are temporarily outside these countries).
7. The final exclusion applies to injury arising out of wrongful discharge from employment, to coercion, and to discrimination in violation of law. A mandatory endorsement, *employers liability insurance endorsement* (WC 00 03 16), to the standard workers compensation and employers liability insurance policy was issued in 1988 to clarify this exclusion. The

endorsement specifies that coverage does not apply to "damages arising out of coercion, criticism, demotion, evaluation, reassignment, discipline, defamation, harassment, humiliation, discrimination against or termination of any employee, or any personnel practices, policies, acts, or omissions." This exclusion is necessary because Part One includes a reimbursement provision that applies to excess benefits payable if the insured discharges, coerces, or discriminates against an employee in violation of the workers compensation law. If Part Two did not include a similar exclusion, some people might erroneously assume that it would cover these injuries.

***We Will Defend.*** The insurer's right and duty to defend the insured are stated in this section. This provision expressly disclaims defense of claims not covered and defense of claims after the limits of liability have been exhausted.

***We Will Also Pay.*** This paragraph is identical to the provision in Part One specifying the additional costs of defense assumed by the insurer.

***Other Insurance.*** As in Part One, the other-insurance provision calls for contribution by equal shares. If more than one insurance policy or self-insurance plan applies, each insurer (or self-insurer) contributes equally with every other insurer until the loss is paid or the insurance is exhausted.

***Limits of Liability.*** Separate limits of liability for accident and disease are shown on the information page and are explained in this section. Disease limits include a policy aggregate and a limit per-employee. The terms "bodily injury by accident" and "bodily injury by disease" are defined in this section and are defined to be mutually exclusive. This prevents two sets of limits (one for accident and one for disease) from applying to the same loss. The standard limits of liability mentioned earlier in the description of the information page are $100/100/500. These limits can be increased using the percentage factors found in the National Council *Basic Manual.* The increase in premium is equal to the percentage shown in the manual multiplied by the total premium and subject to the minimum also shown in the manual. Exhibit 10-4 shows these percentages for various levels of increased limits of liability.

***Recovery From Others.*** The same paragraph that explains the insurer's subrogation under Part One is repeated under Part Two.

***Actions Against Us.*** This provision stipulates that the insured has no right of action against the insurer under Part Two unless the insured has complied with all the terms of the policy and the amount of the insured's obligation has been established.

**Exhibit 10-4**
Table for Increased Limits—Employers Liability Insurance*

| Limits of Liability (000 omitted) | Percentage | Minimum Premium for Increased Limits |
|---|---|---|
| $100/100/1,000 | .70% | $150.00 |
| 100/100/2,500 | 1.20% | 200.00 |
| 100/100/5,000 | 1.70% | 250.00 |
| 100/100/10,000 | 2.40% | 300.00 |
| 500/500/500 | 1.90% | 100.00 |
| 500/500/1,000 | 2.20% | 150.00 |
| 500/500/2,500 | 2.70% | 200.00 |
| 500/500/5,000 | 3.20% | 250.00 |
| 500/500/10,000 | 3.90% | 300.00 |
| 1,000/1,000/1,000 | 3.30% | 150.00 |
| 1,000/1,000/2,500 | 3.80% | 200.00 |
| 1,000/1,000/5,000 | 4.40% | 250.00 |
| 1,000/1,000/10,000 | 5.00% | 300.00 |

*Adapted with permission from the National Council on Compensation Insurance, *Basic Manual for Workers Compensation* and *Employers Liability Insurance*, 2nd reprint, p. R-18.

**Part Three—Other States Insurance.** Some insureds require additional workers compensation coverage for contingencies such as when an employer may expand operations into states unknown at the time the policy is issued. The 1954 workers compensation policy met that need with the addition of a *broad form all states endorsement.* The 1984 policy uses the more appropriate name, other states insurance, for this coverage and incorporates it within the standard provisions policy form as Part Three. It is activated by making an appropriate entry on the information page. Such coverage applies neither in the monopolistic fund states of Nevada, North Dakota, Ohio, Washington, West Virginia, and Wyoming, nor in any other states where the insurer is not licensed to write workers compensation insurance.

***How This Insurance Applies.*** As Part Three explains, other states insurance applies only if Item 3.C of the information page lists one or more states. That entry designates the states where this coverage applies either by specifically listing them or by referring to them as "all states except..." followed by the names of those states where the insurer cannot or does not wish to provide coverage. If a state is designated in Item 3.C and the insured begins operations in that state, the policy provides the same coverage as if that state were listed in Item 3.A.

***Notice.*** The policy informs the insured to "tell us at once if you begin work in any state listed in item 3.C of the information page." Since insureds may not always remember to give such notice whenever Part Three coverage applies, underwriters should be alert for such states appearing on premium audit reports. The appropriate state filings must be made if required, and the renewal updated. If there is separate workers compensation coverage in an additional state, the appropriate exclusion endorsement can be attached to the policy excluding this work and/or state.

**Part Four—Your Duties If Injury Occurs.** Part Four explains the policy conditions relating to the duties of the insured. These conditions obligate the insured to give prompt notice of injury, claims, or suit to the insurer not only to protect the insured's own rights, but to give the insurer a chance to identify and investigate claims or suits to protect its rights. Part Four also requires that the insured cooperate with the insurer and that the insured attend hearings and trials at the request of the insurer. The insured shall also help in the securing of witnesses. The insured cannot, except at his or her own expense, voluntarily make any payment, assume any obligation, or incur any expenses except for the immediate medical and other services at the time of injury as required by the workers compensation law. The insured also cannot do anything after the injury occurs to interfere with the insurer's right of recovery from others.

The failure of the insured to comply with one or more of the policy conditions will *not* relieve the insurer of its responsibilities to the injured employee or the survivors of the deceased employee under the workers compensation law. The purpose of the law is to protect the injured employee, and any denial of coverage would defeat that purpose. In addition, the insurer does not reserve the right to be reimbursed by the insured in these cases.

**Part Five—Premium.** Part Five of the standard provisions policy form explains how the premium is determined. Since workers compensation and employers liability insurance premiums are determined by manual rules, a single sentence incorporating the manuals into the policy contract by reference would suffice. Insureds, however, rarely see the manuals, and to be bound by unfamiliar documents is not comforting. Part Five provides a simple explanation of premium determination procedures.

***Our Manuals.*** This paragraph establishes the role of company manuals in determining premiums and stipulates that the manuals and the premium may change during the policy period.

***Classifications.*** This paragraph introduces the concept of classification. More importantly, it tells the insured that the classifications and rates shown on the information page may change if they do not accurately describe the work covered by the policy.

***Remuneration.*** Remuneration as a premium basis is described in this section. As the policy stresses, included is the remuneration of the insured's employees and executive officers and of employees of uninsured contractors and subcontractors.

***Premium Payments.*** According to this paragraph, the insured is responsible for the payment of all premium when due.

***Final Premium.*** This provision tells the insured how the final premium is determined. It explains why the final premium may be different from the estimated premium. It also shows how the premium will be determined on cancellation of the policy.

***Records.*** This paragraph obligates the insured to keep records of information needed to compute premium and to provide them when requested.

***Audit.*** This provision explains the insurer's right to examine and audit the insured's records during business hours at any time during the policy period and within three years after expiration insofar as such records relate to the policy. It also states that rate service organizations have the same rights.

**Part Six—Conditions.** The remaining conditions of the policy, further limiting or defining the rights and obligations of the parties to the insurance contract, appear in Part Six.

***Inspection.*** This condition gives the insurer permission to inspect a policyholder's workplaces and operations. These inspections enable the insurer to determine that safe practices are in use and proper precautions are taken for the safety of employees and visitors.

Although this condition states that the insurer is permitted to inspect workplaces, the policy does not oblige the insurer to perform inspections. When such services are performed, however, the policy indicates that this does not constitute an undertaking to *warrant* that any workplaces, operations, machinery, or equipment inspected are safe or healthful.

***Long-Term Policy.*** If the policy is written for more than one year, each year is considered to be separate as far as policy provisions are concerned, and premium is computed in accordance with the manual rules and rates in effect for that year. An exception is a three-year fixed-rate policy, which would carry an endorsement modifying this provision.

***Transfer of Your Rights and Duties.*** Although it is possible to transfer or assign the policy to cover a new interest if the insurer consents in writing, it is generally preferable that a new policy be issued and the old policy canceled. This provision also clarifies the extension of coverage to the insured's legal representative in the event of death of the insured.

***Cancellation.*** Cancellation of the policy is generally permitted; however, some compensation laws restrict the insurer's right of cancellation. This condition outlines the cancellation right of the insurer and insured and would be subject in all cases to any requirements of the workers compensation law. In general, the insured may cancel the policy by mailing or delivering to the company a *written notice* that states when the cancellation shall be effective. The insurance company may cancel the policy by mailing or delivering to the insured a written notice stating when such cancellation shall be effective. The policy expressly stipulates that the insurer's cancellation cannot occur less than ten days after delivery of the notice.

In essence, it is possible for the insured to cancel the policy virtually without any notice. The insurer, however, must provide at least ten days' notice before its cancellation becomes effective. The reason for this provision is to permit the insured time to obtain a new policy. Upon cancellation, premium adjustment should be made as soon as possible (some states set limits) in accordance with cancellation provisions. Many states also require that the workers compensation agency be notified of the cancellation.

***Sole Representative.*** This condition was added to the new policy to identify the specific insured, under a multi-employer policy, who is authorized to act on behalf of the other insureds. When there is more than one insured, the sole representative is the insured first named in Item 1.

## Endorsements

Despite the flexibility offered by the standard workers compensation policy, a number of situations require standard policy provisions to be modified. These modifications may be accomplished by adding an appropriate endorsement to the policy. Standard endorsement forms have been developed to meet certain special situations in the most convenient manner. An endorsement forms part of an insurance contract amending the provisions of the policy to which it is attached. Endorsements may be attached to the policy from the beginning, or they may be added at any time during the policy period.

Standard endorsements to workers compensation policies are

primarily of two types: (1) those that extend or limit the coverage provided and (2) those that incorporate special provisions affecting the determination of premiums.

A six-digit numbering system identifies specific workers compensation endorsements. The *experience rating modification factor endorsement,* for example, is WC 00 04 03. The WC establishes that the endorsement applies to workers compensation and employers liability insurance. The first two digits refer to the applicable state, 00 indicating that the endorsement applies countrywide. Other endorsements may use a two-digit state code or "89" for miscellaneous endorsements, notices, and related transactions. A "99" indicates a company-specific endorsement. The middle two digits indicate the different types of endorsements as follows:

01—Federal coverages and exclusions
02—Maritime coverages and exclusions
03—Other coverages and exclusions
04—Premium endorsements
05—Retrospective premium endorsements
06—Miscellaneous endorsements

Whenever relevant, the endorsement heading includes the word coverage or exclusion. The last two digits indicate the sequence within each of these six general categories.

**Modifications of Coverage.** Endorsements modifying coverage either add forms of coverage to the standard policy or exclude certain coverages that the insured does not need or has insured elsewhere. Some of the more common coverage and exclusion endorsements are described here.

***Voluntary Compensation and Employers Liability Coverage Endorsement (WC 00 03 11).*** As mentioned, the workers compensation laws of most states exempt some types of employment from statutory workers compensation benefits. The most commonly exempted occupations are farm labor, domestic employment, and casual labor. In some cases the law does not apply to employers with fewer than a certain minimum number of employees. The workers compensation laws of some states do not apply to partners or sole proprietors. Even when such persons are not entitled to workers compensation benefits by law, the same benefits may be voluntarily extended to them by the insurer and employer in two ways:

1. By complying with all the provisions of the law including any required notification and filings and adding the appropriate classification to the policy. No further endorsement is required in this case. This procedure actually brings the exempted

employees within the provisions of the workers compensation law. This is permitted in most states.
2. By using the voluntary compensation endorsement, which adds an entirely different coverage to the policy.

A sample voluntary compensation endorsement appears in Exhibit 10-5. The voluntary compensation endorsement amends the standard policy to include an additional coverage called *voluntary compensation.* The additional coverage *does not* make employees subject to the workers compensation law, but it obligates the insuring company to pay on behalf of the insured an amount equal to the compensation and other benefits that would have been payable to such employees if they were subject to the workers compensation law designated in the endorsement.

The endorsement states certain conditions that must be met *by the persons entitled to the benefits* before the insurer will pay (or will continue to pay). These include a written release of responsibility, transfer of the right of recovery from the responsible parties, and cooperation with the insurer. If the party claims damages in a lawsuit, the duty of the insurer to pay the voluntary compensation benefits ceases, and employers liability coverage applies. Paragraph F of the voluntary compensation endorsement extends employers liability insurance to bodily injury covered by the endorsement in the states shown under "State of Employment" in the "Schedule" appearing on the endorsement. The insurer will defend the insured against the employee's suit and pay any settlement awarded subject to the stipulated limits of liability on the information page.

*Payroll.* The insured must segregate the payroll of employees covered under the voluntary compensation endorsement because such payroll must be shown separately.

*Rates.* The rates for voluntary compensation coverage may be shown under "Designated Workers Compensation Law" in the voluntary compensation endorsement schedule, or they may be shown on the information page. The manual stipulates that the rates charged should be those for the state shown under "Designated Workers Compensation Law."

*Limits of Liability.* Item 3.B on the information page designates the limits that apply for the employers liability portion of this coverage. If limits higher than the standard limits are desired, it is necessary to adjust the workers compensation rates. Rule VIII-B.3 of the *Basic Manual* includes a table (different from that in Exhibit 10-4) showing the proper adjustment for various limits. This adjustment is in addition to the adjustment described earlier to reflect the increased limits for the employees liability coverage.

**Exhibit 10-5**
Voluntary Compensation and Employers Liability Coverage Endorsement*

**WORKERS COMPENSATION AND EMPLOYERS LIABILITY INSURANCE POLICY** **WC 00 03 11**

**1st Reprint** Effective April 1, 1984 **Standard**

**VOLUNTARY COMPENSATION AND EMPLOYERS LIABILITY COVERAGE ENDORSEMENT**

This endorsement adds Voluntary Compensation Insurance to the policy.

A. **How This Insurance Applies**

This insurance applies to bodily injury by accident or bodily injury by disease. Bodily injury includes resulting death.

1. The bodily injury must be sustained by an employee included in the group of employees described in the Schedule.
2. The bodily injury must occur in the course of employment necessary or incidental to work in a state listed in the Schedule.
3. The bodily injury must occur in the United States of America, its territories or possessions, or Canada, and may occur elsewhere if the employee is a United States or Canadian citizen temporarily away from those places.
4. Bodily injury by accident must occur during the policy period.
5. Bodily injury by disease must be caused or aggravated by the conditions of your employment. The employee's last day of last exposure to the conditions causing or aggravating such bodily injury by disease must occur during the policy period.

B. **We Will Pay**

We will pay an amount equal to the benefits that would be required of you if you and your employees described in the Schedule were subject to the workers compensation law shown in the Schedule. We will pay those amounts to the persons who would be entitled to them under the law.

C. **Exclusions**

This insurance does not cover:

1. any obligation imposed by a workers compensation or occupational disease law, or any similar law.
2. bodily injury intentionally caused or aggravated by you.

D. **Before We Pay**

Before we pay benefits to the persons entitled to them, they must:

1. release you and us, in writing, of all responsibility for the injury or death.
2. transfer to us their right to recover from others who may be responsible for the injury or death.
3. cooperate with us and do everything necessary to enable us to enforce the right to recover from others.

If the persons entitled to the benefits of this insurance fail to do those things, our duty to pay ends at once. If they claim damages from you or from us for the injury or death, our duty to pay ends at once.

E. **Recovery From Others**

If we make a recovery from others, we will keep an amount equal to our expenses of recovery and the benefits we paid. We will pay the balance to the persons entitled to it. If the persons entitled to the benefits of this insurance make a recovery from others, they must reimburse us for the benefits we paid them.

**WC 00 03 11** **WORKERS COMPENSATION AND EMPLOYERS LIABILITY INSURANCE POLICY**

**Standard** Effective April 1, 1984 **1st Reprint**

F. **Employers Liability Insurance**

Part Two (Employers Liability Insurance) applies to bodily injury covered by this endorsement as though the State of employment shown in the Schedule were shown in Item 3.A. of the Information Page.

Schedule

| Employees | State of Employment | Designated Workers Compensation Law |
|---|---|---|
| | | |

**Notes:**

1. Use this endorsement to afford voluntary compensation coverage pursuant to Rules II and VIII of the Basic Manual.
2. Use Voluntary Compensation Maritime Endorsement to provide Voluntary Compensation Coverage under Program II of Manual Rule XIII.
3. Work in a monopolistic state fund state should not be included in the Schedule unless employers liability coverage is provided in that state by the Employers Liability Coverage Endorsement.
4. Various uses of this endorsement are illustrated below.

Schedule

| Employees | State of Employment | Designated Workers Compensation Law |
|---|---|---|
| All officers and employees not subject to the Workers Compensation Law. | Any state shown in Item 3.A. of the Information Page | The state where the injury takes place. |
| All domestics, farm and agricultural workers. | Utah | Utah |
| All partners of the insured partnership. | Kansas | Kansas |

***Employers Liability Coverage Endorsement (WC 00 03 03).*** This endorsement is attached to a policy to provide only employers liability coverage in any state, including a monopolistic state fund state, if the insurer is permitted to write such coverage in the state. The endorsement is shown in Exhibit 10-6. When added to a workers compensation policy, the *employers liability coverage endorsement* deletes workers compensation coverage for the state(s) designated in the schedule on the endorsement. For the state named in the schedule, the endorsement converts the policy strictly to employers liability coverage. This coverage applies not only to operations in states designated in the endorsement, but also to operations necessary or incidental thereto. Coverage also applies on a worldwide basis with respect to employees who are citizens or residents of the United States and Canada, and who are temporarily outside these countries and involved in operations necessary or incidental to work in the state named in the schedule.

Although the standard limit of liability is $100/100/500, it can be increased. The premium for the increased limits is calculated according to Rule VIII-B.3 in the same manner and using the same table as for voluntary compensation coverage.

***Contingent Employers Liability—Stopgap Endorsement.*** In certain situations the insurance provided by a monopolistic state fund might not provide coverage in the event of a claim. This endorsement may be added to either a workers compensation or general liability policy to close the gap in coverage. The coverage provided is basically that provided by the employers liability portion of a standard workers compensation and employers liability policy.

When a state fund provides workers compensation insurance, there is no question regarding coverage for injuries to employees if they occur within the state and the employee is regularly employed in that state. However, there may be a question of coverage when the following are true:

- The employee is temporarily engaged in operations in other states.
- The injuries do not come within the scope of the particular law.

In the first situation, compensation coverage is extended by the extraterritorial feature of the Nevada, North Dakota, Ohio, West Virginia, and Wyoming laws. The North Dakota and West Virginia acts restrict the extraterritorial coverage to operations incidental to employment within the state. The Washington law is extraterritorial only regarding federal lands or property within the boundaries of the state of Washington. The stopgap endorsement provides extraterritorial coverage if the state law does not.

When the state fund insurance does not cover an injury because it is not work-related within the scope of the law, the injured employee may still attempt to hold the employer liable for the injury. Even if the claim is groundless, the employer may need employers liability coverage to defend against the claim. The coverage may be provided by private insurers in all states, including those with monopolistic state funds, by means of a stopgap endorsement. Individual insurers usually develop their own forms and rates for stopgap coverage.

***Exclusion Endorsements.*** The workers compensation laws of several states allow executive officers to elect not to have the protection of the law, in which case the *partners, officers and others exclusion endorsement* (WC 00 03 08) can designate individuals not covered by the policy. Thus, their remuneration is not included in the premium base. Similarly, certain jobs or locations can be excluded from the policy coverage by the *designated workplaces exclusion endorsement* (WC 00 03 02) if the relevant state law allows. The underwriter should be assured that employees working on that job or at that job site somehow have coverage provided.

**Premium-Related Endorsements.** In addition to endorsements modifying coverage, there are also endorsements that affect the premium even though the coverage remains the same. Several endorsements of this type are explained in the following pages.

***Anniversary Rating Date Endorsement (WC 00 04 02).*** This endorsement, shown in Exhibit 10-7, is used whenever the *anniversary rating date* differs from the effective date of the policy. If a policy is canceled and rewritten, the new policy, whether issued by the same insurer or another, must carry the classifications and rates applicable on the canceled policy until the normal anniversary date of the canceled policy. Even in most of the states allowing rate deviations, the new policy must carry the rates that applied for that insurer at the original policy inception date until the normal anniversary date. This anniversary rating date requirement promotes uniformity in statistical reporting.

For example, suppose an insurer writes a policy for the period 1 June 1989, to 1 June 1990 using rates effective on 1 October 1988 (latest rates effective on or prior to the inception date of the policy). The policy is canceled on 1 November 1989. An endorsement like the one in Exhibit 10-7 should be attached to the new policy. Rates effective 1 October 1988 will be used from inception date to the normal anniversary rating date, 1 June 1990. After the anniversary rating date, the latest rates in effect on or prior to the anniversary rating date will be

**Exhibit 10-6**
Employers Liability Coverage Endorsement*

**WORKERS COMPENSATION AND EMPLOYERS LIABILITY INSURANCE POLICY** **WC 00 03 03 A**

**1st Reprint** Issued January 10, 1986 **Advisory**

---

**EMPLOYERS LIABILITY COVERAGE ENDORSEMENT**

This endorsement applies only to work in the states shown in the Schedule.

A. Part One (Workers Compensation Insurance) does not apply to work in a state shown in the Schedule.

B. Part Two (Employers Liability Insurance) applies to work in states shown in the Schedule as though they were shown in Item 3.A. of the Information Page.

C. Part Two (Employers Liability Insurance), C. Exclusions is changed by adding these exclusions.

This insurance does not cover:

8. bodily injury to a master or member of the crew of any vessel;
9. bodily injury to any person in work subject to the Longshore and Harbor Workers' Compensation Act (33 USC Sections 901-950), the Federal Coal Mine Health and Safety Act of 1969 (30 USC Sections 931-942) or the Federal Employers' Liability Act (45 USC Sections 51-60), or any amendment to those laws;
10. bodily injury to any member of the flying crew of any aircraft;
11. bodily injury to an employee when you are deprived of common law defenses or are subject to penalty because of your failure to secure your obligations under the workers compensation law of any state shown in the Schedule or otherwise fail to comply with that law.

Schedule

States

**Notes:**

1. Use this endorsement to afford employers liability insurance in any state, including monopolistic state fund states with the exception of Ohio, where the policy does not provide workers compensation insurance. The states are to be listed in the Schedule. Use the Ohio Employers Liability Coverage Endorsement (WC 34 03 01) to afford employers liability insurance in Ohio.

2. The endorsement may be used in a National Council state only if (1) all employees are excluded from the workers compensation law or all employees have elected not to be subject to the law, and (2) there is no state law or regulation making the use of this endorsement illegal. (See Rule II-B-5 of the Basic Manual.)

used. A rate change effective 1 October 1989 would apply for coverage after the anniversary rating date.

*Wrap-up policies,* which cover all subcontractors for the duration of a single job, generally involve the anniversary rating date provisions. The exposure on all such policies must be split before and after the anniversary rating date.

***Experience Rating Modification Factor Endorsement (WC 00 04 03).*** This endorsement is designed to be attached to an experience-rated policy issued before the modification is published. The endorsement, shown in Exhibit 10-8, states that the policy is subject to an experience modification and that it will be endorsed onto the policy when it becomes available.

Unfortunately, modifications have not always been available at the policy effective date (or the anniversary rating date). The premium or loss information needed to calculate the modification has often not been made available to the bureau. In those cases, endorsement WC 00 04 03 is attached to the policy, and the policy is endorsed when the modification becomes available regardless of its effect on premiums.

***Contingent Experience Rating Modification Factor Endorsement (WC 00 04 12).*** Because of the concern about the hardship placed on insureds when the modification results in a substantial additional premium late in the policy period, NCCI revised the *Basic Manual* in January 1990 so that an experience rating modification that results in a premium increase *and* that becomes available more than ninety days past the policy effective date can only be applied prospectively to the remaining portion of the policy period. That is, the policy cannot be endorsed as of its effective date. However, if the experience rating modification results in a premium decrease, the policy should be endorsed as of the effective date. At that same time, NCCI introduced a contingent rating for most risks based on the information available at inception. A new endorsement, *contingent experience rating modification factor endorsement* (WC 00 04 12), is attached when the contingent modification in lieu of the actual modification is applied. Exhibit 10-9 shows this endorsement.

***Aircraft Premium Endorsement (WC 00 04 01).*** The endorsement applies to insureds who own or lease aircraft for the transportation of their personnel in the conduct of their business. Exhibit 10-10 shows an example of this endorsement.

In the Classifications Section of the manual, a note to the classification "Aircraft or Helicopter Operation: Transportation of Personnel" (Code 7421) explains the applicable surcharge. The surcharges apply per passenger seat and are shown under "Miscellaneous

**Exhibit 10-7**
Anniversary Rating Date Endorsement*

**WORKERS COMPENSATION AND EMPLOYERS LIABILITY INSURANCE POLICY** **WC 00 04 02**

**Original Printing** Effective April 1, 1984 **Standard**

**ANNIVERSARY RATING DATE ENDORSEMENT**

The premium and rates for this policy, and the experience rating modification factor, if any, may change on your anniversary rating date shown in the Schedule.

Schedule

Anniversary Rating Date__________(Month)__________(Day)

**Notes:**

1. The anniversary rating date is explained in Rule I of the Basic Manual.
2. Use this endorsement to show the insured's normal anniversary rating date if different from the policy effective date.
3. The insurer may show the anniversary rating date in item 2 or item 4 of the Information Page.



*Reprinted with permission from the National Council on Compensation Insurance.

**Exhibit 10-8**
Experience Rating Modification Factor Endorsement*

| | | |
|---|---|---|
| **WORKERS COMPENSATION AND EMPLOYERS LIABILITY INSURANCE POLICY** | | **WC 00 04 03** |
| **Original Printing** | Effective April 1, 1984 | **Standard** |

**EXPERIENCE RATING MODIFICATION FACTOR ENDORSEMENT**

The premium for the policy will be adjusted by an experience rating modification factor. The factor was not available when the policy was issued. The factor, if any, shown on the Information Page is an estimate. We will issue an endorsement to show the proper factor, if different from the factor shown, when it is calculated.

**Notes:**

1. This endorsement may be used if the insured's experience rating modification factor is not available when the policy is issued.
2. An appropriate typewritten entry may be made in the Information Page instead of using this endorsement.



*Reprinted with permission from the National Council on Compensation Insurance.

**Exhibit 10-9**
Contingent Experience Rating Modification Factor Endorsement*

**WORKERS COMPENSATION AND EMPLOYERS LIABILITY INSURANCE POLICY** **WC 00 04 12**

**Original Printing** Effective January 1, 1990 **Standard**

**CONTINGENT EXPERIENCE RATING MODIFICATION FACTOR ENDORSEMENT**

The premium for this policy will be adjusted by an experience rating modification factor. The factor shown in the schedule is a Contingent Experience Rating Modification factor based on the appropriate experience data available and replaces any prior experience modification factor. We will issue an endorsement to show a revised factor if appropriate additional experience data becomes available. The contingent factor will apply unless a revised factor is subsequently issued.

Schedule

**Notes:**

1. This endorsement may be used when a contingent experience modification factor is used.

2. An appropriate typewritten entry may be made in the Information Page instead of using this endorsement.



* Reprinted with permission from the National Council on Compensation Insurance.

**Exhibit 10-10**
Aircraft Premium Endorsement*

**WORKERS COMPENSATION AND EMPLOYERS LIABILITY INSURANCE POLICY** **WC 00 04 01 A**

**1st Reprint** *Issued May 20, 1986* **Standard**

**AIRCRAFT PREMIUM ENDORSEMENT**

Additional premium is charged for each aircraft shown in the Schedule. The additional premium is not subject to adjustment unless this policy is canceled. You may substitute one aircraft for another without additional charge if the substitute aircraft has no more seats than the aircraft shown in the Schedule.

Schedule

| State | Aircraft | Passenger Seat Charge | Maximum Charge | Estimated Premium |
|---|---|---|---|---|

**Notes:**

1. Use this endorsement to show the additional premium required for classification code 7421.
2. Report passenger seat surcharge under code 9108.
3. Show, in the Schedule, state(s) to which the payroll of classification 7421 is assigned.



*Reprinted with permission from the National Council on Compensation Insurance.

Values" on the state rate pages. The endorsement applies only in jurisdictions where the manual provides for surcharges.

***Premium Discount Endorsement (WC 00 04 06).*** When the estimated advance premium exceeds $5,000 the premium discount endorsement shows how the applicable premium discount is determined. Exhibit 10-11 shows a copy of this endorsement.

The premium discount shown on the endorsement is used in calculating the advance premium, premiums called for by subsequent endorsements, and interim audit premiums. The premium discount percentage is not revised until the earned premium is developed through the final audit.

The endorsement includes a list of the numbers of all policies and the respective estimated standard premiums for all states covered by each policy. The premium discount percentage depends on the total standard premium for all policies listed in the schedule.

Indiana allows the use of the premium discount plan on a selective basis with no filing requirement. If the premium discount is to apply to Indiana, the state name should be entered on the endorsement. Unless Indiana appears on the schedule, the premium discount should not be applied to Indiana premium. The premium discount does not apply to retrospectively rated premiums.

On interstate policies, premium discount percentages can vary by state. Even though the New Jersey standard premium is included in the total policy premium to determine discount percentages for all other states, the discount percentage for New Jersey is based only on the standard premium for New Jersey. Premium discounts do not apply in California.

**Exhibit 10-11**
Premium Discount Endorsement*

| **WORKERS COMPENSATION AND EMPLOYERS LIABILITY INSURANCE POLICY** | | **WC 00 04 06** |
|---|---|---|
| **1st Reprint** | Issued August 10, 1984 | **Advisory** |

**PREMIUM DISCOUNT ENDORSEMENT**

The premium for this policy and the policies, if any, listed in item 3 of the Schedule may be eligible for a discount. This endorsement shows your estimated discount in item 1 or 2 of the Schedule. The final calculation of premium discount will be determined by our manuals and your premium basis as determined by audit. Premium subject to retrospective rating is not subject to premium discount.

Schedule

| | Estimated Eligible Premium | | | |
|---|---|---|---|---|
| | First $5,000 | Next $95,000 | Next $400,000 | Balance |
| 1. **State** | | | | |

2. Average percentage discount:____%

3. Other policies:

4. If there are no entries in items 1, 2 and 3, of the Schedule see the Premium Discount Endorsement attached to your policy number:

**Notes:**

1. Use this endorsement to show the application of Manual Rule VII, Premium Discount, or to identify the insured's policy which shows the application of the Discount Rule.
2. Do not make entries in items 1, 2 or 3 if a policy number is to be shown in item 4.
3. The company has the option of replacing item 1 with the appropriate Table in use by the company. The company may also revise item 1 to conform to Manual Rules applicable to certain states.
4. Item 2 may be used if all eligible premium is developed in one or more states using the same discount.
5. Item 3 is available to list all policies that are combined under the Discount Rule.
6. Use item 4 if premium discount is shown on another policy issued to the insured.



---

*Reprinted with permission from the National Council on Compensation Insurance.

## SUMMARY

The workers compensation and employers liability insurance policy is probably the most standardized liability insurance policy. More so than in any other line of insurance, insurers must compete for workers compensation on the basis of service, and in a few states, price. Understanding the background leading to the enactment of workers compensation laws is essential to understanding and underwriting this line of insurance. Many ambiguous or borderline coverage situations can often be resolved by considering the purpose of the laws and their intent, which is to cover as many work-related injuries as possible. Most insurers can rest assured that any ambiguity will be resolved in favor of the injured worker. Although the requirements that must be met to receive workers compensation benefits are spelled out in each workers compensation law, these too are liberally interpreted in most cases in order to find coverage for an injured party.

This chapter details the coverage provided by the workers compensation and employers liability insurance policy. Probably the most interesting feature of this policy is the lack of any limits or detailed coverage description for the workers compensation coverage. The policy provides that it will pay what the law says it has to pay. Although this makes at least this portion of the policy very easy to understand, it should not, in the underwriter's eyes, reduce the complexity and importance of the whole workers compensation benefit system. It is not a simple system.

The simplicity of the policy provisions should not be misinterpreted to mean that underwriting this line of insurance is simple. Although the underwriting is covered in a subsequent chapter, it should be recognized that it is difficult to underwrite and price a coverage over whose benefits the insurer has little or no control. For this reason, the efforts of the insurer's loss control department to improve risks and thereby prevent injury in the first place become increasingly important.

Because of its mandatory nature and seemingly ever-increasing costs, workers compensation is second probably only to personal auto coverage in attracting the attention of legislators. Underwriters and insurers must understand this and be prepared for the attention this line also gets from the general public and from insureds. By knowing the coverage, the laws, and their history, underwriters will be in a much better position to respond to questions and possibly to make their own suggestions for improving the system.

# Chapter Notes

1. U.S. Chamber of Commerce, *Analysis of Workers Compensation Laws* (Washington, DC, 1989), p. vii.
2. Most compulsory laws have an elective feature. For example, the law may be compulsory as to all employments, but elective with regard to sole proprietors and partners.
3. U.S. Chamber of Commerce, *Analysis of Workers Compensation Laws,* pp. 3-4.
4. U.S. Chamber of Commerce, *Analysis of Workers Compensation Laws,* p. 1.
5. U.S. Chamber of Commerce, *Analysis of Workers Compensation Laws,* p. 7.
6. U.S. Chamber of Commerce, *Analysis of Workers Compensation Laws,* pp. 5-8.
7. Clark v. Waverly Mills, 183 SE 2d 855 (1971).
8. Smith v. Colonial Tire and Auto Service, 207 SE 2d 810 (SC, 1974).
9. U.S. Chamber of Commerce, *Analysis of Workers Compensation Laws,* p. 5.
10. Internal Revenue Code, §3506.
11. Arthur Larson, *Workmen's Compensation for Occupational Injuries and Death,* Desk Edition (New York: Matthew Bender & Company, 1980), §53.30.
12. Hamilla v. Gade, 278 N.Y. 502, 15 NE 2d 438 (1938).
13. Larson, §53.30.
14. Larson, §53.40.
15. Hardware Mutual Casualty Company v. Sprayberry 25 SE 2d 74 (1943).
16. *The Report of the National Commission on State Workmen's Compensation Laws,* July 1972, p. 49.
17. Albert J. Millus and Willard J. Gentile, *Workers' Compensation Laws in Insurance* (New York: Roberts Publishing Corporation, 1976), p. 100.
18. Millus and Gentile, p. 127.
19. Traditionally, this test has been broken down into arising out of and in the scope (or course) of employment. Because the distinction between these two areas is not clear, they have been combined.
20. See Arabian Am. Oil Co. v. Ind. Acc. Comm'n., 94 Cal. App. 2d 388, 210, Pac.2d 732 (Saudi Arabia), and Brown-Pacific-Maxon, Inc. v. Pillsbury, 132 Fed. Supp. 421 (California).
21. Millus and Gentile, p. 135.
22. U.S. Chamber of Commerce, *Analysis of Workers Compensation Laws,* p. viii.
23. U.S. Chamber of Commerce, *Analysis of Workers Compensation Laws,* pp. 18-20.

24. U.S. Chamber of Commerce, *Analysis of Workers Compensation Laws,* p. 22.
25. C.A. Kulp and John W. Hall, *Casualty Insurance,* 4th edition (New York: Ronald Press, 1968), pp. 251-252.
26. *New York Manual of Rules, Classifications and Rates for Workmen's Compensation and Employers' Liability Insurance,* p. 2.
27. Terminology may be a bit confusing here. The workers compensation manual defines the term "standard policy" as the standard provisions workers compensation and employers liability insurance policy *and* the information page. In this text, when referring to the policy form WC 00 00 00 without the information page, the term "standard provisions workers compensation and employers liability insurance policy form" (or just standard provisions policy form) will be used. When referring to the entire policy, including information page, the term "standard policy" will be used.

# CHAPTER 11

# Workers Compensation Premiums and Classifications

In order to properly price and therefore underwrite workers compensation, an underwriter must be familiar with the workers compensation manual and its rules for premium determination and classification. This chapter examines these major areas. Although the actual calculation of the premium is often performed by computer, the underwriter must have an understanding of the exposure base used in workers compensation and what is included within, or excluded from, that base. Many of the rules regarding inclusions and exclusions, how to handle overtime, and so on are the primary concern of the premium auditor. However, there are times when the underwriter must explain to the insured or producer the proper handling of a certain employee's payroll. The underwriter should be able to do this quickly and accurately. How the payroll of certain employees is handled can make a substantial difference in the premium charged some insureds and thus in the profitability of the account.

## THE WORKERS COMPENSATION MANUAL

In addition to the standard workers compensation and employers liability insurance policy and the standard endorsement forms already described, the National Council on Compensation Insurance also developed the *Basic Manual for Workers Compensation and Employers Liability Insurance* (hereafter referred to as the *Basic Manual*). This manual applies in almost forty states and the District of Columbia. There are separate manuals for the independent bureau states of California, Delaware, Michigan, New Jersey, New York, Pennsylvania, and Texas. Despite their unique features, the manuals for these states follow the same general approach as the *Basic Manual.* Naturally, the *Basic Manual* also does not apply in the six states where workers compensation insurance may be provided only through the state fund.

The *Basic Manual* and the manuals of the independent bureau states specify the rules and procedures for writing workers compensation insurance. These uniform rules for all insurers in a state facilitate the rating process, although some states now require each insurer to file the manual independently. Since the premium section of the standard workers compensation and employers liability policy states that "all premium for this policy will be determined by our manuals of rules, rates, rating plans and classifications," the entire manual forms a part of the contract.

The 1980 edition of the *Basic Manual* consists of three parts:

"Part One—Rules"
"Part Two—Classifications"
"Part Three—Rates and State Exceptions"

Pages are numbered separately in each part, and the page numbers begin with a letter indicating the part.

"Part One—Rules" includes pages R1 through R34 plus appendixes. Exhibit 11-1 shows page R1 of the manual as a sample of this part. Exhibit 11-2 provides an outline of the manual rules.

"Part Two—Classifications" includes an alphabetical list of classification descriptions (C pages) and an "Underwriting Guide" (G pages) to assist in locating the proper rating classification.

"Part Three—Rates and State Exceptions" includes the applicable rates by classification for the state as well as any special classifications, special rules, rating plans, or other exceptions that apply in a particular state. In the words of the *Basic Manual,* "Reference should be made to Part Three for Rates, State Special Rules and Special Classifications in conjunction with applying Parts One and Two in a specific state."[1] Exhibit 11-3, page 1 of the Georgia state rate pages, provides an example of this section.

It is imperative for underwriters to be thoroughly familiar with the content and organization of the *Basic Manual.* They should also have it readily available for reference. The manual is as much a part of the insurance contract as the policy itself, and it must be followed explicitly.

## WORKERS COMPENSATION PREMIUMS

Workers compensation insurance protects employers from the losses caused by work-related injuries to, or diseases of, their employees. Therefore, the premium for that protection should reflect the exposure to such losses. That exposure varies considerably, both according to the size of the employer's work force and according to the degree of hazard in the work performed. The traditional workers compensation system establishes equitable premiums by relating the premium to the employer's payroll and by class rating employers according to their business.

With only a few exceptions, the premium base for workers compensation insurance is *payroll* or *remuneration.* These two terms are often used synonymously, which causes no confusion as long as one adheres to the explicit definition provided in the workers compensation manual. Payroll serves as an effective premium base because it (1) varies directly with the exposure covered by the insurance, (2) is relatively easy to determine and verify from available records, and (3) is not readily subject to manipulation by the insured.

Naturally, an employer's exposure to workers compensation losses increases when more employees are added to the payroll. As a result, the payroll records provide a direct measure of the exposure: the larger the total payroll, the greater the exposure. Since not all employees earn the same wage rate, the number of hours worked rather than the remuneration paid might seem to be an even better measure of the exposure. In fact, the Washington State Fund, which is the exclusive insurer for workers compensation in the state of Washington, uses hours worked as the premium base. Other states have also considered using hours worked. While the probability of an accident more directly relates to hours worked, the cost of workers compensation claims does not. Benefit levels depend in part on the injured employee's wage prior to the accident. Thus, payroll would appear to be more directly related to the actual exposure assumed by the insurer.[2]

Payroll records are usually available because they are regularly required for accounting and tax purposes. Hours worked are often recorded as well, but not always with the same degree of accuracy. Required government reports do encourage accurate record keeping for remuneration paid. It is the employee's interest in receiving the full amount earned and the employer's competing interest in controlling costs that provide the most effective check on the accuracy of payroll records. Thus, payroll provides a reliable premium base that is relatively easy to determine from existing records.

Because payroll records must be maintained for tax and accounting purposes, they are also difficult for insureds to manipulate as they might consider doing to reduce their insurance premiums. Payrolls can be verified by reconciliation with federal and state tax returns as well as with financial statements and a variety of other accounting records. An insured may still attempt to manipulate the premium by paying an employee as an independent contractor or by some similar device to

**Exhibit 11-1**
Manual Page R1*

**WORKERS COMPENSATION AND EMPLOYERS LIABILITY** Page R-1

2nd Reprint *Effective April 1, 1984* **RULE I**

## PART ONE—RULES

### RULE I—GENERAL

A. WORKERS COMPENSATION

Workers Compensation as used in this Manual means workmen's compensation, workers compensation or occupational disease.

B. STANDARD POLICY ★

Standard Policy means the Standard Provisions Workers' Compensation and Employers Liability Insurance Policy and the Informations Page issued by the National Council on Compensation Insurance.

C. ENDORSEMENT FORMS

**1. Definition**

Endorsement forms mean standard and advisory endorsements contained in the Policy and Endorsement Forms Manual.

F. EFFECTIVE DATE

**1. Manual**

This Manual applies only from the anniversary rating date which occurs on or after the effective date of this Manual.

**2. Changes**

The effective date of a change in any rule, classification or rate is 12:01 a.m. on the date specified on the manual page. Any change will be issued on a reprinted page and will be designated by a ★. Unless specified otherwise, each change applies only from the anniversary rating date which occurs on or after the effective date of the change.

G. ANNIVERSARY RATING DATE

**1. Definition**

The anniversary rating date is the effective

**2. Standard Endorsements**

A standard endorsement must be used in the form prescribed in that manual.

**3. Advisory Endorsements**

An advisory endorsement is subject to use as determined by the insurance carrier and appropriate regulatory authority.

D. POLICY AND ENDORSEMENT FORMS MANUAL

Refer to the Policy and Endorsement Forms Manual for complete description of coverages and instructions on use of policy and endorsement forms.

E. APPLICATION OF MANUAL RULES

Rules apply separately to each policy, except as allowed by Rule VII-Premium Discount.

month and day of the policy in effect and each annual anniversary thereafter unless a different date has been established by the National Council or other licensed rating organization.

**2. Rewritten Policies** ★

If a policy is canceled and rewritten by the same or another carrier, all rules, classifications and rates of the rewriting carrier which were in effect as of the anniversary rating date shall apply to the rewritten policy until the next anniversary rating date, as established by the rating organization, has been reached. When necessary, use the Standard Anniversary Rating Date Endorsement. (WC 00 04 02).

**3. Long Term Policies**

For application of anniversary rating dates on policies issued for a term in excess of one year, *refer to Rule III-C.*

**Exhibit 11-2**
Outline of Basic Manual Rules

Preface
- A. Organization of manual
- B. Jurisdictions where manual applies
- C. Jurisdictions where manual does not apply

Rule I—General
- A. Workers compensation
- B. Standard policy
- C. Endorsement forms
- D. Policy and endorsement forms manual
- E. Application of manual rules
- F. Effective date
- G. Anniversary rating date

Rule II—Explanation of coverages and methods of insuring
- A. Part One—Workers compensation insurance
- B. Part Two—Employers liability insurance
- C. Part Three–Other states insurance
- D. Voluntary compensation insurance

Rule III—Policy preparation—Insured, policy period, and state of operations
- A. Explanation of terms
- B. Name, address, and other workplaces of insured—Item 1
- C. Policy period—Item 2
- D. State laws designated in the policy—Item 3.A

Rule IV—Classifications—Item 4 of the information page
- A. General explanation
- B. Explanation of classifications
- C. Classification wording
- D. Assignment of classifications
- E. Payroll assignment—Multiple classifications
- F. How to show classifications in Item 4 of the information page

Rule V—Premium basis—Item 4 of the information page
- A. Basis of premium—Total remuneration
- B. Remuneration—Payroll
- C. Estimated payrolls
- D. Whole dollars—Payrolls
- E. Overtime
- F. Payroll limitation

Rule VI—Rates and premium determination—Item 4 of the information page

A. Rates
B. Premium determination
C. Whole dollars—Premiums
D. Loss constant
E. Expense constant
F. Minimum premium
G. Deposit premium
H. Premium modifications—Experience rating plan
I. Premium determination for federal and maritime insurance

Rule VII—Premium discount—Item 4 of the information page

A. Explanation
B. Definitions
C. Retrospective rating
D. Determination of premium discount
E. Combination of policies
F. Large construction projects

Rule VIII—Limits of liability—Item 3.B of the information page

A. Workers compensation and employers liability policy
B. Employers liability insurance—Without workers compensation insurance
C. Voluntary compensation insurance

Rule IX—Special conditions or operations affecting coverage and premium

A. Executive officers
B. Partners and sole proprietors
C. Subcontractors
D. Exclusion of statutory medical benefits—Ex-medical coverage

Rule X—Cancellation

A. Who may cancel
B. Premium determination—Cancellation by the insurance carrier
C. Premium determination—Cancellation by the insured when retiring from business
D. Premium determination—Cancellation by the insured, except when retiring from business
E. Short rate cancellation table for term of one year

*Continued on next page*

Rule XI—Three year fixed rate policy option

A. Eligibility
B. Designation on the information page
C. Rates
D. Minimum premium
E. Deposit premium
F. Earned premium
G. Experience rating plan
H. Cancellation—Premium determination

Rule XII—U.S. Longshoremen's and Harbor Workers' Compensation Act

A. General explanation
B. Workers compensation insurance—Part one
C. Employers liability insurance—Part two
D. Classifications and rates
E. Extensions of the U.S.L.&H.W. Act

Rule XIII—The Admiralty Law and the Federal Employers' Liability Act

A. General explanation
B. Description of coverage programs
C. Coverage
D. Exclusions
E. Limits of liability
F. Classifications and rates
G. Waters not under admiralty jurisdiction

Rule XIV—Domestic workers—Residences

A. Definitions
B. Coverage
C. Name of insured
D. Classifications
E. Rates and premium
F. Minimum premium

Rule XV—Final earned premium determination

A. Actual payroll
B. Premium determination
C. Audit rights of carrier

avoid showing the payments on the regular payroll, but as long as there has been some payment, an alert premium auditor should be able to locate it.

Payroll also provides a premium base responsive to changing economic conditions. If inflation causes loss settlements to rise, it also causes payrolls to increase, thus generating more premium to pay the losses. That natural adjustment process reduces the need for more frequent rate increases.

## Basis of Premium

For the above-mentioned reasons, workers compensation premiums are almost always based on remuneration. When the policy is written, the premium is defined as a certain rate per $100 of remuneration for the policy period. Following the conclusion of the policy period, the actual payroll is used to compute the final earned premium. The *Basic Manual* provides explicit rules regarding the forms of remuneration to be included in determining the total. The following discussion explains these rules and describes several exceptional situations in which remuneration is not the premium base.

**Remuneration.** The National Council's *Basic Manual* stipulates that "premium shall be computed on the basis of the total remuneration paid or payable by the insured for services of employees covered by the policy."[3] Employees covered by the policy are those who might reasonably be considered employees under the applicable workers compensation statute. (Employer-employee relationships were discussed in Chapter 1.) Remuneration for services of employees covered by the policy also implies that the services occurred within the policy period. Total remuneration paid by the insured is a slightly broader concept than most insureds realize. The *Basic Manual* rules, however, explain the concept precisely. Pages G38-G46 of the *Basic Manual* offer guidance in the interpretation of various rules and definitions.

***Remuneration Defined.*** According to the *Basic Manual*, "remuneration means money or substitutes for money."[4] Since the terms payroll and remuneration are often used interchangeably, the *Basic Manual* also includes the explicit definition that "payroll means remuneration."[5]

***Inclusions.*** In addition to ordinary wages or salaries, remuneration includes several other items of compensation. Insureds must sometimes be convinced that such items are counted in the workers

**Exhibit 11-3**
Georgia Rate Page*

**WORKERS COMPENSATION AND EMPLOYERS LIABILITY** **GEORGIA**
**Page 1**
**Original Printing**

*Effective August 1, 1988*
**Advisory Rates**

LEGEND

a Rate for each individual risk must be obtained by Home Office from Rating Organization having jurisdiction.

D Special Disease Rule for this classification—See Rule IV of Manual Supplement—Treatment of Disease Coverage.

E Classification involving specific disease loading. Refer to Home Office for amount.

F Rate provides for coverage under the United States Longshore and Harbor Workers' Compensation Act.

X Refer to special classification phraseology in these pages which is applicable in this state.

Z Classifications not available in this state.

| CLASS CODE | RATE INCL DIS | MIN PREM | CLASS CODE | RATE INCL DIS | MIN PREM | CLASS CODE | RATE INCL DIS | MIN PREM | CLASS CODE | RATE INCL DIS | MIN PREM | CLASS CODE | RATE INCL DIS | MIN PREM |
|---|---|---|---|---|---|---|---|---|---|---|---|---|---|---|
| 0005 | 7.03 | 750. | 1452 | 6.60 | 750. | 2111 | 4.15 | 556. | 2623 | 8.82 | 750. | 3066 | 8.43 | 750. |
| 0008 | 5.47 | 694. | 1463 | 12.18 | 750. | 2112 | 6.27 | 750. | 2651 | 6.36 | 750. | 3076 | 4.75 | 619. |
| 0016 | 7.58 | 750. | 1470 | 8.82 | 750. | 2114 | 4.38 | 580. | 2660 | 3.94 | 534. | 3081D | 4.98 | 643. |
| 0034 | 11.07 | 750. | 1473X | 5.97 | 747. | 2121 | 2.28 | 359. | 2670 | 2.53 | 386. | 3082D | 5.52 | 700. |
| 0035 | 4.56 | 599. | 1474X | 6.50 | 750. | 2130 | 9.73 | 750. | 2683 | 5.34 | 681. | 3085D | 8.81 | 750. |
| 0036 | 10.50 | 750. | 1604EX | 9.25 | 750. | 2131 | 3.82 | 521. | 2688 | 3.27 | 463. | 3091 | 13.18 | 750. |
| 0037 | 10.03 | 750. | 1624E | 6.47 | 750. | 2143 | 8.34 | 750. | 2702X | 33.18 | 750. | 3110 | 7.39 | 750. |
| 0042 | 9.42 | 750. | 1642 | 7.71 | 750. | 2150 | 20.55 | 750. | 2705X‡ | 74.61 | 752. | 3111 | 6.54 | 750. |
| 0050 | 10.85 | 750. | 1654 | 4.96 | 641. | 2156 | 9.90 | 750. | 2710 | 13.07 | 750. | 3113 | 4.46 | 588. |
| 0059D | .64 | — | 1655 | 9.72 | 750. | 2157 | 4.71 | 615. | 2714 | 8.76 | 750. | 3114 | 3.07 | 442. |
| 0065D | .12 | — | 1699 | 2.53 | 386. | 2172 | 1.72 | 301. | 2731 | 8.99 | 750. | 3118 | 4.31 | 573. |
| 0066D | .12 | — | 1701 | 4.20 | 561. | 2174 | 11.88 | 750. | 2735 | 7.84 | 750. | 3119 | 1.71 | 300. |
| 0067D | .12 | — | 1710E | 7.07 | 750. | 2177 | 3.46 | 483. | 2741 | 13.49 | 750. | 3122 | 3.49 | 486. |
| 0079 | 8.43 | 750. | 1741E | 9.83 | 750. | 2211 | 13.40 | 750. | 2747 | 5.31 | 678. | 3126 | 5.98 | 748. |
| 0083 | 9.23 | 750. | 1747 | 7.63 | 750. | 2220 | 3.99 | 539. | 2759 | 10.75 | 750. | 3131 | 4.95 | 640. |

| | | | | | | | | | | | | | | |
|---|---|---|---|---|---|---|---|---|---|---|---|---|---|---|
| 0106 | 18.21 | 750. | 1748 | 5.06 | 651. | 2286 | 3.90 | 530. | 2790 | 2.12 | 343. | 3132 | 6.37 | 750. |
| 0113 | 9.31 | 750. | 1751X | 1.53 | 281. | 2288 | 8.31 | 750. | 2797X | 14.93 | 750. | 3145 | 3.65 | 503. |
| 0169 | 9.23 | 750. | 1803D | 11.48 | 750. | 2300 | 3.53 | 491. | 2802 | 15.06 | 750. | 3146 | 7.14 | 750. |
| 0170 | 5.53 | 701. | 1852D | 10.37 | 750. | 2302 | 2.60 | 393. | 2812 | 7.84 | 750. | 3169 | 7.12 | 750. |
| 0251 | 11.58 | 750. | 1853 | 8.94 | 750. | 2305 | 3.92 | 532. | 2835 | 4.54 | 597. | 3175D | 8.43 | 750. |
| 0400 | 13.08 | 750. | 1860 | 2.78 | 412. | 2361 | 3.27 | 463. | 2836 | 5.08 | 653. | 3179 | 3.04 | 439. |
| 0401 | 17.25 | * | 1924 | 7.68 | 750. | 2362 | 4.97 | 642. | 2841 | 7.10 | 750. | 3180 | 5.88 | 737. |
| 0758b | .28 | — | 1925 | 5.75 | 724. | 2380 | 4.95 | 640. | 2881 | 6.08 | 750. | 3188 | 3.30 | 467. |
| 0759c | 1.19 | — | 2001 | 4.69 | 612. | 2386 | 1.74 | 303. | 2883 | 7.79 | 750. | 3220 | 4.84 | 628. |
| 0770d | .99 | — | 2002 | 8.92 | 750. | 2388 | 3.30 | 467. | 2913 | 5.77 | 726. | 3223 | 9.35 | 750. |
| 0773e | 3.02 | — | 2003 | 4.26 | 567. | 2402 | 8.87 | 750. | 2915 | 6.95 | 750. | 3224 | 6.01 | 750. |
| 0774f | 1.91 | — | 2014 | 11.62 | 750. | 2413 | 8.04 | 750. | 2916 | 7.64 | 750. | 3227 | 4.69 | 612. |
| 0775g | 1.42 | — | 2016 | 3.05 | 440. | 2416 | 10.23 | 750. | 2923 | 4.64 | 607. | 3240 | 7.17 | 750. |
| 0776h | 2.44 | — | 2021 | 1.86 | 315. | 2417 | 4.20 | 561. | 2942 | 3.56 | 494. | 3241 | 6.41 | 750. |
| 0779i | 1.91 | — | 2030 | 11.43 | 750. | 2501 | 3.32 | 469. | 2960 | 11.25 | 750. | 3255 | 6.43 | 750. |
| 0799j | 5.89 | — | 2039 | 6.11 | 750. | 2503 | 1.39 | 266. | 3004 | 5.89 | 738. | 3257 | 5.45 | 692. |
| 0917 | 6.56 | 750. | 2041 | 2.95 | 430. | 2534 | 3.96 | 536. | 3018 | 7.36 | 750. | 3270 | 3.13 | 449. |
| 1005† | 9.89 | 750. | 2065 | 4.98 | 643. | 2570 | 9.52 | 750. | 3022 | 8.19 | 750. | 3300 | 7.40 | 750. |
| 1164E | 8.27 | 750. | 2070 | 8.98 | 750. | 2576 | 8.16 | 750. | 3027 | 4.71 | 615. | 3303 | 10.33 | 750. |
| 1165E | 6.03 | 750. | 2081 | 17.21 | 750. | 2578 | 8.07 | 750. | 3028 | 5.48 | 695. | 3307 | 6.80 | 750. |
| 1169X | 3.47 | 484. | 2089 | 10.38 | 750. | 2585 | 6.28 | 750. | 3030 | 11.89 | 750. | 3315 | 4.86 | 630. |
| 1320 | 6.41 | 750. | 2095 | 7.64 | 750. | 2586 | 2.28 | 359. | 3040 | 11.03 | 750. | 3334 | 2.15 | 346. |
| 1322 | 19.93 | 750. | 2101 | 7.28 | 750. | 2587 | 4.24 | 565. | 3041 | 6.73 | 750. | 3336 | 3.67 | 505. |
| 1430 | 11.03 | 750. | 2105 | 5.66 | 714. | 2589 | 2.96 | 431. | 3042 | 3.81 | 520. | 3365 | 13.87 | 750. |
| 1438 | 12.71 | 750. | 2110 | 6.96 | 750. | 2600 | 4.10 | 551. | 3064 | 7.24 | 750. | 3372 | 6.70 | 750. |

* **0401**—Minimum Premium $100 per ginning location for policy minimum premium computation.

† Code **1005**—Includes a non-ratable disease element of $2.41. See State Exception Rules.

‡ **2705**—An upset payroll of $4.00 per cord shall be used for premium computation in all instances.

Non-Ratable Code and Rate to be used with:

| | | | | |
|---|---|---|---|---|
| b 4758 | d 4770 | f 4774 | h 4776 | j 4799 |
| c 4759 | e 4773 | g 4775 | i 4779 | |

Edition of 8-1-88 (6)

compensation premium base. In general, these inclusions achieve greater equity in the rating system because employers might otherwise gain the services of employees while paying low wages, and thus low premiums, by offering alternate forms of compensation. Rule V-B.2 of the *Basic Manual* lists these additional items that are included in the premium base:

- Commissions
- Bonuses
- Extra pay for overtime work except as provided in Rule V-E
- Pay for holidays, vacations, or periods of sickness
- Payment by an employer of amounts otherwise required by law to be paid by employees to statutory insurance or pension plans, such as the Federal Social Security Act
- Payment to employees on any basis other than time worked, such as piece work, profit-sharing, or incentive plans
- Payment or allowance for hand tools or power tools used by hand provided by employees and used in their work or operations for the insured
- The rental value of an apartment or a house provided for an employee based on comparable accommodations
- The value of lodging, other than an apartment or house, received by employees as part of their pay, to the extent shown in the insured's records
- The value of meals received by employees as part of their pay to the extent shown in the insured's records
- The value of store certificates, merchandise, credits, or any other substitute for money received by employees as part of their pay

***Exclusions.*** The *Basic Manual* also specifically excludes certain items from the total remuneration, which serves as the basis of premium. The most important of these exclusions is for tips and other gratuities. Exclusion of tips is a departure from the previous manual of the National Council and from the manuals of some of the independent bureau states. According to Rule V-B.3, remuneration excludes the following:

- Tips and other gratuities received by employees
- Payments by an employer to group insurance or group pension plans for employees, other than payments covered by Rule V-B.2.e
- The value of special rewards for individual invention or discovery

- Dismissal or severance payments except for time worked or accrued vacation

***Overtime Wages.*** Except in Pennsylvania, Delaware, and Utah, which make no distinction between regular and overtime wages, overtime wages present a special case in calculating the basis of premium. Since employees receive a higher rate of pay for overtime work, their pay is not in direct proportion to the number of hours worked if some of those hours constitute overtime. Generally, the *Basic Manual* rules exclude the *extra pay* so that the basis of premium more directly reflects the actual exposure to employee injuries. However, the rules also contain specific provisions defining overtime and stipulating the records required for such extra pay to be excluded from the premium base. Unless all the conditions of the *Basic Manual* are met, no exclusion of overtime pay is allowed.

The *Basic Manual* states the definition of overtime used in determining the basis of premium:

> Overtime means those hours worked for which there is an increase in the rate of pay:
> a. For work in any day or in any week in excess of the number of hours normally worked, or
> b. For hours worked in excess of 8 hours in any day or 40 hours in any week, or
> c. For work on Saturdays, Sundays, or holidays.[6]

Another restriction presented by the definition is that "in the case of guaranteed wage agreements, overtime means only those hours worked in excess of the number specified in such agreement."[7]

Whereas the wage and hour laws are designed to protect employees from possible abuse, the intent of the *Basic Manual* rule on overtime is to identify those situations in which a higher rate of pay applies because the number of hours worked in the day or week exceeds the number of hours normal and usual to the industry. If a forty-hour work week is normal for the industry, there is no problem. Overtime for workers compensation insurance purposes, however, is not necessarily overtime according to the wage and hour laws.

If, for example, the normal work day is seven hours, the union contract might require one and one-half times the hourly wage rate for any work in excess of seven hours a day. An employee working eight hours might be paid $4 an hour for the first seven hours and $6 for the additional hour. Total wages for the day would be $34. The extra pay, in this case $2, would be deducted in computing the basis of premium so that the remuneration included, $32, is the same as if only the regular rate had been paid for the entire time worked ($4 per hour × 8 hours = $32).

"Premium" pay added to the regular hourly wage rate for work on a night shift or under other special conditions is not considered extra pay for overtime because it does not involve work beyond the normal number of hours. For example, a factory may have two shifts with a $4 per hour wage rate for the day shift and $4.50 per hour for the night shift. Although the insured may argue that the night shift is no more hazardous than the day shift, it is the total payroll that reflects the remuneration the insured must pay to attract the desired labor services. Since the total remuneration reflects the exposure to loss, there is no deduction from the premium base in this case.

Similarly, employees paid on a piece-work basis may receive a higher rate after exceeding a certain production standard. As long as the increased production is accomplished within the normal working hours, the extra pay cannot be deducted from the premium base. Extra pay can be treated as overtime pay only when the employee works more hours per day or per week than the normal limit.

***Payroll Limitations.*** Total payroll has historically served as the basis of premium for workers compensation insurance. However, in 1946 it was observed that highly paid employees, especially those employed in hazardous occupations, sometimes contribute to the existence of a considerable premium on the basis of their salary. In order to limit such a result, a $100 ceiling on the weekly payroll of each individual was introduced in computing the basis of premium. This step provided a remedy for the unusual case without materially diminishing the value of payrolls as a reflection of the exposure since a ceiling of $100 per week was well above the wages paid to most workers at that time.

However, as a result of the subsequent substantial increase in wage levels, a significant volume of payroll gradually became excluded from the premium base because of the limitation. The $100 payroll limitation rule tended to make the premium based on little more than a head count as more and more employees reached the $100 per week wage level.

In order to correct this situation, a program to increase the payroll limitation from an average of $100 per week to an average of $300 per week was developed in the late 1950s. However, the value of payroll as a measure of the exposure similarly diminished under the $300 limitation. As a result, the concept of using total payroll was restored except for executive officers and a few special classifications. Beginning late in 1977, most states returned to unlimited payroll as a basis of premium.

Payroll limitations for executive officers were the same as those for employees until 1977. When unlimited payroll became the basis of the premium for employees, a payroll limitation was retained for executive officers as well as for employees of athletic teams and carnivals. However, because of the continued rise in salaries, fixed dollar limitations rapidly became obsolete. Thus, the National Council began setting the maximum weekly payroll limitation applicable to these high salaried individuals based on the state's average weekly wage rounded to the nearest $100. This amount can automatically be revised as wage levels change each year using the National Council's latest available semiannual call for wage data. The amount of the limitation is reviewed at the time of each general rate revision and adjusted by any indicated change in wage level.

The maximum remuneration applicable for executive officers and employees of athletic teams and carnivals can be found in the state rate pages. The premium base excludes that part of these employees' average weekly pay in excess of the limitation, provided that certain requirements are met.

**Imputed Remuneration.** In a variety of circumstances, individuals receive no remuneration at all or remuneration far more modest than the actual value of their services, yet they are entitled to the benefits of the workers compensation law. In such cases it is necessary to impute the actual value of those services in order to arrive at a premium commensurate with the exposures. The *Basic Manual* stipulates the amount to be included for some situations. For other situations, the remuneration an individual would normally earn for the work performed must be calculated.

***Executive Officers and Owners.*** Special problems arise in determining the appropriate amount on which to base the premium for officers of a corporation or owners of a business. Not only is their compensation likely to be a relatively large amount, but it is also likely to be received in a variety of forms. It may be difficult to distinguish compensation for their labor from income on their investment in the business. It must first be determined whether these individuals are covered by the workers compensation policy since the laws vary from state to state. If so, then an appropriate amount must be determined for inclusion in the premium base.

*Executive Officers.* The president, vice president, secretary, treasurer, or other duly appointed officers of a corporation are employees of that corporation. Except in Oregon and Minnesota for closed corporations, executive officers are entitled to the benefits of the workers compensation law. In more than twenty-five states, however, they may elect *not* to be covered by the workers compensation law. In that case the policy must be properly endorsed (*partners, officers, and others exclusion endorsement*—WC 00 03 08). The remuneration of only those executive officers covered by the policy should be included in the premium base subject to the payroll limitation rules.

The remuneration of executive officers should not be included in the premium base when they are not active in the business and therefore not exposed to its hazards. A National Council interpretation defines two such situations:

- Officers elected for the value of their names or the size of their stock holdings who have no duties and do not enter the premises, except perhaps for directors' meetings.
- Officers who because of age or similar reasons no longer perform any duties and do not enter the premises except perhaps for directors' meetings.[8]

If the officer visits the business frequently, even with no duties, the remuneration should be included.

In some cases an executive officer may receive little or no salary. An officer may be retired from the business or may concentrate on some other business or family activity. Such officers may work only irregularly in the business insured by the policy, but they might still sustain an injury and collect workers compensation. The *Basic Manual* therefore provides that a minimum individual payroll should be included in the premium base for each executive officer. The state rate pages of the *Basic Manual* show the minimum and maximum amount to include in the premium base for each executive officer.

*Partners and Proprietors.* Although partners and proprietors are employers rather than employees, in over half the states they may elect to be covered by the workers compensation law. Partners and proprietors, because they are the owners of the business, may receive a substantial portion of their income in the form of profits rather than a salary. If the premium for partners and proprietors were based on actual salary subject to limitations such as those applicable to executive officers, most partnerships and proprietorships would draw only a minimum amount in salary. Accordingly, a fixed basis of premium provides a reasonable measure of the exposure for such individuals. A majority of the states providing workers compensation coverage to partners and proprietors use a fixed amount rather than minimum and maximums. In 1990, these fixed amounts ranged from $10,400 to $39,000.

***Subcontractors.*** Most workers compensation laws hold a contractor responsible for workers compensation benefits to employees of its uninsured subcontractors. The standard workers compensation policy automatically insures this exposure. Underwriters must therefore ascertain whether or not this exposure exists, and if it does, evaluate it and include the appropriate premium charge if coverage is written. The insured must either prove that the exposure has been insured or pay a premium based on the subcontractor's payroll as well.

*Certificates of Insurance.* Subcontractors may request that their insurer furnish to a third party evidence that they are covered by insurance. A certificate of insurance issued by the subcontractor's insurer may demonstrate that the statutory workers compensation obligation is covered by insurance. Exhibit 11-4 shows an example of such a certificate of insurance.

A certificate of insurance should always indicate coverage for the state and preferably for the location (or locations) in which the work is performed, as well as the period for which coverage is in effect. Some large firms self-insure their workers compensation obligation and may furnish a certificate to that effect.

*Basis of Premium for Subcontractors.* If there is not satisfactory evidence that the subcontractor's obligation is insured, the subcontractor's payroll must be included in the basis of premium. The premium is calculated in the same manner as if the subcontractor's employees were employees of the insured.

If the subcontractor's payroll records are not available, the full subcontract price for the work performed during the policy period should be included in the basis of premium. If investigation reveals that a definite amount of the subcontract price represents payroll, that amount is considered as payroll for the additional premium computation. However, that amount must be at least 50 percent of the contract price in contracts for labor and materials and at least 90 percent of the contract price in contracts for labor only. Exhibit 11-5 outlines the decision process in determining the basis of premium for subcontractors.

***Unsalaried Employees.*** In certain cases individuals may work without receiving any remuneration. If so, it is still possible that they might be covered by the workers compensation law or by a voluntary compensation endorsement. Thus, some premium should be charged for this exposure.

It would seem that individuals who receive no remuneration cannot be employees because a contract of hire appears to be absent. However, there may be some consideration for their services other than monetary compensation. Interns or apprentices may work without pay for a period of training required to enter a particular occupation.

It is also possible that the workers compensation statute of a state specifically includes workers who might not otherwise qualify as employees. If a state does include certain workers by statute, thus creating an exposure for employers of such workers, the underwriter

**Exhibit 11-4**
Certificate of Insurance

SET TAB STOPS AT ARROWS

# Certificate of Insurance

acord®

THIS CERTIFICATE IS ISSUED AS A MATTER OF INFORMATION ONLY AND CONFERS NO RIGHTS UPON THE CERTIFICATE HOLDER
THIS CERTIFICATE DOES NOT AMEND, EXTEND OR ALTER THE COVERAGE AFFORDED BY THE POLICIES LISTED BELOW

| NAME AND ADDRESS OF AGENCY | COMPANIES AFFORDING COVERAGES | |
|---|---|---|
| KLEPPINGER INSURANCE AGENCY<br>400 W. LANCASTER AVE.<br>DEVON, PA. 19028 | COMPANY LETTER A | RELIANCE INSURANCE CO. |
| | COMPANY LETTER B | UNITED PACIFIC INSURANCE CO. |
| **NAME AND ADDRESS OF INSURED** | COMPANY LETTER C | GENERAL CASUALTY INSURANCE CO. |
| DELCHAPSEN & COMPANY, INC.<br>1600 J.F.K. BLVD.<br>PHILADELPHIA, PA. 19103 | COMPANY LETTER D | RELIANCE SPECIAL RISK |
| | COMPANY LETTER E | |

This is to certify that policies of insurance listed below have been issued to the insured named above and are in force at this time. Notwithstanding any requirement, term or condition of any contract or other document with respect to which this certificate may be issued or may pertain, the insurance afforded by the policies described herein is subject to all the terms, exclusions and conditions of such policies.

| COMPANY LETTER | TYPE OF INSURANCE | POLICY NUMBER | POLICY EXPIRATION DATE | Limits of Liability in Thousands (000) | EACH OCCURRENCE | AGGREGATE |
|---|---|---|---|---|---|---|
| A | **GENERAL LIABILITY**<br>[X] COMPREHENSIVE FORM<br>[ ] PREMISES—OPERATIONS<br>[ ] EXPLOSION AND COLLAPSE HAZARD<br>[ ] UNDERGROUND HAZARD<br>[ ] PRODUCTS/COMPLETED OPERATIONS HAZARD<br>[ ] CONTRACTUAL INSURANCE<br>[ ] BROAD FORM PROPERTY DAMAGE<br>[ ] INDEPENDENT CONTRACTORS<br>[ ] PERSONAL INJURY | GL 8-64-44-64 | 2-19-X5 | BODILY INJURY | $ | $ |
| | | | | PROPERTY DAMAGE | $ | $ |
| | | | | BODILY INJURY AND PROPERTY DAMAGE COMBINED | $ 500 | $ |
| | | | | PERSONAL INJURY | | $ |

| | | | | | | |
|---|---|---|---|---|---|---|
| C | **AUTOMOBILE LIABILITY**<br>[X] COMPREHENSIVE FORM<br>[ ] OWNED<br>[ ] HIRED<br>[ ] NON-OWNED | BA 4-01-42-88 | 8-3-X5 | BODILY INJURY (EACH PERSON) | $ | |
| | | | | BODILY INJURY (EACH ACCIDENT) | $ | |
| | | | | PROPERTY DAMAGE | $ | |
| | | | | BODILY INJURY AND PROPERTY DAMAGE COMBINED | $ 500 | |
| E | **EXCESS LIABILITY**<br>[ ] UMBRELLA FORM<br>[ ] OTHER THAN UMBRELLA FORM | LU 7-16-43-16 | 2-19-X5 | BODILY INJURY AND PROPERTY DAMAGE COMBINED | $ 4,000 | $ |
| B | **WORKERS' COMPENSATION and EMPLOYERS' LIABILITY** | ZC 9-83-74-19 | 8-3-X5 | STATUTORY | | |
| | | | | | $ (EACH ACCIDENT) | |
| | **OTHER** | | | | | |

DESCRIPTION OF OPERATIONS/LOCATIONS/VEHICLES

RIGGING AND MILLWRIGHT OPERATIONS

**Cancellation:** Should any of the above described policies be cancelled before the expiration date thereof, the issuing company will endeavor to mail 30 days written notice to the below named certificate holder, but failure to mail such notice shall impose no obligation or liability of any kind upon the company.

NAME AND ADDRESS OF CERTIFICATE HOLDER:

R.J. NELSON & CO.
1800 WHITE HORSE PIKE
ATCO, NEW JERSEY 08048

DATE ISSUED: 9-6-X4

K. ROGER NOGAKI

AUTHORIZED REPRESENTATIVE

ACORD 25 (1-79)

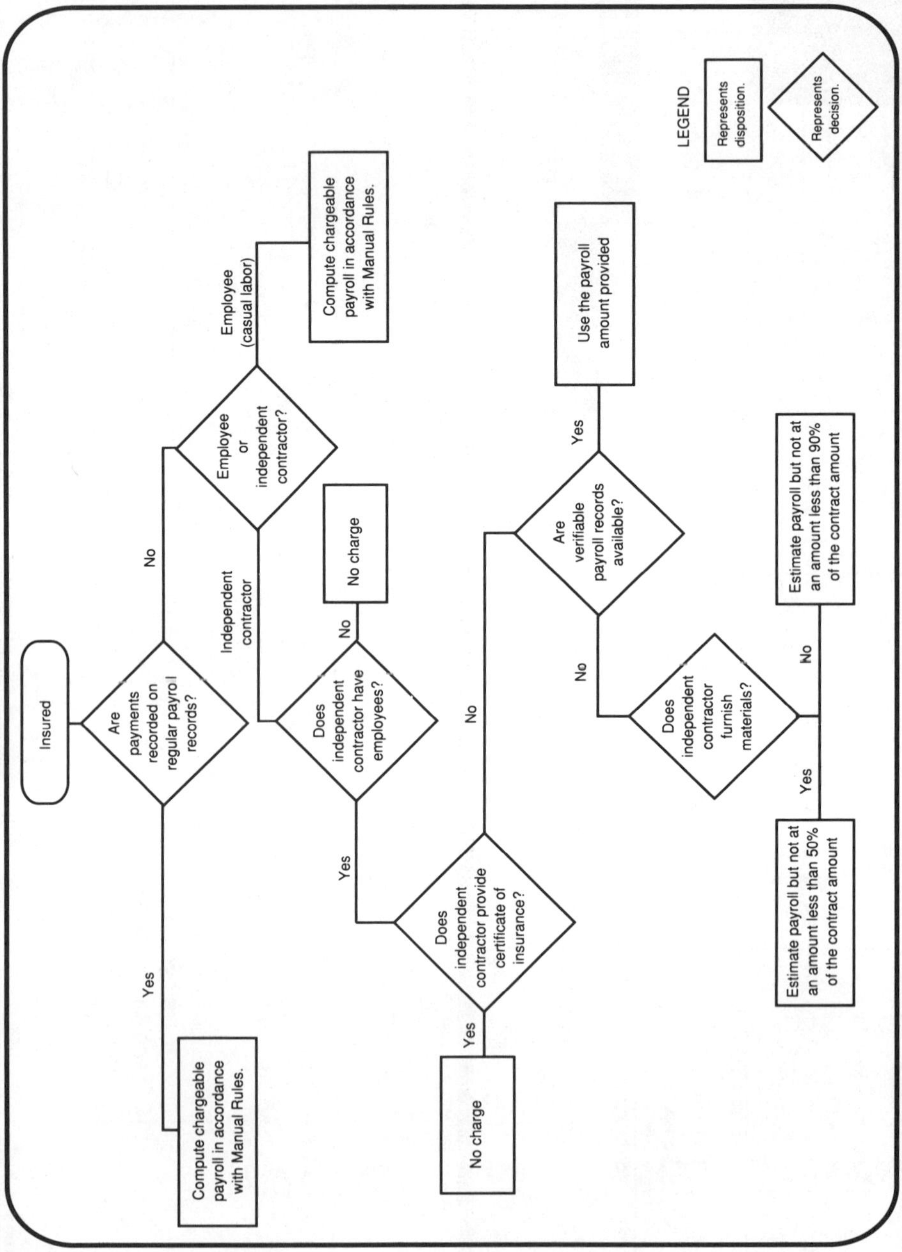


**Exhibit 11-5**
Determining Basis of Premium for Subcontractors

must consider that exposure in the premium base. Cases that frequently arise involve relatives, student nurses, volunteer workers, and welfare recipients.

*Relatives.* The matter of determining what the remuneration of unsalaried relatives would be is a problem that arises from time to time. Whether to include an amount as remuneration would depend upon whether the workers compensation law of the state in which they are working considers them employees. Once it has been determined that an unsalaried relative is considered an employee, it is necessary to determine how much to include as remuneration. If the records show the actual payroll, there is no problem. If not, a good rule of thumb is to include an amount equal to the amount that would normally be received by a regular employee doing the same type of work.

*Student Nurses.* In some hospitals student nurses receive only room and board during their training. A few receive a nominal stipend as well. In other hospitals student nurses pay for their tuition, room, and board.

It is necessary to determine whether the student nurses would be considered employees under the specific conditions of their training in the state involved. If the student nurse is considered an employee, the actual remuneration, if any, should be included plus board and lodging. If no remuneration is paid and no board and lodging is furnished, an amount equal to the starting salary for a beginning trained nurse should be included. Student nurses not considered employees may be provided benefits by means of the voluntary compensation endorsement. When this is done, the endorsement should also indicate the basis of premium.

*Volunteer Workers.* In some states volunteer workers are entitled to benefits under workers compensation laws. Except as otherwise provided (by endorsement or manual rule such as that relating to volunteer firemen), premium will be based on the amount of remuneration normally received by regular employees doing the same or similar work.

Volunteer workers can be provided with benefits equal to those under the act by means of a voluntary compensation endorsement, which would set forth the basis of premium. For example, the schedule of covered employees might include volunteer workers, whose remuneration for premium purposes is calculated at the wage paid regular employees for similar work.

*Welfare Recipients.* In some jurisdictions, welfare recipients are required to "work out" their welfare payments when they are physically able to do so. In states in which the workers compensation statute covers these individuals, a manuscript endorsement similar to the following should be added to the policy: "It is agreed that the premium basis for employees who are also welfare recipients shall be calculated at the wage paid regular employees for similar work."

If a voluntary compensation endorsement is necessary to cover welfare recipients, the endorsement schedule should list them as welfare recipients, whose remuneration for premium purposes is calculated at the wage paid regular employees for similar work.

**Premiums Not Based on Remuneration.** Except in the state of Washington as explained, workers compensation insurance premiums are based almost entirely on the total remuneration to employees. There are only a few cases in which that principle does not apply. These cases involve classifications for which the premium base is specified in the classification description or in footnotes appearing on the state rate pages.

***Per Capita Premiums.*** Premiums for domestic workers in residences are charged per capita. The classifications in the *Basic Manual* for these workers are as follows:

Domestic Workers—Inside—Code 0913
Domestic Workers—Inside—Occasional—Code 0908
Domestic Workers—Outside—including private chauffeurs—Code 0912
Domestic Workers—Outside—Occasional—including occasional private chauffeurs—Code 0909

Rule XIV-D of the *Basic Manual* defines these classifications. The rates shown next to these code numbers on the state rate pages are the rates per each employee falling into that classification rather than the usual rate per $100 of payroll. If full-time domestic workers are employed for less time than the entire policy period, the per capita charge may be prorated according to their period of employment. However, each pro rata charge shall be at least 25 percent of the per capita charge.

***Upset Payroll.*** Upset payroll applies to insureds engaged exclusively in the pulpwood, logging, or lumbering industry. The classification includes the transportation of logs to the mill; construction, operation, maintenance, or extension of logging roads or logging railroads; and drivers. The classification was introduced approximately forty years ago primarily because of the difficulty in obtaining adequate payroll records from the employers in this industry. If adequate payroll records cannot be obtained, the basis of premium for this classification is called an upset payroll, which is based on the number of cords of wood produced.

For example, the state rate page may provide that an upset payroll of $12 per cord for logs up to eight feet long and $10 per cord for logs in excess of eight feet long shall be used for premium purposes. This method realistically approximates the actual payroll. Notice that this is only the payroll figure, and it must be multiplied by the rate.

***Taxicabs.*** A situation similar to upset payroll arises for the taxicab company classification for all but garage employees when there are no verifiable payroll records showing the remuneration of taxicab drivers. In this case the premium is based on the amount per vehicle per policy year for employee-operated vehicles shown in the state rate pages under "Miscellaneous Values." If the owner also leases or rents such vehicles, there is an additional premium calculated on the basis of the amount per vehicle per policy year for leased or rented vehicles also shown on the state rate pages under "Miscellaneous Values." This amount approximates the total earnings from driving one cab.[9]

***Policy Surcharge—Aircraft.*** If the insured uses aircraft for the transportation of personnel, the chance of workers compensation losses is increased. As a result, underwriters should carefully evaluate the exposure before agreeing to provide coverage. This additional exposure may be covered by the *aircraft premium endorsement* mentioned earlier. The premium for this coverage is based on the number of passenger seats in the aircraft. The applicable rate per passenger seat appears in the state rate pages under "Miscellaneous Values."

## Premium Determination

With the exceptions already discussed, the premium base is the insured's total remuneration to employees covered by the policy. The premium for the policy is essentially each $100 of the premium base multiplied by the applicable rate. However, there are additional factors besides the rate that may influence the amount of the premium. These include loss constants and expense constants in some states, minimum premiums, experience modifications, and premium discounts.

**Rates.** It is natural that the rates for workers compensation insurance vary by classification since the losses are much greater in some classifications than in others. The rate is the premium charged for each $100 of payroll. It must be high enough to generate sufficient premium to pay the losses in that classification and to cover expenses. In most states rates are developed by the authorized rating bureau and filed with the state insurance commissioner for approval.

Workers compensation insurance receives special attention from regulatory authorities. Although some states now allow open rating, rates for workers compensation insurance must generally be filed with and approved by state regulatory authorities prior to use even in those states where file-and-use laws apply to other lines of insurance. Bureau rates must be used in some states, while other states permit deviation from bureau rates by a fixed percentage (or perhaps apply a deviation percentage to the *premium* instead of the rate). Such deviations must be filed and approved in advance in most states where deviations are permitted. In some states insurers may use the loss component of the rate developed by the bureau but must use their own expense component.

*The manual rate is the rate filed by the bureau and approved by the commissioner.* For National Council states the manual rate for each classification is shown after its code number on the state rate pages of the *Basic Manual.* For independent bureau states, the manual rate for each classification appears on the rate pages of the manual for that state.

In some cases, *(a) rates* may apply. The symbol (a) in the rate column means that the rate for that classification must be obtained from the rating organization. An (a) rate is prepared on an individual basis using a weighted average combination of other rates according to the insured's operations revealed in an inspection report. Classifications with (a) rates generally have such unusual exposures that the rates do not have the same degree of statistical credibility as manual rates.

In states permitting percentage deviations from bureau rates, the resulting rate may be termed the *authorized rate.* According to the *Basic Manual,* "authorized rate means the manual rate or any other rate that has been established by the National Council or other licensed rating organization."[10]

The rate for a classification code number followed by the symbol "D" or "E" includes a disease loading (A "d' was formerly used instead of an "E"). Such loadings reflect specific disease hazards inherent in the operations described by those classifications. Examples of such disease hazards are silicosis and asbestosis. With bureau approval the disease loading may be removed from a manual rate when the substance for which the disease loading was established is not present in the insured's operations.[11] The presence or absence of such a substance can materially affect the underwriting of the risk, especially if rates are thought to be inadequate.

**Loss Constant.** Experience has shown that the cost per unit of exposure is higher for small employers than for large ones. In an effort to equalize the loss ratios for small and large employers, a loss constant is added to the premium for policies with annual premiums under $500. While in some states the loss constant may be the same for all rating classes, in other states the loss constant may vary by industry group. For example, the loss constants for the three industry groups may be

(1) manufacturing, $15; (2) contracting, $8; and (3) all others, $5. The loss constant for each classification appears next to its code number on the state rate pages. Certain classifications, however, do not have loss constants. As of this writing (early 1990), the loss constant has been eliminated in all but four states and has been combined with the expense constant in one other state. The underwriter should check the manual to determine whether the loss constant applies in a given state.

The loss constant applies per state per policy. A loss constant is charged whenever the earned premium, exclusive of the expense constant for any state, is less than $500 unless such addition would increase the premium to an amount in excess of $500. In that event, only such part of the loss constant shall be added as will bring the amount of the premium to $500, not including the expense constant.[12] For any state in which the insured's operations develop more than $500 in premium, no loss constant applies.

If only one classification applies in a state, the loss constant for that classification should be charged. If more than one classification applies in a state, the loss constant for the classification with the highest loss constant applies.[13]

Loss constants should be stated on the information page on the basis of estimated payrolls. However, loss constants are subject to adjustment upon audit. They should be charged only for those classifications developing premium. If the insured had no operations during the policy period in any state shown in the declarations, no loss constant should be charged for that state.

If a policy is canceled, the pro rata or short rate (depending on who canceled) portion of the loss constant is added subject to the $500 limitation. In a short-term policy the full loss constant is charged except that it may be prorated if (1) the short term policy is issued to replace a binder or (2) the short term policy is issued solely to establish concurrence with other policies of insurance.[14] Loss constants are *not* subject to experience rating modifications. If the minimum premium becomes the final premium for the policy, a loss constant should not be added because it is already included in the minimum premium for each classification.

**Expense Constant.** The expense loading in workers compensation rates does not provide enough premium to cover the expense of issuing and servicing policies with small premiums. The expense constant is an additional premium charge that helps to cover the expenses of issuing, recording, and auditing common to all policies regardless of size. If a state has an expense constant in effect, it applies to all policies, not merely to small ones.

The expense constant can be found in the state rate pages under

"Miscellaneous Values," and it should be shown on the information page. Since the expense constant is included in the calculation of the minimum premium for each policy, it should not be added if the minimum premium becomes the final premium for the policy.[15] It is not subject to premium discount, experience rating modification, or retrospective rating adjustment.[16] For short-term policies the full expense constant should be charged except in those cases mentioned in the preceding section on the loss constant. In addition, the pro rata portion of the expense constant shall not be less than $15 in those cases.[17]

**Minimum Premiums.** A minimum premium is the lowest amount for which a policy may be written. It is stated as the lowest total policy premium for any policy period not exceeding one year. The minimum premium for a classification provides the insuring company with enough premium to cover the usual cost of issuing and servicing a policy. It is stated on the information page on an estimated basis. The minimum premium for any classification includes the loss and expense constants. It is not subject to experience rating. The minimum premium is subject to pro rating on short-term policies under either of the two conditions described in the preceding section on the loss constant.

Unless the classification is (a) rated, the minimum premium appears on the state rate pages opposite the code number for each classification. The (a) rated minimum premiums are developed by the underwriter subject to the approval of the bureau having jurisdiction.

**Experience Rating Plan.** The experience modification is calculated by the bureau and forwarded to the current insurer. The purpose of the experience modification is to tailor the state manual rate to the policyholder's experience based upon the premium and loss record of certain prior years. This modification rewards employers who are relatively successful in controlling losses and penalizes those who are not. The experience modification is used to calculate the estimated premium at policy inception and at the time the final premium adjustment is calculated. As accidents occur less frequently or as their severity diminishes, the policyholder's experience modification becomes a factor of less than one and reduces the insured's overall premium for the current year. This is called an *experience credit.*

*Illustration:*

| | |
|---|---|
| Estimated annual premium (before modification) | $90,000 |
| Experience modification | .90 |
| Estimated modified premium | $81,000 |

If the loss record of the policyholder has not been favorable, the experience modification calculated by the bureau will prove to be a factor greater than one and, as a consequence, will cause the workers compensation premiums to increase. This is called an *experience debit.*

*Illustration:*

| | |
|---|---|
| Estimated annual premium (before modification) | $90,000 |
| Experience modification | 1.15 |
| Estimated modified premium | $103,500 |

The workers compensation bureau having jurisdiction calculates the experience modification based on a formula involving the payroll and losses for each policyholder. The experience period used in calculating an experience modification for a risk generally consists of three complete years of loss experience ending one year prior to the effective date of the modification. For example, the year 1 January 19X9 to 1 January 19X0 would be calculated by the bureau using payroll and losses for the three-year period 1 January 19X5 to 1 January 19X8. The year 1 January 19X8 to 1 January 19X9 is not used until the following year. This method, which uses payroll and losses for three consecutive years, has the effect of averaging the years. As a result, there are still fluctuations, but not the substantial fluctuations that could occur if only one year of experience were used. The most recently expired year is not included in this calculation because the reporting mechanism for payroll and losses cannot provide this information fast enough to do so. Under the unit statistical reporting plan used by NCCI, the premium and losses must be first reviewed at eighteen months after the effective date of the policy and filed no later than twenty months after the effective date of the policy. The use of that information, therefore, cannot be included in the calculation of the current year's modification.

An insured qualifies for experience rating if the payrolls developed during the experience period produce a stipulated minimum premium at the manual rates in force on the date for which the rating is to be established. The minimum varies, but a $3,500 annual premium is used in many states.

The application of this plan to each qualified insured is mandatory regardless of whether a debit or a credit modification results. It is the intent of this plan to rate on the normal anniversary date, and it is not permissible to alter an existing policy by cancellation or rewriting or by any extension of a policy term for the purpose of enabling an insured to qualify for, or avoid, the application of this plan. The use of the experience rating worksheet as a source of underwriting information is examined in the next chapter.

**Premium Discount.** Premium discount allows an insured to receive a credit adjustment in relation to the total earned premium.

Premium discounts are based on the theory of graduating expenses according to the size of the premium. In most states a premium discount plan has been adopted whereby an insured owing a total standard premium of $5,000 or more is entitled to a discount. The *standard premium* for a state means the premium determined on the basis of authorized rates for each classification plus any appropriate additional charge such as experience rating modification, schedule rating modification, loss constants, and minimum premiums. The expense constant is excluded from the determination of the standard premium. The *total standard premium* means the total premium for all states covered under the policy. It should be noted that premium discounts do not apply to standard premiums included in a retrospective rating plan.[18] Separate policies issued to an insured by a single insurer or by two or more insurers under the same management may be combined for the purpose of applying premium discounts.[19] If a policy includes coverage in one or more states that have approved the premium discount plan, and the policy develops total standard premium in excess of the stipulated minimum amount, the standard premium is subject to premium discount. The premium discount varies depending on whether the policy is written for a single state or multiple states. Exhibit 11-6 illustrates the computation of the premium discount when there is only one state covered.

## CLASSIFICATION OF WORKERS COMPENSATION EXPOSURES

The pricing of workers compensation insurance policies involves not only determining the total payroll reflecting the loss exposures covered by the policy but also assigning the payroll to appropriate classifications. This assignment is necessary because the rates for workers compensation insurance vary considerably according to the classification. Class rating isolates the potential causes of loss associated with a particular business and its environment. Thus, employers in hazardous businesses pay higher rates for the workers compensation insurance, which provides benefits to their injured employees. In theory, therefore, each class of business bears its own share of the losses from work-related injuries and diseases. To achieve this result, however, it is necessary for both premiums and losses to be accurately and consistently assigned to the proper classes.

Novice underwriters may ask why a knowledge of classification is necessary when most applications already show a class code number and the exposure units assigned to it. However, it is the responsibility of the underwriter to see that the policy is correctly priced. Just as an

**Exhibit 11-6**

Premium Discount—Single State Policy

**STATEMENT OF PREMIUM ADJUSTMENT**

| NAME AND ADDRESS OF INSURED | NAME AND ADDRESS OF COMPANY |
|---|---|
| FIBI'S Furniture, Inc.<br>Sofa, CT 06598 | Colonial Crafts Mutual<br>Hebron, CT 06248 |
| NAME AND ADDRESS OF AGENCY<br>Thomas Hooker Insurance Agency<br>Charter Oak, CT 06499 | POLICY NUMBER: 81 WC 234567<br>KIND OF POLICY:<br>POLICY PERIOD (MONTH-DAY-YEAR TO MONTH-DAY-YEAR): 7/1/X0 TO 7/1/X1<br>DATE: |
| AGENCY CODE: Z—1636 | AUDIT PERIOD: SAME TO<br>TYPE OF AUDIT: ☐ FIELD ☐ MAIL ☐ ESTIMATE |

| CODE | DESCRIPTION/LOCATION | • BASE/AMOUNT | RATE | PREMIUM | PREVIOUSLY BILLED | ADDITIONAL RETURN |
|---|---|---|---|---|---|---|
| 2881 | Furniture Assembling—Wood | 2466289 | 4.85 | 119615 | | |
| 2883 | Furniture Mfg.—Wood | 1312714 | 9.72 | 127596 | | |
| 8044 | Furniture Store | 404218 | 3.25 | 13137 | | |
| 8810 | Clerical | 101222 | .30 | 304 | | |
| | | | | 260652 | | |
| 0063 | Prem. Disc. (Table 4) | | 15.5% | (40401) | | |
| | | | | 220251 | | |
| | Total Premiums | | | 220251 | 216000 (Deposit) | 4251 (Additional premium due) |

underwriter verifies the underwriting information on the application, so should the classifications assigned be verified. Too often a classification is used either because it was the classification on the previous insurer's policy or because it had the lower rate of the two classifications the producer thought might be applicable. Although the producer is familiar with the risk and has the information about the risk needed to assign the proper classification, the producer may not know the manual rules regarding various classifications.

The rules and classification definitions spelled out in the workers compensation manual applicable in the particular state are designed to attain consistency in classification assignments. In assigning classifications, underwriters must be logical and must follow these rules and definitions. This section describes the workers compensation manual and other guides to classifications, explains the rules regarding classification procedures, and separately discusses construction classifications since they are handled differently from other risks.

## Classification Guides

While experience gives underwriters a familiarity with workers compensation classifications that helps them to assign classifications, even the most experienced underwriter must frequently refer to standard sources to ensure that the correct classifications are assigned in every case. The existence of state exceptions and other subtle variations as well as continual revisions would overtax anyone's memory. The only way to be absolutely certain of a classification is to reread the definition in a classification reference.

Classification references fall into two groups. The fundamental reference is always the workers compensation manual that applies in a given jurisdiction. In addition, there are a number of other references that supplement the manual with alternative arrangements of classifications and additional explanations and interpretations.

**The Workers Compensation Manual—Part Two.** *The Basic Manual for Workers Compensation and Employers Liability Insurance* issued by the National Council on Compensation Insurance applies in all but thirteen states. Six of those thirteen states have monopolistic state funds for workers compensation insurance. The remainder use manuals similar to the *Basic Manual,* but that are issued by independent state bureaus. Part Two of the manual is divided into three separate sections, each of which helps to point to the correct classification.

***Classifications Section.*** This section, page C1 to C54 in the *Basic Manual* and often referred to as C pages, is an alphabetical listing of the classifications established by the National Council. Exhibit 11-7 shows one of these classifications. The description of each classification listed is a phrase perceived as most applicable for the operation. Following that definition is the classification code number. The classification definition frequently coincides with the job title assigned to workers by insureds in that business. The term is usually readily recognizable by both the insured and insurer as an adequate identification of the exposure.

The entire phrase in boldface upper case type together with the classification code number fully identifies the classification. Any reference to a classification on the information page or premium billings should include, as a minimum, all words appearing in boldface, upper case type.

Any part of the classification description appearing in light face type and any notes immediately following the classification description

**Exhibit 11-7**
Example of a Classification Description

> STORE:
>
> HARDWARE .................................. 8010
>
> Applies to wholesale or retail stores.

form part of the *classification definition.* These notes are an integral part of this overall classification. *Notes can explain, extend, or limit the classification definition.* Notes often explain or identify an element of the operation that is not readily apparent in the job description or job title. Notes can extend the classification definition by identifying an element that might appear to go beyond the basic classification, but which is in reality an important segment of that particular business activity. Notes can limit the classification by excluding elements that appear to be a constituent part of the exposure being defined.

Classifications are listed in alphabetical order. Unfortunately, however, classification definitions occasionally begin with a different word than the underwriter anticipates, and thus, they are not always readily found. The other classification guides can help to overcome this problem.

***Underwriting Guide, Classification Section.*** This section is, as its name implies, a guide for anyone involved in classifying workers compensation exposures. It is an expansion of the listing of classifications and includes pages G1-G22. This guide was prepared to help classify operations not specifically identified by the classification definitions.

This section of the "Underwriting Guide" provides an alphabetical listing of businesses with corresponding classification code numbers. Even though a business may be called by a name different from the one used in the classification definition, this listing points to the correct classification. A good example would be a bakery business specializing in making doughnuts and only doughnuts. The insured might consider this business quite different from the many varied operations of a large commercial bakery. This section includes a listing, "Doughnut Mfg," which does not appear in the classification section. The assigned code number and consequent rate, however, are the same as for the bakery classification. In that situation, an insured might be mollified by being labeled a doughnut manufacturer instead of a bakery. In this situation the *Basic Manual* provides a reference to the more acceptable

**Exhibit 11-8**
Extract from Underwriting Guide

| | |
|---|---|
| Beer Vat Coating with Chemicals | 3726 |
| Berry, Fruit Farms or Vineyards—See "Farms" | |
| Bicycles—retail sale or rental—including repair | 8010 |
| Blast Furnace Erection | 5057 |
| Blast Furnace Repair and Relining—masonry | 5022 |

terminology as well as to proper classification. All of the rules pertaining to the assigned classification apply to the business.[20]

An underwriter attempting to classify a bicycle shop might turn to the portion of the "Underwriting Guide" shown in Exhibit 11-8. The entry for bicycles refers to Code 8010, the classification code for hardware stores that appeared in Exhibit 11-7.

This section of the "Underwriting Guide" can be regarded as a second source in the quest for proper classification assignments. A definition that seems "close but not quite" in the classification section may be confirmed by reference to the entries in the "Underwriting Guide." Conversely, the phraseology of a classification in the "Underwriting Guide" may cause the underwriter to rethink the original assumptions made to classify a risk, thus helping to find a better, more applicable classification.

***Underwriting Guide, Interpretation Section.*** An additional part of the "Underwriting Guide" is the Interpretation Section. Although it is included in the G pages of the manual (pages G23-G46), it can be considered separately. The Interpretation Section has two parts, classifications and all other.

*Classifications.* The classifications listed in this segment also appear in the C pages and in the Classification Section of the "Underwriting Guide" listing. The purpose is to clarify those classifications. An expanded definition may be found within these pages.

The identification of the various available uses for the multifaceted "stores" classification alone establishes this section as an invaluable aid. Exhibit 11-9 shows the interpretation of the hardware store classification. This interpretation explains the other operations included within this classification.

Underwriters should become familiar with this section and recognize it as a resource for validating some of the more uncertain classification assignments. Knowing where to find the necessary interpretations is a major advantage.

*All Other.* This segment may be considered an appendix to "Part One—Rules." The interpretations further define many of the rules and procedures of the manual. Subsections in this segment include the following:

- Auditing
- Basis of premium
- Manual rules—miscellaneous
- Overtime
- Payroll limitation
- Premium discount plan
- Experience rating
- Retrospective rating

**The Workers Compensation Manual—Part Three—Rates and State Exceptions.** The last section of the manual is the state rates and exceptions pages. These pages vary in content according to the states for which they apply. Their format is similar in that they contain the special classifications and rules that apply in that state as well as the workers compensation rates for each classification code. There may also be procedural notes, interpretations, rulings, and administrative data relevant to the workers compensation law of the particular state. Exhibit 11-10 shows that in Wisconsin, retail and wholesale hardware stores must be assigned different classifications. Obviously, it is essential for underwriters to have a thorough knowledge of the state pages for the states within which they work.

**Other Classification References.** Although the *Basic Manual* or the corresponding manual for the jurisdiction is the fundamental reference for classifications, additional references are often useful in determining the classification for an operation. Many of these references are issued by the National Council. Others come from a variety of sources. Even though they may be less authoritative, they have other advantages that make them useful. Some of the most common classification references are discussed in the following subsections.

***Scopes of Basic Manual Classifications.*** The *Scopes Manual* is a fairly recent addition to the list of reference materials published by the National Council to aid in classifying an insured. The *Scopes Manual* first includes a reference section that simply lists the classes in alphabetical order with the corresponding code number. The majority of the *Scopes Manual* is a numeric listing of all the codes contained in the manual. Only one code number is shown on each page (although some codes require more than one page). In addition to listing the code number, each page shows the correct phraseology for the classification name, cross-referenced phraseology and footnotes for the classification

**Exhibit 11-9**
Sample Page from Interpretation Section*

**Page G30**
**1st Reprint**
**(Corrected)**

**WORKERS COMPENSATION AND EMPLOYERS LIABILITY**

*Issued July 1, 1982*

**Operations Not Covered:**

1. Dealers in ladies' handbags shall be assigned to Code 8017—"Retail Stores NOC."
2. Stores principally engaged in selling sporting goods such as camping, fishing, hunting, baseball, football, bowling or basketball equipment or supplies and incidental clothing shall be assigned to Code 8017—"Sporting Goods Stores."
3. Stores engaged principally in the mail order sales of clothing, wearing apparel, or dry goods to individuals shall be assigned to Code 8032—"Clothing Stores—wholesale."

**Hardware Stores** . . . . . . . . . . . . . . . . . . . . . . . . . **8010**

★ **Ship Chandlers—no Mfg.** . . . . . . . . . . . . . . . . . . . **8010**

This classification applies to wholesale or retail stores. (Minnesota: Retail—Code 8036; Wholesale—8029) (Wisconsin: Retail—Code 8010; Wholesale—Code 8018)

**Operations Covered:**

This classification applies to wholesale or retail dealers engaged principally in selling articles such as nails, screws, bolts, washers, gaskets, brackets, locks, hinges, electrical outlet boxes, switches, in this classification.

Other types of risks included in this classification are wholesale dealers in the following articles:

1. Radio or Television Parts.
2. Automobile Parts and Accessories.
3. Aircraft Parts and Accessories.
4. Air Conditioning or Refrigerator Parts.
5. Oil Burners and Parts.
6. Cutlery.
7. Sewing Machine Heads and Parts.

**Operations Not Covered:**

1. Stores engaged principally in the retail selling of paint, wallpaper and allied supplies, kitchenware, china and glassware, or sporting goods shall be assigned to Code 8017—"Retail Stores NOC."
2. Stores engaged principally in the retail selling of automobile accessories or parts shall be assigned to Code 8046—"Automobile Accessories Stores—retail." (Minnesota: Code 8036)
3. Repair or installation of household electrical appliances, phonographs, radios and television sets by separate employees at or away from the store, shall be assigned to Code 9519—"Household Appliances—installation, service or repair." (Wisconsin: If any operations conducted

fuses, plugs, sockets, hand or machine tools, portable electric tools, plumbing fittings and garden tools, supplies and equipment including lawn mowers and snow plows.

In addition, hardware stores usually sell a wide variety of incidental "non-hardware" items such as paint, wallpaper and allied supplies, household electrical appliances, phonographs, radios and television sets, kitchenware, china and glassware, sporting goods and automobile accessories or parts.

Such stores may also rent floor scraping or polishing machines, rug and upholstery cleaning machines and similar equipment.

This classification also includes "ship chandlers" who are dealers in ship supplies and equipment such as engine room equipment, lifeboat supplies, navigational instruments, deck gear and other ship stores.

Other types of retail stores or operations assigned to this classification are:

1. Stores selling parts and supplies for radio, television or phonograph equipment.
2. Bicycle Stores—including rental and incidental repair work.
3. Locksmiths—including installation, repair or replacement of locks in existing buildings.

Stores engaged principally in the wholesale or retail mail order sales of hardware are included away from the store, assign Code 8010 to entire operation.)

4. When a store has separate employees engaged in sharpening or repairing ice skates, lawn mowers or cutlery, such operations shall be assigned to Code 3632— "Machine Shops NOC." (Minnesota: Code 8036; Wisconsin: refer to bureau)
5. Wholesale or retail dealers principally engaged in selling plumbers' supplies such as tubs, sinks, radiators, tanks, boilers, and other plumbing fixtures or equipment shall be assigned to Code 8111— "Plumbers' Supplies Dealers."
6. Wholesale or retail dealers principally engaged in selling wire, cable or metal conduit shall be assigned to Code 8106— "Iron or Steel Merchants."
7. Wholesale or retail dealers principally engaged in selling metal pipe, rods, tubes, sheet metal, iron, steel or non-ferrous metals shall be assigned to Code 8106— "Iron or Steel Merchants."
8. Wholesale dealers in welding supplies such as tanks, torches, welding rods and face masks shall be assigned to Code 8018— "Welding Supplies Stores—wholesale—NOC." (Wisconsin: Code 8111)
9. Stores engaged principally in the sale of major household electrical appliances, shall be assigned to Code 8044— "Store: Furniture." (Wisconsin: Code 8010)

**Exhibit 11-10**
Extract from Wisconsin State Pages "Special Classifications"

STORE:

| | |
|---|---|
| HARDWARE—RETAIL—& Drivers | 8010 |
| HARDWARE—WHOLESALE | 8018 |

(this is not given for all classifications), and a detailed description of the "scope" of the classification. The preface to the *Scopes Manual* explains that the scope description for each classification was derived from (1) material contained in National Council classification files, (2) National Council underwriting committee decisions, and (3) National Council underwriting staff interpretations. The manual is semiannually updated. Underwriters have found the *Scopes Manual* to be helpful in determining the operations included within the scope of a certain classification. The final section of the *Scopes Manual* is a listing of classifications that apply only in certain states.

***Classification Code Book.*** The National Council *Classification Codes for Workers Compensation and Employers Liability* (hereafter referred to as the *Classification Code Book*) combines two different arrangements of worker compensation codes in one manual. The first section, "Classification Codes by Numerical Sequence," is printed on white pages. The second section, "Classification Codes by Schedules and Groups," is printed on yellow pages.

*Classification Codes by Numerical Sequence.* This section lists the same classifications shown in the *Basic Manual.* The listing, however, is numerically arranged by code number. Exhibit 11-11 shows a sample page.

There are three columns of statistical numbers to the left of the listed classifications. The first column contains the schedules and group codes that appear in the "Classification Codes by Schedules and Groups" (yellow pages). These numbers relate to the different levels at which the classification system segregates occupations. The first and second digits indicate the schedule, and the third digit represents the group.

The second column shows the compensation and employers liability code (C&EL code) number listing. These numbers determine the order in which the classifications are listed and helps to find the classification description corresponding to a particular code number when only the code number is known. Since some of the code numbers are assigned to multiple classification descriptions, the listing by code number also helps to define the range of operations included within a classification. Although in most instances the initial code number and corresponding classification description are appropriate for the operation, a more apt classification description may sometimes be listed as an alternative under the same code number.

If the classification has been discontinued, the code number is followed by a capital D. When experience from the discontinued class is assigned to a new class, that new class code is shown in parentheses after the classification description. If no new code number is shown, risks formerly in the discontinued classification must be individually classified according to the specific operations involved. Also shown in parentheses for many classes is the date the classification was erected and the date the classification was discontinued (if applicable). The *Basic Manual* should be consulted for the exact classification wording that should be used on the policy since the classification phraseologies are abbreviated.

The third column lists the manufacturers and contractors liability insurance code (M&C code) that corresponds to the listed classification. The term M&C is still used as the heading for this column although the term is no longer used under the ISO simplified policies. Two numbers are shown in this column, one over the other. The top number is the general liability classification code under the "old" general liability program; the bottom number is the code under the simplified program. Notice that the workers compensation code is shown in cross-reference only to the bottom code number. While this is not a definitive listing of all the possible general liability classifications (there are other possible correlations in many instances), this "cross-reference" can be helpful by providing additional insights to classification of the risk. Limited space is why only one general liability classification is shown.

*Classification Codes by Schedules and Groups.* This section of the *Classification Code Book* arranges classifications by main industry divisions called *schedules.* These are further subdivided into *groups* of classifications having generally similar or related characteristics.[21]

The index to this section lists thirty-seven schedules. The schedule numbers do not correlate to the "work field" numbering system of the U.S. Department of Labor or to other more prominent numbering designation symbols. They stem from the system devised by the National Council. The thirty-seven separate schedules represent distinct and recognizable industries. The subdivision of the schedules into groups organizes together businesses using similar technology or performing similar operations.

As stated, the schedule is represented by a two-digit number, and

**Exhibit 11-11**
Sample Page from *Classification Codes Book* (Numerical Sequence)*

**Page 50**
**Original Printing**

*Issued July 1, 1987*

**CLASSIFICATION CODES**

| STATISTICAL NUMBERS Sched.& Group | C. & E.L. Code | M. & C. Code | CLASSIFICATION |
|---|---|---|---|
| 347 | *7997 | 59991/10071 | Store: Automotive Parts—wholesale or combined wholesale and retail & drivers (TX) (E: 3-81) |
| 342 | *7998 | 52511/13716 | Hardware Stores—retail (NY) and (TX) (E: 1-33) |
| 342 | *7999 | 52511/13716 | Hardware Stores—wholesale (NY) (E: 7-39) |
| 342 | *7999 | 52511/13716 | Hardware Stores—wholesale or combined wholesale and retail (TX) (E: 1-33) |
| 341 | 8000D | — | Department Stores—retail (D: 6-34) (8039) |
| 341 | 8001 | 59991/12841 | Florist—store—& drivers |
| 347 | 8002 | 65121/xxxxx | Automobile Rental Co.—all other employees & counter personnel, drivers (E: 7-81) |
| 373 | *8003 | — | Aircraft or Helicopter Operation: Air Carrier—Ticket Sellers and Information Clerks at airports or heliports (AK) (E: 1-84) |
| 053 | 8005D | — | Milk Dealers—store or depot only (D: 12-15) (2070) |
| 343 | *8017 | 59991/18434 | Retail Store—NOC—no service of food (NY) (E: 1-58) |
| 343 | *8017 | 79300/10160 | Billiard Hall (MN) (E: 6-81) |
| 343 | 8018 | — | Store: wholesale—NOC |
| 343 | *8018 | 50991/14068 | Store: Hide Dealer (MN) (E: 6-81) |
| 343 | *8018 | — | Warehousing—Groceries only (AR) |
| 343 | *8019 | — | Temporary Labor Service—Mercantile Operations—all employees engaged in retail and wholesale store operations, & drivers (TX) (E: 1-74) |
| 343 | 8020D | — | Cigar Stores—retail (D: 3-17) (8017) |
| 340 | 8021 | 50421/15223 | Meat, Fish or Poultry Dealer—wholesale |
| 340 | *8021 | 50421/15223 | Meat or Poultry Dealer Wholesale (ME) (E: 3-81) |
| 343 | 8022D | — | Piano or Organ Dealers (Store only) (D: 3-17) (8044) |
| 053 | 8023D | — | Milk Depots—incl. preparation of product for distribution (D: 7-26) (2070) |

| | | | |
|---|---|---|---|
| 340 | 8006 | 54131/13671 | Grocery Store—retail (Not available in CA) |
| 341 | 8007D | — | Dry Goods Stores—retail exclusively (D: 6-49) (8008) |
| 341 | 8008 | 56991/11125 | Store—Dry Goods—Clothing, Wearing Apparel—Retail |
| 341 | 8009D | — | Store Risks—wholesale exclusively (D: 8-22) (8032) |
| 342 | 8010 | 52511/13716 | Store—Hardware—wholesale or retail (Not available in CA, MN, NY and TX) |
| 343 | 8011D | — | Wine and Spirit Merchants—wholesale (D: 1920 Rev.) (8018) |
| 343 | 8012D | — | Wine and Spirit Merchants—no bar, packages only (D: 3-17) (8017) |
| 341 | 8013 | 59711/14655 | Store—Jewelry—wholesale or retail |
| 341 | 8014D | — | Tailor Stores—retail (D: 12-15) (8008) |
| 343 | 8015D | — | Furniture Stores—wholesale or retail (D: 12-38) (8044) (Retained in CA) |
| 123 | *8015 | — | Copying or Duplicating Service—All Employees, Clerical, Salespersons (AZ) (E: 2-85) |
| 340 | *8017 | — | Delicatessen—Retail (AK) (E: 4-86) |
| 343 | 8017 | 59991/18434 | Store Risks—retail NOC |
| 340 | *8017 | — | Grocery, Tea or Coffee Dealer—Retail —& Salespersons (AZ) |
| 340 | *8017 | — | Household Furnishings or Wearing Apparel Dealer—Retail—& Salespersons (AZ) |
| 340 | *8017 | — | Stores—retail—NOC (CA) (E: 4-72) |
| 340 | *8024 | 50421/15223 | Seafood Dealer—Wholesale (ME) (E: 3-81) |
| 056 | 8026D | — | Distributing Stations for Breweries (2121) |
| 279 | *8028 | — | Equipment or Machinery Rental Yards—not dealers in new or used equipment—all employees (CA) (E: 1-87) |
| 342 | *8029 | 52511/13716 | Hardware Store—wholesale (MN) (E: 9-26) |
| 340 | 8030D | — | Delicatessen Stores (E: 9-17) (D: 12-50) (8006) (Retained in NJ) |
| 340 | 8031 | 54211/15224 | Store—Meat, fish or poultry—retail (Re-E: 6-37) |
| 341 | 8032 | 50341/11126 | Store—Clothing, Wearing Apparel or Dry Goods—wholesale (E: 8-22) |
| 340 | 8033 | 54131/13671 | Store—Meat, Grocery and Provision (combined)—retail—NOC (Re-E: 6-37) (Not available in CA) |
| 340 | 8034D | — | Store: Grocery—wholesale (E: 12-50) (Not available in CA) (D: 7-77) (8018) (Retained in AZ, MA, MN, MO, NJ, NY, OK and TX) |
| 340 | *8034D | — | Grocery Stores—wholesale or combined wholesale and retail (NJ) (E: 7-41) (D: 1-51) |
| 342 | *8036 | 52511/13716 | Hardware Store: Retail exclusively (MN) |
| 343 | *8038 | 59991/18433 | Store Risks—retail—NOC—serving food (TX) (E: 2-30) |
| 341 | 8039 | 53111/12356 | Store—Department—retail (E: 6-34) |
| 341 | *8039 | — | Department Store—retail (TX) (E: 12-58) |



*Reprinted with permission from the National Council on Compensation Insurance.

the group by a one-digit number following those two digits. Terminology is somewhat confusing with regard to this numbering system since one often refers to the group by the entire three-digit number. For example, Group 241 refers to Gases and Miscellaneous Inorganic Chemicals, which is a subset of Schedule 24, Chemicals. Under Schedule 24 there are seven groups:

240—Chemical and Dyestuff Rating Plan
241—Gases and Miscellaneous Inorganic Chemicals
242—Extracts, Drugs and Medicine
243—Paint, Ink and Polishes
244—Vegetable Oils and Animal By-Products
245—Coal, Wood and Petroleum Products and Distillation
246—Explosives and Ammunition

Within each group, the active classes, state specials, and discontinued classes are shown with classifications within each in alphabetical order. Discontinued classes are indicated by a D in this section also. The classification to which the experience of the discontinued classification was assigned is shown in parentheses. Classification phraseologies are abbreviated in this section also. Exhibit 11-12 shows a page from this section of the *Classification Code Book.*

This reference can help an underwriter find the appropriate classification when the only starting point is the general nature of the activity. After narrowing the possibilities to the probable schedule and group, the underwriter can then scan all the classifications within the group and study the definitions of those that seem likely to apply.

***Workers Compensation Insurance Premium Audit Reference Book.*** The National Council issues the *Workers Compensation Insurance Premium Audit Reference Book* (hereafter referred to as the *Audit Reference Book*) solely as a reference and guide. As such, it carries less authority than the manuals. Its first page cautions that "the contents of this book are to be used solely for reference or guide purposes" and stipulates that individual insurers "may provide the auditors with specific instructions pertaining to any interpretation appearing in this book."[22]

The *Audit Reference Book* contains a wealth of information and interpretations issued for individual states. Although intended for auditors, it can also be of help to underwriters in classifying risks. It provides addresses of rating organizations for each of the states, an alphabetical listing of classifications, a summary of state exceptions, the rulings and interpretations of the National Council arranged alphabetically by subject, and guidelines explaining significant rules and procedures. The final sections cover interstate experience rating and insurer audit and test audit examples.

***Circular Letters, Manual Amendment Bulletins, and Manual Amendment Pages.*** The National Council and state rating bureaus issue circular letters informing the user of changes or alterations when necessary. These circular letters are a means of informing subscribers of rate increases or decreases and their consideration or pending implementation. Pending law amendments are outlined therein. Circular letters sometimes report changes in procedures that are under consideration or that have been submitted to government bodies for approval. They also provide notice of classification code changes and explanations of the reasons for such changes.

Manual amendment bulletins notify recipients of pending changes in the manual. These changes have usually been proposed and are awaiting a final decision on implementation. In some cases, the bulletin gives the effective date of the change.

The follow-up to manual amendment bulletins is the manual amendment page. The manual amendment page is exactly what its name implies, an amended page that replaces a current page in the manual. Manual amendment pages should be inserted in the correct location on receipt and the change noted. Underwriters should study the new page and compare it to the old page to grasp the application of the change and its rationale.

***Commercial Lines Manual.*** Another reference is the *Commercial Lines Manual (CLM)* issued by the Insurance Services Office. The *CLM* was described earlier and is mentioned here because it may offer some insight into workers compensation classifications.

The advantages of the *CLM* stem in many instances from the correlation of workers compensation and general liability classification descriptions of exposures. This correlation exists because if two risks have similar exposures, the classifications describing those risks are likely to be similar. The *CLM* also provides "a second opinion." The underwriter searching for the most applicable classification may often find this second opinion a stimulus for thought. Following the workers compensation manual, the underwriter may have reached a classification assignment about which there is some doubt. Through cross referencing the workers compensation classification to the *CLM* classification, the underwriter notes in the classification terminology or the attendant notes a distinction or interpretation that may trigger a "chain of thought" that can lead either to a different, more relevant classification or to a confirmation of the original assignment.

***Manuals in Use by the Company.*** Each insurance company employing premium auditors usually has its own auditor's manual and

**Exhibit 11-12**
Sample Page from *Classification Codes Book* (Schedules and Groups)*

**CLASSIFICATION CODES** — *Issued July 1, 1987* — **Page 25** **Original Printing**

**Group 221**—Continued

Discontinued

| | | |
|---|---|---|
| Potteries—mfg. electrical porcelain ware—excluding mining and clay digging | 4058D | (4062) |
| Potteries—mfg. floor, wall or fireplace tile—decorative, not structural | 4055D | (4062) |
| Potteries—mfg. glazed or porcelain earthenware—excluding manufacture of retorts, sewer or drain pipe, electrical porcelain or fireproofing tile | 4049D | (4061) |
| Potteries—mfg. sanitary porcelain earthenware | 4051D | (4061) |
| Terra Cotta Mfg.—for decorating purposes | 4054D | (4053) |

**SCHEDULE 23—GLASS PRODUCTS**

**Group 230—Glass Mfg.**

| | |
|---|---|
| Glass Mfg.—& drivers | 4101 |
| Incandescent Lamp Mfg. (CA) | 4112 |
| Electronic Tube or Transistor Mfg. (CA) | 4112 |
| Television or Cathode Ray Tube Mfg. (NJ) | 4115 |

**SCHEDULE 24—CHEMICALS**

**Group 240—Chemical and Dyestuff Rating Plan**

| | |
|---|---|
| Chemical and Dyestuff Rating Plan | 4800-23<br>4860-83 |
| Acid Mfg. | 4815 |
| Ammonium Mfg | 4812 |
| Ammonium Nitrate Mfg. | 4811 |
| Synthetic Rubber | 4804 |

State Specials

| | |
|---|---|
| Chemical Mfg.—incl. Mixing, Blending and Packaging (CA) | 4829 |
| Chemical Mixing, Blending and Repackaging Only (CA) | 4828 |

Discontinued

| | | |
|---|---|---|
| Glass Mfg.—blown sheet window glass—& drivers | 4102D | (4101) |
| Glass Mfg.—Sheet Glass Mfg.—rolled glass, not polished | 4103D | (4101) |

**Group 231—Miscellaneous Glass Products**

| | |
|---|---|
| Cathedral or Art Glass Window Mfg. | 4133 |
| Glass Window Mfg.—stained | 4133 |
| Glass Merchant | 4130 |
| Glass Mfg.—cut | 4113 |
| Glassware Mfg.—no automatic blowing machines | 4111 |
| Glassware Mfg.—NOC | 4114 |
| Incandescent Lamp Mfg. | 4112 |
| Radio Tube Mfg. | 4112 |
| Mirror Mfg. | 4131 |

State Specials

| | |
|---|---|
| Glass Mfg.—cut (MN) | 4114 |
| Glassware Mfg.—No Automatic Blowing Machines (MN) | 4114 |

**Group 241—Gases and Miscellaneous Inorganic Chemicals**

| | |
|---|---|
| Oxygen or Hydrogen Mfg.—& drivers | 4635 |
| Acetylene Gas Mfg.—& drivers | 4635 |
| Carbonic Acid Gas Mfg.—& drivers | 4635 |
| Hydrogen or Oxygen Mfg.—& drivers | 4635 |
| Salt, Borax or Potash Producing or Refining—& drivers | 4568 |
| Borax, Salt or Potash Producing or Refining—& drivers | 4568 |
| Potash, Salt or Borax Producing or Refining—& drivers | 4568 |

State Specials

| | |
|---|---|
| Acid Mfg.—sulphuric, hydrochloric or nitric only (MD, NJ, NY and TX) | 4536 |
| Ammonia Mfg.—nitrogen hydrogen fixation processes (CA, KS, KY, MN, MS, NY, NC and TX) | 4585 |
| Ammonium Nitrate Mfg. (CA, FL, KS, MN, MS, NY, NC, OK and TX) | 4586 |
| Bleaching Powder Mfg. (NY) | 4527 |
| Chlorine or Alkali Mfg. (NY) | 4527 |
| Silica Gel Mfg. (MD) | 4584 |

Discontinued

| | | |
|---|---|---|
| Acetylene Gas Mfg. | 4636D | (4635) |



*Reprinted with permission from the National Council on Compensation Insurance.

related company manuals. Obviously, the auditor should study these company manuals and know how to use them; but underwriters can also benefit from these manuals. Company procedures vary within the insurance industry, and the underwriter should be thoroughly grounded in the procedures preferred by a particular company.

Many companies have also compiled excellent classification interpretation manuals that further explain classification assignment methodology. These manuals may carry the weight of final authority within that company, and the underwriter is well-advised to be familiar with their uses and contents.

***Internal Bulletins.*** Insurance company internal bulletins are, as the name implies, applicable to the operations and procedures of each individual insurer. Underwriters should be aware of all such bulletins as they may assist the process of classification. Their applicability is determined by the company.

***PAAS Classification Guides.*** The Premium Audit Advisory Service (PAAS) publishes classification guides that describe the operations contemplated by particular classifications, list state exceptions and compare workers compensation to general liability classifications. The PAAS educational bulletins can also help in resolving classification problems. Exhibit 11-13 shows a sample page from the PAAS *Classification Guide.*

## Classification Rules

"Part One—Rules" of the *Basic Manual* states the rules to be followed in the assignment of classifications. Any business may involve many different operations in a variety of combinations. Some of these operations may be extremely hazardous, while others are not. Some may be very minor and incidental to other operations. In some situations it may be equitable to rate some of the insured's operations separately from the others. The classification rules attempt to delineate classification procedures, which are both equitable and easily applied.

**Classifications Explained.** As the *Basic Manual* explains, "The object of the classification system is to group employers into classifications so that the rate for each classification reflects the exposures common to those employers."[23] With certain exceptions, that rate is an average for all employees of the business even though some may be involved in much more hazardous activities than others. In general, therefore, "it is the business of the employer within a state that is classified, not the separate employments, occupations or operations within the business."[24] The rules specify certain situations,

**Exhibit 11-13**
Sample Classification Description from PAAS *Classification Guide**

85 JOHN STREET, NEW YORK, NY 10038—212/669-0511

PAAS
PREMIUM AUDIT ADVISORY SERVICE

CLASSIFICATION GUIDE

Topic GLASS WINDOW MFG. - STAINED          File No. 4133

WC INDUSTRIAL GROUP 231

| | CODE | MANUAL REFERENCE GLASS WINDOW MFG. - stained |
|---|---|---|
| WC | 4133 | Includes glass mfg.<br><br>STATE EXCEPTIONS: CA, DE, MI, PA |
| | | MANUAL REFERENCE Glass or Glassware Manufacturing |
| GL | 54077 | This classification includes cut, polished plate, rolled, ribbed, colored, figured, wire and machine or manually blown sheet window glass. |

<u>CONTEMPLATED OPERATIONS</u>

This classification contemplates the manufacture of the type of glass products described including the manufacture of the glass itself. The manufacturing process will generally include the coloring or staining of the glass, cutting the sheets to desired sizes and shapes and fitting with lead.

<u>OPERATIONS ASSIGNED BY ANALOGY (State Exceptions Not Shown)</u>

Cathedral or Art Glass Window Mfg.

<u>OPERATIONS WHICH MUST BE SEPARATELY CLASSIFIED (State Exceptions Not Shown)</u>

| | |
|---|---|
| Glass Mfg. | 4101 |
| Glass Mfg. - cut | 4113 |
| Glass Merchant | 4130 |
| Glassware Mfg. - No automatic blowing machines | 4111 |
| Glassware Mfg. NOC | 4114 |
| Glazier - Away from Shop | 5462 |
| Mirror Mfg. | 4131 |

<u>STATE EXCEPTIONS TO NCCI CODE 4133</u>

| | | |
|---|---|---|
| <u>CALIFORNIA</u> | <u>This classification applies, but with the following wording:</u> | |
| | Cathedral or Art Glass Window Mfg. - Including glass manufacturing | 4133 |
| <u>DELAWARE</u> | <u>This operation is assigned to the following classification:</u> | |
| | Glassware Mfg., NOC | 535 |
| <u>MICHIGAN</u> | <u>This operation is assigned to the following classification:</u> | |
| | Glass Window Mfg. - stained Includes glass mfg. | 4114 |
| <u>PENNSYLVANIA</u> | <u>Same as Delaware.</u> | 535 |

<u>GENERAL LIABILITY - Operations Which Must be Separately Classified</u>

| | |
|---|---|
| Glass Dealers and Glaziers | 13590 |

*Reprinted with permission from Premium Audit Advisory Service.

such as construction operations and insureds conducting separate businesses, that require assigning additional classifications.

Once the underwriter has been given the insured's gross payroll, he or she must determine the *basic classification* appropriate for the insured's business. The payroll of employees belonging to *standard exception classifications* must be separated from the gross payroll, as must the remuneration of employees performing operations defined as *general exclusions.* Unless the rules allowing additional classifications apply, the remaining payroll is then assigned to the basic classification. The essential point for the underwriter to remember is that all payroll goes into the basic classification unless the rules provide an explicit reason otherwise. Therefore, underwriters must thoroughly know and be readily able to apply these rules.

***Basic Classifications.*** The "Classifications Section" (C pages) of the *Basic Manual* alphabetically lists approximately 600 classifications. Other than the standard exception classifications, each one describes a particular business. All classifications in the *Basic Manual* other than standard exception classifications are basic classifications. Basic classifications describe the business of an employer. It is the underwriter's responsibility to determine which basic classification best describes the business of the employer within the state so that the employer's exposure base and loss experience may be pooled with all similar businesses.

The basic classification is often called the governing classification although that term is relevant only when additional classifications are permitted. In that case, "the *governing classification* at a specific job or location is the classification, other than a standard exception classification, that produces the greatest amount of payroll."[25] It is necessary to determine the governing classification first because the payroll of all employees not explicitly mentioned elsewhere in the rules must be included in the governing classification.

***Standard Exception Classifications.*** Some occupations are so common that they have been established as separate classifications. The *Basic Manual* defines these occupations as standard exception classifications. Employees falling within the definition of these standard exception classifications are not included within a basic classification *unless* the basic classification specifically includes those employees. For example, the classification "Church: Professional Employees & Clerical" (Code 8868) includes clerical employees even though they would otherwise be considered standard exceptions. The payroll for employees in these standard exception classifications is not included within the definition of payroll for general liability purposes. Except for drafting employees, there are no corresponding general liability codes for these standard exceptions.

If the insured has any employees meeting all the criteria of a standard exception, the payroll for these employees should be deducted from the basic classification and assigned to the appropriate standard exception classification. Standard exception classifications vary somewhat in different states. The National Council *Basic Manual* lists as standard exceptions clerical employees; drafting employees; drivers, chauffeurs, and their helpers; and salespersons, collectors, or messengers—outside.

*Clerical Office Employees (Code 8810).* The *Basic Manual* defines clerical employees as "employees engaged exclusively in bookkeeping, in record keeping, in correspondence, or in other office work where books and other records are kept or correspondence is conducted."[26] A further restriction is that this classification may include only "employees who work in areas physically separated from other operations by structural partitions and in which work of clerical office employees as defined in this rule is performed exclusively."[27] If an employee is not physically separated from other operations or has any other duty in addition to clerical functions, that employee cannot be included within the clerical classification. Instead, the total payroll of that employee must be assigned to the highest rated classification of the operations to which the employee is exposed. Executives often do not meet this definition of clerical employees since their responsibilities may require them to leave the office, and their duties are not exclusively clerical.

*Drafting Employees (Code 8810).* This classification applies only to "employees engaged exclusively in drafting and confined to office work."[28] The entire payroll of employees exposed to any other operations must be assigned to the highest rated classification of operations to which they are exposed.

*Drivers, Chauffeurs, and Their Helpers (Code 7380).* This classification covers "employees engaged in such duties on or in connection with a vehicle. This classification also includes garage employees, stablehands, and employees using bicycles in their operations."[29] On occasion, a business contracts with another entity to obtain transportation or delivery services. Unless there is satisfactory evidence that the workers compensation obligation toward any drivers, chauffeurs, or helpers involved has been insured by the owner of the vehicles, the total actual payroll of such drivers, chauffeurs, or helpers must be included as payroll of the insured employer who contracted for such services. That payroll would be assigned to the standard exception classification or to another classification if required by its definition in the same way as if those drivers, chauffeurs, or helpers were employees of the insured.

*Salespersons, Collectors or Messengers—Outside (Code 8742).* Employees in this classification are engaged in duties away from the employer's premises. This classification does not apply to employees who deliver merchandise because they are treated as drivers even though they also collect or sell. If they walk or use public transportation to make their deliveries, they are included in the governing classification. The making of occasional courtesy deliveries of small amounts of the merchandise sold, however, does not mean that the salesperson classification should not be used.

***General Inclusions.*** Some operations are a normal and necessary part of a business even though they at first seem to be distinct from the business itself. For example, an employees' cafeteria involves processes and skills different from those of a manufacturing operation, but the cafeteria employees are probably few, and they encounter many of the same hazards as everyone else in the plant. The rules provide, therefore, for the payroll of such employees to be included in the basic classification. These operations are called *general inclusions.* According to the *Basic Manual,* they "appear to be separate businesses, but they are included within the scope of all classifications other than the standard exception classifications."[30] The following are considered these types of operations:

- "Commissaries and restaurants for the insured's employees." The cafeteria employees at the factory belong with the factory classification. Such operations receive a separate classification only when distinct operations are separately classified because they involve construction, erection, lumbering, or mining (see the subsequent section on classifying construction operations).
- "Manufacture of containers such as bags, barrels, bottles, boxes, cans, cartons or packing cases by the employer for use in the operations insured by the policy." This operation might include the insured's shipping department or other operations necessary for the distribution of the insured's product. Only a separate enterprise supplying containers to other firms would be separately classified.
- "Hospitals or medical facilities operated by the insured for its employees." The remuneration of plant doctors, nurses, and first aid attendants is included in the basic classification.
- "Maintenance or repair of the insured's building or equipment by the insured's employees." A janitor's remuneration is included in the basic classification.
- "Printing or lithographing by the insured on its own products."

Unless the insured performs construction or erection work, the rules allow only three situations in which a general inclusion operation may be separately classified. One is if the operation constitutes a separate and distinct business of the insured as provided in Rule IV-D. Second, the operation must be separately classified if it is specifically excluded by the wording of the basic classification. Finally, if the insured's principal business is described by a standard exception classification, then the operation that would otherwise be a general inclusion must be classified separately.

***General Exclusions.*** Just as general inclusions describe operations normal for any business, general exclusions are operations so unusual that they are excluded from basic classifications. They usually involve hazards much more severe than the normal operations of the business. General exclusions are separately classified unless specifically included in the wording of the basic classification.[31] If the classification definition merely refers to "all employees," these operations must still be excluded. To some extent, forcing a separate classification should mirror the underwriter's increased interest in and concern about these operations. Even though the operations should be separately classified and rated, the underwriter must still decide if the exposure presented is one the insurer wants to cover. General exclusions are the following:

- "Aircraft operation—all operations of the flying and ground crews." The operations of piloting a plane, serving as a member of the crew, or servicing the plane on the ground must be separately classified.
- "New construction or alterations by the insured's employees." New construction includes both erection of new buildings and additions to existing buildings. Alterations might include structural changes or the erection or removal of store fronts or interior partitions. This exclusion also applies to extraordinary repairs, such as replacement of heating and cooling systems, plumbing, or electrical wiring. If the premises have not been previously occupied, new construction also includes installation of machinery, equipment, and fixtures. Painting in connection with any of these activities also belongs in this general exclusion.
- "Stevedoring, including tallying and checking incidental to stevedoring." Any tallying or checking clerks in warehousing or freight handling enterprises, however, would be included in those classifications. This exclusion does not apply in New York.
- "Sawmill operations—sawing logs into lumber by equipment such as circular carriage or band carriage saws, including

operations incidental to the sawmill." This exclusion does not apply in California.

- "Employer operated day care service."

The rules for general inclusions and for general exclusions apply to all classifications within the scope of their respective definitions except for construction or erection operations. Construction or erection operations constitute their own specialized handling.

**Classification Wording.** A question often arises as to the extent of the classifications as they have been established. Rule IV-C provides guidance for interpreting classification definitions.

***Captions and Notes.*** When captions or notes appear, they form part of the classification definition. Captions precede related classifications and apply to all of them. Notes follow the classification description and further restrict the definition and control the use of the classification.

***Words and Phrases.*** When ordinary words are used in classification phraseology, they should be given their ordinary meanings. Some words and phrases that are frequently used in the various classifications are defined by Rule IV-C of the *Basic Manual.*

*All Employees, All Other Employees, All Operations, or All Operations to Completion.* If any classification includes any of these phrases, then *no* other classification shall be assigned to that operation unless specifically indicated by the classification wording. The standard exception and general exclusions rules still apply, but otherwise there is no division of payroll.

*Clerical.* This term means clerical office and drafting employees as defined in Rule IV-B.2.a and IV-B.2.b.

*Drivers.* This term is also defined by the rule regarding standard exception classifications (Rule IV-B.2.c).

*Includes or &.* Either indication means that the classification contains the operations or employees specifically designated. Employees or operations included in such a classification will not be assigned to any other classification even though there are classification descriptions that apply. A classification phrase occasionally reads "includes clerical" or "& drivers." In these instances the standard exception classifications do *not* apply and those codes cannot be used.

*No or Not.* These words preclude applying a classification to an insured with operations described by the phrase following the words no or not.

*NOC.* These letters stand for "not otherwise classified." Any classification designated as NOC should be used *only* when no other classification more specifically or accurately describes the insured's business.

Classifications with this phraseology can fit a variety of operations for which there is no other applicable classification. These classifications can also be a stumbling block if the underwriter discovers such a classification early in the process and fails to look further. Whenever classification assignments seem questionable, NOC classifications should be considered a last resort. A classification containing NOC is frequently the most appropriate, but the underwriter should make certain that the business is indeed "not otherwise classified."

For example, a carpentry contractor engaged in remodeling work and room additions on houses should be classified as "Carpentry—Detached one or two family Dwellings" (Code 5645). However, one underwriter argued that such activities might be more accurately classified as "Carpentry NOC" (Code 5403). The crux of the argument was that since there is no carpentry code for remodeling, the carpenter is engaged in carpentry operations that are not otherwise classified. However, the object of the classification system is that "each classification reflects the exposures common to those employers." Exposures implicit in building a house or a room addition or in doing remodeling work on a residential dwelling are common to both a general carpentry contractor working on residences and to a remodeling carpentry contractor working on residences. Thus, in this example the exposure of the insured is adequately described by "Carpentry—Detached one or two family Dwellings" (Code 5645). On the other hand, "Carpentry NOC" (Code 5403) contemplates the rather different exposures faced by commercial contractors.

This example demonstrates how the failure to consider the objective of the classification system can lead to accepting an NOC classification too quickly.

*Or.* The word "or" in classifications also means "and."

*Salespersons.* This term means the standard exception classification defined in Rule IV-B.2.c.

*To Be Separately Rated.* If a classification requires operations or employees "to be separately rated," all such operations or employees are classified separately according to Rule IV-D.4. This phrase usually appears in the notes that accompany the basic classification description.

**Assignment of Classifications and Payroll.** As mentioned, classification procedures attempt to assign the one basic classification that best describes the business of the employer within a state. With certain exceptions, each classification includes all the various types of labor found in a business. Thus, "it is the business which is classified, not the individual employments, occupations or operations within a business."[32]

***Classification of Separate Legal Entities and Business Not Described by a Classification.*** A business to be classified is normally a separate legal entity. If a policy covers more than one entity, each separate legal entity insured is assigned to the basic classification that describes its entire business within a state. This procedure applies even if the business is conducted at more than one location. If there is no classification that describes the business, the classification that most closely describes the business will be assigned.

Other than standard exceptions, general exclusions, mercantile operations, farm operations, and construction and erection businesses, it makes no difference how many separate operations or locations are involved as long as the total operation is described by a single manual classification. It is this one classification that applies to the total operation. This principle was formerly referred to as the "single enterprise" rule. The 1980 *Basic Manual* restates the rule, but the intent remains the same as the 1934 manual provision. Such a "single enterprise" may have either one operation or a number of separate operations that are normally a part of the same business. The underwriter must assign a *single* classificaton that most accurately describes the entire operations of the insured. *No* other classification can be assigned to *any* portion of a single enterprise's operations even if another classification specifically describes the operation in question or if the operation in question is at another location unless the separate location or operation has employees defined as standard exceptions or general exclusions only.

Some businesses are best described by one of the standard exception classifications. For a bank or an insurance company, for example, the greatest amount of payroll would be assigned to the clerical employee classification. In that case, "the operations of all employees not included in the definition of the standard exception classification shall be assigned to the separate basic classification which most closely describes their operations."[33] Thus, a bank's maintenance and security employees should be assigned to "Buildings—Operation by Owner or Lessee" (Code 9015), and a bank's cafeteria employees should be assigned to "Restaurant NOC" (Code 9079).

The classification for mercantile operations is separately determined for each location. In that case, however, there can be *no interchange of labor* (explained later) between locations.

***Assignment of Additional Basic Classifications.*** If a classification requires operations or employees to be separately rated, or if an employer operates a secondary business within a state, an additional basic classification may be assigned under certain conditions. The 1934 manual referred to this situation as a "multiple enterprise." The 1980 *Basic Manual* specifies the following necessary conditions for assigning additional basic classifications:

a. The secondary business is conducted as a separate undertaking or enterprise. This condition does not apply if the classification wording requires the assignment of an additional classification for specified employees or operations. For example, some classifications direct that certain operations are to be separately rated.
b. Separate payroll records are maintained for each business.
c. Each business is physically separated by structural partitions and is conducted without interchange of labor.
d. The assignment of the separate classification is not prohibited by wording of that classification or any other classification assigned to the policy.

If all of the above conditions do not exist:

(1) All employees shall be assigned to the classification applicable to the principal business if the classification for the principal business carries a rate which is the same or higher than that for the classification of the secondary business.
(2) The secondary business shall be assigned to the classification which describes that business if such a classification carries a rate higher than that applicable to the principal business.
(3) The principal business is the business with the greatest amount of payroll, excluding standard exceptions or general exclusions operations.

e. Policies with more than one classificaton may involve employees working in connection with the several classifications. Payroll assignment for such employees is subject to Rule IV-E.[34]

The intent here is to encourage the underwriter to scrutinize those operations, occupations, or employments within an insured's business that are not normal or usual to such an enterprise. It is the business of the insured that is classified, but if there is within the insured's business an operation that could be considered unusual for that business, then the exposures of that operation may be considered, and thus classified, separately.

***Miscellaneous Employees.*** "Miscellaneous employees are those who perform duties conducted in common for separate operations subject to more than one basic classification. The payroll of any miscellaneous employees shall be assigned to the governing classification." Miscellaneous employees might include the following:

- General superintendents
- Maintenance or power plant employees, such as janitors, porters, cleaners
- Boiler-tenders or stokers

- Elevator operators
- Shipping or receiving clerks
- Yard workers

Consider, for example, a four-story factory with two floors devoted to a general job machine shop and two floors devoted to plastic goods manufacturing. "Machine Shop NOC" (Code 3632), applies to the machine shop. One of the three plastics manufacturing classes applies to the plastic goods manufacturing operation. The elevator operators, porters, and cleaners serving all four floors will be assigned to the governing classification, which could be either Code 3632 or the plastics manufacturing classification, depending on which produces the larger amount of payroll.[35]

***Interchange of Labor.*** Some employees who would not be considered miscellaneous employees may perform duties directly related to more than one basic classification. An example is an employee who on occasion interchanges between operations subject to more than one basic classification. Suppose, for example, one of the machine shop employees worked for the plastic goods manufacturer two days a week. "When there is such an interchange of labor, the entire payroll of employees who interchange shall be assigned to the highest rated classification representing any part of their work."[36] In a five-day week the employee's time card for that week may show three days in the machine shop and two days in the plastic goods shop. If the rate for the plastic goods manufacturer classification is higher than the rate for the machine shop, then the entire payroll of that employee would be assigned to the plastic goods manufacturer classification even though the employee actually spent less time there than in the machine shop.

The exceptions to this rule are that "for construction, erection, stevedoring, part-time aircraft operations in connection with Code 7421—Aircraft Operations, or trucking when such operations constitute a secondary business conducted as a separate enterprise, the payroll of an individual employee may be divided and allocated to more than one such classification, provided the entries on the original records of the insured disclose an allocation of each such individual employee's payroll. An estimated or percentage allocation is not permitted."[37]

***Normal Versus Incidental Operations.*** The essential purpose of the rules and interpretations enumerated in "Part One—Rules" of the *Basic Manual* and herein specified could be summarized as an attempt to recognize what is normal and what is incidental to a business enterprise. It is the operations, occupations, and employments normal to a business that determine which classifications or rules apply. The basic classifications all anticipate inclusion of the normal activities that are not standard exceptions or general exclusions. The operations, occupations, and employments that prove incidental to a business test the underwriter's power of judgment. Is an incidental operation of the insured's subject to consideration as a secondary business? Is this a contingent operation likely to occur within normal parameters of the insured's business? Does this seemingly incidental exposure coming in the regular course of business but not viewed as the primary or governing exposure significantly alter the overall thrust of the business? Is it subordinate to the main activity, or does it contribute to a subtle change requiring a classification other than that initially apparent?

## Construction Classifications

The National Council *Basic Manual* includes nearly 100 classifications describing construction or erection operations. The diversity of construction operations and the related hazards justify this multitude of classifications despite the resulting complications for underwriters. The theory of classification is to group insureds with similar loss exposures so that each group pays its share of workers compensation losses. In other cases the grouping reflects the business of the insured. The construction business, however, is so varied that equity requires separate rating of the distinct operations within the construction field. Without that provision, an electrical contractor would have to share the losses of the building wreckers and bridge painters, thus making it very difficult to stay in business as a result.

Rates effective in one state, for example, ranged from $6.31 per $100 of payroll for interior carpentry work to $52.76 for iron or steel erection of frame buildings not over two stories. One would naturally expect a high rate for such a hazardous operation. It is, in fact, only slightly higher than the rates for stunt flying and bridge painting. In contrast, the rate for clerical workers in that same state is $0.38 per $100 of payroll, and for photoengraving, only $0.93. Thus, rates for construction classifications not only tend to be much higher than rates for the majority of businesses, but they also tend to vary widely from one classification to another within the construction field.

**Classification Procedures.** Rule IV-D.8 of the National Council *Basic Manual* is a significant exception to the general classification procedures for workers compensation insurance. This rule provides for separate classification of distinct construction or erection operations as long as separate payroll records are maintained for each operation.

***Distinct Operations.*** Construction projects involve many phases and require the services of several skilled trades. Separate parts of the project are often executed by subcontractors specializing in certain types of construction work. Even when the general contractor hires and directly supervises workers, building codes and union contracts often require certain operations to be performed exclusively by members of a particular building trade. As long as payroll records show which employees did the work and what their wages were, each distinct operation should be assigned to the classification that best describes it.

The normal requirement for nonconstruction operations of physical separation by structural partitions does not apply to the assignment of additional basic classifications for construction or erection operations. It is common in a construction project for different operations to be executed at the same time. Masons, electricians, carpenters, and plumbers often rub elbows while working on the same building. Even so, they perform distinct operations, which should be assigned to separate classifications.

***Separate Payroll Records.*** Distinct operations can be separately classified only if separate payroll records are maintained for each operation. These records must show the actual time worked, not a percentage of total time. Under no circumstances may there be an allocation of payroll to workers compensation classifications on a percentage basis. The *Basic Manual* stipulates that "any such operation for which separate payroll records are not maintained shall be assigned to the highest rated classification which applies to the job or location where the operation is performed."

The assignment of separate classifications requires the contractor's payroll records to show more detail than would be necessary in other businesses because they must show the time worked in, and payroll amounts for, each distinct operation. Underwriters may want to contact the premium audit department to suggest a visit between the premium auditor and the insured when the risk is written so that records will be properly maintained. Premium auditors should suggest suitable accounting procedures to the insured when appropriate and explain how adequate records might reduce the total premium charged.

***Scope of Classifications.*** Although distinct construction operations should be assigned to separate classifications, each classification may include incidental operations within its scope. For that reason, the *Basic Manual* rules state the following:

> A separate construction or erection classification shall not be assigned to any operation which is within the scope of another classification assigned to such a job or location.[38]

For example, concrete construction normally requires carpenters to build wooden forms for the concrete. Although building forms is essentially carpentry work, it is an integral part of concrete construction. The workers building the forms are exposed to the same hazards and subject to the same supervision as those pouring the concrete.

Incidental operations may also involve the interchange of labor. The supervisor may switch workers from one task to another as necessary. Maintaining separate time and payroll records in such situations would be totally impractical. Thus, the classifications are designed to include within their scope any additional, associated operations.

For this reason, work performed by an *insured* subcontractor may be assigned a separate classification (on the subcontractor's policy) when the same work performed by employees of the general contractor comes within the scope of a different classification. For example, a contractor building a house employs carpenters to erect the frame. Their payroll is assigned to the classification "Carpentry—Detached One or Two Family Dwellings" (Code 5645). When it is time to install the finished floors in the house, the contractor may either direct those same carpenters to lay the floor or hire a subcontractor who specializes in flooring to do the work. In the first case, laying the floor comes within the scope of the carpentry classification. The carpenters may work on the rough frame one day and the finished floor the next, or move on to the next house as directed by the supervisor. Regardless of whether they lay floors part of the time, their entire payroll should still be assigned to the carpentry classification. Even if the general contractor had separate crews for the framing and finishing work, both crews would still be assigned to the carpentry classification. In the second case the workers specialize in laying floors and perform no other carpentry operations for the general contractor at that location. Their payroll should be separately classified as "Carpentry—Installation of Finished Wooden Flooring" (Code 5437). This example illustrates that it is not the kind of work, but each *distinct* operation, that is classified.

***Subcontractors.*** The separate classification of distinct construction or erection operations creates an additional complication in the case of subcontractors. Any subcontractor with the workers compensation obligation adequately insured may qualify for separate classification as a distinct operation under its own policy.[39] For example, in a project described by the classification "Sewer Construction" (Code 6306), some portions of the work, such as excavation, may be subcontracted. The National Council has ruled the following in this case:

> ... such subcontracted work shall be classified on the basis of the classification describing the particular type of work involved. Thus, the subcontractor who only performs excavation work in connection with the construction of a sewer would be classified under "Excavation," Code 6217 rather than under "Sewer Construction," Code 6306.[40]

However, if the subcontractor does not have insurance, the principal contractor has the workers compensation obligation toward employees of the subcontractor as if they were employees of the principal contractor. Thus, the payroll of the subcontractor's employees should be assigned to the same classification as if they were employees of the principal contractor.

***Division of Single Employee's Payroll.*** Separate classification of distinct construction operations raises another possibility generally not permitted by the *Basic Manual* rules. In a machine shop a timekeeper who spends some time working on the shop floor and some time in an office faces the same hazards as the machinists and must be placed in the same classification despite the many clerical duties. A division of the timekeeper's payroll between the two classifications is not allowed. However, "for construction, erection, stevedoring, part-time aircraft operations in connection with Code 7421—Aircraft Operations, or trucking when such operations constitute a secondary business conducted as a separate undertaking or enterprise, the payroll of an individual employee may be divided and allocated to more than one such classification, provided the entries on the original records of the insured disclose an allocation of each such individual employee's payroll. An estimated or percentage allocation of payroll is not permitted."[41] Naturally the records must show the time actually worked in each operation.

A classification that sometimes causes confusion in this regard is "Contractor—Executive Supervisor or Construction Superintendent" (Code 5606), which applies to "those persons exercising supervisory control through job superintendents or foremen." The class "does not apply to any person who is directly in charge of construction work."[42] Such supervision is a full-time job that requires work in the office as well as at the construction site. Thus, when this classification is used, a single employee's payroll cannot be divided between it and any other classification. A supervisor who spends time *directly* supervising or actually performing any operation other than office or sales work may not be placed in this classification but is placed in the governing class.

There may also be misunderstandings with regard to classifying common laborers. Common laborers may be assigned to assist various construction operations as needed at different stages of the project. If adequate records exist, the laborer's payroll should be assigned to the classifications describing the operations involved. If the records do not show the time devoted to each operation, the laborer's payroll should be assigned to the *highest rated* (not the governing) classification involved. Payroll of common laborers should be assigned to the *governing classification only* when they qualify as miscellaneous employees according to Rule IV-E.1. For example, the payroll of workers engaged in cleanup activities can be assigned to the governing classification since the cleanup duties are common to all the operations at the construction site.

**Contractor's Permanent Yards and Shops.** A special classification, "Construction or Erection Permanent Yard" (Code 8227), is available for contractors maintaining *permanent* yards for storage and maintenance of equipment, and storage of supplies. This can also be used for downtime when employees are assigned yard duties. *This classification may be used only when specifically assigned by the board or bureau having jurisdiction.* To qualify, yards must be permanent locations. If a yard meets this requirement, the payroll for employees' time in the yard belongs in this class. Payrolls for work away from the yard must be assigned to the classification of that operation. For example, a master mechanic who normally works in a yard may be sent to a sewer job site to repair equipment. The payroll for this time, including time going to and from the job, should be assigned to the sewer classification.

On large projects a contractor usually sets up a yard at or adjacent to the job site. Such a yard is considered temporary, and the contractor's permanent yard classification does not apply. A *temporary yard* may become permanent if it continues to be used after completion of the project for which it was originally established. For example, a road contractor may secure a job several hundred miles away. Land may be leased adjacent to the job site for the storage, repair, and maintenance of equipment to be used on the job. As long as that job is in progress, the yard is considered temporary, and the payroll of the yard employees should be assigned to the appropriate street and road construction classification. After completion of the original job, the contractor may obtain another job in the same area. If the same yard is used for the second job, it might then qualify as a permanent yard.

Fabrication or mill operations are not included in this classification. Fabrication of iron or steel at a permanent yard location should be assigned to the appropriate iron works shop classification depending on whether the material fabricated is structural, ornamental, or decorative. While the cleaning and reconditioning of forms in a permanent yard does come within the permanent yard class, the actual manufacturing of wooden forms at a permanent location should be classified as "Carpentry—Shop Only—& Drivers" (Code 2802). The contractor's permanent yard classification also does not apply to storage, maintenance, or repair of floating equipment such as dredges or pile drivers.

Under normal conditions, the payroll assigned to the permanent yard classification should be only a small percentage (under 10 percent) of a contractor's total payroll. If payroll for the yard operation is more than 10 percent, the underwriter should analyze the operation.

## SUMMARY

This chapter has examined the rather technical rules of workers compensation insurance with which the underwriter must be familiar in order to determine premiums and classify risks. The widespread use of the NCCI *Basic Manual* makes it imperative that the underwriter be familiar with the manual—the ability to quickly locate information can help in his or her own research and in supporting any underwriting decisions that may be questioned by a producer or an insured. The appropriate classification of workers compensation exposures, as in general liability, is critical to the operation of the class rating system. Assigning the exposures of a risk to the wrong class not only affects the premium for that risk, but do so for future risks whose rates are based on the experience of the class. There are a number of sources that help underwriters to classify risks, but the most important is the premium audit department of the insurer, if the premium audit function is handled in house, not by an outside audit firm. Underwriters should develop a close working relationship with premium auditors and should rely on their expertise to help answer classification questions.

The classification of construction operations and maritime operations (considered in the next chapter) is handled somewhat differently from that of other types of risks. This is primarily because of the nature of the operations performed by these risks. Understanding how to handle them can prevent premium collection problems at the time of the final audit.

The following chapter examines risks subject to federal jurisdiction and explores the underwriting considerations in workers compensation. Along with those considerations, the laws, coverage, and manual rules for premium determination and classification presented in this, and in the preceding, chapter create the basis for successful underwriting.

# Chapter Notes


1. National Council on Compensation Insurance, *Basic Manual for Workers Compensation and Employers Liability Insurance* (New York: National Council on Compensation Insurance, 1980), Preface.
2. National Council on Compensation Insurance, *Workers Compensation Insurance Basis of Premium—Payroll vs. Manhours,* 19 June 1978.
3. *Basic Manual,* Rule V-A.
4. *Basic Manual,* Rule V-B.1.
5. *Basic Manual,* Rule V-B.4.
6. *Basic Manual,* Rule V-E.1.
7. *Basic Manual,* Rule V-E.1.
8. *Basic Manual,* p. G38.
9. *Basic Manual,* p. C49.
10. *Basic Manual,* Rule VI-A.4.
11. *Basic Manual,* Rule VI-A.5.
12. *Basic Manual,* Rule VI-D.4.
13. *Basic Manual,* Rule VI-D.5.
14. *Basic Manual,* p. G41.
15. *Basic Manual,* Rule VI-E.4.
16. *Basic Manual,* Rule VI-E.3.
17. *Basic Manual,* p. G41.
18. *Basic Manual,* Rule VII-C.
19. *Basic Manual,* Rule VII-C.
20. *Basic Manual,* "Underwriting Guide," p. i.
21. National Council on Compensation Insurance, *Classification Codes for Workers Compensation and Employers Liability Insurance* (Boca Raton, FL: National Council on Compensation Insurance, 1987), "Classification Codes by Schedules and Groups," p. i.
22. National Council on Compensation Insurance, *Workers Compensation Insurance Premium Audit Reference Book* (New York: National Council on Compensation Insurance, 1983).
23. *Basic Manual,* Rule IV-A.
24. *Basic Manual,* Rule IV-A.
25. *Basic Manual,* Rule IV-B.5.
26. *Basic Manual,* Rule IV-B.2.a.
27. *Basic Manual,* Rule IV-B.2.a.
28. *Basic Manual,* Rule IV-B.2.b.
29. *Basic Manual,* Rule IV-B.2.c.
30. *Basic Manual,* Rule IV-B.3.
31. *Basic Manual,* Rule IV-B.4.
32. *Basic Manual,* Rule IV-D.1.
33. *Basic Manual,* Rule IV-D.7.
34. *Basic Manual,* Rule IV-D.4.

35. *Basic Manual,* Rule IV-E.1.
36. *Basic Manual,* Rule IV-E.2.
37. *Basic Manual,* Rule IV-E.2.
38. *Basic Manual,* Rule IV-D.8.
39. Note that with workers compensation, there is no problem with defining adequately insured as there is with general liability insurance. As explained earlier, there are no limits of liability on the workers compensation coverage portion of the policy and thus no problem with deciding which limits are adequate. If there is coverage, it should be adequate.
40. *Basic Manual,* p. G23.
41. *Basic Manual,* Rule IV-E.2.
42. *Basic Manual,* p. C13 (effective 1 September 1982).

# CHAPTER 12

# Workers Compensation Underwriting Decisions

The rigid structure of the workers compensation insurance system leaves little room for underwriting creativity. The exposure, as Chapter 10 explained, is defined by the workers compensation laws of the state. State law also mandates the benefits for which the insurer is responsible under the policy. Chapter 11 explained the elaborate workers compensation rating system, which involves precise rules for classification and premium determination in order to make certain that policies are issued with all the proper endorsements and classifications. Workers compensation underwriters must know these laws and manual rules. This part of the job requires clear-cut decisions. Despite the highly structured nature of the workers compensation insurance system, however, underwriters must still consider many additional factors in deciding which business to accept. This chapter explores those considerations.

The chapter begins with a discussion of the possible legal jurisdictions for workers compensation cases. While by far most cases of employee injuries come within the state workers compensation laws described in Chapter 10, maritime and certain other employees may be subject to federal laws instead. Different laws can mean different exposures and benefits. Underwriters must therefore be able to recognize those cases in which federal compensation laws might apply.

The remainder of the chapter addresses the other concerns of workers compensation underwriters. Many of the same sources of information used for other lines apply to workers compensation as well, but they must be analyzed from a different perspective. Other sources of information related to job safety records may be required as well. As with other lines of insurance, underwriters carefully examine an applicant's management, finances, loss history, safety program, and caliber of employees. In addition, workers compensation underwriters evaluate the plant and equipment with regard to housekeeping, maintenance, safety features, and frequency of replacement. They also consider the processes and operations performed.

Still another aspect of workers compensation underwriting is the possible application of a merit rating plan. Risks meeting certain eligibility requirements may be subject to the experience rating plan of the applicable rating bureau. Such plans modify the premium for workers compensation coverage by a factor related to the insured's loss history. In some cases, an alternative can be a retrospective rating plan, which incorporates a modifier reflecting the actual experience during the policy period. In some states, schedule rating offers still another alternative. In a dynamic, competitive environment, these aspects of pricing can present the most interesting challenges of workers compensation underwriting.

## COMPENSATION INSURANCE UNDER FEDERAL JURISDICTION

The discussion in Chapter 10 centered on insurance for an employer's liability under state workers compensation laws. There are many situations, however, in which employee injury claims come within federal rather than state jurisdiction. Federal laws entitle certain groups of employees to compensation for work-related injuries without regard to fault. In such cases, the principle is the same as under state workers compensation laws. The difference is the schedule of benefits and thus the applicable rates for insurance coverage under the federal laws. Other groups of employees falling exclusively under federal jurisdiction may sue employers for damages resulting from work-related injuries.

Maritime compensation exposures often appear unexpectedly. These surprises may result from the producer's or underwriter's limited familiarity with the nature of the operations insured, from insufficient underwriting information when the coverage was written, or from the insured's venture into a new operation with a maritime exposure after the inception of the policy. The problem is complicated by the fact that most of these situations concern maritime employments in which distinctions between land and water areas and between crew members and harbor workers are especially difficult to draw.

## Federal Compensation and Employers Liability Laws

Federal involvement in the laws governing workers compensation claims began even before the first state workers compensation statute took effect. In 1908, Congress passed two laws concerning the compensation claims of specific groups of employees. Since that time, Congress has enacted several additional compensation statutes, of which the most significant is the United States Longshore and Harbor Workers' Compensation (USL&HW) Act. Before discussing the intricacies of the USL&HW Act and its extensions, this section reviews the other federal legislation.

**Federal Employees' Compensation Act (FECA).** Congress first ventured into the compensation field to provide benefits to federal government employees sustaining work-related injuries. Subsequent legislation broadened the coverage and liberalized the benefits provided by the original act. The Federal Employees' Compensation Division within the Department of Labor administers the claims settlements. Since the federal government retains this exposure, there is no insurance involved. Federal employees thus constitute a substantial group of workers whose job-related injuries do not affect the work of underwriters.[1]

**Federal Employers' Liability Act (FELA).** The Federal Employers' Liability Act, on the other hand, defines a legal liability exposure that underwriters may encounter. The FELA applies solely to employees of interstate railroads and assures them of the same rights to compensation regardless of the state in which an injury occurs. Unlike workers compensation statutes, the FELA does not provide compensation without regard to fault. Rather, the doctrine of comparative negligence applies. The employer thus may not defeat the claim by arguing that the employee's negligence contributed to the injury, but the employee must prove some negligence on the part of the employer. The size of the award then varies in proportion to the degree of each party's negligence.

By enacting the FELA, Congress preempted the legislative interest of states in the compensation of injured interstate railroad workers. Thus, state workers compensation laws do not apply to workers covered by FELA. Employees of other interstate carriers such as bus lines and truckers, however, are subject to state workers compensation laws because Congress has not mentioned them in any legislation.

As a result of a 1939 amendment and subsequent judicial interpretation, the original restriction of the FELA to railroad workers employed in interstate transportation duties has nearly evaporated. In one case the Supreme Court allowed an office clerk to bring suit against her railroad employer under the FELA for an injury resulting from a window breaking in the office. The court ruled that because the plaintiff's duties included filing the drawings for designs of engines, cars, parts, and bridges, those duties substantially furthered interstate commerce.[2] By that line of reasoning, virtually any railroad employee might have the right to seek compensation under the FELA.

The trend in FELA cases has also been toward weakening the burden of proof of the employer's negligence. This trend led one authority to suggest that railroad workers sustaining injuries on the job have "the best of both worlds" under the FELA.[3] That is, they stand an excellent chance of recovering damages, but instead of being limited to the schedule of benefits provided by the workers compensation law, the jury may award them sizable judgments. Of course, there are still cases of injured railroad workers who cannot prove the employer's negligence and thus receive no compensation for injuries.

**Jones Act.** In 1920 Congress amended the general maritime law by permitting sailors to bring a direct negligence action against the owners of a ship and by creating the possibility of an action for wrongful death. The Merchant Marine Act of 1920, commonly called the Jones Act, provided that

> any seaman who shall suffer personal injury in the course of his employment may, at his election, maintain an action for damages at law with the right of trial by jury, and in such action all statutes of the United States modifying or extending the common law right or remedy in cases of personal injury to railway employees shall apply.[4]

Thus, the Jones Act placed sailors in the same best of both worlds situation that interstate railroad workers achieved with the passage of the FELA. As sailors, they are subject to admiralty law and, if injured, have the right to sue their employers for damages in admiralty courts. This is similar to an employers liability suit.[5] Under admiralty law, the sailors have an implied contractual right (as a result of the contract of hire) to transportation back to the home port, and wages, maintenance, and cure (that is, medical treatment) for the duration of the voyage. In addition, admiralty law gives the injured sailor the right to sue for damages if the vessel is unseaworthy. Besides these remedies, the injured sailors have the right (under the Jones Act) of suing the shipowner for damages caused by negligence in the operation of the ship. As under the FELA, the comparative negligence principle applies, and the right to a jury trial is guaranteed. While the injured sailor must prove negligence to establish the employer's liability, the potential for a large jury award is great. Moreover, the proof of negligence requirement has been so broadly interpreted that violation of a safety regulation, for example, suffices.[6] Thus, the prospects for recovery under the Jones Act are excellent, although by no means certain, and the limitations contained in workers compensation statutes regarding both benefit schedules and the exclusion of other remedies do not apply.

The Jones Act provision for a wrongful death action follows the same principles. It also incorporates the FELA provisions and guarantees the right to trial by jury. Since the only obligation under admiralty or maritime law to survivors or heirs of a seaman who died from injuries had previously been for funeral expenses, the Jones Act added significantly to the potential employer's liability in such cases.

While the Jones Act covers "any seaman" injured in the course of employment, it does not provide any definition of the term "seaman." Subsequent legislation, the United States Longshore and Harbor Workers' Compensation Act, restricted the application of the Jones Act, however, by its definition of covered employees. The USL&HW Act provides an exclusive remedy for injured maritime employees but does not include "a master or member of a crew of any vessel." In effect, this legislation divides maritime workers into two categories. Because masters and members of a crew are excluded from USL&HW Act coverage, they may seek the remedies the Jones Act provides for "seamen." Maritime workers, not masters or members of a crew, are covered by the United States Longshore and Harbor Workers' Compensation Act.

Despite this differentiation, cases arise where the employee injured aboard a floating object in the navigable waters claims benefits under the USL&HW Act rather than asking for seamen's benefits. In order to recover seamen's benefits, the employee must prove that he or she is a seaman, and will then be limited to a recovery of only maintenance and cure unless he or she can prove that the injury resulted from either unseaworthiness (admiralty law) or negligence (Jones Act). Lacking such proof, the employee stands to recover a greater amount under the USL&HW Act, which provides benefits without regard to fault or negligence. Since the USL&HW Act gives the employer the burden of proving that the employee is *not* entitled to benefits, the employee in this situation often wins an award. Employees working on floating construction equipment and floating oil drilling rigs can frequently choose between seamen's benefits and compensation benefits according to which will give them the higher award for their injuries. It is even possible for an employee to accept compensation benefits under the USL&HW Act and then claim the status of a seaman in order to sue for a larger award under the Jones Act.[7]

The traditional legal test of seaman status includes three elements. First, the vessel must be *in navigation.* A vessel capable of movement, even if it is at anchor or under repair, is in navigation. Second, the worker must have a permanent connection with the vessel, although that does not require living on board. Third, the worker's duties must be primarily to aid in navigation.[8]

However, as one legal scholar noted, "As the result of hundreds of decisions broadening these concepts, expressions can be found to the effect that the term 'seaman' has now been expanded to the point where it covers practically any worker, from helmsman to bartender, who sustains an injury while working on almost any structure that floats, or once floated, or is capable of floating on navigable waters."[9]

This broadened interpretation stems from a fundamental change in the nature of sea-going activities. The term "vessel" now encompasses most types of man-made, floating objects as well as fishing boats and ships transporting passengers or cargo. The courts have held several kinds of construction equipment, for example, to be vessels. These include barges, dredges, and the like.[10] Thus, the insured's ownership, lease, or charter of any floating equipment should alert the underwriter to the presence of maritime exposures.

## Coverage for Insureds Subject to Admiralty Law and FELA

Rule XIII of the *Basic Manual* states the rules for covering, excluding, or limiting exposures under admiralty law (including Jones Act coverage) and the Federal Employers' Liability Act. Although Part Two of the standard policy applies to these cases of employers' liability (unless excluded), the coverage may be tailored to the needs of the insured by attaching appropriate endorsements.

Terminology in the *Basic Manual* can be somewhat confusing regarding Jones Act coverage. The manual headings refer to admiralty law and to FELA. Because the Jones Act provides FELA remedies to injured sailors, there may be a question as to whether the FELA heading refers also to the FELA remedies provided to injured sailors. It does not. Such remedies are included within the heading of admiralty law. In this discussion of coverage for admiralty law and FELA exposures, the term admiralty law includes any FELA remedies provided to injured sailors.

**Coverage Programs.** The *Basic Manual* allows two different approaches to insuring liability under admiralty law or the FELA. The standard policy is used in either case, and the appropriate endorsements are added.

***Program I.*** The first approach provides Part One coverage (workers compensation insurance) for statutory liability under the workers compensation law of any state designated in Item 3.A of the information page and Part Two coverage (employers liability insurance) for damages under admiralty law or the FELA subject to a standard limit of $25,000. Although this is essentially the coverage provided by the standard policy alone, for clarification the *maritime coverage endorsement* (WC 00 02 01) should be attached to policies insuring maritime operations. An interstate railroad with Program I coverage should have the *Federal Employers' Liability Act coverage endorsement* (WC 00 01 04) attached to the policy, indicating the applicable limits of liability.

***Program II.*** The second approach provides the same coverage as Program I with the addition of voluntary compensation coverage. Under this coverage the insurer offers to settle a claim strictly in accord with the workers compensation law designated in the endorsement as if the claim were subject to that law instead of the laws of negligence. The designated law may be either the workers compensation statute of a particular state or the USL&HW Act. If the injured employee rejects the offer of settlement, then employers liability coverage applies to the employee's claim or suit, with the same standard limit of liability as for Program I.

To provide Program II for operations subject to admiralty law, the policy should include both the maritime coverage endorsement and the *voluntary compensation maritime coverage endorsement* (WC 00 02 03). Taken together, these endorsements provide voluntary compensation coverage for masters and members of crews, define the territorial limits, and clarify the limits of liability that apply. The rates stated in the policy for maritime voluntary compensation must reflect the limits of liability stated in the schedule of the maritime coverage endorsement.

To provide Program II for employments subject to FELA, the Federal Employers' Liability Act coverage endorsement is attached as for Program I. In addition, the voluntary compensation and employers liability coverage endorsement (WC 00 03 11) is attached.

**Admiralty Law Coverage Option.** The maritime coverage endorsement excludes from coverage the insured's traditional maritime liability to provide transportation, wages, maintenance, and cure to injured sailors. However, such coverage may be included by entering a premium charge in Item 2 of the schedule on the endorsement. The additional premium for including this optional coverage is computed by using an (a) rate.

**Exclusions.** If the insurer does not intend to provide coverage for admiralty law exposures, such coverage may be excluded by attaching the *maritime exclusion endorsement* (WC 00 02 02). Similarly, FELA liability may be excluded by attaching the *Federal Employers' Liability Act exclusion endorsement* (WC 00 01 05).

Unless these endorsements form part of the policy, employers liability coverage applies to any admiralty law or FELA exposures present in the insured's operations, and the appropriate premium charge applies. Either of these exclusion endorsements might specify certain states in which the endorsement applies, meaning that coverage is excluded only in those states.

Insureds occasionally assert that the existence of protection and indemnity (P&I) coverage (a type of ocean marine coverage) serves to exclude vessel crewmen from workers compensation coverage. That assertion is incorrect since an *unendorsed* workers compensation policy contains no such exclusion. There would thus be duplicate coverage. If the maritime coverage endorsement is attached to the policy, however, an injury also covered by P&I coverage is excluded. Similarly, a maritime exclusion endorsement would exclude claims for bodily injury to a master or member of a crew of a vessel.

## Premium Determination for Insureds Subject to Admiralty Law and FELA

Premium charges for admiralty law and FELA exposures are determined using the special classifications established for these operations. The rates for those classifications assume that the standard limit of liability applies. If increased limits of liability apply, the premium is adjusted according to the manual rules. If the insured's operations are not under admiralty or FELA jurisdiction, the special classifications may still be used, subject to the applicable state rules.

**Classifications and Rates.** Rule XIII-F of the *Basic Manual* defines the classifications for maritime and railroad operations. The "Classifications Section" of the *Basic Manual* merely refers to Rule XIII for the descriptions of these classifications. For each operation described, there are three separate classifications. One corresponds to Program I coverage for the operation. The other two are for Program II coverage with either state law or the USL&HW benefits designated. The rates for these classifications appear in a separate section on the state rate pages.

Where maritime operations may create a USL&HW exposure, the policy should include the *Longshoremen's and Harbor Worker's Compensation Act coverage endorsement* (WC 00 01 06) to provide such coverage. As long as the insurer receives a sufficient premium for the coverage, it would normally be willing to cover a claim under state or federal compensation laws should an employer be found to be subject to such a law. This assumes that the rates are adequate, which is not always the case.

Excavation and dredging often come under maritime jurisdiction. Excavation or dredging contractors may be engaged to dig drainage or navigation channels, or to maintain existing channels at the proper depth. Material may be dredged from existing waterways for use as fill at construction sites. Dredging often produces sand, gravel, or seashells for use as building materials or in making concrete. Dredging equipment may be of the bucket or suction types. It may be permanently mounted on a vessel or pontoon designed for the purpose, or it may consist of conventional excavation equipment, such as a crane with dragline, temporarily placed on a barge. As long as the equipment remains on shore, even if it is dredging a navigable waterway, no maritime exposure exists. When the equipment is mounted on a vessel in navigable waters, however, the operating crew becomes subject to admiralty jurisdiction.

Construction of underwater foundations and tunnels may involve caissons to hold back mud and water while excavation and construction proceeds. Work in the caisson itself is not maritime. However, caissons often require the use of vessels as tenders, and the employees working on the tenders in navigable waters are subject to admiralty law. Thus, there are many construction operations that may involve an admiralty classification. When there is a possibility of USL&HW Act exposure, payrolls should be assigned to the highest rated classification that is applicable. Because of the liberal benefits, most insurers underwrite all maritime exposures very carefully.

**Waters Not Under Admiralty Jurisdiction.** An insured may conduct operations described by an admiralty classification on waters not under admiralty jurisdiction. For example, employees of fishing or boating operations on inland lakes would be subject to the state workers compensation law. A standard policy without endorsements for maritime operations covers this exposure. The rules are those that apply to statutory workers compensation coverage.

In National Council states, the appropriate classification for such operations is the admiralty classification describing the operation corresponding to Program II coverage for the location involved. In Pennsylvania and Delaware, a separate dredging classification exists for coverage under the state workers compensation law only. USL&HW coverage may be included by applying the percentage increase factor (explained in the next major section) to the rate for this classification. Admiralty coverage for dredging operations may be insured under the same policy, however, only if the separate classifications and rates for the operations subject to state and admiralty jurisdictions are clearly subdivided.

## The USL&HW Act and Its Extensions

Because admiralty jurisdiction barred the application of state workers compensation laws to most maritime workers while working on board vessels in navigable waters, Congress moved to fill the gap by enacting a federal compensation law. The United States Longshoremen's (later changed to Longshore) and Harbor Workers' Compensation Act (USL&HW Act), passed in 1927, applied the principle of the workers compensation laws to certain maritime workers.

As other gaps in compensation coverage appeared, Congress extended the provisions of the USL&HW Act. The most significant legislative development, however, was the 1972 amendment of the act redefining its coverage of maritime workers and substantially increasing the benefits under the original act and its extensions. Judicial decisions have clarified many of the troublesome issues involved, but it would be naive to assert that all ambiguities have been resolved.

**The United States Longshore and Harbor Workers' Compensation Act.** Since it was modeled after the New York Workmen's Compensation Law, the United States Longshore and Harbor Workers' Compensation Act applies essentially the same principles of compensation to those workers excluded from the protection of state laws. The USL&HW Act provides compensation without regard to fault for eligible maritime workers injured in the course of employment. The act was initially intended to be the exclusive remedy for such injuries. Because in practice, however, it did not do so, the 1927 act was extensively amended in 1972. The 1972 amendments removed some legal problems and introduced others, prompting further amendments in 1984, including the change in the title of the law to a nonsexist form.

Although injured longshore and harbor workers could not directly sue their employers, *third-party-over actions* had become common. Prior to 1972, an employee of a stevedoring firm injured while loading or unloading a vessel could sue the ship's owner on the grounds that the injury resulted from the unseaworthy condition of the vessel. The ship owner might then recover any damages awarded to the employee from the employer because of the implied indemnity covering the stevedoring work on the vessel. This third-party-over action produced the same result as if the employer paid damages in excess of the USL&HW benefits directly to the employee.

The 1972 amendments to the USL&HW Act eliminated the right of maritime workers to sue shipowners under the unseaworthiness doctrine and the right of a shipowner to bring a third-party-over action against the employer. To make this restriction more palatable to maritime workers, the amendments also significantly increased the benefits and extended the jurisdiction of the act.

The 1984 amendments clarified the definition of covered employees and many benefit provisions. It is this amended act that is analyzed here in terms of the employer's obligation, the persons eligible for benefits, the injuries covered, and the benefits provided.

***Employer's Obligation.*** Every employer under the USL&HW Act must secure the payment of compensation in one of two ways. One way is to obtain insurance coverage from any insurer authorized to write workers compensation insurance and approved by the secretary of labor. The other way is to become a self-insured employer by furnishing to the secretary of labor satisfactory proof of the financial ability to pay compensation directly and to receive the authorization to do so. This authorization normally requires the deposit of a security bond or other suitable guarantee. Employers who have failed to secure compensation required under the act face fines of up to $10,000 and prison terms of up to one year.

***Persons and Employments Covered.*** The USL&HW Act substantially covers all maritime employment in whole or in part on the navigable waters of the United States except the master or members of the crew of a vessel. Like workers compensation statutes, the act defines the term, employee, when used in the USL&HW Act as follows:

> any person engaged in maritime employment, including any longshoreman or other person engaged in longshoring operations, and any harbor-worker including a ship repairman, shipbuilder, and shipbreaker, but such term does not include—
>
> "(A) individuals employed exclusively to perform office clerical, secretarial, security, or data processing work;
>
> "(B) individuals employed by a club, camp, recreational operation, restaurant, museum, or retail outlet;
>
> "(C) individuals employed by a marina and who are not engaged in construction, replacement, or expansion of such marina (except for routine maintenance);
>
> "(D) individuals who (i) are employed by suppliers, transporters, or vendors, (ii) are temporarily doing business on the premises of an employer described in paragraph (4), and (iii) are not engaged in work normally performed by employees of that employer under this Act;
>
> "(E) aquaculture workers;
>
> "(F) individuals employed to build, repair, or dismantle any recreational vessel under sixty-five feet in length;
>
> "(G) a master or member of a crew of any vessel; or

"(H) any person engaged by a master to load or unload or repair any small vessel under eighteen tons net;

if individuals described in clauses (A) through (F) are subject to coverage under a State workers' compensation law.[11]

The act also excludes from coverage "an officer or employee of the United States or any agency thereof or of any State or foreign government or of any political subdivision thereof."[12]

The act otherwise provides compensation benefits in cases of disability or death of an employee, but only if the disability or death results from an injury occurring on the navigable waters of the United States (including any adjoining pier, wharf, dry dock, terminal, building way, marine railway, or other adjoining area customarily used by an employer in loading, unloading, repairing, dismantling, or building a vessel).[13]

Thus, the question that most often arises is whether the USL&HW Act or a state workers compensation law applies. It is possible for an employee to be engaged in maritime operations (such as building a marina) on non-navigable waters wholly within one state and therefore covered by the state rather than the federal act. It is also possible and quite common for an employee to be engaged in operations related to the loading or unloading of a ship, but executed on land rather than on water. In that case the problem is where to draw the line between land and water, and thus between state and federal jurisdiction. Prior to 1972, federal jurisdiction stopped at the water's edge. The USL&HW Act applied at one end of the gangplank, but not at the other. Although the line was clear, employees loading or unloading ships crossed into and out of federal jurisdiction several times a day. In addition, as a result of the advent of containerized operations, more of the work of transferring cargo takes place on shoreside areas than had formerly been the case. Thus, longshore workers once protected by the USL&HW Act were no longer under its jurisdiction merely because of the modernization of operations.

The 1972 amended act expanded federal jurisdiction landward to correct these problems. So as not to extend unintended coverage to any worker who happened to come into the dock area, however, the amended act linked coverage to maritime employment. For the act to apply, two criteria must be met. The injured worker must be an employee according to the definition of the act, *and* the injury must have occurred upon navigable waters as defined by the act. These two requirements can be summarized as tests of *status* and *situs*, respectively.

*Status.* The USL&HW Act expressly includes as a "person engaged in maritime employment" any member of several classes of workers, the first of which is "any longshoreman or other person engaged in longshoring operations." A worker who can be characterized as a "longshoreman" within the ordinary meaning of that term, employed as such at the time of the injury, has the status required by the act without further inquiry concerning particular duties.[14] The worker's union affiliation may indicate the status of a longshoreman, but it is not conclusive proof either way.

Even a worker not employed as a longshoreman is covered by the act if "engaged in longshoring operations." Such operations include two subcategories: (1) *stevedoring operations* (the immediate loading and unloading of vessels) and (2) *terminal operations* (the other cargo-handling activities associated with stevedoring operations). Longshoring operations may be regarded as all operations necessary to the transfer of cargo between land and water modes of transportation that are performed by workers associated with that transfer rather than with the transportation itself. The test is essentially whether the employee's work relates directly to the cargo or to the equipment or premises used to handle it. Stevedoring cargo checkers, talliers, and clerks who document cargo movement are *not* excluded as "office clerical." They are covered by the act.

The definition of employees covered by the USL&HW Act also specifically mentions ship repairmen and shipbuilders. These terms include the many trades or crafts represented within the labor force of a shipyard. Thus, all shipyard workers—welders, burners, machinists, carpenters, electricians, painters, sandblasters, crane operators, their assistants, and many others—are shipbuilders or ship repairmen. All functions that contribute to the enterprise should be considered shipbuilding or ship repairing, and the employees who perform these functions should thus be regarded as covered harbor workers.[15] As with longshoremen, a shipbuilder or ship repairman retains that status even while temporarily assigned to nonmaritime work. It is the general occupation rather than the precise duties at the time of injury that establishes the status of maritime employment.

Although construction and repair of commercial vessels generally meets the *status* requirement, certificates of exemption from coverage under the USL&HW Act are issued by the secretary of labor when state act coverage is available and when work is done on small vessels only. *Small vessels* are defined as commercial barges under 900 lightship displacement tons; and tugboats, towboats, crew boats, supply boats, fishing vessels, or other work vessels are similarly defined if they are less than 1,600 tons gross. Military vessels, Corps of Engineers dredges, and U.S. Coast Guard vessels are not included in the exempt vessels definition. The term *displacement* refers to the weight of the empty barge in long tons; and the term *gross tons* refers to the size of the vessel, counting each 100 cubic feet as one gross ton.

The USL&HW Act also lists shipbreakers among covered harbor workers. Shipbreaking includes all facets of the scrapping of a vessel, from the stripping of nonferrous fittings and parts from the hull to the reduction of the hull to pieces of steel of a convenient size, and the associated functions of moving and piling the scrap and loading it for shipment out of the waterfront scrapyard. All workers in this industry should be considered covered employees.

All harbor workers, whether expressly mentioned in the act or not, are included unless they are members of the crews of vessels or engaged by the master to load, unload, or repair a vessel under eighteen tons net. For example, linesmen, vessel watchmen, gangplank attendants, marine inspectors and surveyors, divers, marine construction workers, ship cleaners and chandlers, and others whose employment is clearly identified with the water or the waterfront, but who are not members of the crews of vessels, have the status of maritime employees within the act's coverage.

Workers who load or unload small vessels that cannot be considered "ships" are also maritime employees. The performance of such operations is just as much maritime when it relates to small vessels as when it relates to large ones. Any doubt concerning this conclusion should be dispelled by the act's specific exclusion of "any person engaged by the master to load or unload or repair any small vessel under eighteen tons net." The specification that the exclusion applies only to those "engaged by the master" constitutes a clear indication that those engaged by others—the owner or, far more usually, a marina operator, boat repair yard, or other employer performing such services for the owner under contract—*are* covered employees.

The 1984 amendments specifically exclude building, repairing, or dismantling recreational vessels less than sixty-five feet in length from coverage under the USL&HW Act. The factories are normally at inland locations, and the repair facilities are usually at inland boat dealers or on inland lakes or rivers that are not navigable, so this exclusion is logical.

However, a few recreational vessel construction and repair facilities are located on or near navigable waters. These operations may continue to be under the USL&HW Act for that part of the work done on vessels while floating in navigable waters or on dry docks, building ways, or marine railways adjacent to those waters. These workers would be deemed to fall under the admiralty jurisdiction and would not be covered by a state act as would those workers at inland locations. Building or repair of pleasure craft more than sixty-five feet in length usually does meet the *status* test for coverage under the USL&HW Act.

The definition of employee in the amended USL&HW Act limited the persons within the act's protection at the *newly covered shoreside* areas, but it was not meant to withdraw in any way the act's previous coverage of maritime employees.[16] The Supreme Court used this reasoning to conclude that a sewer construction worker directing the unloading of materials from a supply barge in the Hudson River was a maritime employee.[17] Thus, all employment actually performed upon navigable waters of the United States should be regarded as *maritime employment* whether or not it bears an immediate relation to commercial shipping operations.

The significance of the status test appears most readily in longshoring operations that extend some distance from the water. Any worker performing cargo-handling duties on the water is an employee within the terms of the act while doing so. Whether such an employee retains the act's protection while ashore depends on the facts of the case. The determination in such a case should be based on the degree to which the worker's shoreside presence is merely incidental to the work on the water. If it is, the worker retains employee status while ashore.

*Situs.* The landward extension of the USL&HW Act's jurisdiction to areas adjoining navigable waters provides full protection to workers engaged in maritime operations whether they are on land or water at the time of injury.

In general, the locations at which longshoring operations are conducted can be readily identified as piers or marine terminals. Because of the large scale on which modern shipping is conducted and particularly because of the large holding areas required for handling containerized cargo, it is not unusual for marine terminals to cover many hundreds of acres. Such terminals come within USL&HW jurisdiction. It is neither necessary that the precise location of an injury be one used for loading or unloading operations nor that it immediately adjoin the water. It suffices that the overall area that includes the location is part of a terminal adjoining the water.[18]

Where additional space is not available immediately adjacent to the previously established boundaries of a waterfront pier or terminal and where a number of stevedoring companies work at the same terminal, such facilities as *gear lockers,* buildings in which stevedoring equipment is maintained and stored, may be located outside the fenced boundaries of a terminal. Because such facilities exist solely for the loading and discharging of ships, they should be regarded as extensions of the terminals. Hence, although they do not themselves adjoin the water, they are parts of terminal complexes that do, and are thus within the act's jurisdiction.

The USL&HW Act expressly includes any dry dock, building way, or marine railway within its jurisdiction. A *dry dock* includes both a floating dock and a graving dock, and the cranes, scaffolds, and appurtenant structures with them. A *building way* or *marine railway* includes the land adjacent to the incline or track system that is devoted to the construction or repair of vessels on the ways. Some shipyards have systems of lateral-transfer tracks on which vessels removed from the water can be shifted around the yard; the entire area covered by such a system is a marine railway within the scope of the act. Similarly, the area for shipbuilding or repairing should not be limited to a particular location or locations, but should be regarded as the entire, overall facility devoted to covered activities. The relevant area is the entire shipyard or other facility customarily used in loading, unloading, repairing, or building a vessel. Such facilities include nearby locations functioning as part of the same facility even if they are separated from the main facility by roads or fences.

It is logical that construction and repair of commercial vessels always meet the *situs* test for coverage under the USL&HW Act. A commercial shipyard must be located on a navigable waterway since commercial vessels move in and out; and any waterway that supports commercial vessel traffic is navigable by definition. Similarly, the construction and repair of recreational vessels more than sixty-five feet in length also usually meets the *situs* test. Since few large yachts are used on non-navigable waters, virtually all of these operations are on navigable waters and covered by the federal act.

The extension of USL&HW jurisdiction to land areas adjoining the navigable waters of the United States created a "twilight zone" where either state or federal law may apply. The Supreme Court has ruled that this is an area of concurrent jurisdiction. According to the Court, injured shipyard workers are not barred from compensation under the state law merely because the USL&HW Act might also apply.[19] Nor does an award under one law exclude possible compensation under the other law as long as proper credit for the first award is taken into account.[20]

In doubtful situations underwriters should assume that USL&HW jurisdiction might apply. As long as its benefit levels are higher, injured workers will tend to seek compensation under the USL&HW Act. Moreover, the act provides that in the adjudication of a claim "it shall be presumed, in the absence of substantial evidence to the contrary ... that the claim comes within the provisions of the Act."[21] Thus, the burden is on the employer to demonstrate that coverage clearly does not exist rather than on the claimant to demonstrate that coverage applies.

***Injuries and Diseases Covered.*** The definition of injury used in the USL&HW Act represents an amalgamation of the corresponding sections of the New York Workmen's Compensation Law.

> . . . "injury" means accidental injury or death arising out of and in the course of employment, and such occupational disease or infection as arises naturally out of such employment or as naturally or unavoidably results from such accidental injury, and includes an injury caused by the willful act of a third person directed against an employee because of his employment.[22]

Thus, any work-related accident and virtually any disease somehow associated with the employment qualifies for compensation if the employee has suffered any impairment as a result.

***Benefits.*** The benefits provided by the USL&HW Act are essentially the same as those provided by state workers compensation laws. Following the 1972 amendments, however, USL&HW benefits tended to be more liberal than those provided in many states. As a result, where there is a question of jurisdiction, injured workers have been more inclined to seek USL&HW benefits.

**Insurance for USL&HW Act.** With appropriate endorsements, the standard workers compensation and employers liability policy can provide coverage for the USL&HW exposure. Rule XII of the National Council's *Basic Manual* delineates the procedures for insuring exposures under the act.

The United States Longshore and Harbor Workers' Compensation Act uses the same principles as the state workers compensation laws. A complication arises because an employer may be subject to both the USL&HW Act and the state workers compensation law at the same time. While both of these exposures may be insured, they must be separately covered and hence separately rated.

Although the USL&HW Act is a workers compensation law, it may not be entered in Item 3.A of the information page on a workers compensation policy. Instead, USL&HW coverage is provided by adding the *Longshoremen's and Harbor Workers' Compensation Act coverage endorsement* (WC 00 01 06) to the standard workers compensation policy.

This endorsement amends the definition of "workers compensation law" to include the USL&HW Act with respect to operations in any state in the endorsement's schedule. The policy then applies to those operations as though the state were listed in Item 3.A of the information page. Even a monopolistic fund state, for example, may be listed on the endorsement to provide USL&HW coverage for operations in that state. The manual applicable in the state named in the information page governs the policy, but the insurer must also agree to abide by the rules and regulations of the Labor Department's Office of Workers Compensation Programs.

The endorsement broadens the coverage of the standard workers compensation policy to apply to a similar, but separate, statutory obligation of the employer. Part one of the policy, according to which the insurer promises to "pay promptly when due the benefits required" of the insured by the workers compensation law, includes USL&HW benefits by virtue of this endorsement. When the policy is endorsed to provide USL&HW coverage for the insured's operations, the insurer pays any benefits awarded under the USL&HW Act regardless of the location of the injury.

USL&HW coverage requires additional premium charges calculated according to the manual rules explained in the section "Premium Determination." If the insurer intends to provide USL&HW coverage and to collect the additional premium, the policy should include the Longshoremen's and Harbor Workers' Compensation Act coverage endorsement. If the insurer does not intend to provide such coverage, the *Longshore and Harbor Workers' Compensation Act exclusion endorsement* (WC 00 01 07) should be added to the policy.

**Extensions of the USL&HW Act.** In addition to maritime workers, other groups of employees outside the jurisdiction of state workers compensation laws have also been covered by federal law. These include employees of government contractors at overseas installations, civilian employees of the armed forces, and workers on offshore drilling rigs on the outer continental shelf. In each case Congress extended the provisions of the USL&HW Act to apply to these workers.

***Defense Base Act.*** Many civilians work at American military installations around the world. State workers compensation laws do not apply outside the United States, and the Federal Employees' Compensation Act only covers direct employees of the federal government. The Defense Base Act applies to the employees of government contractors outside the continental United States. Employees who are not U.S. citizens may be exempted by a waiver if it is approved by the secretary of labor. The Defense Base Act extends the provisions of the USL&HW Act to these overseas employees of government contractors. Jurisdiction under the act is precisely stated, and there have been few legal questions in its application. This coverage is provided by endorsement WC 00 01 01.

***Nonappropriated Fund Instrumentalities Act.*** A 1942 Supreme Court decision held that an army exchange was an integral part of the

War Department subject to the same legal immunities and thus exempt from a state gasoline tax.[23] This decision raised the possibility that post exchange employees might thus come under the civil service laws. The Civilian Employees of Nonappropriated Fund Instrumentalities Act clarified this question by explicitly excluding such employees from the civil service laws and from the Federal Employees' Compensation Act.[29] The act provides instead for the compensation of injured employees of nonappropriated fund instrumentalities according to the terms of the USL&HW Act. Employees covered by this law are those who are not compensated from funds appropriated by Congress, but who are employed *by instrumentalities of the United States* (under the Defense Base Act, the covered employees work for a contractor under contract with an agency of the United States government). For the most part, these are civilian employees of the armed forces working in post exchanges, ship service stores, service clubs, day care centers, and similar ancillary operations at air, naval, and military bases. This coverage is provided by endorsement WC 00 01 08.

***Outer Continental Shelf Lands Act.*** In recent years the outer continental shelf has been an active area for petroleum exploration and production. Outer continental shelf lands are beyond the boundaries of the states and thus come under federal jurisdiction. The outer continental shelf includes all submerged lands extending seaward from the three-mile territorial limit. Along the Atlantic Coast the average distance from the shore to the outer edge of the continental shelf is about seventy miles. In some places it reaches nearly 250 miles.

The Outer Continental Shelf Lands Act extends the provisions of the USL&HW Act to employees conducting operations on the outer continental shelf under a federal lease or other authorization relating to exploration, development, removal, or transportation by pipeline of natural resources. It does not apply to masters or members of a crew of any vessel or to employees of the federal, state, or any foreign government. This coverage is provided by endorsement WC 00 01 09.

**Premium Determination.** Premiums for coverage under the USL&HW Act or its extensions are based on payroll. Thus, premium determination follows essentially the same procedure for USL&HW coverage as for state workers compensation act coverage. However, there are certain additional considerations involved in both the basis of premium and the classifications and rates for USL&HW coverage. With one significant exception, the basis of premium rules in the workers compensation manual are the same for USL&HW coverage. That exception involves overtime pay for stevedores (not for all maritime work).

Although the same payroll serves as the premium base whether

USL&HW coverage or state coverage applies, the structure of the classification and rating system provides the additional premium for broadening the coverage to include USL&HW benefits. For certain classes designated by the letter *F* following the classification code number, this is accomplished directly by basing the rates for those classifications on USL&HW loss experience. For the remaining classifications, it is accomplished through a percentage increase factor that is applied to the state-coverage-only rate to increase it to reflect the USL&HW exposure.

***F* Classifications.** Certain classifications describe freight handling, stevedoring, or other operations that normally come within USL&HW jurisdiction. These classifications are indicated by the letter *F* following the classification code number. An example is the classification "Freight Handling NOC" (Code 7350F). The manual rates for these *F* classifications apply to coverages under either the USL&HW Act or a combination of the USL&HW Act and the state act, and have been calculated accordingly. Thus, the manual rate for an *F* classification multiplied by the premium base produces the premium required for USL&HW Act coverage or the premium required for a combination of USL&HW Act and state act coverage.

Some freight-handling operations, however, may be performed at railroad yards, airports, or warehouses in locations not adjoining the navigable waters of the United States. For coverage under the state compensation law only, there are *non-F* classifications describing the same operations as an *F* classification but carrying a rate appropriate for state coverage only. For example, the classification "Freight Handling NOC" (Code 7360) describes the same operation as the Code 7350F classification, but it contemplates coverage only under state law.

***Non-F* Classifications.** Any operation listed in the *Basic Manual* classification section could conceivably be performed on the navigable waters of the United States and thus be subject to the USL&HW Act. Although painting ship hulls is a distinct operation, painting the cabin walls of an ocean liner is the same operation as painting the rooms of a house. However, painters on an ocean liner would be under USL&HW jurisdiction. If any of the insured's operations described by a *non-F* classification involve some employees subject to the USL&HW Act, the *Basic Manual* rates and minimum premiums for these classifications must be increased by the *United States Longshore and Harbor Workers' Compensation Coverage Percentage* found under "Miscellaneous Values" on the state rate pages.

## Impact on Underwriting

One might ask why underwriters care whether an employee is subject to a state law or one of the several federal laws explained. Pricing is not an issue because the insurer collects (usually at audit) the premium due, and any injured employees receive the appropriate benefits mandated by law. However, there are still several underwriting concerns.

First, the workers compensation policy treats each of the various laws differently, and the policy does not even cover the FECA. Thus, to provide the proper coverage and to receive an adequate premium (assuming the filed rate is adequate), the underwriter must make sure all exposures are identified, all appropriate endorsements are attached, and the proper classifications and rates are shown.

Second, the identification and evaluation of exposures, an integral step in the underwriting decision-making process, is not always an easy task. That is, many employees are "borderline" in the sense that they may come under any one or more of several applicable laws. To properly evaluate the exposure, the underwriter must know the law applicable to each employee.

Even if an insurer has failed to charge the proper premium, the policy will in most cases provide benefits to the injured employee. The insurer must then go back, properly classify and rate the policy, and collect the premium due. In some cases, collecting may be difficult.

Finally, some insurers may avoid any workers compensation exposures falling under federal jurisdiction because of insufficient underwriting expertise or reinsurance restrictions. Employments covered by the USL&HW Act require expertise in underwriting, claims handling, premium auditing, and loss control. Even an underwriter with many years of experience, but no experience in handling maritime exposures, would find it difficult to evaluate such exposures. Reinsurance treaties may also contain restrictive provisions regarding coverages such as those to insure the USL&HW Act exposure.

An underwriter may discover USL&HW Act exposures in many typical construction and erection operations. Too often, this discovery results from a claim. Underwriters must always be alert to the existence of maritime exposures. They may be indicated in many ways, including to whom certificates of insurance are issued, type of equipment owned, a list of jobs in progress, claims under other coverages, and so on. Some producers located near navigable waters attach a Longshore and Harbor Workers Compensation Act coverage endorsement to every workers compensation policy, just to be safe. The endorsement is attached even if such exposures are not contemplated when the policy is issued. In such situations, the underwriter should convey to the producer that when a maritime exposure is anticipated, it must be clearly indicated.

## UNDERWRITING WORKERS COMPENSATION

Underwriting workers compensation insurance involves the same principles and processes as underwriting commercial auto and general liability. In addition, the types of information gathered is the same as are the sources from which this information is derived. This section describes the information used to underwrite workers compensation insurance and then explores some of the additional factors considered.

### Sources of Information

Most of the sources of information identified in Chapter 3 apply to workers compensation. These include the application, the producer, the insured's financial reports, the premium auditor, claims personnel, and loss control reports. As with the underwriting of commercial auto and general liability, the size and complexity of the risk often determines the amount and depth of information needed to make a decision. In addition, insurer underwriting guidelines usually describe the types of risks that the insurer prefers to write (and prefers not to write) and the information that the insurer deems necessary. The sources common to workers compensation and other lines include some workers compensation-specific information. Underwriters also use additional sources specific to workers compensation insurance.

**Application.** The importance of the application and the information it provides has already been emphasized. Prior premiums and losses, prior insurer information, the length of time the insured has been in business, and so on are just as important in workers compensation as they are in other lines of commercial liability insurance. In addition, the application for workers compensation insurance contains questions aimed at uncovering information regarding the possibility of injury to employees. These include the use of aircraft and watercraft, exposure to flammables and caustic chemicals, underground work, age of employees, and so on. Some of these questions are also asked to elicit information for rating and classification purposes. Exhibit 12-1 shows a sample of the questions that might be asked on a workers compensation application.

Many of the questions asked for workers compensation are similar, or even identical, to the questions asked for other coverages. However, the underwriter must often look at the answers from a different perspective, depending on the coverage.

**Exhibit 12-1**
Workers Compensation Exposure Identification Questions*

| | | YES | NO | | | YES | NO |
|---|---|---|---|---|---|---|---|
| 1. | Does applicant own, operate or lease aircraft/watercraft? | | | 9. | Any group transportation provided? | | |
| 2. | Do operations involve storing, treating, discharging, applying, disposing, or transporting of hazardous material? (e.g., landfills, asbestos, wastes, fuel tanks, etc.) | | | 10. | Any employees under 16 or over 50 years of age? | | |
| 3. | Any work performed underground or above 15 feet? | | | 11. | Any employees over 60 years of age? | | |
| 4. | Any work performed on barges, vessels, docks, bridge over water? | | | 12. | Any part time or seasonal employees? | | |
| 5. | Is applicant engaged in any other type of business? | | | 13. | Is there any volunteer or donated labor? | | |
| 6. | Are sub-contractors used? | | | 14. | Any employees with physical handicaps? | | |
| 7. | Any work sublet without certificates of ins.? | | | 15. | Do employees travel out of state? | | |
| 8. | Is a formal safety program in operation? | | | 16. | Are athletic teams sponsored? | | |
| | | | | 17. | Are pre-employment physicals required? | | |
| | | | | 18. | Any other insurance with this insurer? | | |
| | | | | 19. | Any prior coverage declined/ cancelled/non-renewed (Last 3 years.)? | | |

* Reprinted with permission from ACORD Corporation, ACORD Form 130-S (3/88).

For example, most commercial liability insurance applications ask if there are part-time employees hired by the insured. A part-time employee is often less well trained than a full-time employee. Lack of experience or training may result in the employee taking shortcuts or not performing the job as it should be performed. From a general liability insurance standpoint, this behavior can lead to products liability claims. Lack of experience or training can also be responsible for the fact that a part-time employee may not understand the importance of protective clothing. The failure to wear that clothing can increase the possibility of injury, and consequently, the possibility of workers compensation claims. So, from a workers compensation standpoint, as in general liability, any information about the use of part-time employees is important in evaluating an applicant. Part-time employees are often not listed on the application for commercial auto insurance as drivers. The resulting inability of the insurance company to evaluate these persons can allow persons with poor driving records to operate insured vehicles, thus increasing the employer's and insurer's exposure. Even an insured with a good driver safety program may fail to secure the driving record of part-time employee drivers since "they were only going to be driving a couple of weeks." Thus, the same information can give the underwriter some insight into the exposures presented for many different coverages. What the underwriter does with this information once gathered depends on the coverage, the answers to other questions, and the insurer's guidelines.

**Loss Control (Inspection) Reports.** Most insurers order loss control reports on all workers compensation risks "of any reasonable size." "Reasonable size" is defined differently by different insurers. However, since many insurers prefer not to write workers compensation policies that generate less than a certain amount of premium, a loss control report is ordered on the majority of workers compensation risks.

The information contained in a workers compensation loss control report includes the more general financial information, background information, loss history, and safety program information. The report also contains information specific to workers compensation. Any information related to the questions shown earlier on the workers compensation application would be beneficial to the underwriter. In some cases, the underwriter may specifically request additional information. For example, if there is an exposure to caustics, the underwriter may want to know exactly what type, the extent of the exposure, recommendations as to the proper protection, and so on.

Insurers differ somewhat on the "major" areas to be covered in a loss control report. In general, three major areas of information specific to workers compensation include the employee work force, the plant and equipment, and the operations or processes that take place. Each is examined later in this chapter. Other insurers may look at different areas, but still include much of the same information.

Exhibit 12-2 shows a detailed report used by one insurer. The areas focused on by that insurer are management, supervision, and operations. To use this report, the loss control representative evaluates aspects of each of these major areas on a numerical scale. Each score is then totaled. The scale used to evaluate the total score is excellent = 90-100, good = 77-89, fair = 54-76, and poor = 0-53. Additionally, if recommendations have been made, the score after the insured has complied with all the recommendations is also shown.

The loss control department also functions as a source of information in other ways. For instance, if an insurer writes a substantial amount of coverage for a certain class of risks, the loss control department might compile the operating and loss information it has learned about for this class into a fairly technical manual. The manual would include information about safety devices, quality control, hiring practices, and other operations related to the desirability of a risk. The insurer could use this manual to develop recommendations for improving a given risk or class of risks. If the recommendations are followed, what may be considered an undesirable class of business by other insurers would become acceptable for the insurer whose loss control department researched that class.

**Background Resource Publications.** Most of the background resource publications described in Chapter 3 are useful in underwriting workers compensation. They include the *Best's Loss Control Engineering Manual* (*LCEM*) and *Best's Underwriting Guide* (*BUG*). Each classification description in these two resources contains a hazard index for workers compensation. In addition, the *BUG* has a column for underwriting comments related to this index. Exhibit 12-3 reprints the *BUG* workers compensation exposure description for the antique dealers classification. This classification has a hazard index of 6 for workers compensation (on a scale of 1 to 10, 10 being the least desirable). The underwriting comments column notes that the index would be lower for risks that do not do repair or refinishing work. Following the description of the workers compensation exposure in Exhibit 12-3 are questions pertaining to workers compensation from the *BUG* underwriting checklist for this class.

In addition to these publications, there are many safety-related technical manuals and reports that provide information on underwriting workers compensation. There are so many manuals because the majority of studies on loss control, accident prevention, and so on have

**Exhibit 12-2**
Exposure Evaluation Report—Workers Compensation*

(Must be completed on each pre-survey or first survey and updated on each re-survey)

*Name* ______________________________ *Engineer* ______________

Location ______________________________ Date ______________

| A. MANAGEMENT | EXCELLENT | GOOD | FAIR | POOR | SCORE AS IS | SCORE W/RECS. COMPL'D |
|---|---|---|---|---|---|---|
| 1. STATEMENT OF POLICY (Form F70-132) | Annual, Written Communication to all employees. Meeting with Supervisors to affirm or reaffirm the policy. (7) | Written policy to Supervisors. (5) | General Awareness or Loss Control Policy by employees. (3) | No policy of Loss Control by management and no one designated for Loss Control Activity. (0) | | |
| 2. EMPLOYEE SELECTION (Form F70-32) | Job — Placement Physicals given all employees. Employee placed in job commensurate with his physical capabilities. Check references. (5) | Job placement physicals given. (4) | Job placement application of employees indicating past illnesses or injuries. (3) | No application form indicating injuries or illness. (0) | | |
| 3. PLANT SAFETY RULES (Form F70-172) | Rules are printed and enforced. Rules developed by employees, supervision and management. Rules are part of new employee orientation updated annually. (5) | Rules are printed and distributed to employees, developed by management and enforced. (4) | Rules are posted on bulletin boards. (3) | No written rules. (0) | | |
| 4. DISASTER AND EMERGENCY PLAN (Form F70-217) | Formal plan in writing covering riots, fires, tornados, etc., communicated to all Personnel. Practice alerts on 6 month basis. (3) | Plan in writing for disasters and communicated. (2) | Plan in writing. (1) | No plan. (0) | | |
| 5. MANAGEMENT INVOLVEMENT | Management reviews Loss Control Reports and follows up on hazard control and entire program. (5) | Knows Losses and communicates to supervisors. (4) | Knows Losses that have transpired. (3) | No knowledge of loss exposure. (0) | | |

*Continued on the next page*

| B. SUPERVISION | | | | SUB-TOTALS | | |
|---|---|---|---|---|---|---|
| 1. SUPERVISOR TRAINING (Supervisor Education Manual) | All Supervisors complete a formal training course, in addition attend quarterly supervisor seminars. (7) | All supervisors attend quarterly supervisor seminars. (5) | Attend one day general safety meeting per year. (3) | No program for education. (0) | | |
| 2. NEW EMPLOYEE TRAINING | Formal program (in writing) on new employee training. Explanation of rules, explanation of special hazards. Follow-up training and enforcement. (5) | Training on the job and follow-up explanation of rules. (4) | Training by fellow employees. (3) | No formal training. (0) | | |
| 3. PHYSICAL HAZARD INSPECTION (Form F70-7) | Written program in effect and a formal program for follow-up. Results are part of supervisors monthly report to top management. (7) | Written program in effect and follow-up program. (5) | Using form for physical hazard survey. (3) | No program. (0) | | |
| 4. ACCIDENT INVESTIGATION (Form F70-39) | Completes supervisor report of accident and makes changes to remove hazard and reinstructs his people. Makes changes in procedures as necessary. (6) | Completes supervisor report of accident and makes the physical changes necessary to remove hazard. (5) | Completes a supervisor report of accident. (4) | No accident investigation by supervisor. (0) | | |
| **C. OPERATIONS** | | | | SUB-TOTALS | | |
| 1. HOUSEKEEPING | There is a planned place for everything and everything is in its place. Aisles properly marked and clear. (5) | Most materials are neatly stored. Aisles are marked and clear. (4) | Aisles marked but not observed. Enough room but materials poorly stored. Cleaned up by clean-up man when needed. (3) | No program and a problem exists. (0) | | |
| 2. MACHINE GUARDING | All points of operation guarded and properly adjusted. Proper procedures for set-up men. (7) | All points of operation guarded and in use. Some out of adjustment. (5) | Most machines guarded but some not in use. (3) | Machines not guarded. (0) | | |
| 3. POWER TRANSMISSION GUARDING | All chains, sprockets, gears, overhead conveyors, etc. are protected by guards. (5) | Codes are followed, but improvements can be made. (4) | Most areas guarded, but not enforced. (3) | Open gears, belts, etc. (0) | | |

Carry forward to other side

| C. OPERATIONS (Continued) | EXCELLENT | GOOD | FAIR | POOR | SCORE AS IS | SCORE W/RECS. COMPL'D |
|---|---|---|---|---|---|---|
| | | | | Carried forward | | |
| 4. PLANT MAINTENANCE AND GENERAL PHYSICAL HAZARD PROTECTION | All equipment is on a maintenance schedule. Floors are in excellent repair. Guard rails are well designed and maintained. New processes are checked with safety director before operation of equipment. (4) | Evidence of good maintenance. Guarding generally in evidence and well maintained. (3) | Guards in place but not well maintained. (2) | No evidence of effective controls. Floors not even, slippery surfaces, stairs without railings, unprotected openings in floors, etc. (0) | | |
| 5. PERSONAL PROTECTIVE EQUIPMENT | Proper equipment furnished, employees trained in use. Enforced program. Follow-up by supervisor and safety personnel. (4) | Proper equipment issued by management. Most of employees using equipment. (3) | Proper equipment issued by management. (2) | None provided or not adequate. (0) | | |
| 6. MATERIAL HANDLING | All jobs are analyzed and mechanized equipment is provided where needed and proper instruction is given for use. Jobs are designed to reduce handling through use of conveyors, etc. (5) | Mechanized equipment is adequate and in use. Can use more study on methods. Instruction is given. (4) | Mechanization for only large and bulky items. (3) | Improper practices in evidence and little effort to control. (0) | | |
| 7. VENTILATION | Exceeds standards in all exposure areas. Periodic checks for adequacy are made. New processes are analyzed. (5) | Meets standards in all exposure areas. No program to recheck. (4) | Minimum standards in most areas. (3) | Below minimum I.H. standards where exposures exist. (0) | | |
| 8. NOISE CONTROL | Analysis has been made and equipment designed to reduce noise levels below minimum levels. Employees are all checked and an audiometric program is in effect. (5) | Analysis has been made. Processes have been engineered and personal protective equipment is issued and used. No audiometric program. (4) | Personal equipment issued. Not used where necesary. (3) | Noise exposure and no controls. (0) | | |
| 9. FIRE CONTROL | — Flammable liquids control<br>— Meeting N.F.P.A. standards<br>— Spray booths properly protected<br>— Automatic extinguishing systems where necessary<br>— Training programs on fire prevention (50 | — Training program for supervisors and employees in fire prevention<br>— Hazards controlled (4) | — Common fire hazards and special fire hazards controlled (3) | No apparent control (0) | | |

*Continued on the next page*

| | | | | | | |
|---|---|---|---|---|---|---|
| 10. FIRST AID | Nurse and/or doctor.<br>Records kept and analyzed.<br>First aid room and all necessary first aid materials. (5) | — Records kept<br>— Trained first aid personnel<br>— Most necessary first aid materials<br>— First aid room (4) | — Records kept<br>— First aid kits at central location (3) | — No records kept (0) | | |
| | | | | SUB-TOTALS | | |
| | | | | GRAND TOTALS | | |
| | | | | TOTALS W/URG. RECS., COMPL'D | | |
| | | | | TOTALS W/ALL RECS., COMPL'D | | |

NOTE:

1. If no exposure exists, rate in excellent category.
2. If the account is too small for formal training, rate in excellent category if employees are well trained.
3. Use for any size account.
4. Engineer will date and initial on back page on each call.
5. Use absolute values only—DO NOT RATIO.

COMMENTS: ______________________________

| LOSS CONTROL ENGINEER CALLS | MO. | YR. | INITIALS | MO. | YR. | INITIALS | MO. | YR. | INITIALS |
|---|---|---|---|---|---|---|---|---|---|
| | | | | | | | | | |
| | | | | | | | | | |
| | | | | | | | | | |
| | | | | | | | | | |

*Reprinted with permission of Sentry Insurance.

**Exhibit 12-3**

*Best's Underwriting Guide*—Antique Dealers Classification*

## Workers Compensation

The insured may hire a few employees to help with the sales and deliveries of antiques. Other, larger operations may have several locations and large sales staffs. Injuries may result from opening boxes with razor blades or knives. Employees may trip over materials or equipment. Slips and falls on waxed or littered floors are possible. During the course of delivery, or while moving stock within the shop, employees may suffer strains and sprains, including back injuries and hernias. Are employees trained in proper materials-handling techniques? Delivery personnel also are exposed to vehicular accidents.

Does the insured perform repair or restoration work? What materials are used? Lacquers may contain amyl-acetate and benzene. Both are irritating to mucous membranes and possess a narcotic effect if inhaled frequently. Turpentine oil can cause serious irritation of the kidneys. Severe injuries, including blindness, may occur if lacquers or thinners are splashed into the eyes. Epoxy resins found in glues should be used in well ventilated areas. If not used with caution, epoxy resins can cause serious burns, skin rashes, eye injuries and unconsciousness. Are employees properly trained for working with such materials? Are workers equipped with appropriate personal protective equipment? For more information on possible exposures in this area refer to Furniture Refinishing and Upholstery Shops.

The Fire exposure is increased with the presence of these liquids. Is the work area equipped with an adequate number of accessible, properly illuminated exits? (See also Fire and E.C.)

Does the dealer participate in out-of-town exhibits? Do any of the insured's employees travel to other states or foreign countries to make purchases? The frequency and radius of travel must be given serious consideration.

If the value of the merchandise is or is perceived to be considerable, the shop may be a prime target for criminals. Employees both on and off the premises may be exposed to injury during a robbery attempt.

## Underwriter's Checklist

- Are good housekeeping practices employed? Are premises kept uncluttered and is there ample room to move about the shop?
- Does the insured do repair or restoration work? Is the work area in the same building as the antique shop?
- What chemicals, paints and refinishing materials are kept on hand? What are their health and physical hazards? How are they stored?
- Are workers using chemicals, paints and refinishing materials issued proper personal protective equipment?
- Does the insured keep cash on the premises?
- What does an analysis of prior loss experience reveal?

*Adapted with permission from *Best's Underwriting Guide* (Oldwick, NJ, A.M. Best Company, 1989), Antique Dealers Classification, pp. 3,5.

focused on employee injuries. Two examples of such manuals are the *Accident Prevention Manual for Industrial Operations*—National Safety Council, and *Occupational Injuries and Illnesses in the United States by Industry*—U.S. Department of Labor, Bureau of Labor Statistics.

Like several of the publications described in Chapter 3, it is unlikely that an underwriter would refer to these two manuals (or any similar manual) in evaluating an individual risk. More likely, such manuals would be used by underwriting management as a basis for underwriting guidelines. However, if such manuals were available to an underwriter, they could assist in the underwriting of an unfamiliar class of business.

**Experience Rating Exhibits (Worksheets).** If an organization has been in business long enough and has had sufficient premium, it is likely that the organization is eligible for experience rating. Through experience rating, an organization's workers compensation class rate is adjusted upward or downward by an *experience rating modification factor* (often called an *experience mod*) that reflects the insured's loss experience. *If the risk is eligible, experience rating is mandatory.* The experience rating worksheet is developed, and the experience rating modification factor is calculated by the applicable rating bureau and sent to the *insurer of record* (that is, the insurer that the bureau shows to be providing coverage). If the risk is an applicant, the underwriter may ask the applicant to obtain a copy of the current experience rating worksheet from the present insurer so that it may be evaluated. The calculation of the modification is described in detail later in this chapter.

Exhibit 12-4 shows a sample experience rating worksheet for an organization. There are many ways in which the underwriter can use the information shown on the worksheet. In most cases it verifies information the underwriter already has either on an application (new business) or in the underwriting file (renewal business).

The first thing the underwriter should do after receiving the worksheet is to verify that it is for the correct organization. The simplest way to do so is to check the risk identification number on the worksheet. In addition, the first two digits of the risk identification number itself also indicate the one state in which the insured operates (an *intrastate* experience modification) or that the insured operates in more than one state (an *interstate* experience modification).

For new business, the name on the worksheet should be checked. If the name on the worksheet differs from the name on the application or if additional organizations appear (such as subsidiary organizations or related organizations with the same ownership), the underwriter should

**Exhibit 12-4**
Workers Compensation Experience Rating Worksheet*

**WORKERS COMPENSATION EXPERIENCE RATING**

NAME OF RISK ABC CORPORATION — RISK IDENT. NO. 990-123-456 — STATE ANY — EFFECTIVE DATE 01/01/X0

| 1 CODE | 2 ELR | 3 D-RATIO | 4 PAYROLL | 5 EXPECTED LOSSES | 6 EXP-PRIM LOSSES | 7 CLAIM DATA | 8 IJ | 0 F | 9 ACT INC LOSSES | 10 ACT PRIM LOSSES |
|---|---|---|---|---|---|---|---|---|---|---|
| CARRIER 99999 | | | POLICY X6 X6 X6 | | | EFF-DATE | 01/01/X6 | | EXP-DATE | 01/01/X7 |
| 1463 | 2.02 | .36 | 86,703 | 1,751 | 630 | X60024 | 5 | F | 12,280 | 5,000 |
| 5515 | 2.08 | .34 | 2,478,337 | 51,549 | 17,527 | X60010 | 2 | 0 | 47,136# | 5,000 |
| 5606 | 0.58 | .37 | 137,447 | 797 | 295 | 10 | | * | 4,146 | 4,146 |
| 8227 | 1.02 | .34 | 109,350 | 1,115 | 379 | | | | | |
| 8810 | 0.06 | .38 | 244,940 | 147 | 56 | | | | | |
| POLICY-TOTAL | | | 3,056,777 | (SUBJECT PREMIUM = 99,529) | | | | | 174,162 | |
| CARRIER 99999 | | | POLICY X7 X7 X7 | | | EFF-DATE | 01/01/X7 | | EXP-DATE | 01/01/X8 |
| 1463 | 2.02 | .36 | 93,806 | 1,895 | 682 | X70124 | 2 | 0 | 285,586# | 5,000 |
| 5506 | 1.45 | .36 | 1,503,170 | 21,796 | 7,847 | 4 | | * | 1,836 | 1,836 |
| 5515 | 2.08 | .34 | 985,941 | 20,508 | 6,973 | | | | | |
| 5606 | 0.58 | .37 | 111,429 | 646 | 239 | | | | | |
| 8227 | 1.02 | .34 | 95,686 | 976 | 332 | | | | | |
| 8810 | 0.06 | .38 | 244,009 | 146 | 55 | | | | | |
| POLICY-TOTAL | | | 3,034,041 | (SUBJECT PREMIUM = 98,152) | | | | | 287,422 | |
| CARRIER 99999 | | | POLICY X8 X8 X8 | | | EFF-DATE | 01/01/X8 | | EXP-DATE | 01/01/X9 |
| 1463 | 2.02 | .36 | 508,210 | 10,266 | 3,696 | X80013 | 5 | F | 5,714 | 5,000 |
| 5506 | 1.45 | .36 | 1,586,986 | 23,011 | 8,284 | X80179 | 5 | F | 20,714 | 5,000 |
| 5515 | 2.08 | .34 | 1,586,986 | 33,099 | 11,223 | 6 | | * | 3,380 | 3,389 |
| 5606 | 0.58 | .34 | 496,456 | 2,879 | 1,065 | | | | | |
| 8227 | 1.02 | .34 | 277,377 | 2,829 | 962 | | | | | |
| 8742 | 0.17 | .34 | 32,307 | 55 | 19 | | | | | |
| 8810 | 0.06 | .38 | 398,223 | 329 | 91 | | | | | |
| POLICY-TOTAL | | | 4,886,545 | (SUBJECT PREMIUM = 151,097) | | | | | 29,808 | |
| | (A) 0.30 | (B) | (C) EXPECTED EXCESS (D-E) 113,259 | (D) 173,614 | (E) 60,355 | (F) ACTUAL EXCESS (H-I) 105,066 | (G) 22,200 | | (H) 139,428 | (I) 34,362 |

* Total to Policy Year of all cases $5,000 or less
\# Limited loss

| | (11) PRIMARY LOSSES | (12) STABILIZING VALUE | (13) RATABLE EXCESS | (14) TOTALS | (15) EXP MOD |
|---|---|---|---|---|---|
| ACTUAL | (I) 34,362 | (C) x (1-W) + (G) 101,481 | (A) x (F) 31,520 | (J) 167,363 | (J) (K) .85 |
| EXPECTED | (E) 60,355 | 101,481 | (A) x (C) 33,978 | (K) 195,814 | REVISED PLAN |

PAGE NUMBER
DATE

*Adapted with permission from *Understanding the Changes Introduced By The Revised Workers Compensation Experience Rating Plan* (New York: National Council on Compensation Insurance, 1989), p. 9.

determine the exact name and form of organization of the applicant. The importance of properly naming the insured was explained in Chapter 1.

For new business, the effective date of the modification (referred to as the *anniversary rating date*) should be checked against the effective date of the policy. In most cases, the two are the same, but there are times when the dates may not agree. To simplify rating and premium auditing, the two dates should be the same. Short-term (or long-term) policies can be written to make the two dates coincide at renewal.

For new business, the worksheet can be used to verify other information shown on the application, including prior insurers (a code number is shown), loss history, and classification codes. The classification codes shown for the most recent year should agree with the classification codes shown on the application. In addition, the underwriter should review the two other years shown on the worksheet to see if any other codes have been applicable for this risk. If additional or different codes are shown, the underwriter should determine the types of operations represented by these codes and determine why they are not shown on the application. An insured may list a lower rated classification in order to save money, or the insured could have changed operations, discontinued or introduced certain products, and so on. The underwriter should receive a satisfactory explanation from the insured about the reasons for using different classifications.

It is possible that the insured does not show a certain hazardous type of operation on the application because such work is not anticipated during the next year. However, if that classification code appears on the experience rating worksheet, it could indicate that the insured is willing to undertake that work given the opportunity. Because that work is extremely hazardous, the insurer may be unwilling to provide coverage to the insured. If the classification code does not appear on the experience rating worksheet, the underwriter might not know about such operations until after the work begins (for example, when a claim is submitted) or even after it is finished (for example, the classification code appears on the final audit).

For renewal business, the loss history and classification codes should also be checked against the insurer's records primarily to see that they are correct, not so much to obtain new information (since such information should be in the insurer's files). In addition, the payroll amounts shown for each classification can be double-checked. It is possible that the loss history will not perfectly match the application or insurer's records, but any material discrepancies should be resolved.

For new and renewal business, the experience rating worksheet can alert the underwriter to additional locations of the insured's business. It is possible that the insured has shown operations in only one state, but the experience rating worksheet shows several states.

Just because an underwriter has handled an account for a number of years is no reason to assume that all information on the worksheet is correct. Material discrepancies can arise from clerical errors, failure to report a claim, failure to report a change in reserve, failure to report a change in payroll as a result of a revised premium audit, and so on. Regardless of the cause of the error, all errors should be corrected and a new modification calculated.

As Chapter 3 explained, underwriters are not only interested in the total dollar amount of losses, but also in trends in losses. The worksheet displays the loss history such that trends in losses are easy to detect. In addition to showing three years of loss history as is usually provided on the application, the experience rating worksheet provides a breakdown of losses by size (the exact breakdown will be described later). Some indication of claim frequency and severity can be discerned from the information on the worksheet.

The worksheet also shows payroll by classification for three years. Trends in payroll can also help the underwriter in the evaluation of a risk. If payroll is increasing rapidly each year, the underwriter may wish to check the payroll estimates shown on the policy to verify that they are realistic. The approximate percentage of total payroll in each class can also be checked against policy estimates. The payroll breakdown by class may give the underwriter an idea of the direction in which the insured's operations are headed. Certain operations may be taking on added importance in the insured's total operations. The underwriter must determine whether or not those classes are desirable. Sudden increases in overall payroll may indicate the addition of staff, the opening of a new plant or location, and so on. All are important to the underwriter in determining the exposures presented by the risk.

A risk with a declining overall payroll may have financial problems. The underwriter would need to check any financial statements obtained or financial analyses performed to further investigate this possibility. Sudden drops in payroll may indicate that a plant was closed. Such a drop should probably also be accompanied by a drop in losses. If losses have continued to increase as payroll has decreased, the underwriter must determine why. In many cases, the announcement of a plant closing is accompanied by a sudden increase in workers compensation claims as laid-off workers seek other sources of income, sometimes with the help of the union.

**OSHA Records.** Since 1971 every employer who is subject to the Williams-Steiger Occupational Safety and Health Act of 1970 (which is a large number of employers) is required to keep occupational

**Exhibit 12-5**
OSHA Log, Form 200—Columns 1–6

| Extent and Outcome of INJURY | | | | | |
|---|---|---|---|---|---|
| Fatalities | Nonfatal Injuries | | | | |
| Injury Related | Injuries With Lost Workdays | | | | Injuries Without Lost Workdays |
| Enter DATE of death<br><br>Mo./day/yr. | Enter a CHECK if injury involves days away from work, or days of restricted work activity, or both. | Enter a CHECK if injury involves days away from work. | Enter number of DAYS away from work. | Enter number of DAYS of restricted work activity. | Enter a CHECK if no entry was made in columns 1 or 2 but the injury is recordable as defined above. |
| (1) | (2) | (3) | (4) | (5) | (6) |

injury and illness records for his or her employees in the establishment at which the employees usually report to work. Every employer must maintain (1) a log of recordable occupational injuries and illnesses, and (2) supplementary records of each occupational injury or illness. There are several recording forms; however, the basic form is referred to as the OSHA log, Form 200. The first six columns (columns A-F) of information on Form 200 are general information items such as the case or file number, date of injury or illness, employee's name, occupation of the injured employee, the department to which the employee was assigned, and a description of the injury or illness. The next six columns (columns 1-6) identify the extent and outcome of injuries. Notice in Exhibit 12-5 that the form provides a frequency count for the number of fatalities and nonfatal injuries; then, nonfatal injuries are divided among those involving lost work days and those without lost work days. OSHA defines a *recordable case* as referenced in column 6 as one involving an occupational death, occupational illness, or an occupational injury involving loss of consciousness, restriction of work or motion, transfer to another job, or medical treatment (other than first aid). Many of these terms are further defined on the reverse side of the OSHA Form 200. The third section (columns 7-13) of the log requests information on the type, extent, and outcome of illness. It is shown in Exhibit 12-6.

The OSHA log can be of material assistance to the underwriter when no records would otherwise be available to document the

**Exhibit 12-6**
OSHA Log, Form 200—Columns 7–13

| Type, Extent of, and Outcome of ILLNESS | | | | | | | | | | | | |
|---|---|---|---|---|---|---|---|---|---|---|---|---|
| Type of Illness | | | | | | | Fatalities | Nonfatal Illnesses | | | | |
| CHECK Only One Column for Each Illness (*See other side of form for terminations of permanent transfers.*) | | | | | | | Illness Related | Illnesses With Lost Workdays | | | | Illnesses Without Lost Workdays |
| Occupational skin diseases or disorders | Dust diseases of the lungs | Respiratory conditions due to toxic agents | Poisoning (systemic effects of toxic materials) | Disorders due to physical agents | Disorders associated with repeated trauma | All other occupational illnesses | Enter DATE of death. Mo./day/yr. | Enter a CHECK if illness involves days away from work, or days of restricted work activity, or both | Enter a CHECK if illness involves days away from work. | Enter number of DAYS away from work. | Enter number of DAYS of restricted work activity. | Enter a CHECK if no entry was made in columns 8 or 9. |
| (7) | | | | | | | (8) | (9) | (10) | (11) | (12) | (13) |
| (a) | (b) | (c) | (d) | (e) | (f) | (g) | | | | | | |

incidence of industrial injury. Before OSHA, only a small percentage of employers maintained accurate occupational injury records. The OSHA log should be available since it is a mandatory requirement of the Occupational Safety and Health Administration. (In most instances, it will be the loss control representative who will actually review the OSHA log.) The information on the log can be used to identify the types of losses that are occurring, their frequency, and their duration in terms of lost work days. It can also be used to verify other loss information submitted with the application.

**Industry Statistics.** Most studies that have been conducted on injuries and loss control have used employees as their "group" of concern. As a result, there is much information on the subject of employee injuries. In addition, as a result of OSHA and other employment-related laws, employers have had to keep more detailed records of employee injuries than they have had to keep for injuries that might be classified as general liability type losses. This section examines how underwriters and insurers can make use of this wealth of information in the underwriting of workers compensation insurance.

In the discussion of products liability underwriting, it was pointed out that many of the statistics on product hazards were more helpful to underwriting management in setting underwriting policy and guidelines than to an underwriter in underwriting a single risk. The same is true for most of the industry statistics on occupational injuries and diseases.

The fact that the widget manufacturing industry (1) has an injury/illness incidence rate of 2.7 per 100 full-time workers, (2) ranks

232nd among all major US occupations in terms of this injury/illness rate, and (3) suffers 75 percent of its occupational injuries as a result of an employee being struck by a falling object does little to help Daryl Underwriter when she receives a submission on a widget manufacturer. This information can, however, be helpful to underwriting management. First, management may decide that because the chances of employee injuries are so minor relative to the premium collected for this classification, this is a relatively desirable class of business to write. In addition, further investigation reveals that loss by a falling object is a result of employees dropping the widgets on their toes. If employees are required to wear steel-toed shoes, approximately 90 percent of these losses would be eliminated. As a result, the underwriting guide to which Daryl would refer when she received this submission would list widget manufacturing as desirable as long as the employer has a policy of requiring employees to wear steel-toed shoes.

The following are some of the sources of information on occupational injuries and illnesses and how they can be used:

- Occupational injury and incidence rates are published by several organizations and include the U.S. Department of Labor, Bureau of Labor Statistics survey (using OSHA definitions); OSHA estimates; National Safety Council estimates based upon National Center for Health Statistics survey, state vital statistics departments, state industrial commissions, and reports by members of the National Safety Council; National Institute for Occupational Safety and Health estimates; *Morbidity and Mortality Weekly Report,* published by the Centers for Disease Control, based upon National Occupational Hazard Survey; and an insurer's own records. Any of these sources can be used by management as a relative measure of the occupational injury exposure inherent in any number of classifications. They can also be used to compare a particular insured's loss history with that of the industry to which it belongs (realistically this would be done only for large risks).
- A listing of injuries by cause or by part of body affected. When identified with a particular occupation or classification, this information can help direct loss control efforts.
- The NCCI assigns classifications to one of four *hazard groups* for use in retrospective rating. The hazard group gives an indication of the relative occupational injury severity normally associated with the classification. Unfortunately, there is no way to compare classifications within the same hazard group.

## Factors to Consider

There are many factors to consider when underwriting workers compensation coverage. Some of these factors have been mentioned in the discussion of sources of information as well as in Chapter 3.

Workers compensation underwriting is much like general liability underwriting except a different group of persons—employees in workers compensation and the public in general liability—is the group of concern with regard to injury. In addition, unlike general liability, workers compensation insurance is not concerned with property damage. One other difference between workers compensation and general liability underwriting is that, in theory at least, employees should be more concerned with their own safety rather than with that of the third party buyer of a product. Hopefully, employees therefore take insurer loss control recommendations for workers compensation more seriously since such recommendations are intended to protect the employee from injury. As most underwriters learn, however, this is not always the case.

This section first reviews factors discussed in the underwriting of other lines of insurance that also relate to workers compensation. It then discusses the two factors that are specifically related to workers compensation coverage, (1) plant and equipment and (2) processes or operations. Although each factor is considered in underwriting other lines of insurance, the emphasis given to these factors by the workers compensation underwriter is somewhat different from that in other lines of insurance.

**Factors Related to All Lines.** As mentioned, many of the factors considered in underwriting commercial auto and general liability are also considered for workers compensation. The following are five such factors:

1. Management
    - managerial expertise
    - concern for safety
    - background
2. Finances
    - profitability
    - position relative to similar firms
    - outlook for growth/survival
3. Loss (claims) history
4. Safety program
    - existence
    - recordkeeping
    - enforcement

  - management support
5. Caliber of employees
  - selection
  - training
  - years of experience
  - concern for safety/quality
  - expertise

As stated, the importance of all these factors has been discussed. However, because loss history greatly affects the desirability of a risk, this factor is reviewed—here from the perspective of a workers compensation underwriter.

For smaller workers compensation risks, the losses are usually too few to develop a frequency trend or to identify any particular type of loss that may be especially problematic. In this case, the underwriter concentrates more on other factors such as management concern for safety, employee selection, and so on since these factors also affect loss experience. The underwriter can also determine the hazards that are historically associated with this type of risk and further determine whether or not the particular risk being underwritten has such hazards. If so, perhaps some form of loss control may help to handle these hazards. Another approach to smaller risks is to question the insured about those few losses that have been incurred. If an employee was injured on a certain piece of equipment, the underwriter may inquire about the type of safety features (guards, for example) on the equipment.

For larger risks, computerized loss summaries for workers compensation insurance are common. Many of them are detailed in terms of the cause of the injury (for example, improper lifting) and the type of injury (for example, strained back). When examining such loss runs, it is easier to detect trends, compare loss incidence rates with industry figures, identify the equipment that is causing problems, and so on. For example, if there appears to be an unusually high number of back strain losses as a result of improper lifting, the underwriter may suggest that loss control representatives instruct employees about the proper methods of lifting.

Exhibit 12-7 is a claims experience report used by one firm. Every injury is listed on such reports. For each injury, detailed information is provided about the claim, the claimant, and the injury. The injury code shown in the exhibit is helpful to the underwriter in that it gives detailed information about the inquiry. There are four sections to the injury code:

- Type of injury
- Part of body

- Nature of injury
- Agency

The key to what is included in each section is presented in Exhibits 12-8, 12-9, 12-10, and 12-11, respectively.

Although not shown in the exhibits, claim reports also show summaries of the total number of claims by year. These summaries are broken down into whether the claims involve medical or indemnity, and whether they are open or closed.

Claims can also be analyzed in terms of frequency and cost with regard to each section of the injury code (that is, by type of injury, part of body, nature of injury, and agency). By examining the summaries of frequency and cost by code, the underwriter is able to identify the injury types or agencies that cost the insurance company the most money. It is possible that a large number of a certain type of injury is expected in the insured's industry. If so, there may be little an insurance company can do. However, if such a large number of a certain type of injury is unexpected but occurring, some type of action should be taken. Underwriters must also consider frequency of occurrence since frequent small injuries are usually a better indicator of a problem than are one or two large injuries.

Exhibit 12-12 is an example of a report analyzing claim frequency and costs with regard to each of the four sections of the injury code produced by the same firm. These reports also usually include a detailed analysis of each claim included in the summary.

**Plant and Equipment.** Plant and equipment (including autos) is the first of two factors that are uniquely related to workers compensation underwriting. Here, the underwriter's concern is the safety of the plant or premises where the employees work and the equipment with which they work. Included in an evaluation of plant and equipment would be an examination of (1) housekeeping, (2) maintenance, (3) safety features, and (4) replacement.

***Housekeeping.*** The term "housekeeping" is used in its broad sense to include the plant layout, cleanliness, and efficiency of plant operations. For example, sweeping up the chips from a woodworking machine would be considered "housecleaning," a narrower term than housekeeping; the installation of an exhaust system to keep the chips off the floor in the first place would be "housekeeping." Thus, the general quality of housekeeping is judged on the overall appearance of cleanliness, and efficiency. Cluttered or slippery floors and stairways may either be the cause of accidents or may intensify the chance of an accident involving adjacent machines and operations. Clean conditions here are of primary importance in the prevention of losses.

The adequacy and layout of aisles has a bearing on the quality of

# Exhibit 12-7
## Claims Experience Report*

0332839 16
PERIOD 01-01-78/12-31-78
QUARTERLY REPORT FOR MAR-78
PAGE 6

SAMPLE COMPANY
PLANT A

| CLAIM NO / INJ DATE | CLAIMANT | SEX | AGE | CLAIM STATUS | RECOVERED COST / INJ CODE | PAYMENTS: COMPENSATION CURRENT / PAID TO DATE | PAYMENTS: MEDICAL CURRENT / PAID TO DATE | PAYMENTS: ALLOCATED CURRENT / PAID TO DATE | PAYMENTS: TOTALS CURRENT / PAID TO DATE | ESTIMATED FUTURE COST: COMPENSATION | ESTIMATED FUTURE COST: MEDICAL | ESTIMATED FUTURE COST: ALLOCATED | EXPECTED TOTAL COST: RECOVERABLE / INCURRED |
|---|---|---|---|---|---|---|---|---|---|---|---|---|---|
| 78000006 | R CLEMSON | M | 46 | N,C* | | | 17.00 | | 17.00 | | | | |
| 11-21-77 | CONT LT HAND | | | | B05E57 | | 17.00 | | 17.00 | | | | 17.00 |
| 78000003 | C CONGEMI | M | 53 | N,R, | | | 29.65 | | 29.65 | | | | |
| 12-07-77 | PAINFUL RT SHOULDER | | | | D03L65 | | 29.65 | | 29.65 | 1,120.00 | 845.35 | | 1,995.00 |
| 77000051 | N PENATI | | 56 | | | | | | | | | | |
| 04-29-77 | PAINFUL BACK | | | | F11L66 | 1,090.81 | 211.49 | | 1,302.30 | 1,119.19 | 378.51 | | 2,800.00 |
| 78000032 | R GIBBS | M | 43 | N | | | | | | | | | |
| 06-06-77 | PAINFUL BACK | | | | D11L57 | | | | | 1,120.00 | 1,000.00 | | 2,120.00 |
| 77000089 | T KELADES | M | 48 | | | 1,004.34 | | | 1,004.34 | | | | |
| 10-03-77 | SEVRE SPR LT FT ANKLE | | | | F08L65 | 2,029.63 | 281.80 | | 2,311.43 | 727.37 | 288.20 | | 3,327.00 |
| 78000007 | J LESHNACK | M | 51 | N,C* | | | 74.35 | | 74.35 | | | | |
| 12-30-77 | CONT RT CHEEK | | | | B01E43 | | 74.35 | | 74.35 | | | | 74.35 |
| 77000105 | D LONG | | | C* | | | 25.00 | | 25.00 | | | | |
| 10-29-77 | CUT RT FOREARM | | | | C04J57 | | 56.60 | | 56.60 | | | | 56.60 |
| 77000062 | S MASHORDA | | 38 | | | | | | | | | | |
| 05-24-77 | LT INGUINAL HERNIA | | | | F20L66 | 1,523.60 | 1,624.98 | | 3,148.58 | 676.40 | 325.02 | | 4,150.00 |
| 78000009 | R MORGAN | M | 62 | N.R. | | | 86.90 | | 86.90 | | | | |
| 11-30-77 | LOW BACK DEGEN ARTH | | | | B11L47 | | 181.90 | | 181.90 | | | | 181.90 |
| 77000050 | M OLINIK | | 57 | | | | | | | | | | |
| 05-13-77 | FRAC LT FOOT | | | | F08I65 | 2,727.00 | 313.75 | | 3,040.75 | 1,213.00 | 399.25 | | 4,653.00 |
| 77000104 | R PAGE | M | 34 | | | 249.25 | 27.80 | | 277.05 | | | | |
| 11-28-77 | CONT TRANSVERSE ARCH RT F | | | | A08E65 | 249.25 | 27.80 | | 277.05 | 1,473.75 | 745.20 | | 2,496.00 |
| 78000021 | V PARTAIN | F | 57 | N | | | | | | | | | |
| 11-15-77 | CONT ABR RT THGH RT ANKLE | | | | A13P65 | | | | | 1,120.00 | 800.00 | | 1,920.00 |
| 77000103 | J POLLIFRONE | M | 43 | | | 465.36 | 80.00 | | 545.36 | | | | |
| 11-17-77 | LAC RT MIDDLE FINGER | | | | A06J57 | 909.57 | 138.75 | | 1,048.32 | 1,402.43 | 521.25 | | 2,972.00 |

CLAIM STATUS LEGEND C CLOSED C* CLOSED THIS PERIOD N NEW R REOPENED L LITIGATION I INVESTIGATION D DENIED CLAIM

0332839

*Adapted with permission of Gates, McDonald & Company, Columbus, OH, 1978.

**Exhibit 12-8**
Key to Accident Analysis Code—Type of Injury*

A. Striking against—bumping, stepping, kicking, pushed or thrown against objects
B. Struck by—falling, flying, sliding, or moving objects
C. Caught in, under, or between—objects moving or stationary, or moving parts of objects
D. Fall on same level
E. Fall to different level
F. Slip (not fall) involuntary bodily reaction—strains, sprains, ruptures, etc.
G. Contact with Temp extremes—burns relating to heat or cold
H. Inhalation, absorption, indigestion (radiation, toxic substances, caustics, asphyxiation poisoning or contact disease)
I. Overexertion—lifting, pulling, pushing, wielding, throwing, or handling of objects
J. Contact with electric current
K. Rubbed or abraded—produced by pressure, vibration, friction, or foreign matter in eyes
L. Vehicle accidents—motor, railway, water, aircraft, etc.
M. Unclassified insufficient data

*Adapted with permission of Gates, McDonald & Company, Columbus, OH, 1978.

every risk. Aisles that are too narrow or congested can cause an employee to be injured by machines or equipment by which the employee is walking. Handling materials in narrow or congested aisles can also lead to injury. Equipment layout providing sufficient space around machines, which permits the safe and efficient performance of work is also important. Congestion at these points is a contributing factor in many accidents. In addition, adequate space and facilities to permit the safe and orderly storage of raw materials in a fashion that minimizes congestion and rehandling can reduce hazards. A properly planned flow of materials, which produces the right quantity of the right materials in the right place at the right time, will increase efficiency while reducing the hazards of rehandling and congestion.

Almost every business activity produces some form of waste, which must be regularly removed to prevent excessive accumulations

**Exhibit 12-9**

Key to Accident Analysis Code—Part of Body*

1. Head—Includes neck
2. Eye
3. Shoulder
4. Arm
5. Hand and/or Wrist
6. Finger
7. Leg—incl. hips, buttock, knee
8. Foot—incl. ankle
9. Toe
10. Ribs and/or Chest
11. Back
12. Abdomen
13. Multiple Parts
    (Applies when more than one major body part has been affected.)
14. Body Parts
    (Not elsewhere classified)
15. Respiratory System
    (Lungs, etc.)
16. Circulatory System (Heart, blood, arteries, veins, etc.)
17. Musculo-skeletal System
    (Bones, joints, tendons, muscles, etc.)
18. Digestive System
19. Excretory System
    (Kidneys, bladder, intestines, etc.)
20. Unclassified
    (Not filed through our office or insufficient information)

*Adapted with permission of Gates, McDonald & Company, Columbus, OH, 1978.

with the accompanying hazards of congestion and cluttered floors, machines, and work areas. In addition, personnel and materials traffic control, which eliminates congestion and cross-traffic, will increase efficiency and reduce hazards.

***Maintenance.*** The buildings in which the work is performed and the equipment used in operations must be well maintained if safe and efficient operation is to be expected. Floors and stairways must be constantly traveled by the employees. Poor conditions resulting from improper maintenance may well be the cause of many accidents and delays in production. Every employee must rely on the proper operation of machines, equipment, and tools used in the job. The sudden failure of some part of a machine may easily result in serious injury to the

**Exhibit 12-10**

Key to Accident Analysis Code—Nature of Injury*

A. Amputation
B. Asphyxiation, Strangulation, Drowning
C. Burn or Scald—(Heat or Chemical)
D. Disorder Due to Repeated Trauma; bursitis, tenosynovitis, etc. (26)[1]
E. Contusions or Crushes
F. Conjunctivitis
G. Concussion, Shock, Prostration
H. Occupational Skin Diseases or Disorders (21)[1]
I. Fractures
J. Cut, Lacerations, Puncture open wound and infections
K. Poisoning (Systemic Effects of Toxic Materials) (24)[1]
L. Strains, Sprains, or Dislocation
M. Dust Diseases of the Lungs Pneumoconioses (22)[1]
N. Ulcerations (Not Skin Disorders)
O. Varicosities
P. Multiple Injuries
Q. Electric Shock, Electrocution
R. Unknown
S. Death
T. Disorders Due to Physical Agents (Other than toxic materials) (25)[1]
U. Respiratory Conditions—Toxic Agents (23)[1]—or Disease
V. All Other Occupational Illnesses (29)[1]

1. These categories conform to the Occupational illness classification required for OSHA reporting.

*Adapted with permission of Gates, McDonald & Company, Columbus, OH, 1978.

operator or fellow employees as well as damage to the product and delay in production. Proper maintenance is not only the repair of equipment that has failed, but also a continuous program to prevent excessive wear and to locate potential trouble. The quality of lighting can intensify or reduce all of the hazards at a plant. When a worker is unable to see clearly, the chances for an accident are increased. Excellent lighting may enable a person to avoid a hazard that otherwise might cause injury.

***Safety Features.*** The equipment used by the insured (including the building in which the employees work) should contain a reasonable amount of the latest safety features or devices. For example, the building should be sprinklered, and guards should be properly installed

**Exhibit 12-11**
Key to Accident Analysis Code—Agency*

41. Air Pressure
42. Chemicals—Cleaning compounds, liquids, gases, fumes
43. Boxes, Barrels, Containers, Skids
44. Clothing—apparel, shoes, jewelry
45. Conveyors (power or gravity)
46. Mineral Items—dirt, clay, sand, stone, ores, dust, etc.
47. Power apparatus—Tools, motors, equipment, etc.
48. Excavations—trenches, tunnels, etc.
49. Furniture, Fixtures, Furnishings
50. Glassware—bottles, sheet, etc.
51. Glass Fibers, cloth, paper
52. Hand Tools (non powered)
53. Hoistering Apparatus — cranes, elevators
54. Heating Equipment — Furnace, stoves, etc.
55. Infections, Parasitic Agents, Poisonous vegetation and disease
56. Ladders (fixed or portable)
57. Machines—metal, wood, plastic, process equipment
58. Mechanical Power Transmission—Belts, flywheels, gears
59. Sharp objects—needles and knives
60. Pressure and Storage Vessels Compressors, gas cylinders, tanks, tires
61. Radiation—x-ray, welding, isotopes
62. Metal Items—plates, rods, metal scrap
63. Vehicles—hand trucks, boats, etc.
64. Wood Items—Logs, lumber, poles, wooden products
65. Working Surfaces — (indoor/outdoor) Incl. objects on floors, roofs, scaffolds, driveways, etc.
66. Miscellaneous
67. Person Other Than Injured
68. Insufficient Data to Determine Agency
69. Recreational Activity
70. Environmental—Noise, extreme temperatures, etc.
71. Food
72. Animals and Insects
73. Building Structures — Doors, walls, ceilings, etc.

*Adapted with permission of Gates, McDonald & Company, Columbus, OH, 1978.

on the equipment. Safety features also include protective clothing and glasses.

The term "reasonable" is used since the underwriter and insurer must use common sense in what to expect in terms of safety features. It is possible to require every employee to wear masks, gloves, and

**Exhibit 12-12**
Industrial Claim Cost Analysis*

SAMPLE COMPANY
PLANT A

ANNUAL FROM 10 - 01 - 77 THRU 09 - 30 - 78
DATE OF RUN 12 - 04 - 78

TYPE OF INJURY

| DESCRIPTION | CLAIMS NO. | CLAIMS % | TOTAL PAID TO DATE | ESTIMATED FUTURE COSTS | EXPECTED COSTS TOTAL | EXPECTED COSTS % |
|---|---|---|---|---|---|---|
| D FALL-SAME LEVEL | 10 | 18.8 | 13,548 | 14,207 | 27,755 | 34.9 |
| F BODILY REACTION | 2 | 3.7 | 14,237 | 4,616 | 18,853 | 23.7 |
| A STRIKE AGAINST | 14 | 26.4 | 6,715 | 9,933 | 16,648 | 20.9 |
| I OVEREXERTION | 3 | 5.6 | 4,786 | 5,191 | 9,977 | 12.5 |
| B STRUCK BY | 14 | 26.4 | 2,036 | 1,660 | 3,696 | 4.6 |
| G TEMP. CONTACT | 1 | 1.8 | 0 | 1,213 | 1,213 | 1.5 |
| C CAUGHT IN | 5 | 9.4 | 517 | 562 | 1,079 | 1.3 |
| K ABRADED | 2 | 3.7 | 52 | 0 | 52 | |
| L VEHICLE ACC. | 1 | 1.8 | 42 | 0 | 42 | |
| M UNCLASSIFIED | 1 | 1.8 | 15 | 0 | 15 | |
| TOTAL | 53 | | 41,948 | 37,382 | 79,330 | |

PART OF BODY

| DESCRIPTION | CLAIMS NO | CLAIMS % | TOTAL PAID TO DATE | ESTIMATED FUTURE COSTS | EXPECTED COSTS TOTAL | EXPECTED COSTS % |
|---|---|---|---|---|---|---|
| 03 SHOULDER | 2 | 3.7 | 11,956 | 5,565 | 17,521 | 22.0 |
| 11 BACK | 7 | 13.2 | 5,089 | 9,113 | 14,202 | 17.9 |
| 08 FOOT | 7 | 13.2 | 4,129 | 6,108 | 10,237 | 12.9 |
| 07 LEG | 3 | 5.6 | 6,027 | 2,942 | 8,969 | 11.3 |
| 04 ARM | 3 | 5.6 | 4,609 | 3,288 | 7,897 | 9.9 |
| 14 BODY PART-NOC | 2 | 3.7 | 3,896 | 2,299 | 6,195 | 7.8 |
| 05 HAND-WRIST | 11 | 20.7 | 3,831 | 2,327 | 6,158 | 7.7 |
| 06 FINGER | 7 | 13.2 | 1,827 | 2,506 | 4,333 | 5.4 |
| 13 MULTIPLE PARTS | 3 | 5.6 | 148 | 3,234 | 3,382 | 4.2 |
| 01 HEAD | 3 | 5.6 | 272 | 0 | 272 | .3 |
| 02 EYE | 4 | 7.5 | 87 | 0 | 87 | .1 |
| 10 RIBS-CHEST | 1 | 1.8 | 77 | 0 | 77 | |
| TOTAL | 53 | | 41,948 | 37,382 | 79,330 | |

NATURE OF INJURY

| DESCRIPTION | CLAIMS NO | CLAIMS % | TOTAL PAID TO DATE | ESTIMATED FUTURE COSTS | EXPECTED COSTS TOTAL | EXPECTED COSTS % |
|---|---|---|---|---|---|---|
| L STRAIN-SPRAIN | 16 | 30.1 | 29,415 | 22,249 | 51,664 | 65.1 |
| E CONTUSION | 13 | 24.5 | 5,274 | 5,507 | 10,781 | 13.5 |
| P MULTIPLE INJ. | 4 | 7.5 | 2,367 | 3,295 | 5,662 | 7.1 |
| I FRACTURES | 2 | 3.7 | 2,768 | 2,612 | 5,380 | 6.7 |
| J CUT-PUNCTURE | 12 | 22.6 | 2,024 | 2,506 | 4,530 | 5.7 |
| C BURN OR SCALD | 1 | 1.8 | 0 | 1,213 | 1,213 | 1.5 |
| F CONJUNCTIVITIS | 4 | 7.5 | 87 | 0 | 87 | .1 |
| R UNKNOWN | 1 | 1.8 | 13 | 0 | 13 | |
| TOTAL | 53 | | 41,948 | 37,382 | 79,330 | |

AGENCY OF INJURY

| DESCRIPTION | CLAIMS NO | CLAIMS % | TOTAL PAID TO DATE | ESTIMATED FUTURE COSTS | EXPECTED COSTS TOTAL | EXPECTED COSTS % |
|---|---|---|---|---|---|---|
| 65 WORK SURFACES | 12 | 22.6 | 22,175 | 20,582 | 42,757 | 53.8 |
| 57 MACHINES | 8 | 15.0 | 5,983 | 5,774 | 11,757 | 14.8 |
| 63 VEHICLES | 3 | 5.6 | 5,771 | 2,380 | 8,151 | 10.2 |
| 64 WOOD ITEMS | 1 | 1.8 | 3,896 | 1,489 | 5,385 | 6.7 |
| 43 CONTAINERS | 3 | 5.6 | 964 | 3,702 | 4,666 | 5.8 |
| 62 METAL-MINERALS | 10 | 18.8 | 1,885 | 1,660 | 3,545 | 4.4 |
| 59 SHARP OBJECTS | 4 | 7.5 | 702 | 582 | 1,284 | 1.6 |
| 54 HOT SURFACES | 1 | 1.8 | 0 | 1,213 | 1,213 | 1.5 |
| 47 POWER APPARATUS | 2 | 3.7 | 259 | 0 | 259 | .3 |
| 66 MISCELLANEOUS | 1 | 1.8 | 119 | 0 | 119 | .1 |
| 53 HOISTS | 1 | 1.8 | 60 | 0 | 60 | |
| 52 HAND TOOLS | 2 | 3.7 | 37 | 0 | 37 | |
| 41 AIR PRESSURE | 1 | 1.8 | 30 | 0 | 30 | |
| 46 DUST | 1 | 1.8 | 22 | 0 | 22 | |
| ALL OTHERS | 3 | 5.6 | 45 | 0 | 45 | |
| TOTAL | 53 | | 41,948 | 37,382 | 79,330 | |

0332839 16

* Adapted with permission of Gates, McDonald & Company, Columbus, OH, 1978.

steel-toed shoes, but that is not always reasonable. It would be reasonable to expect insureds who have employees using company private passenger-type vehicles on a regular basis to purchase vehicles with air-bags, if available. It would not be reasonable to expect every insured to immediately retrofit every vehicle with airbags just because the technology becomes available. Nevertheless, an insured who does so is a more desirable risk not only because of the airbags, but also because of the employer's obvious concern for the safety of the employees.

The underwriter relies heavily on the loss control department in determining what is reasonable in terms of safety features. There are volumes of manuals that tell the loss control representative what is available, necessary, or required for different risks. At the least, the insured should have all safety equipment required by OSHA or similar state organization.

Some equipment may have all the safeguards available for that model, but it is possible that the newer models of the same equipment have more safety features. That is, some equipment is not able to be retrofitted with new safety features. This means that the underwriter needs to consider the insured's policy about replacing equipment, which is covered in the next section.

***Replacement.*** Closely related to considerations of safety features are the plans the insured has for replacing older, possibly obsolete, equipment. The insured's present equipment may be obsolete not in terms of producing a product, but in terms of safety features. Again, what course of action is considered reasonable becomes an issue in this case. An insured who does not replace the equipment in this scenario would not automatically be considered an undesirable risk. However, an insured who replaces the equipment because of an equal emphasis on production and safety would be considered a more desirable risk.

There is not always a direct correlation between equipment age and condition, although it is easy to assume that there is. Many underwriters assume that old equipment is in poor condition unless they are shown otherwise. This is often the case, but not always. A piece of equipment that is not heavily used and that is well maintained can be kept in very good condition for many years. Conversely, few underwriters question the condition of a relatively new piece of equipment—another misguided assumption. Intense, heavy use of a piece of new equipment, combined with improper maintenance, can very quickly downgrade the condition of new equipment.

An insured should have a plan for regularly replacing equipment or at the least for regularly inspecting equipment to see if it needs replacing. Without a plan, equipment is usually not replaced until it breaks. Such neglect can often lead to injuries.

**Processes and Operations.** At the heart of workers compensation underwriting is evaluating what it is that the insured or applicant does. An employer that has only clerical employees presents a much different exposure than an employer whose employees paint water towers, but the evaluation is more complex than that. Even two water tower painting contractors can differ greatly in terms of underwriting desirability.

If the insured is a manufacturer, the underwriter is interested in the production processes. What raw materials are used? How dangerous are these materials and processes? Are chemicals used in the manufacture of the product? If so, what are they and are they hazardous to employees working with them? Although two manufacturers may produce the same product, one may have a highly mechanized operation that presents little exposure of employees to injury. The other may still involve primarily manual processes that create a greater exposure because they increase the chance of employee injuries. In some cases, these two risks may carry the same workers compensation rate because the same classification would apply to each. In other cases, there may be two different classifications to address the different degrees of exposure to injury.

If the insured is a contractor, the underwriter would be interested in the type of work performed. Broad labels like "building contractor," "plumbing contractor," and so on are insufficient not only for underwriting purposes but also for rating purposes. The underwriter needs to know about the types of buildings and plumbing, the breakdown between new construction and building repairs or additions, the breakdown between installation of plumbing in new buildings or repair of plumbing, and other related significant operations. Carpentry, for example, may be a sufficient description of operations for some purposes, but not for underwriting. There are six different carpentry classifications in the *Basic Manual* and probably at least that many more different variations of those classes not reflected in the manual.

The amount of subcontracted work and whether the insured requires certificates of insurance from subcontractors is important. The insured may have a quality work force and look desirable, but if the insured uses a number of uninsured subcontractors (for whom the insured would be liable for workers compensation insurance) with a transient work force, the underwriter may form a completely different picture about the desirability of the insured.

To a large extent, the differences in processes or operations should be reflected by the rates charged the different classifications. However, the rates for each class (or perhaps overall) are not always adequate. In addition, as was true with maritime exposures, some insurers simply prefer not to write certain types of risks. Although the rates for the logging classification may be adequate, for example, an insurer may prefer not to write risks of this type because of (1) inexperience in this line, (2) the very small number of such risks in the territory (thus preventing the insurer from having a spread of risk), or (3) reinsurance considerations.

Although the production processes or operations are central to workers compensation underwriting, this is the area in which some underwriters are the weakest. This weakness stems from a general lack of understanding of different kinds of businesses. It is very difficult to underwrite a risk classified as millwright work when the underwriter does not know what the term means or the type of work encompassed within the classification. This is where publications such as *Best's Underwriting Guide,* the PAAS *Classification Guide,* and other manuals can be invaluable to the underwriter.

## INDIVIDUAL INSURED RATING PLANS

The concept of classification is the grouping of risks with similar occupational hazards. Nevertheless, there will be risks within a classification that present extremely different hazards. This divergence between risks that belong to the same manual classification is found in a great many classifications.

It is the function of an individual insured rating plan to measure, in part, the deviation of a single risk from average conditions. In most risks, the individual insured rating plan will not totally reflect the actual experience, good or bad, unless the risk is large enough to be self-rated. Without individual insured rating plans, insureds with better than average experience would be subsidizing below average risks.

In addition, individual insured rating provides a strong incentive to improve accident prevention. By increasing the premium for the risk that has losses greater than the average in its class, and by reducing the premium for a risk that has losses less than the average in its class, insureds are encouraged to practice loss control. The manual premium in compensation insurance may be modified by experience rating or retrospective rating.

### Experience Rating

To the extent that an employer has statistically reliable experience that differs from average experience, these differences should be recognized in the rates for that employer. This is accomplished through experience rating, where a firm's experience is used to vary its future premiums. Experience rating is a form of *prospective* rating (past losses affect current premiums) as contrasted with *retrospective* rating (current losses affect current premiums), discussed in the next section.

Experience rating is a mathematical device by which actual losses for a three-year period are compared with "expected losses" for the same period to establish an experience modification or factor, which when applied to the current premium, will either increase or decrease the premium otherwise computed.

The experience rating plan of the National Council is the one used in the majority of states.[25] The eligibility requirements vary by state, but in general (1) the payroll developed in the last year or the last two years of the experience period must have produced a certain premium or (2) if more than two years are used to determine eligibility, there must have been a certain minimum average annual premium.[26] As of April 1990, the minimums for the first requirement range from $3,500 to $12,000, and the minimums for the second part of the requirement range from $1,750 to $6,000. These minimums are periodically adjusted to reflect inflation and to prevent risks that are really too small from being included.

As mentioned, if a risk is eligible, it must be experience rated; that is, the program is mandatory. Because it is mandatory and because the modification calculated by the bureau is the modification that must be used by any insurer, experience rating cannot be used as a competitive tool by an underwriter as can schedule rating and retrospective rating.

**Experience Period.** The experience period used in calculating the experience modification is normally the three years ending one year before the experience modification is to be effective. For example, Exhibit 12-13 shows that for an experience modification effective 1 January 19X9, the experience period would be 1 January 19X5 to 1 January 19X8.

There are several reasons for the one-year lapse between the end of the experience period and the effective date of the experience modification. Most injuries sustained in the current policy period are so recent that their ultimate cost may be very uncertain immediately after the close of that policy period. Second, the experience period must end far enough in advance of the policy period during which the modification will apply so that there is enough time to gather the loss data, perform the necessary calculations, publish the experience modification, and issue the renewal policy—all prior to the inception date of the policy.[27]

**Exhibit 12-13**
Experience Period Determination

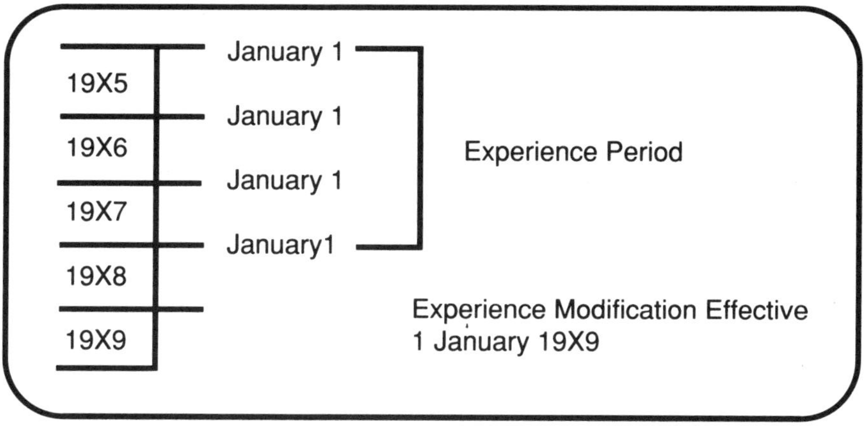


**Change in Ownership or Operations.** The experience used is the risk's entire experience in all operations during the experience period. This includes operations not usual or common to its business, operations of uninsured contractors doing work for the risk, and operations discontinued during the course of the experience period. Additionally, payrolls and losses of a risk while it is self-insured may be included.

Neither a change in management, in the form of organization (partnership to corporation), nor in name affects the use of experience unless there has been a change of ownership. This is true even if a risk has completely changed the nature of its operations during the experience period. For example, a manufacturer of metal goods may convert to plastics manufacturing during the experience period without affecting the experience modification. The assumption is that a change of ownership, on the other hand, may have such a significant effect on loss control as to invalidate past experience as an indicator of future experience. If a change of ownership does occur, the insurer must report the details of the change to the applicable bureau so that the continued use of the modification can be determined. There are also circumstances when several separate risks may be combined for experience rating. When a person, a group of persons, or a corporation holds a majority interest in two or more separate risks, the loss experience of the individual risks can be combined to produce a common experience modification.

**Calculating an Experience Modification.** Although the underwriter does not actually calculate the experience modification, he or she must understand how it is done and the meaning of the various pieces of information on the experience rating worksheet. Very simply, experience rating compares a risk's actual losses during the experience period with the losses expected of that type of risk. The actual calculation is complicated because, in order to make the program as equitable as possible for all insureds, it considers many more variables so that each risk's experience is reflected.

The following sample calculation of a modification is based on the worksheet shown in Exhibit 12-14. As illustrated, most of the information on the worksheet is broken down according to policy year. As mentioned in the section on using the worksheet as a source of underwriting information, this year-by-year breakdown not only helps the underwriter to detect trends, but it also facilitates the verification of losses and other relevant information.

***Payroll and Expected Loss Information.*** Columns 1 and 4 of the worksheet list the applicable classification codes for the risk and the payroll assigned to each code. Columns 2 and 3 show the expected loss rate (ELR) and the D-ratio, respectively, for each classification code. The class codes, ELR, and D-ratio are shown for each of the three years of the experience period. The *expected loss rate* is the expected losses for each classification per $100 of payroll. Each classification has its own ELR. In the exhibit, class code 1463 carries an ELR of 2.02, and code 8810 carries an ELR of 0.06. Code 1463 is asphalt works, and code 8810 is clerical. It is logical that the ELRs of these classifications are substantially different. When the expected loss rate is applied to the payroll figures shown on the worksheet, the result is the expected losses as shown in Column 5. This column is totaled to represent expected losses for the three years of the experience period, which is shown in box (D) at the bottom of Column 5.

The expected loss rate is derived from the current manual rates. The manual rate for each class is modified to remove the insurer expense component. A second modification is then made to reflect the differences between the losses that were expected during the experience period and those that will be expected during the time the rate will be used (that is, the policy period to which the experience modification factor will apply). The details of this second step are beyond the scope of this text. However, among the factors considered are loss development factors, trend factors, factors to reflect loss limitations used in the experience rating calculation, and factors to reflect changes in benefits.

Both the actual and expected losses used in calculating an experience modification are split into two parts—primary and excess. The *primary losses* are more reflective of loss frequency, whereas the

**Exhibit 12-14**

Workers Compensation Experience Rating Worksheet*

**WORKERS COMPENSATION EXPERIENCE RATING**

NAME OF RISK ABC CORPORATION — RISK IDENT. NO. 990-123-456 — STATE ANY — EFFECTIVE DATE 01/01/X0

| 1 CODE | 2 ELR | 3 D-RATIO | 4 PAYROLL | 5 EXPECTED LOSSES | 6 EXP-PRIM LOSSES | 7 CLAIM DATA | 8 IJ 0 F | 9 ACT INC LOSSES | 10 ACT PRIM LOSSES |
|---|---|---|---|---|---|---|---|---|---|
| CARRIER 99999 | | | POLICY X6 X6 X6 | | | EFF-DATE | 01/01/X6 | EXP-DATE | 01/01/X7 |
| 1463 | 2.02 | .36 | 86,703 | 1,751 | 630 | X60024 | 5 F | 12,280 | 5,000 |
| 5515 | 2.08 | .34 | 2,478,337 | 51,549 | 17,527 | X60010 | 2 0 | 47,136# | 5,000 |
| 5606 | 0.58 | .37 | 137,447 | 797 | 295 | 10 | * | 4,146 | 4,146 |
| 8227 | 1.02 | .34 | 109,350 | 1,115 | 379 | | | | |
| 8810 | 0.06 | .38 | 244,940 | 147 | 56 | | | | |
| POLICY-TOTAL | | | 3,056,777 | (SUBJECT PREMIUM = 99,529) | | | | 174,162 | |
| CARRIER 99999 | | | POLICY X7 X7 X7 | | | EFF-DATE | 01/01/X7 | EXP-DATE | 01/01/X8 |
| 1463 | 2.02 | .36 | 93,806 | 1,895 | 682 | X70124 | 2 0 | 285,586# | 5,000 |
| 5506 | 1.45 | .36 | 1,503,170 | 21,796 | 7,847 | 4 | * | 1,836 | 1,836 |
| 5515 | 2.08 | .34 | 985,941 | 20,508 | 6,973 | | | | |
| 5606 | 0.58 | .37 | 111,429 | 646 | 239 | | | | |
| 8227 | 1.02 | .34 | 95,686 | 976 | 332 | | | | |
| 8810 | 0.06 | .38 | 244,009 | 146 | 55 | | | | |
| POLICY-TOTAL | | | 3,034,041 | (SUBJECT PREMIUM = 98,152) | | | | 287,422 | |
| CARRIER 99999 | | | POLICY X8 X8 X8 | | | EFF-DATE | 01/01/X8 | EXP-DATE | 01/01/X9 |
| 1463 | 2.02 | .36 | 508,210 | 10,266 | 3,696 | X80013 | 5 F | 5,714 | 5,000 |
| 5506 | 1.45 | .36 | 1,586,986 | 23,011 | 8,284 | X80179 | 5 F | 20,714 | 5,000 |
| 5515 | 2.08 | .34 | 1,586,986 | 33,099 | 11,223 | 6 | * | 3,380 | 3,389 |
| 5606 | 0.58 | .34 | 496,456 | 2,879 | 1,065 | | | | |
| 8227 | 1.02 | .34 | 277,377 | 2,829 | 962 | | | | |
| 8742 | 0.17 | .34 | 32,307 | 55 | 19 | | | | |
| 8810 | 0.06 | .38 | 398,223 | 329 | 91 | | | | |
| POLICY-TOTAL | | | 4,886,545 | (SUBJECT PREMIUM = 151,097) | | | | 29,808 | |
| | (A) 0.30 | (B) | (C) EXPECTED EXCESS (D-E) 113,259 | (D) 173,614 | (E) 60,355 | (F) ACTUAL EXCESS (H-I) 105,066 | (G) 22,200 | (H) 139,428 | (I) 34,362 |

* Total to Policy Year of all cases $5,000 or less

\# Limited loss

**PAGE NUMBER**

**DATE**

| | (11) PRIMARY LOSSES | (12) STABILIZING VALUE | (13) RATABLE EXCESS | (14) TOTALS | (15) EXP MOD |
|---|---|---|---|---|---|
| **ACTUAL** | (I) 34,362 | (C) x (1-W) + (G) 101,481 | (A) x (F) 31,520 | (J) 167,363 | (J) (K) .85 |
| **EXPECTED** | (E) 60,355 | 101,481 | (A) x (C) 33,978 | (K) 195,814 | REVISED PLAN |

*Adapted with permission from *Understanding the Changes Introduced By The Revised Workers Compensation Experience Rating Plan* (New York: National Council on Compensation Insurance, 1989), p. 9.

*excess losses* are more reflective of loss severity. As mentioned in an earlier chapter, underwriters are more concerned with loss frequency because it is a better predictor of future losses than is loss severity. Breaking down losses into their primary and excess components in experience rating also reflects this increased emphasis or weight given to loss frequency.

The *D-ratio* in Column 3 represents the portion or percentage of the *expected* losses that are classified as *primary.* Thus, multiplying the amount of expected losses shown in Column 5 by the D-ratio gives the *expected primary losses* shown in Column 6. This column is also totaled for the three years of the experience period. The result is shown as in box (E) the box at the bottom of Column 6. *Expected excess losses* are simply the expected losses minus the expected primary losses. This figure is shown as item (C) in the box at the bottom of Column 4.

***Actual Losses.*** Columns 7 through 10 reflect information on the insured's losses. Column 7 lists either claim numbers for claims over $5,000 or the number of claims for all claims below $5,000.

Column 8 gives more information about the insured's losses. Under the portion of the column labeled IJ, an injury code is shown. This code tells the type of loss involved for claims over $5,000. The definition of each code used is found in the *Workers Compensation Statistical Plan* manual of NCCI. In this case, a 2 indicates a permanent total disability and a 5 indicates a claim for temporary total or temporary partial disability benefits. An *F* indicates that the amount is a final amount for the claim, that is, the claim is closed. An *O* indicates that the claim is still open. As shown in the footnote on the form, an asterisk indicates that the figure is a total of all claims $5,000 or less. The figure at the bottom of Column 8 in box (G) is not the total of that column. This figure will be explained later.

Column 9 shows both the actual dollar amount of each loss for losses over $5,000 and the policy year total for all losses under $5,000. The "#" to the right of two of the losses indicates that the amount of that loss is limited. That is, in order to lessen the impact of large single- and multiple-claim accidents, the experience rating calculation places a per claim limit on the amount of loss included in the calculation. The limit is referred to as the *individual loss limitation.* This limit varies by state and equals 10 percent of the *state reference point* (SRP). The SRP is based on an index of each state's benefit levels. In this example, the loss limitation is equal to $45,679 (this is not shown on the experience rating worksheet).

The figure shown at the bottom of Column 9 in Box (H) is not the total of that column. It is the total of all losses less than the individual loss limitation amount plus $45,679 for each of the two limited losses.

Column 10 shows the primary portion of the losses shown in Column 9. The primary portion is the first $5,000 of a single loss. The amount over $5,000 is the excess portion. The total for this column is shown at the bottom of the column in box (I). Subtracting box (I), actual primary losses, from box (H), actual losses subject to the individual loss limitation gives the *actual excess losses,* shown in box (F) at the bottom of Column 7.

***W Value.*** Box (A) is the W value or *weighting value.* The W value is used to determine how much of the actual excess loss amount will enter into the formula for calculating the experience modification. The W values are found in the *Experience Rating Plan Manual;* they vary from 0.07 for smaller insureds (based on expected losses) to 0.63 for larger insureds. Thus, the entire amount of excess losses is never used for an insured (the previous version of the experience rating plan did allow insureds with over $5,000,000 in expected losses to use 100 percent of the actual excess losses). In box (A) in the sample worksheet, the W value is 0.30.

***B Value.*** The $22,200 shown in box (G) is the B value, also known as the *ballast value, ballast element,* or *stabilizing element.* The last term best describes the use of this number. The B value is used to limit the effect of adverse loss experience on the experience modification of a risk. The B value is added to both the actual losses and the expected losses used in the formula to determine the modification. The B value ranges from $7,500 for smaller insureds (based on expected losses) to $504,999 for larger insureds. The effect of the B value is to keep the experience modifications closer to 1.00; that is, it reduces fluctuations in the modification. The B values are found in the *Experience Rating Plan Manual.*

***Actual Losses Used in Formula.*** The experience modification is determined by comparing adjusted actual losses plus the B value to expected losses plus the B value. *Adjusted actual losses* are the actual primary losses plus a weighting of the actual excess and expected excess losses. The weighting depends on the W value described earlier.

The insured's actual excess losses shown in box (F) are multiplied by the W value to determine the amount of *actual ratable* (*weighted*) *excess losses.* This calculation is shown in the top box of column 13 at the bottom of the page.

The complement of the W value (that is, 1-W) is then multiplied by the expected excess losses. To this is added the B value. It was explained earlier that the W value increases with the size of the risk as measured by total expected losses. Thus, as the risk gets larger, a greater percentage of the risk's own excess loss experience is used in the formula, and less of the expected excess losses is used. That is, the insured's experience is considered to be more credible. The sum of the B value plus (1-W) multiplied by the expected excess losses is called the *stabilizing value* and is shown in column 12 at the bottom of the worksheet.

The numerator of the experience rating formula, which shows actual losses, is the following (in the order shown on the experience rating worksheet):

Actual Primary Losses + [(1-W)(Expected Excess Losses)] + B value + [(W)(Actual Excess Losses)]

In some formulas, the B value is added at the end, but the result is the same.

***Expected Losses Used in the Formula.*** The denominator of the experience rating formula is very similar to the numerator. The denominator is equal to the expected losses plus the B value. Although the boxes at the bottom of the worksheet seem to indicate a more difficult-to-calculate amount of expected losses, the result of the formula for expected losses that appears in the boxes is simply expected primary losses plus expected excess losses. The formula also shows that W is multiplied by the expected excess losses, and 1-W also is multiplied by the expected excess losses. Combining these two operations results in expected excess losses being multiplied by 1, which is equal to expected excess losses. To these expected losses is added the same B value used in the numerator (again, it can be added anywhere in the formula).

Below is the complete formula for calculating the experience modification:

$$\frac{\text{Actual Primary Losses} + [(1\text{-W})(\text{Expected Excess Losses})] + \text{B value} + [(\text{W})(\text{Actual Excess Losses})]}{\text{Expected Primary Losses} + [(1\text{-W})(\text{Expected Excess Losses})] + \text{B value} + [(\text{W})(\text{Expected Excess Losses})]}$$

In the sample worksheet, the formula results in a modification of .85, which means that the insured will be charged 85 percent of the manual rate—a 15 percent credit. A modification of 1.15 would have meant that the insured would be charged 115 percent of the manual rate—a 15 percent debit.

The experience rating formula limits the maximum credit modification available to an insured depending on the insured's expected loss size. For smaller risks, the plan also places a cap on the maximum debit for a risk. This cap ranges from 1.60 (that is, a 60 percent debit) to 2.00 based on the insured's expected loss size. There is no cap on the maximum debit for larger risks.

Because the W value never reaches 1.0 and because the B value is included in the formula for all insureds' modifications, no insured's experience is viewed as 100 percent credible. That is, no insured's modification is based solely on its own actual experience (referred to as *self-rated*). Under the previous version of the experience rating plan, some insureds were self-rated.

## Retrospective Rating

With the advent of premium discount in the mid-thirties as a formal, filed method of reducing expenses according to premium size, plans to "retrospectively rate" certain insureds' premiums were simultaneously introduced by both stock and mutual companies on a formal, filed basis. The first plans filed were plans *A, B,* and *C,* and in 1959, plan *J* was introduced. These are called *tabular plans,* which means that the factors are fixed and found in a table of rating factors. These plans are now known as *Retrospective Rating Options I, II, III,* and *IV,* respectively. All insureds with the same premium size subject to this rating plan would have their premiums retrospectively rated using the same factors—the only difference would lie in the level of losses incurred. The tabular plans are reserved for workers compensation.

Retrospective rating is optional and should be used, according to the *Retrospective Rating Plan Manual,* only when elected by the insured and accepted by the insurer. In practice, insurers sometimes offer retrospective rating as an alternative to not writing coverage at all.

Unlike experience rating, which bases current premiums on past losses, retrospective rating bases current premiums on the losses incurred during the current period. The intent is to charge a premium reflective of the losses incurred plus a "loading" to represent insurer's expenses and premium taxes. While experience rating does provide an incentive for practicing loss control, the results of any loss control efforts are slow to be reflected in the experience modification. However, they are almost immediately reflected by retrospective rating. If loss control efforts reduce losses in a given year, the premium for that year is reduced. Similarly, if the insured fails to control losses, that experience is reflected in a higher premium paid for that year.

Eligibility requirements for retrospective rating are much higher than for experience rating. A risk is eligible for a one-year retrospective rating plan if it develops an estimated standard premium of $25,000. *Standard premium* means the premium for the risk based on the filed rates and subject to experience modification, loss constants, and minimum premiums, but without the application of the premium discount or the expense constant. Retrospective rating options can be written on a one- or three-year basis and can be used on an intrastate as well as an interstate basis.

An additional option, Rating Option V (formerly plan D), is available for workers compensation and certain other lines singly or in combination. Option V is a very flexible rating plan that permits the selection of loss conversion factors and maximum and minimum premiums, thus allowing an infinite number of combinations. Because of its flexibility, Option V is called a *nontabular plan.* The plan can include, in addition to workers compensation, general liability, auto liability, auto physical damage, and burglary and glass insurance. Because Option V usually does include lines in addition to workers compensation and applies to larger insureds, this rating plan is not explained in this chapter.

**Premium Calculation.** Retrospective rating is not a stand-alone system. It is a rating formula that is superimposed on the guaranteed cost premium that otherwise would be applicable. Remember that even though experience rating is based on the insured's loss experience, it is based upon previous loss experience and once the modification is determined at the beginning of the year, the insured's rate for coverage is guaranteed. That is, the rate will not change even though the final premium will vary with the insured's payroll. This is called a *guaranteed cost premium.*

A policy written on a retrospective rating basis will have a *retrospective premium endorsement* attached. The endorsement varies depending on the options selected. The endorsement for a one-year plan under Options I, II, III, or IV is WC 00 05 01, shown in Exhibit 12-15. The endorsement states exactly which plan is selected and makes reference to any necessary tables that are a part of the plan.

In the following explanation of premium calculation for retrospective rating, the "Table of Rating Values" is mentioned several times as a source for certain factors. There are a number of these tables. At the beginning of the section in the manual that contains these tables is a state reference chart. The chart lists which tables (one for a one-year plan and one for a three-year plan) to use for each state and the effective date of use. For example, the chart may state that for Alabama, Tables XXV and XXVI should be used, effective 1 November 19X6, and Tables XXIX and XXX should be used, effective 1 January 19X8. Because different states use different tables (there is not a different table for each state, however), figures shown on these tables are said to "vary by state."

## Exhibit 12-15
Retrospective Premium Endorsement*

**WORKERS COMPENSATION AND EMPLOYERS LIABILITY INSURANCE POLICY** **WC 00 05 01**

**Original Printing** Effective April 1, 1984 **Standard**

### RETROSPECTIVE PREMIUM ENDORSEMENT
### RATING OPTIONS I, II, III or IV—ONE YEAR PLAN

This endorsement is added to Part Five (Premium) because you chose to have the cost of the insurance rated retrospectively. You chose the one year Rating Option shown in the Schedule. This endorsement explains the rating plan and how the retrospective premium will be determined.

This endorsement applies in the states listed in the Schedule. It determines the retrospective premium for the insurance provided during the rating plan period by this policy and any policy listed in the Schedule. The rating plan period is the one year period beginning with the effective date of this endorsement.

The amount of retrospective premium depends on five standard elements and two elective elements.

A. **Retrospective Premium Standard Elements**

The five standard elements are explained here.

1. Standard premium is the premium we would charge during the rating plan period if you had not chosen retrospective premium rating, but with two exceptions. Standard premium does not include the expense constant charge or the premium discount credit.
2. Basic premium is less than standard premium. It is standard premium multiplied by a percentage called the basic premium factor. The basic premium factor varies depending on the Rating Option you chose, the total amount of standard premium, and the states where the insurance is provided. The basic premium factors are shown in the Tables of Rating Values that form a part of this endorsement.
3. Incurred losses are all amounts we pay or estimate we will pay for losses, interest on judgments, expenses to recover against third parties, and employers liability loss adjustment expenses.
4. Converted losses are larger than incurred losses. A converted loss is an incurred loss multiplied by a percentage called the loss conversion factor. Loss conversion factors vary by state. They are shown in the Tables of Rating Values that form a part of this endorsement.
5. Taxes are a part of the premium we collect. Taxes are determined as a percentage of basic premium and converted losses. The percentage is called the tax multiplier. It varies by state and by Federal and non-Federal classifications. The tax multipliers are shown in the Schedule.

B. **Retrospective Premium Elective Elements**

Two other elements are included in retrospective premium if you elected to include them. They are the excess loss premium for the loss limitation, and the retrospective development premium. They are explained here.

1. The election of a loss limitation means that the amount of incurred loss to be included in the retrospective premium is limited to an amount called the loss limitation. The loss limitation applies separately to each person who sustains bodily injury by disease and separately to all bodily injury arising out of any one accident.

   The charge for this loss limitation is called the excess loss premium. Excess loss premium is a percentage of standard premium multiplied by the loss conversion factor. The percentage is called the excess loss premium factor. Taxes are added to excess loss premium just as they are for other elements of retrospective premium.

   Excess loss premium factors vary by state, by classification, and by the amount of the loss limitation. If you chose this elective element, the loss conversion factor, the loss limitation, the excess loss premium factors, and the states where they apply are shown in the Schedule.

2. The retrospective development element is used to help stabilize premium adjustments. The premium for this element is charged with the first three calculations of retrospective premium, and is called the retrospective development premium. It is a percentage of standard premium multiplied by the loss conversion factor. The percentage of standard premium is called the retrospective development factor. Taxes are added to retrospective development premium just as they are for other elements of retrospective premium.

   Retrospective development factors vary by state, by electing a loss limitation, and by first, second, and third calculations of retrospective premium. If you chose this elective element, the retrospective development factors are shown in the Schedule.

C. **Retrospective Premium Formula**

Insurance policies listed in the Schedule will be combined with this policy to calculate the retrospective premium. If the policies provide insurance for more than one insured, the retrospective premium will be determined for all insureds combined, not separately for each insured.

1. Retrospective premium is the sum of basic premium, converted losses, and taxes, plus the excess loss premium and retrospective development premium elective elements if you chose them.
2. The retrospective premium will not be less than the minimum retrospective premium. The retrospective premium will not be more than the maximum retrospective premium. The minimum and maximum retrospective premiums vary by state, by the Rating Option you chose, and by the amount of standard premium. The minimum and maximum retrospective premiums may be determined from the Tables of Rating Values that form a part of this endorsement.
3. If this endorsement applies to more than one policy or state, the standard premium, minimum premium, and maximum premium will be the sum of the standard premium, minimum premiums, and maximum premiums, respectively, for each policy and state.
4. The retrospective premium, including the minimum retrospective premium and the maximum retrospective premium, will be increased by a percentage called the non-stock adjustment factor. This factor varies by state and amount of standard premium. The non-stock adjustment factors may be determined from the Tables of Rating Values that form a part of this endorsement.

D. **Premium Calculations and Payments**

1. We will calculate the retrospective premium using all loss information we have as of a date six months after the rating plan period ends and annually thereafter. We will have the calculation verified by the appropriate rate service organization at your request.

   We may make a special valuation of the retrospective premium as of any date that you are declared bankrupt or insolvent, make an assignment for the benefit of creditors, are involved in reorganization, receivership, or liquidation, or dispose of all your interest in work covered by the insurance. You will pay the amount due us if the retrospective premium is more than the total standard premium as of the special valuation date.
2. After a calculation of retrospective premium, you and we may agree that it is the final calculation. No other calculation will be made unless there is clerical error in the final calculation.
3. After each calculation of retrospective premium, you will promptly pay the amount due us, or we will refund the amount due you. Each insured is responsible for the payment of all standard premium and retrospective premium calculated under this endorsement.

E. **Work In Other States**

If any of the policies provide insurance in a state not listed in the Table of States, and if you begin work in that state during the rating plan period, this endorsement will apply to that insurance if this rating plan applies in that state on an interstate basis. The retrospective premium standard elements, and the elective elements you chose, will be determined by our manuals for that state, and added to the Schedule by endorsement.

F. **Cancelation**

1. If any insurance subject to this endorsement is canceled, the effective date of cancelation will become the end of the rating plan period for all insurance subject to this endorsement unless we agree with you, by endorsement, to continue the rating plan period.
2. If we cancel for nonpayment of premium, the maximum retrospective premium will be based on the standard premium for the rating plan period, increased pro rata to 365 days.
3. If you cancel, the standard premium for the rating plan period will be increased by our short rate table and procedure. This short rate premium will be the minimum retrospective premium and will be used to determine the basic premium.

   The short rate premium will be used to determine the excess loss premium and retrospective development premium if you chose these elective elements.

   The maximum retrospective premium will be based on the standard premium for the rating plan period, increased pro rata to 365 days.
4. Section F.3. will not apply if you cancel because:

   a. all work covered by the insurance is completed;

   b. all interest in the business covered by the insurance is sold; or,

   c. you retire from all business covered by the insurance.

Schedule

1. Retrospective Rating Option______.
2. Other policies subject to this Retrospective Premium Endorsement: __________________________________________
3. Loss limitation: $
4. Tables of Rating Values listed in the Table of States are attached to and are part of this Retrospective Premium Endorsement.

**TABLE OF STATES**

| State | Applicable Table of Rating Values | Excess Loss Premium Factors: State (Other than "F" Classes) | Excess Loss Premium Factors: Federal ("F" Classes Only) | Tax Multiplier: State (Other than "F" Classes) | Tax Multiplier: Federal ("F" Classes Only) | Retrospective Development Factors: 1st | Retrospective Development Factors: 2nd | Retrospective Development Factors: 3rd |
|---|---|---|---|---|---|---|---|---|
| | | | | | | | | |

**WORKERS COMPENSATION AND EMPLOYERS LIABILITY INSURANCE POLICY** **WC 00 05 01**

**Original Printing** Effective April 1, 1984 **Standard**

**NOTES TO RETROSPECTIVE PREMIUM ENDORSEMENT**
**RATING OPTIONS I, II, III OR IV—ONE YEAR PLAN**

1. This endorsement may be used for Options I, II, III and IV of the Retrospective Rating Plan. It is designed for a one year rating plan period.
2. Paragraph C.4. of the endorsement should be omitted by a company not using the non-stock adjustment factor.
3. Show the applicable Rating Option in item 1 of the Schedule.
4. Identify by policy number any other policy to be combined with this policy for retrospective rating. Other policies should be endorsed with the Retrospective Premium Endorsement (Short Form) to show that they are subject to this endorsement.
5. Show the amount of the loss limitation, if applicable, or enter "none," "does not apply," or other appropriate text if a loss limitation was not elected. If the limitation applies in some but not all states, name, in item 3 of the Schedule, the states where it applies.
6. The Table of Rating Values may be printed on the Schedule or printed separately. If printed on the Schedule, item 4 of the Schedule should be omitted.
7. The Schedule shows a Table of States that may be printed at the beginning or end of the Schedule or may be printed separately. If printed separately, an appropriate attachment clause should be included on the Schedule, such as: "This Schedule includes the attached Table of States." The display of information on the Table of States may be rearranged by the company.

5 of 5



* Reprinted with permission

At the policy inception, the insured pays the standard premium. Approximately six months after the policy expiration, the losses are valued and a retrospective premium is computed. This premium is compared to the standard premium already paid, and the insured either receives a return premium or pays an additional premium. This computation of the retrospective premium and adjustment of premium is called the *first computation* and *first adjustment.* Exhibit 12-16 illustrates this process.

However, losses may remain open for many years after the policy expiration. One year after the first adjustment, the losses are again valued, and another retrospective premium is computed. Again, the insured either pays an additional premium or receives a return premium based on previous payments made to the insurer. This process continues annually until all claims are settled or until the insurer and the insured agree to make the most recent computation the *final computation* even if some losses remain open. After this point, no further calculations are made unless there was a clerical error in the final computation.

The formula used in calculating the retrospective premium is

**Exhibit 12-16**
Retrospective Rating Adjustment

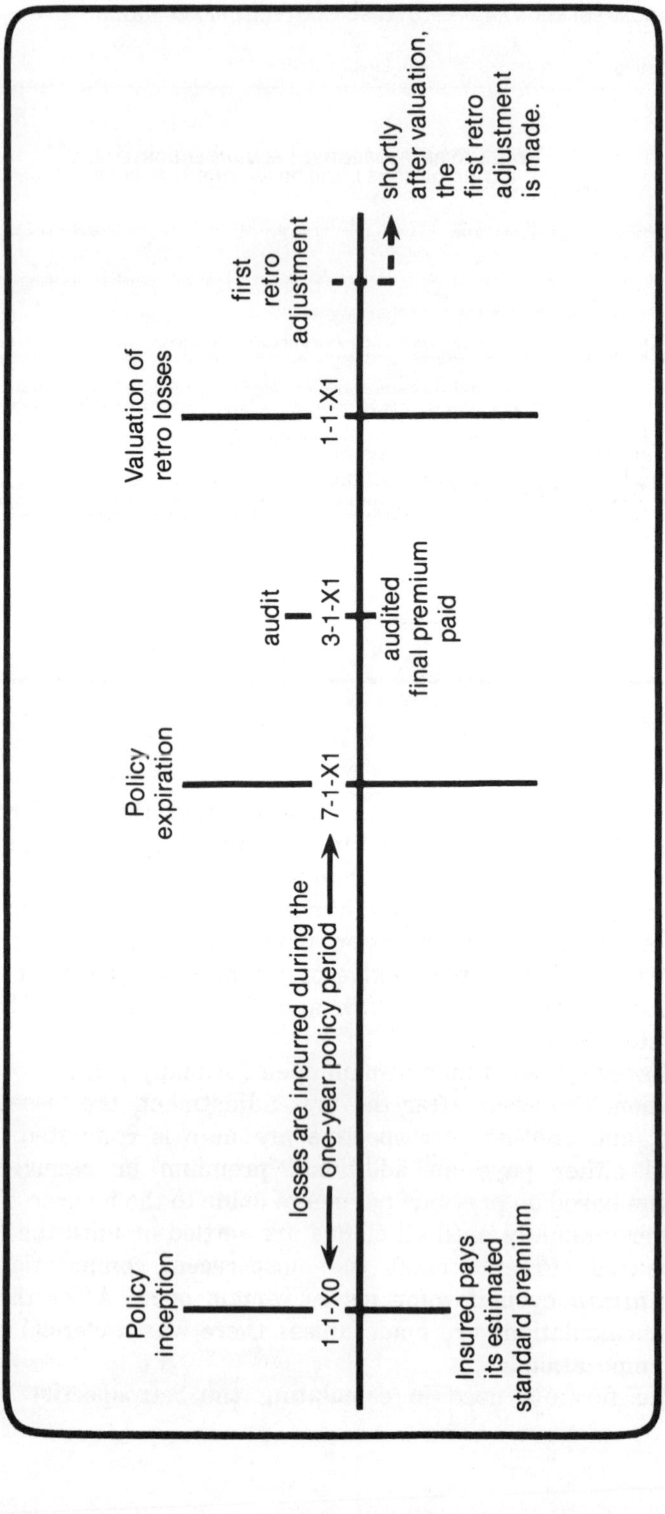

shown in Exhibit 12-17. Briefly, the sum of the basic premium plus converted losses multiplied by the tax multiplier produces the indicated retrospective premium, subject to a maximum and minimum premium. Each of these aspects of the formula is examined in the following sections along with two other aspects of retrospective rating.

***Basic Premium.*** The basic premium is the standard premium multiplied by the *basic premium factor.* The standard premium, as defined earlier, is the experience rating modified manual premium to which neither the premium discount credit nor the expense constant charge has been applied. The basic premium factor is a percentage of less than one that varies according to the rating option chosen, the total amount of standard premium, and the states in which coverage is provided. The factors are shown in the table of rating values found in the *Retrospective Rating Plan Manual* and are referenced in the retrospective premium endorsement.

The basic premium provides for such insurer expenses as underwriting, acquisition, loss control, premium auditing, and general administration. In addition there is an adjustment in the basic premium for the presence of minimum and maximum premium limitations and an allowance for the insurer's profit or contingencies. As the amount of the standard premium increases, the basic premium factor decreases, thus reflecting the economies of scale with regard to insurer expenses. The basic premium does not allow for the premium tax or claims administration expenses. These are accounted for elsewhere in the formula.

***Converted Losses.*** The next aspect of the retrospective rating formula is the converted losses. Converted losses are equal to actual incurred losses times a loss conversion factor. The *loss conversion factor* covers the insurer's claims adjustment expenses and the overall costs of the insurer's claims services such as the investigation of claims and the filing of claim reports. Loss conversion factors vary by state and are shown in the table of rating values in the manual. As subsequently explained, actual incurred losses may be limited.

***Tax Multiplier.*** The last item in the retrospective rating formula is the tax multiplier. This covers the licenses, fees, assessment (including those for subsidy of the assigned risk market), and taxes the insurer must pay on the premiums it collects. The multiplier logically varies by state and is found in the state rate pages of the *Retrospective Rating Plan Manual.*

***Minimums and Maximums.*** The retrospective premium calculated by the formula to this point is subject to a minimum and a maximum. Both vary according to the plan selected, and both are stated as a percentage of the standard premium. The percentages are found in the

**Exhibit 12-17**
The Retro Formula

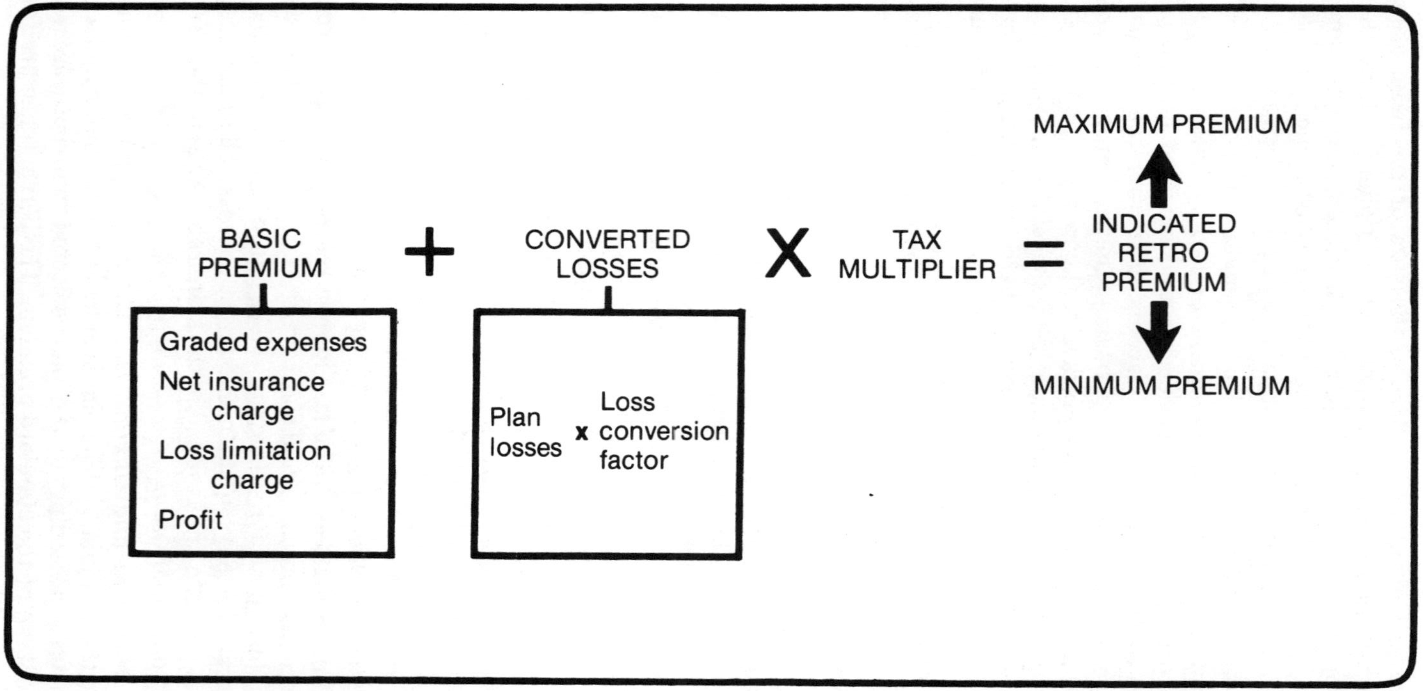

same table of rating values in which the basic premium factors and the loss conversion factors are found.

***Excess Loss Premium.*** As mentioned, the incurred losses used in the retrospective premium calculation can be limited. That is, the amount of a single loss included in the formula can be subject to some maximum. This option is available only to those insureds whose total standard premium subject to the retrospective rating plan is at least $100,000. In addition, the limitation of losses for rating purposes in no way affects an insurer's responsibility to pay the entire loss.

The intent in limiting losses is to avoid the possibility of one or more very expensive losses having an undue influence on the retrospective premium. The logic is similar to that used in explaining why there is a loss limitation in experience rating. The difference is that the use of a loss limitation in retrospective rating is elective, and the amount is at least partly variable (that is, the insured can select a certain limit, but only from a list of possible limitations stated in the manual). The loss limitation in experience rating is mandatory, or in other words, cannot be selected by the insured.

The following formula is used to determine the excess loss premium:

Standard premium × Excess loss premium factor × Loss conversion factor

The only component not yet defined is the *excess loss premium factor.* This factor is equal to the excess loss factor minus the excess loss adjustment amount. The *excess loss factors* are found on the state rating pages of the *Retrospective Rating Plan Manual.* Within each state, they vary according to the hazard group (as explained earlier, there are four) into which the risk falls and the loss limitation chosen. The *excess loss adjustment amount* is found on the table of rating values and varies by standard premium and the loss limitation chosen.

The manual states that the excess loss premium factor should in no case be less than 10 percent of the excess loss factor. The excess loss premium should be multiplied by the tax multiplier.

***Retrospective Development Premium.*** This elective feature of retrospective rating is intended to stabilize the premium adjustments as a result of the retrospective premium computations. It anticipates future increases in costs and is included in only the first three adjustments. The following formula is used to determine the retrospective development premium:

Standard premium × Retrospective development factor × Loss conversion factor

The retrospective development factor is found on the state rate pages of the *Retrospective Rating Plan Manual.* The factor for each state varies by adjustment (that is, first, second, or third) and whether or not there is a loss limit. The retrospective development premium should also be multiplied by the tax multiplier.

**Comparison of the Tabular Plans.** In rating Option I, the insured cannot pay more than the standard premium. The minimum premium that would be realized for a risk with good experience (for example, a 30 percent loss ratio) is the highest of all tabular plans' minimum premiums. That is, the minimum is not much below the standard premium. Thus, the insured can realize only a slight savings, with good experience, over a guaranteed cost plan with premium discount. In Option II, the minimum is much lower and the maximum, much higher. The swing between the two extremes can be substantial. Considerable savings are possible with good experience, and substantial penalties are possible if losses are excessive. The high maximum appeals to underwriters and may enable them to accept a risk with unfavorable loss experience. Additionally, the low minimum permits underwriters to be competitive on risks with good control over losses. Option III is much like Option II. The maximum is the same, and the basic premium is slightly higher. However, Option III does not have a stated minimum. The minimum is equal to the basic premium times the tax multiplier. The truly superior risk can achieve its lowest premium with this plan. Rating Option IV is a hybrid of Options I, II, and III. It has a higher minimum and lower maximum than Options II or III. This is a more moderate approach. This plan would appeal to the risk with better than average loss experience that did not want to take the chance of a high maximum premium if the loss experience should be unusually poor.

**Uses of Retrospective Rating.** Unlike experience rating, which is mandatory for qualified risks, retrospective rating is optional and must be agreed to by the insured and the insurer. The advantage of retrospective rating is pricing flexibility. The underwriter has some control over the insured's premium level. The provision for losses in the standard premium may be inadequate or excessive for certain risks. Retrospective rating permits the underwriter to recognize these deviations from the norm.

Through retrospective rating, the underwriter can offer an incentive for loss control because the premium for the current period is based on the insured's experience during the current period and thus produces a premium that responds quickly to changing conditions. Retrospective rating is a way to offer a lower premium to a superior account with the ability to control losses.

A significant change in operations may cause losses to vary from normal. For example, when an insured opens a new plant or closes an existing plant, experience has shown that losses will usually be higher than average. Retrospective rating is useful in this case since the manual rate and experience rating will not account for these higher losses in the short run. If the insured has a change in operations, the underwriter may be uncertain about the effect on expected losses and may therefore want the upward pricing flexibility between the standard premium and the maximum premium. In contrast, a change in operations may result in significant improvement in a risk, and the risk may be penalized through experience rating for past losses. Under the rules of experience rating, if a material change in ownership takes place, the insured loses the past modification, which will be detrimental if the modification is favorable. If the insured firm is acquired by another, the insured firm may take on the modification of the acquiring company. There are also times when an underwriter will insure a division or subsidiary of a company. The experience modification used on the insured subsidiary will be the modification of the controlling company, and the modification may not reflect the true experience of the insured division or subsidiary. In these cases, the underwriter could use retrospective rating to make up for the deficiencies or excessive premium that may develop.

Because of significant hazard variation within a class, some risks quite naturally fall into the high or low hazard end of the classification. Retrospective rating is a technique to adjust the premium in recognition of this variation in hazard. In addition, the adjustment can be made rather quickly for insureds new in the business rather than waiting for the less sensitive experience rating to reflect hazard differences. An example would be plumbing contractors classified as Plumbing, NOC. This class includes the industrial plumber handling 20-inch pipe and the household plumber who installs ½-inch pipe. If the industrial plumber is retrospectively rated, his or her higher-than-average expected losses can be anticipated and priced accordingly.

Some industries have an occupational injury frequency-severity pattern where few injuries occur but where there is a potential for occasional severe claims. For example, the class for salespersons, collectors, or messengers is of this general type. It is reasonable to expect good loss experience in most years with an occasional extremely poor year. The use of a one-year retrospective rating plan for such risks may create some hardships for the insurer. For example, a risk may have a return premium for five consecutive years due to favorable experience. Even if there is extremely poor experience in the sixth year, the additional premium paid at the time of adjustment may not be large enough to make the account profitable over the six-year period (possibly due to a low maximum premium). A possible solution to this problem would be the use of a three-year retrospective rating plan, which combines premiums and losses over three years in determining any retrospective premium adjustment.

Scientific and technological change can also affect the workers compensation exposure. For example, new toxic chemicals, materials, and processes may affect workers in a way that is not anticipated by the manual rate. The emergence of nontraumatic hearing loss, cumulative injury, and the effects of asbestos are some examples of this phenomenon. These circumstances may cause late developing claims, sometimes well after retrospective adjustments have been finalized. When insuring industries that may be affected by such changes, the underwriter must consider whether the rate reflects the consequent exposures to loss.

Even when using retrospective rating, the loss experience for a risk for any one year is very difficult to predict. Some insurers try to counter the wide variance in experience from year to year for smaller risks (due to an inadequate number of exposure units) by establishing a higher requirement for eligibility than the $25,000 standard premium requirement of the manual. By insuring risks with more exposure units and hence a higher standard premium, the insurer hopes to increase the predictability of losses and decrease the yearly fluctuation in experience.

## Schedule Rating

A third individual insured rating plan, schedule rating, is available in less than a dozen states. Under schedule rating, the premium for a risk can be modified to reflect characteristics of the risk *that are not reflected in its experience.* Although schedule rating is often used in other lines of insurance as a competitive tool and there is usually little documentation to justify the schedule credit (other than those situations where the producer has agreed to reduce the commission rate), the schedule rating section of the *Experience Rating Plan Manual* states, "All schedule debits and all schedule credits shall be based on evidence that is contained in the file of the carrier at the time the schedule debit or credit is applied."[28]

The maximum modification (debit or credit) varies by state. Two states use 15 percent, and the rest use 25 percent. The minimum eligibility requirements also vary and range from $750 to $2,500 annual premium amounts. The manual lists the reasons or factors for which a schedule debit or credit can be given. For each of them, there is a range of percentage debits or credits that can be given. For example, for conditions related to the premises, the range may be a 6 percent debit to a 6 percent credit. The total of all factors cannot exceed the maximums stated in the manual. The following are the factors listed in the manual:

- Premises
- Classification peculiarities
- Medical facilities
- Safety devices
- Employees—selection, training, supervision
- Management—cooperation with insurer
- Management—safety organization

Underwriters should know if schedule rating is allowed in their jurisdictions. If it is, they should know the state rules regarding the plan, the documentation required, and their insurer's guidelines regarding the use of schedule rating.

## SUMMARY

While most employments are subject to state workers compensation laws, some employments are subject to federal laws, the most widely known of which is the United States Longshore and Harbor Workers Compensation Act. The determination of who is covered by this law and who is covered by the law of a certain state can be a confusing issue. Situs and status tests help in this effort. However, the underwriter should remember that as with so many other principles in commercial liability underwriting, this determination is ultimately made by the courts.

The underwriting of workers compensation coverage involves many of the factors also considered in underwriting other lines of commercial liability insurance. For example, the underwriter looks for an insured who has well-trained, qualified, safety-conscious employees. Workers compensation underwriters also consider factors unique to the workers compensation exposure, such as the plant and equipment as well as the production processes.

Although there is probably less pricing flexibility in workers compensation than most other commercial liability lines, the underwriter does have some tools available—retrospective rating and schedule rating. These two individual insured rating plans can be a competitive tool, but experience rating cannot. This neither lessens the importance of experience rating nor diminishes the importance of the experience rating worksheet as a source of underwriting information.

# Chapter Notes


1. Before 1982, District of Columbia government employees were covered by FECA. Private employees working in the District of Columbia were covered by USL&HW. These employees are now covered by two separate District of Columbia Workers' Compensation Acts. The act that applies to government employees still closely resembles FECA.
2. Reed v. Pennsylvania Railroad Company, 351 U.S. 502, 76 S. Ct. 958 (1956).
3. Arthur Larson, *Workmen's Compensation for Occupational Injuries and Death,* Desk Edition (New York: Matthew Bender & Company, 1981), § 91.70.
4. Merchant Marine Act, 41 Stat. 1007 (1920), 46 U.S.C. § 688 (1975).
5. The term admiralty is derived from the English practice in which the admiral was in charge of the seas and all navigation thereon. The admiral set up the courts and established the rules and regulations.
6. Kernan v. American Dredging Co., 355 U.S. 426, 78 S. Ct. 394 (1958). Millus and Manes, *Longshoremen's Act,* pp. 53-54.
7. Grant Gilmore and Charles L. Black, Jr., *Law of Admiralty* (Mineola, NY: Foundation Press, 1975), pp. 434-436.
8. Larson, *Workmen's Compensation,* § 90.21. Gilmore and Black, *Law of Admiralty,* pp. 331-334.
9. Larson, *Workmen's Compensation,* § 90.21.
10. Gilmore and Black, *Law of Admiralty,* p. 47. Larson, *Workmen's Compensation,* § 90.23.
11. United States Longshore and Harbor Workers' Compensation Act, as amended, Public Law No. 92-576 (27 October 1972), 86 Stat. 1251, and as further amended, Public Law No. 98-426 (28 September 1984), 98 Stat. 1639, § 2(3).
12. USL&HW Act, § 3(a).
13. USL&HW Act, § 3(a).
14. Northeast Marine Terminal Co. v. Caputo, 432 U.S. 429, 97 S. Ct. 2348 (1977).
15. Alabama Dry Dock & Shipbuilding Co. v. Kininess, 554 F.2d 176 (5th Cir. 1977).
16. U.S. Department of Labor, Office of Workers Compensation Programs, *Guidelines for Determination of Claims under Amended Longshoremen's Act,* Program Memorandum No. 58 (5 August 1977).
17. Director, OWCP v. Perini North River Associates, 103 S.C. 634 (1983).
18. Dravo Corp. v. Maxin, 545 F. 2d 381 (3d Cir. 1976), Larson, *Workmen's Compensation,* § 89.30.
19. Sun Ship, Inc. v. Pennsylvania, 100 S. Ct. 2432 (1980).
20. Larson, *Workmen's Compensation,* § 89.50.
21. USL&HW Act, § 20.
22. USL&HW Act, § 2(2).

23. Standard Oil Company v. Johnson, 316 U.S. 481, 62 S. Ct. 1168 (1942).
24. Albert J. Millus and Joseph F. Manes, *The Longshoremen's and Harbor Workers' Compensation Act and Its Extensions* (New York: The Roberts Publishing Corp., 1978), pp. 222-240.
25. This section is intended to summarize the major aspects of experience rating. If the reader desires more information, the National Council *Experience Rating Manual* has a good description of the program in addition to the rules and procedures. The National Council also publishes two pamphlets that further describe experience rating—*The ABCs of Revised Experience Rating* and *An In-depth View of Experience Rating.* Several definitions and explanations in this section are based on these publications.
26. The requirements listed are for *intrastate* rating (that is, for a risk that only conducts operations within a single state). The requirements and some of the mechanics of *interstate* rating (that is, the risk conducts operations in two or more states) are a bit more complicated and will not be described in this text.
27. In fact, the statistical reporting plan used in workers compensation requires the first report of losses for a certain policy period to be valued as of eighteen months after the month the policy is effective and to be filed no later than twenty months after the policy effective date. Thus, a policy effective in January 19X3 would have its losses reported to the bureau sometime between June and August 19X4. It would therefore be impossible to calculate an experience modification in time for a January 19X4 renewal. Because losses can be first reported as late as August, it is easy to see how any delay in reporting or how problems in calculating the modification could make it difficult to have the modification ready in time for the January 19X5 renewal.
28. National Council on Compensation Insurance, *Experience Rating Plan Manual* (Boca Raton, FL: National Council on Compensation Insurance, 1984), p. A-7, 1st reprint, effective 1 January 1987.

# CHAPTER 13

# Miscellaneous Commercial Liability Concepts

This final chapter examines the underwriting of several, less widely written lines of commercial liability insurance. Although some underwriters may never underwrite these lines, the underwriting considerations apply to other lines as well. In addition, the commercial liability underwriter should be familiar with all types of commercial liability insurance to best address the needs of insureds.

This chapter first examines the underwriting of surety bonds, emphasizing the underwriting of contract bonds. Although the underwriting of contract bonds is specialized, many of the techniques used in contract bond underwriting can also be used in the underwriting of other lines of insurance. The most important aspect of underwriting bonds is financial analysis. If an insurer's bond department is willing to provide contract bonds for a risk, seldom will the commercial liability underwriter find a financial reason for refusing to write the liability coverages. Bond underwriters must closely review the risk's financial status and work plans. Contract bond underwriting is also important to the commercial liability underwriter since many commercial accounts request contract bonds along with their other property and liability insurance coverages.

The chapter then examines the underwriting of two professional liability lines of insurance—for physicians and surgeons and for agents and brokers. The number of claims for medical malpractice have recently escalated. Stories of doctors retiring from practice or limiting their practice because of the cost of insurance are no longer big news items. An understanding of the factors that enter into the underwriting of physicians and surgeons professional liability insurance is important for all commercial liability underwriters.

The underwriting of agents and brokers errors and omissions coverage emphasizes loss control efforts directed particularly toward proper office procedures, including recordkeeping. If an agency establishes appropriate office management policies and procedures, the chances of an errors and omissions claim is greatly reduced. Although there will always be a need for the staff of the agency to be professionally competent (that is, in terms of coverage knowledge and risk management alternatives), clerical errors such as failing to renew or to request an endorsement are a leading cause of loss.

## SURETY BONDS

*Suretyship* is a technique used to assure one party, the *obligee,* that another party, the *principal,* can fulfill an obligation he or she has undertaken to perform. It is a risk transfer technique similar to insurance. However, the party who is making the guarantee, the *surety,* has not always been an insurance company. The surety is an entity, most often a corporation, who joins with the principal to guarantee some action of that principal through a surety bond. Failing to perform, the principal is said to be in default, at which time the surety is called upon to honor its guarantee.

It must be remembered that the principal is primarily responsible for fulfilling a specific contractual obligation; the surety is not. The surety may make some kind of payment in lieu of completing that obligation or may engage others who will complete it. In many situations, money damages are the only method the surety can use to honor its guarantee to the obligee if the principal fails to fulfill its obligation.

A contract already exists between the principal and the obligee; the surety bond becomes an additional contract among three parties. This additional contract guarantees the principal's compliance with the terms of the original principal-obligee contract. However, at common law, the surety has the right to be indemnified by the principal for any loss suffered as a result of default. Therefore, the surety company should not suffer a true loss if the surety underwriter has handled the situation properly. The surety underwriter's job is to ascertain that the principal can perform the obligations he or she has agreed to accept, or, upon failing to perform, to indemnify the obligee for that failure from net worth. In reality, surety insurers do suffer losses in spite of the best efforts of their underwriters.

The degree of exposure to loss that exists in bonds varies so greatly that distinct sections of surety obligations must be studied separately. The surety underwriter may be asked to guarantee that buildings will be completed to the satisfaction of the owner (in full compliance with plans and specifications as set forth under the contract), that a person will abide by the rules of the permit that has been granted, that any judgment rendered will be paid, that grass will grow by a guaranteed date, and that obligations to suppliers and subcontractors will be paid on time. Some bonds that cover activities with low loss frequency, and for small amounts, are written with little underwriting except the recommendation of the producer. Other bonds, particularly contract bonds such as efficiency guarantees, are not written freely for even the best potential clients because the nature of the obligation makes performance almost impossible.

The importance of the surety in fulfilling its role of risk-bearer shifts considerably from the first type of obligation to the second. In the case of the "freely written" bonds, the surety is merely endorsing a candidate for consideration; in the other case, the surety may be instrumental in changing the nature of the obligation to protect the principal. The obligee, of course, is intent on protecting himself or herself from any and all possible failures of the principal. It sometimes happens that the surety, in order to do its job of guaranteeing the principal's action, must help the principal establish the ground rules—which may mean altering the contract and changing the obligation. This, however, does not happen very often.

## The Nature of the Principal's Obligation

Inherent in every bonding situation is the belief in the honesty of the principal and his or her ability to perform. Without this assumption, the obligee would never agree to engage the principal. This assumption also extends to the surety as a partner of the principal. For the principal, the ability to perform refers to the contract into which the principal and obligee have entered. For the surety, the ability to perform refers to the promise to pay a sum of money if the principal is unable to perform its obligations under that contract. An obligee's evaluation of the principal is based upon the principal's financial strength and work record. This obligee's evaluation of the surety is based upon the surety's investigative procedures, financial stability, and historical bonding experience. In most cases, the ability of the principal to secure a bond provides sufficient evidence to the obligee of the principal's ability to perform.

Although most bonds are for *fixed* amounts that are known when the bond is written, some bonds provide *variable* amounts, and others have an *open penalty* in which the only limit is the extent to which the surety may legally obligate itself. Bonds whose exact limits are not known are not as freely written as those whose limits are known. This holds true in all surety lines. In contract bonds, this is significant not only in monetary terms but also in performance requirements. If specific tests can be met, or specific designated parts are to be installed, the bond is more readily available than if general terms are given and either specific or nonspecific results are required. Considerably more is required to guarantee the *efficient operation* of an item than the more common guarantee of *delivery* of that item. Think of the difference in exposure to loss in these two examples of job descriptions:

1. Remodel laundry building and furnish washing machines and clothes dryers for a state mental institution and provide a maintenance guarantee for twenty years. Machines will be operated by patients under supervision.
2. Construct two-story addition to county court house as per specifications prepared by architects and engineers (attached).

The first job is much smaller in size but definitely has a higher risk of failure and requires a stronger financial condition than the latter. The first job requires, among other things, that the principal remain in business for the twenty years of the maintenance period.

## The Nature of the Surety's Guarantee

The nature of a surety's guarantee is so unusual that by law, a bond must be formally written for one party to be held liable for the "debt, default, or miscarriage" of another. Conditions are set forth in writing which, if met, void the obligation. It is said that an oral binder has no meaning in corporate suretyship.

However, many characteristics of the bond are *not* included in the document itself. One primary item often not fully explained is the choices for satisfying the obligations of the surety. For example, in contract bonds an option used frequently to fulfill the surety's obligation is to let the obligee rebid the remaining work, with the surety paying the excess over what had originally been contracted. This method allows the owner freedom of market, removes the original contractor from the picture, and releases the surety from obligation once it has made the payment.

*Forfeiture* is another method of fulfilling a surety bond. It is also one of the harshest measures that can exist for the principal. Bonds with forfeiture clauses are usually financial guarantee bonds. The forfeiture clause provides the surety with no alternative to immediate forfeiture of the bond amount. For example, an electric utility may require such a bond from a commercial customer. If the customer does not pay its utility bill within a certain number of days, the utility may call on the surety for immediate payment. In most cases, the surety will be indemnified by the customer (principal). In bonds that do not require forfeiture, it is not common to default. Many other options can be used to give the principal the opportunity to work out solutions to the obligee's problems without causing any undue *financial* stress on the principal.

Surety bonds are *joint and several* obligations. If the principal goes bankrupt, it might be conceivable that its debts will be forgiven, and therefore it cannot be compelled to complete obligations that include payment of debts. Since the bond is joint *and* several, however, *each of the several parties* is equally joined to the obligation. The surety can be held to an obligation even when the principal might be released. The principal and surety can be jointly or individually held responsible. However, the surety always has a right to reimbursement from the principal, even if the surety is sued individually. The exception occurs where the surety steps in and pays obligations not legally those of the principal. The joint and several nature of the obligation is for the convenience and protection of the obligee, not the principal.

Why then is it so important to underwriters that so many applications or indemnity agreements be signed? While the right to sue exists, it is expensive and time consuming to exercise. The indemnity agreement commonly used by underwriters is to instruct principals about items not contained in the bond form, but which can be used to mitigate, control, or speed up settlements of losses for the surety's benefit without forcing additional legal costs. Under an indemnity agreement, the surety can sometimes obtain relief without a lengthy legal proceeding because of the more rapid resolution of a contractual obligation than would be possible by asserting the common law relief of indemnity.

An additional precaution for sureties is to have at their exclusive disposal the necessary funds for disbursement. Collateral requirements are based on the principal's financial strength. Some financial guarantee bonds are written *only* with full collateral, and the function of the surety on these obligations is to arrange for the safekeeping and proper disposition of the collateral. The surety can quickly handle transactions of this nature without a formal trust.

Unlike most forms of insurance, the surety cannot be released from one of its bonds. Conditions permitting cancellation of bonds are much more restrictive than in traditional insurance. Even nonpayment of premium is not granted as a valid reason for terminating a bond. This concept strengthens the value of the surety guarantee and also warns the surety should individual principals waiver in their desire to perform as they have agreed. The nonpayment at least gives the surety the chance to defend itself or to protect itself once the premium is delinquent.

## Types of Surety Bonds

There are many different ways to group surety bonds. Generally, surety bonds are divided into four major categories: (1) public official bonds, (2) court bonds, (3) license and permit bonds, and (4) contract bonds. There are several other bonds that might best be placed in a miscellaneous category. These include federal surety bonds and financial guarantee bonds. Fidelity bonds, which are often included in discussions of surety bonds, are different enough in nature that they are described in a separate text for the AU program. This chapter concentrates on contract bond underwriting since it is by far the largest line of surety bonds. However, the other types of bonds are briefly described.

**Public Official Bonds.** Public official bonds are required of most elected officials who handle public funds, and many appointed officials as well. The single most outstanding characteristic of public official bonds is that they are generally for *faithful performance* of duty, not just for honesty. Malfeasance, misfeasance, and nonfeasance of official duties are included under a bond if monetary damages can be proven. Generally, most losses are caused by dishonest individuals. Sometimes the dishonest individual is not the one bonded but a subordinate for whom the bonded individual is responsible.

The degree of risk associated with different bonded officials varies considerably. A notary public does not have the opportunity to embezzle substantial funds as does the city treasurer. The hunting and fishing license agent has a seasonal responsibility, but the sheriff's is year-round. Tax collectors need insurance to protect them in case of robbery and burglary, but other municipal officers might not have the same need.

Public official bonds do not protect the individual who is bonded; instead, they protect the governmental body that requires the bond. This poses a unique problem because in some cases there is no statutory provision dictating when and how the official can be relieved of responsibility if he or she so wishes. Officials cannot limit their liability without leaving office, and yet they cannot leave office without fulfilling their duties. Meanwhile, the bond continues to guarantee faithful performance.

Generally, the governmental body that requires the bond is the only one that can present a claim. It can only make a claim as prescribed by law, but the law gives the exclusive criteria for claim situations, and the bond is required to conform to the law. The surety cannot protect itself in any way from the legal requirements. Regardless of the limitations the surety prints in its form, the law dictates what the bond should cover.

The surety is told the bond amount and the bond is usually set for the term of office. Despite all the legal entanglements from which there is no escape, most surety companies are eager to write public official bonds as they have proven profitable.

***Underwriting Public Official Bonds.*** The application is usually the only substantial source of underwriting information for public official bonds. It contains personal references, banking facilities to be used, audit procedures used for the office, and a few financial questions. Reliance on the reputation of the official is paramount. A brief review of the training and work experience of the individual is occasionally conducted, and a clearance of accounts of the prior official is often required to screen carryover problems. It is impossible to be sure no hidden problems exist within the ranks of subordinates, but checking the records and clearing the predecessor will help spot major problems in most instances.

As with most surety obligations, an underwriting criterion is the worth of the individual bonded. In public official bonds, the personal assets of the individual must be depleted before any funds have to be expended by the surety. However, many public officials who may be responsible for a great deal of money may have little net worth. Most officials are capable of performing the tasks they have been elected to perform. Most will follow the rules for keeping their accounts in the prescribed fashion. Most will be willing after their term of office has expired to turn over the securities, books, papers, and records pertinent to the office they have held. And finally, most will become aware of and comply with all rules relating to disbursements of public funds.

A great deal of class underwriting has been done on public official bonds since surety companies have insisted that sound accounting practices be instituted and proper audits be carried out regularly. This has helped control some losses that could not be avoided.

***Loss Control for Public Official Bonds.*** The liability of public officials can be limited in a number of ways. One way is to have the governmental body to whom the public official reports designate the official depository of funds and securities. In this way, the obligation in choosing the depository has not been left with the bonded public official. This is essential to prevent the individual from being responsible should the bank fail. Another way of controlling losses for public official bonds is to require insurance against robbery and burglary or broad form crime insurance so that monies in the custody of the public official will be insured if they are lost. The need for protection in this case may extend to the insuring of all employees for whose conduct the official is responsible. Probably the most conventional method used to control losses is to require the governmental body to make annual audits so that losses will be discovered while they are still small.

**Judicial Bonds.** Generally, judicial bonds offer a guarantee similar to that of public official bonds. That is, the bond guarantees that a person or organization will faithfully perform certain duties prescribed by law or by a court, or will show financial responsibility for the benefit of another until the court reaches a final decision. Upon the principal's failure to perform, the surety would step in and pay for damages. Judicial bonds generally fall into two groups, fiduciary bonds and court bonds.

***Fiduciary Bonds.*** A *fiduciary* is a person who occupies a position of trust or who manages the affairs or funds of another. The principal (fiduciary) should be experienced in the duties for which he or she has been appointed and generally must be represented by qualified counsel in order for a surety company to safely underwrite the bond. This is necessary because the duty of a fiduciary is to handle the affairs of another in a legally prescribed manner. In all instances this means that the fiduciary must not engage in any risky, unprofitable operations or investments. In some states a list prescribes the kinds of investments that can be legally obtained. Advice of counsel on matters such as this is essential.

The responsibilities of a fiduciary also include some form of reporting either annually or at the end of the term of service. The term will not expire until the obligation of the bond has been performed. In many cases, the term of the fiduciary may extend over a number of years, in which case it may be advisable to call for a periodic accounting to be prepared by the attorney. Such accountings are common in connection with *guardian bonds* (bonds issued to a person who legally has the care of a person and/or a person's property because of the inability of that person to manage his or her own affairs). By frequently delivering to the court an accounting of all activities undertaken to date or since the last accounting, the fiduciary is able to obtain the court's approval for those actions (while the records are still available) and be exonerated for those activities before the term of service of the fiduciary is expired.

The bond itself is often required by the court to be on its own form, although many courts accept the form used by the surety company. The bond is usually set by the court in a fixed amount based upon the value of the personal property expected to be received by the fiduciary (real estate cannot validly be sold without court order). If it is found that the bond amount is not large enough, an additional bond may be required. The bond is for the term the fiduciary will serve, with a short-term obligation being easier to underwrite and accept. There is no cancellation provision in the bond form—only the court can relieve the fiduciary of his or her responsibilities.

Most fiduciary bonds are underwritten by means of data obtained on the application, which includes a very brief financial statement, and to a great extent by relying on the ability of the counsel of the principal. Some underwriters assert that they underwrite law firms more than they underwrite the principal.

***Court Bonds.*** In numerous kinds of litigation, bonds are required of one of the parties bringing suit to protect the other party. A surety bond giving this guarantee is called a *court bond* and may be required by law or by rule of court.

There are many types of court bonds, but plaintiff's and defendant's bonds are the most widely known.

*Plaintiff's bonds* are required of people entering complaints at law against others. To have the bond written, plaintiffs must have also begun building a case to the extent that an attorney will represent them. Most sureties will review the financial status of plaintiffs for whom they are writing bonds.

*Defendant's bonds* are required of people engaged in suits initiated by plaintiffs. They find themselves in the position of wanting to regain possession of something someone has obtained from them, and over which litigation is already in effect. Defendant's bonds are usually required to (1) retain or regain possession of property (that has been attached at the insistence of the plaintiff) pending the outcome of the suit, or (2) to suspend the execution of a judgment, order, or decree of the court while the defendant seeks reversal of an unfavorable judgment in a higher court. This last type of proceeding creates additional concern for underwriters in that the defendant has already lost the case. Consequently, many surety underwriters will only consider writing defendant's bonds with full collateral.

Why then does anyone wish to have a court bond when he or she is a defendant and full collateral is being required? The reason is that in most instances, there is no alternative. Since the defendant cannot obtain a surety bond without depositing collateral with the surety, the true cost of the defendant's court bond is a service fee designed to overcome the expenses of collection, handling, safekeeping, and filing of papers of collateralized bonds. Considering the low premium charge, the system is probably to the advantage of all concerned. The court is not designed or geared for accepting collateral, does not have to engage in the additional task of determining whether collateral is adequate, and does not have to obtain premises for the safekeeping of such collateral.

The results of court cases are extremely useful sources of underwriting information. Defendants must be more carefully underwritten than plaintiffs, and therefore, an application (including a brief form of financial statement) may often be all that is required of a plaintiff. But for a defendant, some form of collateral may be required. However, in no instance can the underwriter assume that the case will go in favor of the principal. In every case, the bond must be underwritten with the possibility that the principal will lose and will have to pay the face amount of the bond. The face amount of the bond is generally set by the court such that the value of the property in question, plus an amount for costs and damages, is included in the amount.

**License and Permit Bonds.** Innumerable guarantees are required of business persons today as there is regulation for virtually every type of business. For most firms, among the requirements that cause them to be licensed is that surety must be provided to stand behind the firm's promise to conduct business as required by statute or administrative ruling. The scope of the bond required varies according to the law, the locality, the nature of the guarantee, and the parties who have a right of action under the bond.

License and permit bonds are defined by one surety company as bonds required by the federal government or by any state, county, municipality, or other political subdivision as a condition precedent to the issuance of a license to engage in a certain business or activity, or the granting of a permit to exercise a particular privilege. In order to understand the obligation of the bond, the underwriter must understand the law requiring the bond, the bond form, and any regulation promulgated by the enforcing authority. Most such bonds could be included in one or more of the following groups:

- *Compliance or Privilege Bonds.* Compliance or privilege bonds are given to public bodies for purposes of regulation and limitation and to guarantee that the business will be conducted, or the privilege exercised, in compliance with the building and trade codes. The bond penalties are usually nominal and can be written freely for applicants who are known, well regarded, and recommended by the producer. Examples include contractors' license bonds and liquor license bonds.
- *Good Faith Bonds.* Bonds in favor of public bodies and that protect the general public against fraud, misrepresentation, and unfair practices of the licensee-principal are good faith bonds. Examples are car dealer, collection agency, employment agency, and pawnbroker bonds. Greater caution in underwriting is called for in this class, but bonds may be issued for established

businesses of good reputation and a reasonable amount of financial worth.

- *Buyers' Bonds.* Buyers' bonds are given to public bodies guaranteeing generally to pay or account for a sum of money, or in effect, to guarantee that the principal will remain in business. Examples are commission merchant, dealer in agricultural products, livestock auctioneer, livestock dealer, and milk dealer bonds. Underwriting considerations should be a clear loss history, favorable references, plus a sound financial condition.
- *Tax Bonds.* Tax bonds guarantee the payment of taxes levied under the laws or ordinances by which such bonds are required. In retail sales, the tax is collected from the public, but generally the tax money is commingled with all other business funds and loses its identity so that the surety then becomes liable for the successful operation of a business. These bonds are outright financial guarantees and include the following: cigarette tax, gasoline or fuel tax, liquor tax, and sales tax. The laws requiring these bonds should be read carefully, the principal's reputation and moral background must be above reproach, and its net worth substantial.

**Contract Bonds.** Many underwriters feel that underwriting contract bonds is the only real underwriting done by surety underwriters, even though many other bonds, particularly the financial guarantee bonds, also require skill in financial analysis. It is with contract underwriting that the intricacies of accounting become intertwined with those of business, presenting perhaps the greatest challenge to the underwriter.

The major contract bonds include bid, performance, payment, and maintenance bonds. The nature of contract bonds is summarized in Exhibit 13-1. Supply bonds are an additional, miscellaneous type of contract bond.

Contract bonds are not confined to construction operations. They would also be required by the municipality that advertises for bids from firms that may be interested in handling its trash collections. Contract bonds are frequently confused with construction contract bonds, since most contract bonds are predominantly used for construction purposes, and bonds of this type generate the most premium volume for sureties. Because most contract bonds are used in public construction work, the types of contract bonds are discussed below in terms of construction contract bonds.

***Bid Bonds.*** A bid bond is furnished to an owner (obligee) of a project. It promises that the contractor or construction firm (principal)

**Exhibit 13-1**
Contract Bond Comparison*

| Bid Bond | Performance Bond | Payment Bond | Maintenance Bond |
|---|---|---|---|
| **Obligee (Insured)** | | | |
| The owner or party who is calling for the bid | The owner of the property or the person who is having the work done | Same as performance bond | Same as performance bond |
| **Principal (Persons Bonded)** | | | |
| The bidder | The contractor | The contractor | The contractor |
| **What Is Guaranteed** | | | |
| That the bidder will enter into the contract and post a performance bond if the bid is accepted | That the work will be completed by the contractor according to plans and specifications | That the project will be free of liens—that is, all bills for labor and materials will be paid | That the work will be free from defects in materials and workmanship for a certain specified period |
| **When Required** | | | |
| Public work projects; a certified check may be substituted for the bond | Public work projects | Public work projects | Whenever specified in the contract |
| **Underwriting Considerations** | | | |
| The character, capacity, capital, and experience of the contractor; also information on work under bid | The qualifications of the contractor, i.e., character, capacity, capital, and experience, as well as copy of work specifications | Same as performance bond | Same as performance bond; also, term of bond |

* Adapted from FC & S Bulletins, Casualty/Surety (Cincinnati: National Underwriter Company, October 1973), pp. Bonds Con-1, 2.

bidding for a contract will, if the bid is accepted, enter into a contract and furnish the other necessary contract bonds. If the bid is accepted and the contractor fails to provide such bonds or refuses to perform the work, the obligee in most instances is entitled to be paid the difference between the amount of that contractor's bid and the bid that is finally accepted. A sample bid bond is shown in Exhibit 13-2.

***Performance Bonds.*** When a bid is accepted, the contractor who is awarded the work must not only enter into a contract with the owner, but also must furnish the other bonds that may be required for completion of work. These usually include a performance bond and a payment bond, although the two are sometimes combined under one bond form. A maintenance bond may also be required as a guarantee that the completed work is free from defects for a certain period. Like the payment bond, the guarantee of the maintenance bond may also be included within the conditions of the performance bond. Maintenance bonds are discussed later in the chapter.

The performance bond guarantees that the owner will be indemnified for any loss stemming from the failure of the contractor to perform the work according to the contract, plans, and specifications—which may or may not be subject to statutory provisions.

If a contractor defaults or is ready to default under a performance bond, a surety has five options it can exercise. It can (1) complete the contract using the existing contractor, (2) complete the contract using a replacement contractor, (3) provide the existing contractor with financial assistance sufficient to prevent default, (4) have the owner for whom work is being done make arrangements for completion of work with any losses payable by the surety up to the penalty amount or (5) pay over the penalty amount of the bond to the obligee.

A surety *may* elect to complete a contractual obligation, using the existing contractor or a replacement contractor. However, it is not compelled to do so, since the usual form of performance bond does not guarantee the completion of work by *the surety.* A sample combined performance and payment bond is shown in Exhibit 13-3.

***Payment Bonds.*** In addition to having work completed according to specifications, most owners expect that such work, when completed, will be free of any liens. A guarantee for the latter is especially important to owners of projects because suppliers of labor and materials who go uncompensated usually can apply a mechanic's lien to the property. A *mechanic's lien* is a right granted by statute to those who seek to secure the value of their work or services that is in the form of additions on real estate.[1] When a lien is placed on such property, the owner does not have clear title to it until all debts are

## Exhibit 13-2
Bid Bond

# THE AMERICAN INSTITUTE OF ARCHITECTS



*AIA Document A310*

# Bid Bond



KNOW ALL MEN BY THESE PRESENTS, that we
(Here insert full name and address or legal title of Contractor)

as Principal, hereinafter called the Principal, and
(Here insert full name and address or legal title of Surety)

a corporation duly organized under the laws of the State of
as Surety, hereinafter called the Surety, are held and firmly bound unto
(Here insert full name and address or legal title of Owner)

as Obligee, hereinafter called the Obligee, in the sum of

Dollars ($ ),

for the payment of which sum well and truly to be made, the said Principal and the said Surety, bind ourselves, our heirs, executors, administrators, successors and assigns, jointly and severally, firmly by these presents.

WHEREAS, the Principal has submitted a bid for
(Here insert full name, address and description of project)

NOW, THEREFORE, if the Obligee shall accept the bid of the Principal and the Principal shall enter into a Contract with the Obligee in accordance with the terms of such bid, and give such bond or bonds as may be specified in the bidding or Contract Documents with good and sufficient surety for the faithful performance of such Contract and for the prompt payment of labor and material furnished in the prosecution thereof, or in the event of the failure of the Principal to enter such Contract and give such bond or bonds, if the Principal shall pay to the Obligee the difference not to exceed the penalty hereof between the amount specified in said bid and such larger amount for which the Obligee may in good faith contract with another party to perform the Work covered by said bid, then this obligation shall be null and void, otherwise to remain in full force and effect.

Signed and sealed this day of 19

_(Principal)_ _(Seal)_

_(Witness)_

_(Title)_

_(Surety)_ _(Seal)_

_(Witness)_

_(Title)_

settled. In fact, property has been sold in order to settle debts that have been secured by mechanics's liens.

To avoid mechanic's liens where they are permissible and to provide a method whereby unpaid bills of creditors can be secured where mechanic's liens cannot be filed, owners of projects frequently request a payment bond in addition to the performance bond.[2] A payment bond—often referred to as a *labor and materials bond* or a *labor and materials payment bond*—guarantees that bills incurred by a contractor for labor and materials will be fully paid at the completion of the project.

A payment bond is often required for federal, state, or local government work. Such a bond also is often suggested with private work.

***Maintenance Bonds.*** Many jurisdictions have statutes, ordinances, or covenants that require a certain degree of care in the construction of property. In addition, construction contracts often specify that contractors must remedy any unsatisfactory work due to faulty work or defective materials. To comply with these laws and specifications, contractors may be required to provide obligees with a maintenance bond that guarantees that faulty work will be corrected or defective materials replaced.

Generally, a performance bond includes this maintenance guarantee for one year after the work is completed, without additional premium. Even when a separate maintenance bond is required along with a performance bond, there is usually no additional charge by the surety for the maintenance bond. However, when a contractor does not have to furnish a performance bond, but still has to produce a maintenance bond, or when the contractor must guarantee certain work and materials for periods longer than one year, the maintenance bond requires an additional charge.

There are a number of ways by which contractors can become implicated in lawsuits involving faulty work. They may perform work that is done properly only to find out later that certain materials they used had latent defects. For example, green lumber can eventually warp or split, bricks of improper mix can retain moisture, and concrete products can fail to meet specifications relating to strength.

Plans and specifications prepared by the contractor or others, such as architects, may be misleading or inappropriate for the type of work that is being done. There may be times, too, when contractors are brought into suit because of the faulty work of subcontractors, especially when the latter are not asked to supply performance and maintenance bonds. Contractors may be implicated by accepting certain responsibilities under exculpatory or hold harmless agreements. There

## Exhibit 13-3
Performance/Payment Bond

THE AMERICAN INSTITUTE OF ARCHITECTS



*AIA Document A312*

# Performance Bond

Any singular reference to Contractor, Surety, Owner or other party shall be considered plural where applicable.

CONTRACTOR (Name and Address):

SURETY (Name and Principal Place of Business):

OWNER (Name and Address):

CONSTRUCTION CONTRACT
Date:
Amount:
Description (Name and Location):

BOND
Date (Not earlier than Construction Contract Date):
Amount:
Modifications to this Bond: ☐ None ☐ See Page 3

CONTRACTOR AS PRINCIPAL
Company: (Corporate Seal)

Signature: ______________________
Name and Title:

SURETY
Company: (Corporate Seal)

Signature: ______________________
Name and Title:

(Any additional signatures appear on page 3)

*(FOR INFORMATION ONLY—Name, Address and Telephone)*

AGENT or BROKER:

OWNER'S REPRESENTATIVE (Architect, Engineer or other party):

**1** The Contractor and the Surety, jointly and severally, bind themselves, their heirs, executors, administrators, successors and assigns to the Owner for the performance of the Construction Contract, which is incorporated herein by reference.

**2** If the Contractor performs the Construction Contract, the Surety and the Contractor shall have no obligation under this Bond, except to participate in conferences as provided in Subparagraph 3.1.

**3** If there is no Owner Default, the Surety's obligation under this Bond shall arise after:

**3.1** The Owner has notified the Contractor and the Surety at its address described in Paragraph 10 below that the Owner is considering declaring a Contractor Default and has requested and attempted to arrange a conference with the Contractor and the Surety to be held not later than fifteen days after receipt of such notice to discuss methods of performing the Construction Contract. If the Owner, the Contractor and the Surety agree, the Contractor shall be allowed a reasonable time to perform the Construction Contract, but such an agreement shall not waive the Owner's right, if any, subsequently to declare a Contractor Default; and

**3.2** The Owner has declared a Contractor Default and formally terminated the Contractor's right to complete the contract. Such Contractor Default shall not be declared earlier than twenty days after the Contractor and the Surety have received notice as provided in Subparagraph 3.1; and

**3.3** The Owner has agreed to pay the Balance of the Contract Price to the Surety in accordance with the terms of the Construction Contract or to a contractor selected to perform the Construction Contract in accordance with the terms of the contract with the Owner.

**4** When the Owner has satisfied the conditions of Paragraph 3, the Surety shall promptly and at the Surety's expense take one of the following actions:

**4.1** Arrange for the Contractor, with consent of the Owner, to perform and complete the Construction Contract; or

**4.2** Undertake to perform and complete the Construction Contract itself, through its agents or through independent contractors; or

**4.3** Obtain bids or negotiated proposals from qualified contractors acceptable to the Owner for a contract for performance and completion of the Construction Contract, arrange for a contract to be prepared for execution by the Owner and the contractor selected with the Owner's concurrence, to be secured with performance and payment bonds executed by a qualified surety equivalent to the bonds issued on the Construction Contract, and pay to the Owner the amount of damages as described in Paragraph 6 in excess of the Balance of the Contract Price incurred by the Owner resulting from the Contractor's default; or

**4.4** Waive its right to perform and complete, arrange for completion, or obtain a new contractor and with reasonable promptness under the circumstances:

**.1** After investigation, determine the amount for which it may be liable to the Owner and, as soon as practicable after the amount is determined, tender payment therefor to the Owner; or

**.2** Deny liability in whole or in part and notify the Owner citing reasons therefor.

**5** If the Surety does not proceed as provided in Paragraph 4 with reasonable promptness, the Surety shall be deemed to be in default on this Bond fifteen days after receipt of an additional written notice from the Owner to the Surety demanding that the Surety perform its obligations under this Bond, and the Owner shall be entitled to enforce any remedy available to the Owner. If the Surety proceeds as provided in Subparagraph 4.4, and the Owner refuses the payment tendered or the Surety has denied liability, in whole or in part, without further notice the Owner shall be entitled to enforce any remedy available to the Owner.

**6** After the Owner has terminated the Contractor's right to complete the Construction Contract, and if the Surety elects to act under Subparagraph 4.1, 4.2, or 4.3 above, then the responsibilities of the Surety to the Owner shall not be greater than those of the Contractor under the Construction Contract, and the responsibilities of the Owner to the Surety shall not be greater than those of the Owner under the Construction Contract. To the limit of the amount of this Bond, but subject to commitment by the Owner of the Balance of the Contract Price to mitigation of costs and damages on the Construction Contract, the Surety is obligated without duplication for:

**6.1** The responsibilities of the Contractor for correction of defective work and completion of the Construction Contract;

**6.2** Additional legal, design professional and delay costs resulting from the Contractor's Default, and resulting from the actions or failure to act of the Surety under Paragraph 4; and

**6.3** Liquidated damages, or if no liquidated damages are specified in the Construction Contract, actual damages caused by delayed performance or non-performance of the Contractor.

**7** The Surety shall not be liable to the Owner or others for obligations of the Contractor that are unrelated to the Construction Contract, and the Balance of the Contract Price shall not be reduced or set off on account of any such unrelated obligations. No right of action shall accrue on this Bond to any person or entity other than the Owner or its heirs, executors, administrators or successors.

**8** The Surety hereby waives notice of any change, including changes of time, to the Construction Contract or to related subcontracts, purchase orders and other obligations.

**9** Any proceeding, legal or equitable, under this Bond may be instituted in any court of competent jurisdiction in the location in which the work or part of the work is located and shall be instituted within two years after Contractor Default or within two years after the Contractor ceased working or within two years after the Surety refuses or fails to perform its obligations under this Bond, whichever occurs first. If the provisions of this Paragraph are void or prohibited by law, the minimum period of limitation available to sureties as a defense in the jurisdiction of the suit shall be applicable.

**10** Notice to the Surety, the Owner or the Contractor shall be mailed or delivered to the address shown on the signature page.

**11** When this Bond has been furnished to comply with a statutory or other legal requirement in the location where the construction was to be performed, any provision in this Bond conflicting with said statutory or legal requirement shall be deemed deleted herefrom and provisions conforming to such statutory or other legal requirement shall be deemed incorporated herein. The intent is that this Bond shall be construed as a statutory bond and not as a common law bond.

**12 DEFINITIONS**

**12.1** Balance of the Contract Price: The total amount payable by the Owner to the Contractor under the Construction Contract after all proper adjustments have been made, including allowance to the Contractor of any amounts received or to be received by the Owner in settlement of insurance or other claims for damages to which the Contractor is entitled, reduced by all valid and proper payments made to or on behalf of the Contractor under the Construction Contract.

**12.2** Construction Contract: The agreement between the Owner and the Contractor identified on the signature page, including all Contract Documents and changes thereto.

**12.3** Contractor Default: Failure of the Contractor, which has neither been remedied nor waived, to perform or otherwise to comply with the terms of the Construction Contract.

**12.4** Owner Default: Failure of the Owner, which has neither been remedied nor waived, to pay the Contractor as required by the Construction Contract or to perform and complete or comply with the other terms thereof.

**MODIFICATIONS TO THIS BOND ARE AS FOLLOWS:**

(Space is provided below for additional signatures of added parties, other than those appearing on the cover page.)

CONTRACTOR AS PRINCIPAL
Company: (Corporate Seal)

Signature: ______________________
Name and Title:
Address:

SURETY
Company: (Corporate Seal)

Signature: ______________________
Name and Title:
Address:

THE AMERICAN INSTITUTE OF ARCHITECTS

*AIA Document A312*

# Payment Bond

Any singular reference to Contractor, Surety, Owner or other party shall be considered plural where applicable.

CONTRACTOR (Name and Address):

SURETY (Name and Principal Place of Business):

OWNER (Name and Address):

CONSTRUCTION CONTRACT
Date:
Amount:
Description (Name and Location):

BOND
Date (Not earlier than Construction Contract Date):
Amount:
Modifications to this Bond: ☐ None ☐ See Page 6

CONTRACTOR AS PRINCIPAL
Company: (Corporate Seal)

Signature: ____________________
Name and Title:

SURETY
Company: (Corporate Seal)

Signature: ____________________
Name and Title:

(Any additional signatures appear on page 6)

*(FOR INFORMATION ONLY—Name, Address and Telephone)*
AGENT or BROKER:

OWNER'S REPRESENTATIVE (Architect, Engineer or other party):

**1** The Contractor and the Surety, jointly and severally, bind themselves, their heirs, executors, administrators, successors and assigns to the Owner to pay for labor, materials and equipment furnished for use in the performance of the Construction Contract, which is incorporated herein by reference.

**2** With respect to the Owner, this obligation shall be null and void if the Contractor:

**2.1** Promptly makes payment, directly or indirectly, for all sums due Claimants, and

**2.2** Defends, indemnifies and holds harmless the Owner from claims, demands, liens or suits by any person or entity whose claim, demand, lien or suit is for the payment for labor, materials or equipment furnished for use in the performance of the Construction Contract, provided the Owner has promptly notified the Contractor and the Surety (at the address described in Paragraph 12) of any claims, demands, liens or suits and tendered defense of such claims, demands, liens or suits to the Contractor and the Surety, and provided there is no Owner Default.

**3** With respect to Claimants, this obligation shall be null and void if the Contractor promptly makes payment, directly or indirectly, for all sums due.

**4** The Surety shall have no obligation to Claimants under this Bond until:

**4.1** Claimants who are employed by or have a direct contract with the Contractor have given notice to the Surety (at the address described in Paragraph 12) and sent a copy, or notice thereof, to the Owner, stating that a claim is being made under this Bond and, with substantial accuracy, the amount of the claim.

**4.2** Claimants who do not have a direct contract with the Contractor:

.1 Have furnished written notice to the Contractor and sent a copy, or notice thereof, to the Owner, within 90 days after having last performed labor or last furnished materials or equipment included in the claim stating, with substantial accuracy, the amount of the claim and the name of the party to whom the materials were furnished or supplied or for whom the labor was done or performed; and

.2 Have either received a rejection in whole or in part from the Contractor, or not received within 30 days of furnishing the above notice any communication from the Contractor by which the Contractor has indicated the claim will be paid directly or indirectly; and

.3 Not having been paid within the above 30 days, have sent a written notice to the Surety (at the address described in Paragraph 12) and sent a copy, or notice thereof, to the Owner, stating that a claim is being made under this Bond and enclosing a copy of the previous written notice furnished to the Contractor.

**5** If a notice required by Paragraph 4 is given by the Owner to the Contractor or to the Surety, that is sufficient compliance.

**6** When the Claimant has satisfied the conditions of Paragraph 4, the Surety shall promptly and at the Surety's expense take the following actions:

**6.1** Send an answer to the Claimant, with a copy to the Owner, within 45 days after receipt of the claim, stating the amounts that are undisputed and the basis for challenging any amounts that are disputed.

**6.2** Pay or arrange for payment of any undisputed amounts.

**7** The Surety's total obligation shall not exceed the amount of this Bond, and the amount of this Bond shall be credited for any payments made in good faith by the Surety.

**8** Amounts owed by the Owner to the Contractor under the Construction Contract shall be used for the performance of the Construction Contract and to satisfy claims, if any, under any Construction Performance Bond. By the Contractor furnishing and the Owner accepting this Bond, they agree that all funds earned by the Contractor in the performance of the Construction Contract are dedicated to satisfy obligations of the Contractor and the Surety under this Bond, subject to the Owner's priority to use the funds for the completion of the work.

**9** The Surety shall not be liable to the Owner, Claimants or others for obligations of the Contractor that are unrelated to the Construction Contract. The Owner shall not be liable for payment of any costs or expenses of any Claimant under this Bond, and shall have under this Bond no obligations to make payments to, give notices on behalf of, or otherwise have obligations to Claimants under this Bond.

**10** The Surety hereby waives notice of any change, including changes of time, to the Construction Contract or to related subcontracts, purchase orders and other obligations.

**11** No suit or action shall be commenced by a Claimant under this Bond other than in a court of competent jurisdiction in the location in which the work or part of the work is located or after the expiration of one year from the date (1) on which the Claimant gave the notice required by Subparagraph 4.1 or Clause 4.2.3, or (2) on which the last labor or service was performed by anyone or the last materials or equipment were furnished by anyone under the Construction Contract, whichever of (1) or (2) first occurs. If the provisions of this Paragraph are void or prohibited by law, the minimum period of limitation available to sureties as a defense in the jurisdiction of the suit shall be applicable.

**12** Notice to the Surety, the Owner or the Contractor shall be mailed or delivered to the address shown on the signature page. Actual receipt of notice by Surety, the Owner or the Contractor, however accomplished, shall be sufficient compliance as of the date received at the address shown on the signature page.

**13** When this Bond has been furnished to comply with a statutory or other legal requirement in the location where the construction was to be performed, any provision in this Bond conflicting with said statutory or legal requirement shall be deemed deleted herefrom and provisions conforming to such statutory or other legal requirement shall be deemed incorporated herein. The intent is that this

Bond shall be construed as a statutory bond and not as a common law bond.

**14** Upon request by any person or entity appearing to be a potential beneficiary of this Bond, the Contractor shall promptly furnish a copy of this Bond or shall permit a copy to be made.

**15 DEFINITIONS**

**15.1** Claimant: An individual or entity having a direct contract with the Contractor or with a subcontractor of the Contractor to furnish labor, materials or equipment for use in the performance of the Contract. The intent of this Bond shall be to include without limitation in the terms "labor, materials or equipment" that part of water, gas, power, light, heat, oil, gasoline, telephone service or rental equipment used in the Construction Contract, architectural and engineering services required for performance of the work of the Contractor and the Contractor's subcontractors, and all other items for which a mechanic's lien may be asserted in the jurisdiction where the labor, materials or equipment were furnished.

**15.2** Construction Contract: The agreement between the Owner and the Contractor identified on the signature page, including all Contract Documents and changes thereto.

**15.3** Owner Default: Failure of the Owner, which has neither been remedied nor waived, to pay the Contractor as required by the Construction Contract or to perform and complete or comply with the other terms thereof.

**MODIFICATIONS TO THIS BOND ARE AS FOLLOWS:**

(Space is provided below for additional signatures of added parties, other than those appearing on the cover page.)

CONTRACTOR AS PRINCIPAL
Company: (Corporate Seal)

Signature: ____________________
Name and Title:
Address:

SURETY
Company: (Corporate Seal)

Signature: ____________________
Name and Title:
Address:

are also many situations in which contractors are clearly negligent in the performance of their work.

The fact that there is no relationship between a maintenance bond guarantee and products-completed operations insurance needs to be clearly stated. If the contractor is found to be responsible for defective work that is the subject of a maintenance bond, the work must be remedied at the contractor's own expense. Many contractors are not aware that faulty work is uninsurable, judging from the number of disputes and court decisions involving completed operations liability insurance claims. Nevertheless, most liability insurance policies, standard or nonstandard, exclude claims for property damage to work performed or to materials that are used in that work. Most such work is therefore done at a loss since there is usually no insurance for this exposure. As a result, sureties are careful to bond only contractors that are financially capable of repairing or replacing defective work or materials since they are, in fact, attesting to that capability by issuing maintenance bonds.

***Supply Contract (Supply) Bonds.*** A supply contract involves an agreement for furnishing and delivering materials or supplies at an agreed price, usually without any obligation to install whatever is to be delivered. Most such contracts are between private enterprise and federal, state, or local governmental bodies. A supply contract bond is required by those governmental bodies (obligees) from their suppliers (principals) guaranteeing the performance agreed upon in a supply contract. Since, for the most part, these bonds are required by the government, they are statutory in form.[3]

Those who wish to obtain supply contracts, whether they are manufacturers, wholesalers, or dealers, must submit bids, a situation like that of contractors who wish to obtain public work contracts. Typically, the lowest bidder must be selected. When a bidder, or supplier in this case, fails to furnish whatever is required according to the contract specifications, he or she is liable for the difference between the bid price and the cost of buying those materials or supplies on the open market.[4]

There may be times when the materials covered by a supply contract are not readily available on the open market. Equipment made to order by a manufacturer is an example. Unless the commitment to supply the equipment can be met, the manufacturer may be subject to extraordinary damages, including costs for the delay involved in having some other firm complete the contract.

Sureties must determine whether or not suppliers have the equipment to fulfill the contract, as well as sufficient sources from which materials or supplies are to be obtained. Depending upon the material or commodity in question, it is also important for the surety to determine whether or not the supplier has a fixed price contract from the materials source. The price of steel and copper, for example, fluctuates from week to week, and a supplier without a fixed price contract may be in financial trouble if the price for supplying that material eventually exceeds the price for which the supplier has agreed to sell it. In other words, a supplier may have to fulfill a contract at a loss. How much a supplier can withstand in terms of losses thus becomes an important point for the surety to consider.

## Underwriting Contract Bonds

Most contract bonds are similarly underwritten and require the underwriter to be aware of the same considerations. Most of the factors mentioned in the following explanation of a performance bond are equally applicable to all types of contract bonds.

The sources of information for contract bond underwriting are much the same as for other lines of insurance. Because the contractor's financial condition is the crucial consideration in contract bond underwriting, the sources of financial information are extremely important.

Previous sureties can be an important source of information. A contractor and surety develop a very close, almost personal, working relationship. This relationship usually results in more timely service by the surety as the contractor's firm prospers and as the underwriter becomes more and more familiar with the contractor's work. As a result, contractors do not usually change sureties as quickly as they might change insurers for their other insurance coverages. When a surety is changed, the new surety underwriter should check with the previous underwriter to see if there were any problems. A refusal by a surety to issue new bonds may be the reason for the contractor's decision to change sureties. The contractor may therefore be looking for a "more cooperative" surety that will continue to issue bonds, and the underwriter should be aware of this fact.

The underwriter requires a completed application and current financial statements from the contractor in order to evaluate the submission. Because contract bond underwriting is a process that is repeated every time a bid is contemplated and every time a new fiscal period is completed, the information contained in these statements must be updated throughout the life of the bond.

Underwriters of contract bonds must generally consider three factors:

1. The nature of the underlying contractual obligations of the principal

2. The extent of the surety's obligations upon default by the principal
3. The qualification of the principal in terms of character, capacity, and capital

**Nature of Underlying Contractual Obligation.** Of primary concern to the contract bond underwriter is the contract document into which the principal has entered with the obligee. The contract is first presented in the form of bid specifications. The underwriter must carefully review the contract to verify not only that the type of work specified is the type with which the principal is familiar, but also that there are not terms within the contract with which it would be difficult to comply. Considerations regarding the terms in the contract might include the following:

- Clauses untested in the courts
- Requirements to use minority subcontractors
- Completion requirements
- Penalties or damages for late completion or noncompliance with contract terms
- Maintenance guarantees
- Efficiency guarantees
- Greater-than-normal *retainages* (amount withheld by owner until all work is completed or guarantees met)
- Warranties
- Method of payment
- Schedules

The appendix to this chapter reprints an article explaining many of these features and how they affect the ability of a contractor to complete a job to specifications.

**Extent of Surety's Obligation Upon Default.** The second major underwriting consideration is the extent of the surety's obligations upon the default of the principal. The options for the surety under the contract were covered earlier. In addition, most of the obligations of the surety are spelled out by the contract document itself. Relevant provisions would be those related to damages, penalties, completion dates, and so on. In addition, the underwriter must ascertain that the principal has other adequate coverage such as liability and property insurance. The lack of insurance to respond to a liability suit can just as easily cause default by a principal as can the inexperience of the principal in a certain line of work. Verifying the existence of other insurance would also include a review of any indemnity or hold harmless agreements entered into by the principal and the adequacy of the principal's insurance to respond to these agreements.

**Qualifications of the Principal.** In addition to determining the principal's obligations and the extent of the surety's obligation, the underwriter must consider the principal's qualifications in terms of *character, capacity,* and *capital,* the three Cs of bond underwriting.

***Character.*** The character of a bond applicant—whether an individual, partnership, joint venturer, or corporation—is judged by the traits of integrity, reliability, and leadership or drive needed to accomplish goals despite difficulties. The reasons are obvious.

Many court cases have been instituted by suppliers of materials who were not paid. Other cases arise as a result of shortcuts that cause defective work. In the end, correcting the situation may cost more than the contractor can afford. And, finally, there are cases involving contractors who are just unreliable. They may, for example, remain away from their work for long periods, or they may not have the stamina needed to cope with problems and pressures that frequently occur in construction work.

***Capacity.*** Another important factor that must be considered by surety underwriters is the capacity of the principal. In this context, "capacity" refers not to financial, but to the principal's technical or professional ability to perform the required work. To assess the principal's capacity, the surety must consider a number of points:

1. *The surety must consider the type of work to be done, and whether it is in line with the principal's expertise.* A contractor that has been engaged in the construction of single-family dwellings may be suspect if the job sought involves the construction of a large commercial building. The reason should be obvious. The work, for one thing, may require additional and expensive labor and expertise. The contractor also may lack the experience required in estimating all costs of labor and materials for complex jobs. Too, some of the work will probably have to be subcontracted, and the principal's knowledge and experience in subcontracting is something that should not be ignored. Much of this information can be gathered by contacting the owners of previously completed work or architects and engineers who worked on the contractor's projects.
2. *The surety must consider the type of equipment and tools that are owned or may be required.* An important task here is to determine whether the equipment is in good shape and properly maintained, and whether such equipment and tools are appropriate for a given job. If the equipment is poorly maintained, this gives some indication of the contractor's work habits. Moreover, if the equipment is old, in need of repair, or otherwise inadequate for the work to be performed, this may

indicate the contractor's need for funds to replace it. This may be further complicated if the contractor is still paying for old equipment, and the additional payments for new or rented equipment are more than the contractor can handle financially. Of concern to most underwriters is how the contractor obtains equipment. Renting is one alternative, rental purchase is another, and installment purchase is a third. Some underwriters prefer to see equipment purchased outright because it is a good indication of the contractor's financial status and shows that the contractor's cash flow will not be affected by payments. The contractor immediately knows the effect of the purchase on his or her financial condition.

3. *The surety must consider the amount of work in progress.* The surety will want to know what jobs the contractor may have in progress and whether or not they are bonded. It is not at all unusual for a contractor to encounter difficulties by taking on too many jobs at the same time.
4. *The surety must consider the administrative abilities of the contractor.* This ability may overlap with various other character traits. The contractor's ability to properly administer a job is a key to determining whether or not the work can be satisfactorily completed.

***Capital.*** No measure of a principal's qualifications is more important than that of capital—financial resources, financial strength, and credit standing. Unless the principal has sufficient capital, the surety will not issue the bond. This stands to reason since adequate capital is necessary for the performance of any contract. A surety that grants such a bond indicates that the principal is qualified in a number of ways—including financially—to meet certain obligations.

A surety assesses a principal's capital by examining its financial statements. The balance sheet indicates to the surety the financial standing of the principal at any given point in time. The profit and loss statement or income and expense statement shows the results of operations for the accounting period. Both financial reports indicate the profitability of the business and, when compared with reports of previous years, whether the contractor is growing. A review of the statements will also give the surety some indication of the amount of work a contractor can safely assume.

The surety also uses other tools in determining the financial stability of contractors. The goal is to determine whether the contractor is financially competent to undertake a certain venture, and whether the principal can satisfy any debt that may unexpectedly occur.

*Financial Records.* Many sureties expect to see at least the last three year-end statements, and if the year ended more than six months prior, they will expect an interim statement. This interim statement may not have to be audited by a certified public accountant (CPA), but spot checks (verification) of assets may be completed by the underwriter. Fiscal year-end statements are expected to be audited by a CPA, and if they are not, the underwriter will be required to verify the statement before any bonds are written. The extent to which the underwriter must go in order to verify the statement is based on the financial strength of the contractor and the size of the bonds to be written.

Credit reports are also ordered on most risks to verify information included with the submission and to further check the insured's financial performance record. Because the underwriting of bonds is a continuous process until the job is completed, the underwriter must also review updated financial information during the life of the bond. Even though an underwriter cannot cancel a bond if it appears that the insured's financial status becomes questionable, the sooner an underwriter detects possible problems, the faster, easier, and more cheaply can these problems be corrected.

Many sureties also question bankers about three different aspects of the contractor's finances.

- Current balances for the contractor.
- Confirmation of current loans (including amounts and payments).
- Authorization for future loans. If there is, the underwriter will usually ask the contractor to furnish copies of the authorization.

*Financial Resources Not Found on Statements.* Although plant and equipment items are found on the balance sheet of a firm, they represent one major asset that is often overrated by the contractor and that cannot be clearly determined from information in the financial statements. Another financial statement item that is difficult to evaluate is the "status of work in process," which gives the financial status of ongoing work. Such items are traditionally valued by standard accrual methods of accounting and do not reflect the estimated profit or lack of profit without some analysis. For example, accounts receivable indicate that the contractor has an asset, but it may only be a paper asset, which should have a corresponding paper liability. Accounting records do not always reflect the liability, but once the contractor has billed the owner, the amount billed is considered an asset. In fact, the contractor may have overbilled the customer by front-end loading the profit. Thus, the underwriter will use a *status of contracts* or *status of work in process* report similar to that shown in Exhibit 13-4 to analyze billings and costs and to compare the contract price with estimated costs to complete. This information, which is used to adjust assets and liabilities shown on the financial statements, is probably the single most significant item for the underwriter to consider when dealing with large contractors. Work in process gives indications of the trend of the contractor's business, not just a static picture of where it was last year, or at the fiscal year-end.

**Monitoring the Contractor.** The underwriter has many different types of information that relate to the contractor. During the life of the bond, the underwriter must readily assimilate this information and then keep it available for future reference. One surety company uses a form shown in Exhibit 13-5 for this purpose. Some of the information reflects summary data from items previously discussed, and some information cannot be obtained until the bid results are obtained. The results of the bidding and the results of subcontract bidding also have places on this form. Bids that reflect differences in excess of 10 percent generally need an explanation. Bids differing by more than 15 percent may mean that the bid amount should be recomputed and other bonding restricted until the contractor is proven capable of making a profit on this job. It is also possible that the surety will elect to forfeit the bid bond if the contractor cannot complete the job for the bid price and the amount of the difference between bid prices is more than the amount of the bid bond. This action is not frequent. The contractor will still be expected to pay the penalty since the surety usually has an indemnity agreement with the contractor.

Also on the memorandum in Exhibit 13-5 is a section on work on hand or work in process. This is not meant to be a complete analysis of this area but rather, a brief list of the uncompleted amount of work, including work under bid but not yet awarded. A review of this work gives some indication of the size of the resulting work program if the contractor is successful on all outstanding work including the current bid. Undertaking too large a work program is one of the quickest ways for a contractor to get in financial or managerial difficulties. Also, the financial strength of most contractors does not contemplate large deviations from the specifications, although change orders are to be expected. If the work program and the job size are both reaching the higher limits of the contractor's financial capabilities, underwriters are well advised to restrict future bidding to smaller jobs until, by completing the work program, the contractor proves that these larger jobs and larger programs can be profitably handled.

Although underwriters have used rules of thumb regarding acceptable size of jobs or programs, they must do so with caution. For

**Exhibit 13-4**
Status of Contracts Form

STATUS OF CONTRACTS

Name and Address of Contractor

Uncompleted Contracts
as of 19

| Contract Description and Location | I<br>Contract Price Including Approved Change Orders | II<br>Contractor's Estimated Cost At Time of Bid (1) | III<br>Total Amount Billed to Date Including Retainage (2) | IV<br>Total Costs To Date | V<br>Revised Estimated Remaining Costs To Complete (3) | VI<br>Estimated Completion Date |
|---|---|---|---|---|---|---|
| 1. | | | | | | |
| 2. | | | | | | |
| 3. | | | | | | |
| 4. | | | | | | |
| 5. | | | | | | |
| 6. | | | | | | |

Contracts Completed During Last Fiscal Year or Since Last Status of Contracts Report

| Contract Description and Location | Final Contract Price | Total Cost | Gross Profit or Loss |
|---|---|---|---|
| | | | |
| | | | |
| | | | |
| | | | |
| | | | |
| | | | |
| | | | |

1. Include contractor's original estimated total cost plus cost of all change orders and extra work orders approved to date.
2. Do not include "claims" or "disputed items." If desired, attach an explanation.
3. See instructions on reverse side.

This Information Prepared

By ______

Date ______, 19 ______

Remarks:

## Exhibit 13-5
## Contract Bond Underwriting Memorandum

| | | | | |
|---|---|---|---|---|
| APPLICANT | NAME AND ADDRESS | ☐ INDIVIDUAL<br>☐ PARTNERSHIP<br>☐ CORPORATION<br>☐ JOINT VENTURE | SUBMITTED BY | DATE |
| | | | UNIFORM COMMERCIAL CODE FILING?<br>☐ YES ☐ NO<br>☐ BLANKET ☐ SPECIFIC | |
| OBLIGEE | NAME AND ADDRESS | | APPROVED | DECLINED |
| PROJECT | | | REMARKS: | |

| BOND DATA | | OTHER BIDDERS | BIDS |
|---|---|---|---|
| | BID DATE | | $ |
| | BID BOND | | $ |
| | PERF. BOND | | $ |
| | PAYT. BOND | | $ |
| | MAINT. (NO. YRS) | ENGINEER'S ESTIMATE | $ |

| | | | |
|---|---|---|---|
| CONTRACT PRICE<br>$ | WORK SUBLET DESCRIPTION | BONDED? | AMOUNT |
| COMPLETION TIME | | | |
| PENALTY<br>$ | | | |
| PAYMENTS (How Made? Cash?) | | TOTAL | $ |

| WORK ON HAND (INCLUDE OUTSTANDING BIDS AND THOSE TO BE BID.) | DESCRIPTION AND LOCATION OF WORK | COST PLUS OR LUMP SUM | BIDS IN LINE? | CONTRACT PRICE | % COMP | AMT. UNCOMPLETED |
|---|---|---|---|---|---|---|
| | | | | $ | | $ |
| | | | | $ | | $ |
| | | | | $ | | $ |
| | | | | $ | | $ |
| | SPECIAL EQUIPMENT—SPECIAL HAZARDS? (For Either New Job or Work on Hand) | | | PLUS NEW CONTRACT | | $ |
| | | | | TOTAL UNCOMPLETED WORK | | $ |

| Experience | | | | |
|---|---|---|---|---|
| | LARGEST PREVIOUS CONTRACT | CONTRACT PRICE<br>$ | KIND OF WORK | DATE COMPLETED |
| | LARGEST PREVIOUS WORK PROGRAM: | AMOUNT<br>$ | KIND OF WORK | DATE PERFORMED |

| Financial Information (STATEMENT ON REVERSE SIDE) | | | | | |
|---|---|---|---|---|---|
| | BANK CREDIT (Amt., Name of Bank, How Secured) | | | D & B RATING | STATEMENT DATE |
| | | CURRENT ASSETS | $ | TOTAL ASSETS | $ |
| | INDEMNITY | CURRENT LIAB. | $ | TOTAL LIAB. | $ |
| | | NET QUICK ASSETS | $ | NET WORTH OR STKHLD'S EQUITY | $ |

example, one underwriter might use a guideline that a single job size or uncompleted program not exceed ten times available working capital. Others, however, have been warned against using this specific rule of thumb. The choice of guidelines depends on insurer (surety) philosophy, the underwriter, and the situation. A careful analysis of net quick assets, balanced with the review of net worth, and a comparison of those figures in a prior accounting period indicates trends more valuable than rules of thumb. For these considerations, some underwriters prefer the use of ratios, while others prefer to stay with dollar amounts. National financial averages such as those published by Dun & Bradstreet provide the underwriter with additional information for comparison purposes. Locality differences, labor negotiations pending, and individual contractor characteristics must be considered.

**Indemnity Agreements.** Primary among the features considered in the underwriting process is the strength of indemnitors. Generally, these are the majority owners (and spouses) of the firm but can also be third parties. Individual assets outside the firm may help make a strong case better, but they never make a weak case sound. An *indemnitor* is one who agrees to stand behind the contractor and lend financial support to the surety on behalf of the contractor. If owners are not willing to stand behind their own firms, it is unlikely that the surety will wish to continue the relationship. The purpose of requiring written indemnity is to ease and increase the ways for the surety to obtain relief if it is needed. In many instances the surety has a right at law to be reimbursed for the loss it pays, but some owners would like to hide behind a corporate shell to avoid personal losses. If they will not willingly indemnify a surety, they may not find a surety willing to bond their firm.

**Extending a Line of Credit.** At some point, a contractor may want an indication of the size of work program the surety feels can be handled and how big a job it is willing to bond. Most underwriters can indicate ranges of job sizes and work programs that are within the realm of possibility for the surety's bond program for the contractor.

Apart from telling the contractor that a certain line of credit has been extended, the producer and the underwriter come to terms on how much they believe the contractor can handle. They do not tell the contractor since their agreement is not a formal credit extension, but the contractor usually knows what his limits are. If he does not know this, he may think he can assume more work than he can realistically handle, an assumption that would greatly concern the underwriter.

When the surety does extend a line of credit for future jobs, the contractor should expect that the surety will limit the work to be undertaken to jobs that are similar to past jobs and that the surety will look for the contractor to show continued financial success. It is also likely that the surety will analyze work in process. The extra work associated with preparation of documents when a line is extended makes the system less than attractive for any but the largest of contractors who frequently give bids and who would be regularly organizing this information in any event. These contractors, however, are generally big enough that they do not require a formal extension of a line of credit. Interoffice discussions between underwriters may be reduced on cases where a line of credit has been extended, but the reduction is so minor the contractor is probably never even aware of it.

## MEDICAL PROFESSIONAL LIABILITY INSURANCE

Much has been written about who professionals are and what occupations are considered professions. There is not total agreement on either point. Ronald C. Horn, in *On Professions, Professionals, and Professional Ethics* (one of the texts in the CPCU program), describes seven desirable characteristics that make an occupation a profession:

1. A commitment to high ethical standards;
2. A prevailing attitude of altruism;
3. Mandatory educational preparation and training;
4. Mandatory continuing education;
5. A formal association or society;
6. Independence; and with reservations,
7. Public recognition as a profession.[5]

Horn further comments that these characteristics are not absolute. No profession meets all perfectly. Some occupations not considered to be professions meet many of the criteria, and there are differences in the degree to which the "recognized" professions meet the criteria.

An important point to remember is that it may seem easy to sit back and say that occupation A is a profession, while B is not, but in the end, as far as the insurer is concerned, it is up to the courts to decide whether someone is a professional and whether he or she is in an occupation considered a profession. Up to the present time, the courts have tended to expand the definitions of professionals and professions. At the same time, there has been an increased tendency on the part of the public to sue those who have been traditionally viewed as professionals. Two decades ago, it was unusual for a person to sue his or her family doctor. The doctor was a family friend. Today, as medicine becomes more and more specialized, it also becomes more and more depersonalized. There is little hesitation before a patient sues the doctor, especially when the doctor is a specialist with whom the patient has had no previous dealings and with whom the patient contemplates no further dealings.

## Professional Liability Claims

Some of the factors involved in the reporting and settlement of professional liability claims are quite important to the underwriting of the line and are discussed below.

**Out of Court Settlements.** Most liability claims against persons insured are settled out of court. Additionally, the option to settle out of court under most liability policies rests with the insurance company that provides the applicable liability coverage. In auto insurance, for example, when the insured/defendant is at fault, if the plaintiff/claimant will settle for $50,000 (and if $50,000 is within the policy limits), the liability insurer has complete freedom to settle for that amount out of court. The insured has no voice in the decision.

Historically, however, there has been a different pattern in professional liability. An out of court settlement is, in a sense, an admission of guilt or negligence, and for a professional, such an admission could have a serious impact on the reputation of the insured. Consider, for example, a general surgeon who removes what is believed to be a diseased organ that subsequently proves to be normal. Although the negligence is quite clear, the public admission of negligence that an out of court settlement implies might significantly affect the ability of the surgeon to attract patients in the future. The surgeon may wish the claim to be resolved through the legal process because the court might find in his or her favor. Conversely, an out of court settlement might be preferred to avoid publicity.

In the past, professional liability policies almost always included a condition that required the insured (the professional) to consent to any out of court settlement. Unlike an auto liability case, before an out of court settlement was possible the insurer needed the permission of the insured.

The trend is moving away from this pattern. In most areas of professional liability, claims have become so large and so serious that insurance companies insist on the right to settle out of court without the consent of insureds. At present, some professional liability policies contain the traditional condition and some do not. It should be obvious that the difference is significant to the professional liability underwriter.

**Res Ipsa Loquitur.** Because professionals are reluctant to testify against one another, the doctrine of *res ipsa loquitur* (the thing speaks for itself) applies in many professional liability trials. Consider the example of a surgeon who sews up an incision, leaving a pair of scissors inside the patient. If the patient sues the surgeon for malpractice (a form of professional liability), the normal rules of procedure for a negligence trial demand that the plaintiff (patient) prove that the defendant (surgeon) was negligent. But the patient usually has no witnesses to support the negligence claim. The patient cannot testify to the surgeon's negligence because the patient was unconscious during the surgery. It is also unlikely that other members of the surgical team will testify against the surgeon who heads the team.

At that point, the plaintiff's attorney may argue that the doctrine of *res ipsa loquitur* applies. In effect, the attorney is saying that since scissors are not usually found in the human body, the burden of proof (or the burden of persuasion) shifts from the plaintiff to the defendant. It becomes the duty of the defendant to prove that the scissors are in the incision for some reason other than the surgeon's negligence. If the judge accepts this argument, the jury will be instructed that unless the surgeon proves that he or she was not negligent, it must find for the patient.

**The Claims Reporting "Tail."** In most lines of insurance, claims are reported promptly. When a serious auto accident occurs, it takes only a few moments to determine whether or not someone has been injured or killed and if property has been damaged. When a building burns, the process of determining the amount of damage can begin, literally, as soon as the ashes begin to cool. The result is that most property damage claims can be settled within weeks, and the amounts involved in even serious bodily injury claims can be reasonably estimated shortly after the accident.

The nature of professional liability, on the other hand, is that many injuries will not be recognized or claims reported until years after the professional act occurred. Consider a physician who mistreats a patient. The effect on the body of the patient might not show itself for five years, and it will be at that time that the claim for damages is filed. Experience has taught professional liability underwriters that although some malpractice claims will be reported within a few months or a year of treatment, some will not be reported for three, four, or five years. According to the National Association of Insurance Commissioners malpractice closed claim study, 84.5 percent of all claims are reported within twenty-four months of occurrence. At thirty-six months, 93.7 percent are reported; and by five years, 98.1 percent are reported.[6] A second lag, that from report to disposition, occurs in professional liability claims as well as in many nonprofessional liability lines.

In response to the lag between the event and the reporting of a claim, medical professional liability insurers introduced policies written on a claims-made basis. Medical professional liability insurance was one of the first lines in which this coverage was used and is currently one of the lines in which its use is most prevalent. Although some of the specifics are different, most of the concepts about claims-made coverage introduced in Chapter 8 are equally applicable to medical professional liability insurance.

## Legal Doctrines

Certain legal doctrines take on a special, and sometimes different, meaning when applied to professional liability claims, especially those for medical professional liability. These doctrines include the proof of negligence, statutes of limitations, the use of expert testimony, and informed consent.

**Application of Negligence Concept.** The same concept of negligence used in cases against nonprofessionals explained in Chapter 2 is also used in cases against professionals. The difference lies in the idea of the standard of care. The professional is held to a higher standard of care than is a nonprofessional. The professional has usually mastered some specialized body of knowledge, presents himself or herself as having done so, and is therefore held responsible for having done so. For example, an insurance producer who advertises that he has completed courses in workers compensation and is an expert and professional in the area would probably be held to a higher standard of care by a court than would an insurance producer selling all lines and not advertising a specialty in any one area.

**Statutes of Limitations.** Statutes of limitations, as the name implies, are legislative creations. They designate the time period within which legal actions can be brought. The purpose is to protect defendants from old or outdated claims brought after a lapse of time has increased the difficulty of obtaining evidence. In most cases involving bodily injury, the requirement to bring a timely action does not place an unreasonable burden upon the plaintiff. With most injuries, the injury itself and the existence of negligence as a cause are ascertainable at the time of the occurrence.

As mentioned, however, in medical cases and to an extent in all professional liability situations, the person damaged may not be aware that an injury has occurred. To partially mitigate the severity of the statutes' bar to recovery, the courts have said that the date of the occurrence of the negligent act and therefore the point in time from which the statute of limitations begins is the "end of treatment."[7] In addition, a physician's knowledge of a mishap was defined by one court as "fraudulent concealment" (fraud universally nullifies the statutes).[8] These distinctions became less necessary as the *discovery rule* was developed to deal with the problem of fairness created by the statutes. Under this rule, the cause of action runs from the time the plaintiff discovers or, by exercise of reasonable diligence, should have discovered, that an injury has been suffered. The rationale behind the rule is simple:

> Where a choice must be made between the defendant's problem of lost evidence, faded memories and missing witnesses on the one hand, and a deprivation to the plaintiff of any and all remedy for the wrong done. . .on the other, the law must be construed in favor of the blamelessly ignorant plaintiff and against the interests and conveniences of the wrongdoer.[9]

The rule was originally used in cases where a foreign body, such as a sponge or surgical instrument, was found within the patient's body cavity. Later, the same reasoning was applied to sterilization cases when the injury—loss of fertility—was not discovered until after the time period specified in the statutes had passed.[10] About three-fourths of the states have applied some form of discovery rule. Since 1975, a number of states under pressure to ameliorate the "malpractice crisis" have modified their laws to specify a maximum period, regardless of circumstances, in which a suit can be brought against health care providers.[11]

The open-ended nature of the discovery rule and the tradition of not beginning the running of the statutes for minors until they reach majority have placed a burden on the medical profession. The judiciary, for the most part, has concluded that extending the statutes by use of the discovery rule does not place an unreasonable burden on defendants. Legislatures, pressed by the medical profession to alleviate the malpractice crisis, have come to the opposite conclusion in many jurisdictions.

**Expert Testimony.** With regard to changes in court procedures that affect the plaintiff's chances for recovery in litigation, the liberalization of the rules regarding the admissibility of expert testimony are the most significant. Expert testimony, of course, is an exception to the general rule barring opinion evidence. Its use is warranted when the subject matter of the testimony is distinctly related to matters beyond the understanding of the average layperson. In medical malpractice litigation, expert testimony is required at every turn (an earlier section describes the reluctance of some doctors to testify against their colleagues). A qualified expert must establish the standard of care required of a provider, document the defendant's departure from the standard, and link the departure to the injury incurred by the plaintiff.

The qualification of an expert witness to testify is tied to the definition of the standard of care required. In the past, the definition of the standard carried a geographic constraint making it more difficult for plaintiffs to pursue their cases. In order to be allowed to testify, the expert medical witness was required to have knowledge of the particular standards existing in the community where the incident giving rise to the claim occurred. Expertise in medicine relevant to the specific injury would not qualify a person to address the court as to the community standard required of the defendant. The *locality rule,* as it was called, defined the duty owed in terms of the ordinary care, skill, and diligence employed by physicians and surgeons in the same general neighborhood and in the same line of practice. This geographic constraint, unknown outside the United States and not developed even here until the late 1800s, was established to protect rural practitioners from being judged by the standards of their urban colleagues who possessed greater skill because of their expanded opportunities for experience.[12]

There were two problems with the locality rule. First, the scarcity of experts in any community both willing and able to testify deprived plaintiffs of their common law right to recover damages through the judicial process. Second, the local standards might be inadequate and unsafe. For these and other reasons, the definition of locality has been expanded in recent years. Typical phrasing requires the witness to possess and exercise the standard employed in the same or similar communities. In turn, the term "community" has been extended and defined as the medical service area or region. In one case, the court held the following:

> . . .the time has come when the medical profession should no longer be Balkanized by the application of varying geographic standards. . .the proper standard is whether the physician has exercised the degree of care and skill of the average qualified practitioner, taking into account the advances in the profession. In applying this standard it is permissible to consider the medical resources available to the physician as one circumstance in determining the skill and care required.[13]

**Informed Consent.** Informed consent means that the patient has been apprised of the nature of the proposed treatment, alternative forms of treatment, and the potential benefits and potential risks. The court's attitude toward informed consent has shifted. At one time the standard was what the average physician would disclose in like circumstances. However, in addition to the possibility of being self-serving, this interpretation requires that the standard for disclosure be established by expert testimony. As a practical matter, physicians who have been helpful on the negligence issues have been unwilling to support the patient-plaintiff on the consent issue.[14] The courts, in many instances, have rewritten the rules governing informed consent to require more complete disclosure to patients of the risks of the various procedures, the alternative forms of therapy available to treat their condition, and the consequences of doing nothing.[15]

## Physicians and Surgeons Professional Liability Insurance Coverage

Professional liability insurance is required to protect the physician or surgeon from liability arising from professional acts or omissions. This insurance differs from other forms of liability insurance in several important respects. First, liability is not restricted to that "caused by accident" but applies broadly to any liability arising from rendering or failing to render professional services. The harm caused to a claimant frequently results directly from what the professional person intended to do but which nevertheless resulted in unintended injury.

Second, in the standard form, the major insuring clause uses the word "injury." There is no reference to *bodily* injury, *personal* injury, or property damage. Although the principal exposure to loss is bodily injury liability, coverage is provided for all injuries including intangible ones such as mental suffering, humiliation, invasion of privacy, and defamation as long as loss derives from an act or omission of a professional nature.

Third, the professional liability insurance provided by most standard insurers writing primary limits has no limit per accident or occurrence and no separate limit for property damage. Coverage was traditionally written with a *limit per claim* and, almost invariably, with an aggregate limit of liability applying for each year of coverage. The per claim wording, although of long standard, was construed to allow separate recoveries up to the per claim maximum (1) for the patient or the patient's estate under a wrongful death action; (2) for the patient's spouse to recover medical expense, loss of service, loss of consortium, and so on; and (3) for the patient's minor children, or, perhaps, other dependent relatives when the claims or suits are brought as separate actions. Insurers sometimes paid their aggregate limit (generally, three times the per claim limit) in cases involving bodily injury to a single patient on this basis. For this reason, some insurers revised the prior "per claim" wording in favor of a limit *per claim per patient* or a limit *per medical incident.*

The insuring clauses and exclusions of professional liability policies are tailored to the needs of the insured. For individual physicians and surgeons, the company agrees to do the following:

> ...pay on behalf of the insured all sums which the insured shall become legally obligated to pay as damages because of injury arising out of the rendering of or failure to render, during the policy period, professional services by the individual insured, or by any person for whose acts and omissions such insured is legally responsible, except as a member of a partnership, performed in the practice of the individual insured's profession described in the declarations including service by the individual insured as a member of a formal accreditation or similar professional board of a hospital or professional society.[16]

A separate insuring agreement with nearly identical language picks up all the liability for the acts and omissions of the partnership.

The first insuring agreement covers all liability arising out of the practice of the insured's profession. It covers personal acts of the insured for all damages that arise from any type of professional service. It covers the liability of the insured for acts and omissions of employees or associates (but not partnership liability, which is handled by a separate insuring agreement). It does not cover the personal liability of the employees or associates for which separate provision must be made.

The following are exclusions under the policy for individual physicians and surgeons:

1. Injury arising out of criminal acts of the insured
2. Liability due to insured's position as proprietor, superintendent, or executive officer of a hospital, sanitarium, or related facility
3. Partnership liability
4. Bodily injury to employees arising out of and in the course of employment by the insured
5. Liability under workers compensation or similar laws

## Underwriting Professional Liability Insurance for Physicians and Surgeons

To properly underwrite medical professional liability, the underwriter must be familiar with the factors likely to increase or decrease an insured's exposure to loss. These factors differ from one subline to the next within this line of insurance as well as from one class (or subclass) to the next within each subline. Although the underwriter should consider these differences and evaluate risks on a case-by-case basis, there are basic characteristics that an underwriter will look for in the evaluation of any professional risk. They include fundamental underwriting information provided by the applicant (personal and educational background, current practice, vicarious liability exposures, and claim history), the applicant's loss control activities, and the presence (or absence) of nonprofessional coverage.

**Underwriting Information (The Application).** Information on a medical professional liability insurance application for a physician or surgeon is required in five areas. They include personal information, educational background, the current medical practice or specialty, vicarious liability exposures, and the applicant's claim history.

***Personal Information.*** Personal information includes name, address, telephone number, social security number (for identification), as well as date and place of birth. Age, while it cannot be used to disqualify an applicant, may suggest a need for closer analysis of the practice and the extent to which the physician has updated his or her knowledge and skills. The physical and mental capacity to carry on an active professional life are assumed to diminish with age, but the underwriter cannot assume or generalize about how age affects a particular person's capacities.

Country of birth is a consideration if medical training and education were not completed in the United States. It may affect a person's ability to communicate with patients and may indicate that the physician may not reside permanently in the U.S. The latter fact could increase the cost of defense of a claim or make rebuttal of allegations against an insured more difficult.

***Educational Background.*** Information about the educational background of the applicant is not limited to the medical school he or she attended. Also required is information about postgraduate training, board certifications, continuing education, and previous practice since graduation.

*Medical School.* The first question about educational background invariably relates to the medical school attended and year of graduation. Medical schools differ in reputation but, with a few historical exceptions, offer the same opportunity for a satisfactory education. With the exception of Canadian schools, the underwriter should not immediately assume that foreign medical graduates (FMGs) have the same foundation in the basic sciences and clinical medicine as graduates of United States schools. Considering the number of foreign medical schools, variation in expertise can be expected. The Educational Council for Foreign Medical Graduates is an organization established to evaluate the competence of foreign medical school graduates in the United States. Certification by this council indicates that an individual has met standards established by the council in a number of areas including use of the English language.

*Postgraduate Training.* Perhaps even more important than the medical school attended is the extent and character of the physician's postgraduate education. Generally, at least one year is spent in an internship in which physicians rotate through the principal medical and surgical departments of a hospital broadening their basic knowledge of medical practice. With the first year completed, the physician then trains for any number of years in a residency program in the specialty that has been chosen. In addition to residency programs, a number of leading medical institutions offer fellowship programs for further training and/or specialization in a particular field. For all these programs, it is important to know where the applicant trained and whether or not the residency programs were completed. One way for foreign medical school graduates to enhance their credentials is to complete an extended residency at one of this country's major teaching hospitals or medical complexes. The length of time in training is linked to competency in private practice.[17] In all of these matters, the type of training received must be noted for later comparison with what the physician actually does in day-to-day practice.

*Board Certification.* Another matter of importance is board certification. The training and experience gained during residency and the first years of practice may qualify a person for certification or recertification by an American Board of Medical or Surgical Specialties after postgraduate education is completed. This is different from state licensure, which is the minimum requirement to practice any type of medicine. Licensure is required, while certification is this country's voluntary mechanism for establishing additional credentials in a particular area of medicine. It is the opinion of many that the board certified specialist is more likely to provide quality care than a noncertified professional.

Applications usually inquire into a physician's membership in other professional associations and specialty societies. Membership in these groups is usually considered desirable, but studies have *not* shown that such membership or activity affects professional competence.[18] Membership in specialty societies requiring extensive continuing education might be more of an advantage.

*Continuing Education.* Information on the extent of a physician's continuing education is another underwriting criterion which has gained acceptance. There is little doubt that practitioners who keep up to date with developments in their area of specialization render a higher quality of medical care than those who do not. In fact, competence has been observed to decline fifteen to twenty years after medical school graduation, a decline presumably based on a failure of many physicians to keep up with emerging trends in medicine.[19] Reading has been observed to be one of the best ways to update medical knowledge, but this is not an easy item to monitor.[20] Active participation in medical audits of a hospital medical staff is another method of keeping skills up to date.

Applications frequently ask whether or not a physician has participated in continuing education programs in recent years, and some ask for the applicant's medical education number assigned by the American Medical Association (AMA). The difficulty here, of course, is appraising the value of continuing education. Additionally, various studies have reached different conclusions about the effectiveness of continuing education on practice habits.[21] All other things being equal, participation in continuing education suggests that the physician will be more competent, although the significance of its effect is difficult to measure.

*Previous Practice After Formal Training.* Final questions in this section of the standard application would ask where the physician has practiced since completion of formal training and in which jurisdictions medical licenses are held. This would include service rendered while in the military or other public service organizations as well as private practice in a locale other than the current one. These questions round out the section and allow the physician or surgeon to give a full account of previous experiences. With this information, the underwriter can see not only that all time is accounted for but also can verify the applicant's professional reputation.

Verifying the physician's responses to many of the questions in this section—as well as the responses to those of the next section—can be done by consulting the county medical society catalogs and various almanacs maintained by national societies.

***Current Practice.*** The third section of the application relates to current practice, and the first questions in this section solicit information to aid in the proper classification of the physician by specialty and rating class. The application usually provides a comprehensive though not exhaustive list of specialties, which the physician checks. These specialties correspond with those for which the ISO has established codes, which in turn roughly correspond to the specialty categories used by the AMA. Once specialty is established, other questions are asked to determine the appropriate classification to which the physician will be assigned.

Other information about current practice includes principal place(s) where offices are maintained. Geographic area, of course, determines rating territory, which is of primary importance. Urban areas traditionally generate greater claim activity than rural areas, and territorial differentials may or may not adequately compensate for these differences.

Hospital affiliation is another consideration in evaluating a practitioner. The application generally asks where and what type of privileges are maintained. If a physician is active on the medical staff of a facility connected with a medical school or affiliated with a medical school with respect to a residency program, the quality of medical care provided is likely to be above average. Of course, such a physician may be involved in diagnosing and treating a patient population giving rise to greater exposure than another physician practicing in a community hospital without the same visibility and reputation, so the preferred risk is not easily selected. If a physician's medical privileges have been revoked or restricted or if a physician has been placed on probation for any reason, a thorough explanation and investigation are required. In fact, checking on the good standing of any physician at the hospitals where privileges are or have in the past been maintained is good practice. It is particularly important when the physician is unknown in the underwriter's community.

Other standard inquiries include whether or not a physician's license to prescribe or dispense narcotics has been refused, suspended, or revoked; whether the physician has ever been treated for alcoholism, narcotics addiction, or mental illness; whether the physician has incurred or become aware of any chronic illness or physical defect that impairs, or could tend to impair, the ability to practice medicine; and whether or not the physician has ever been convicted of any crime. A final question is whether any insurer has ever canceled, declined coverage, or refused renewal for professional liability insurance in recent years. If any of these questions is answered in the affirmative, further investigation is in order.

Some insurers ask if the physician specializes in weight control work (other than by diet or exercise) that does not comply with the highest standards of the medical profession. Others ask to what extent surgical procedures done at the office or other similar nonhospital facilities include the administration of anesthesia (other than topical or by means of local infiltration). A positive answer here would alert the underwriter and require further investigation.

Other questions would be related to patient load, gross income, and advertising practices. The answers to these questions can be used in conjunction with other information to evaluate the character of a physician's practice. A credit report can sometimes be useful as can an inspection of the premises where the applicant conducts his or her principal practice. Finally, reputation can be checked by informal inquiry. Most insurers specializing in this line are able to accomplish this without being obtrusive.

When underwriting a risk, the underwriter must determine if the rate prescribed is adequate. That is, even considering the differentiation in rates according to medical specialty, does the rate (which applies per doctor/by specialty) reflect the exposure presented? There are many intraspecialty variables that affect the adequacy of the premium.[22] Included among them are the patient load, whether or not, and how much, surgery is performed, extent of referrals, types of treatments, and so on. Physicians close to retirement who have reduced their work load, stopped performing surgery, and avoid hazardous procedures present a much different exposure than a doctor in the same specialty that is at the peak of his or her career and is involved in all aspects of the particular specialty.

***Vicarious Liability Exposures.*** The fourth section of the application requests information regarding liability that may arise because of the personal acts of others connected with the insured physician's practice.

*Sole Proprietor, Partnership, or Corporation.* The first question is whether the physician practices as a sole proprietor, a one-person corporation, a medical partnership, or as a medical service corporation or professional association composed of more than one physician. The second question concerns the persons the physician employs or supervises, and the third concerns the physician's involvement in certain types of business enterprises, primarily with respect to the ownership and operation of hospitals or clinics with bed and board facilities.

The first is a coverage question—does the physician need coverage for his or her partnership or corporation exposure in addition to coverage for his or her personal interests? To provide coverage for the partnership or corporation, most insurers require that all partners or members (stockholders) of the professional corporation also be insured by that insurer. This requirement, although desirable from an underwriting standpoint, obviously complicates the provision of insurance to established physician groups where the individuals are not all in the same insurance company.

*Physician Employees.* The vicarious liability a physician incurs because of persons employed is another exposure that requires consideration. A physician or physician group may employ other physicians, as well as other professional and paraprofessional personnel for whom the practitioner or group is responsible under the doctrine of *respondeat superior.* (Of course, even without the vicarious aspects of liability, the physician or group could be held directly liable for negligence in the selection of unqualified personnel.) An employed physician in this context should be distinguished from the employee/stockholder or partner of a professional corporation or partnership who is more appropriately referred to as a "member" of the corporation or partnership rather than an "employee." The optimal situation, of course, is for the physician employee to be insured in the same insurance company as the physician employer. In fact, unless this is the case, some insurers will not cover the employer's vicarious liability for the acts of a physician employee. At a minimum, the underwriter must have the physician employee complete an application to see that he or she is well qualified and should collect such additional premium as the situation warrants.

*Nonphysician Employees.* In addition to physicians, other classes of professionals and paraprofessionals may be employed. They include registered nurses (RNs), licensed practical or vocational nurses (LPNs or LVNs), radiology and laboratory technicians, physical, occupational, and inhalation therapists, and a variety of others. The type and number of employees is generally related to the physician employer's or physician group's specialization. For instance, a cardiologist may employ a technician certified in electrocardiography, and a neurologist may employ a technician certified in electroencephalography.

Physician assistants (PAs) may also increase a practitioner's exposure, depending on what the assistant does. The possible range is fairly broad. In rural areas, the PA may work in locations remote from the supervising physician for days at a time, much like the nurse practitioner. In urban medical centers they work directly under the physician or surgeon doing whatever is requested. For example, working for an orthopedist may involve anything from removing casts to setting simple fractures not requiring the physician's full attention. However, a PA can get involved in much more complex procedures, and it is generally assumed that the risk of a PA varies directly with the risk of the physician or surgeon being assisted.

Pathologists and radiologists are two classes of specialists that routinely employ a large number of technicians. Individually, each technician does not create a significant exposure, but taken as a group, they may. If the radiological or clinical laboratory is not connected with any hospital facility, a slight additional charge may be made to cover the contingent liability the physician incurs in employing these personnel. If the physician supervises employees of another organization (generally a hospital), the situation is again more complex. Some insurers simply ignore this additional exposure, while others go to the opposite extreme, either declining coverage or making an additional charge for every employee supervised. The data on losses in this area are not readily available, so it is unclear what the appropriate response really is.

***Claim History.*** The fifth and final section of the physicians' application concerns claims or suits in which the practitioner may have been involved. The application asks for information about the medical facts of the case, including but not limited to the name, age, and sex of the patient; the dates and type of treatment and/or surgery that led to the allegations; the nature of the actual allegations in the claim; and whether or not suit was ever filed. If the case is recent, within about the last five years, it is appropriate that the applicant submit complete copies of office and hospital records for the review of the underwriter and/or the underwriter's medical consultant. In addition to these matters, it is important to know what other physicians or hospital(s) were involved in the claim and the current status of the case. Status here means whether or not the claim is open and, if so, whether the physician's insurer has indicated a desire to settle. If applicable, information on the amount of the claimant's settlement demand or the defendant's settlement offer should be included or developed by the underwriter. If the claim has been closed, the manner of disposition should be indicated as well as the amount, if any, paid by the applicant's policy and the total paid by the policies or resources of all other defendants. To facilitate checking this information, the insurer defending the physician should be indicated as well as the policy number of the contract under which the claim is being handled. Although some insurers provide special forms for providing claim information, the more common request is for the physician to provide a comprehensive description typed under his or her own letterhead.

The analysis of this claim information requires access to personnel with medical and legal backgrounds. It requires an appraisal not only of what happened in a particular set of circumstances, but of what these facts imply about the physician's practice of medicine. The warning signs to watch for include the performance of procedures outside the physician's areas of competence; the inability to recognize limitations; the delay or refusal to call in consultants; incomplete workups and diagnostic decisions that are not only incorrect but unfounded; inadequate and unorganized medical records; carelessness and inattention to established medical protocols; and, finally, attitudes that indicate insensitivity toward patients.

**Loss Control.** Loss control has always been important to medical professionals. The following are some of the many fairly simple steps a physician can take to reduce the chance of being successfully sued:

- Physicians should not tell their patients or the patients' attorneys about the existence of professional liability insurance. Merely mentioning the insurance could encourage a lawsuit or encourage a demand for higher damages.
- Physicians should not perform operations until the hospital charts have been checked to be sure of the patients' identities and of the operations to be performed.
- Physicians should not make any statements which might be construed as admission of fault.
- Physicians should maintain a sound attitude, professional manner, and tactful approach toward each patient and the patient's family.
- Physicians should not make it a habit to diagnose and instruct patients over the phone. Such instructions can easily be misunderstood.
- Physicians should carefully delegate and supervise the duties of their employees.
- Physicians should frequently check the condition of any equipment used.
- Physicians should maintain a complete and accurate history of each patient's case.
- Physicians should refrain from over-optimistic prognoses and promising too much to the patients.
- Physicians should keep inviolate all confidential matters.
- Fees should be explained completely and understood in advance.
- Physicians should know and abide by any legal duties toward patients.
- If physicians are to be absent from their practice, they should make available or recommend a qualified substitute.
- Physicians should be careful to instruct properly, render sufficient care, and make themselves available to all patients.

The insurer can also do other things that will affect the losses paid. Among them is claim administration, important for the satisfactory settlement of individual cases as well as for its advance notice of emerging trends for actuaries and ratemakers. In addition, insurers should find ways to encourage physicians to report medical injuries when they occur rather than when claims actually arise. This type of reporting (which might not go directly to an insurer) might allow injury control techniques to be applied that are unworkable when emphasis is given only to claims. This type of approach, even more than a change in form from the occurrence to the claims-made basis, could dramatically affect the long-term stability of this market.

**Nonprofessional Coverage.** Professional liability coverage underwriters are also concerned with the nonprofessional coverage carried by their insureds. The distinction between a professional and a nonprofessional exposure is not always clear. For example, is the collapse of an examining table when a patient lies on it during a routine physical examination a professional liability exposure or a premises-operations exposure?

Problems are reduced when the professional and nonprofessional coverages are written with the same insurer, but due to the limited number of professional liability insurers, this is not always possible. A more common practice is to confirm that the physician or surgeon has both coverages with adequate limits. Thus, any questions would more likely arise between the two insurers as to which is responsible rather than a question as to the existence of coverage at all. If there are widely differing limits between the professional and nonprofessional coverages, problems can arise as injured parties (and the doctor defendant) attempt to place the accident causing injury within the coverage of the policy with the higher limits.

## PROFESSIONAL LIABILITY INSURANCE FOR INSURANCE AGENTS AND BROKERS

Professional liability insurance for men and women working in the field of insurance has been the subject of much study and much litigation. Those who study and underwrite professional liability for other professions also gather a great deal of information about professional liability for their own profession. Further, members of the public who deal with agents and brokers do not seem to hesitate to file claims against insurance professionals, perhaps on the assumption that agents and brokers carry large amounts of insurance on themselves.

Selling insurance on behalf of insurance companies is not considered one of the traditional professions such as medicine, law, accountancy, engineering, or architecture, but the legal responsibilities of an insurance agent or broker are beginning to require that he or she perform as a professional. The field of insurance is growing more complex; yet some producers operate without the years of professional education and training that is typical of other professions.

The professional liability of an insurance agent or broker can emanate from two sources. It is possible to be both agent and broker and to have professional responsibilities to both the insurer and the insured. An agent has a duty to the insurer to act only as authorized by contract. The agent is bound to exercise good faith, loyalty, and honesty toward the principal (the insurer). If the agent fails to use reasonable care, diligence, and good judgment and if this failure is the proximate cause of a loss to the insurer, the agent can be found legally liable. The agent is also bound to follow and carry out the principal's instructions. For example, if the agent fails to cancel an unwanted policy or if the agent exceeds the authority given by the insurer, the agent can be legally liable.

Brokers have been held liable for damages when they failed to obtain insurance for a client. The failure to notify a client of the inability to obtain insurance also can result in liability. In the case of *Hardt* v. *Brink,* a broker was held liable to his client because he failed to advise the client of the insurance requirement involved in a lease of premises and of potential liability to a landlord under a lease.[23] The court held that the broker had represented himself as an insurance expert and had assumed the duty of advising his client as to the insurance needs of his business. Many other cases exist where agents or brokers have been found liable to clients. In most states, case law in this field has developed to the point where an insurance agent or broker finds it difficult to defend himself or herself unless the agent has operated in a professionally prudent manner.

As illustrated in the *Hardt* v. *Brink* case, insurance agents and brokers are held to a high standard of care, especially if they hold themselves out as experts or professionals. During recent years, producer associations have stressed the need for continuing education, and state licensing examination have been upgraded. Producers have wide opportunities to increase their professional skills through national educational programs. The courts have taken the position that the public can expect professional performance from men and women who have ample opportunity to acquire professional knowledge and skill.

One of the reasons for an increase in claims against producers is that insurance companies are no longer willing to overlook producers' errors and omissions. In the past, many insurance companies were willing to pay losses caused by agent or broker error, but now these same companies expect the producer to assume that responsibility. Now, most of the burden of careless or unprofessional acts by producers has been transferred to the producer or to the professional liability insurer.

## Agents and Brokers Coverage

Professional liability insurance for agents and brokers is usually called *errors and omissions* (E&O) *coverage.* The agents and brokers E&O policy agrees to pay on behalf of the insured all sums for which the insured becomes legally liable arising from any negligent act, error, or omission of the insured or employees that takes place in the conduct of the business of a general agent, an insurance agent, or a broker. In addition to legal liability, the insurer also agrees to cover defense costs. As is the case with most other professional liability policies today, the E&O policy usually is written on a claims-made basis.

The underwriter should realize that the professional services provided by insurance agents and brokers have expanded greatly from the original task of selling and placing coverage. The concept of full financial services is a reality for many agents and brokers. Professional activities now include notarizing documents, life insurance and mutual fund sales, premium financing, consulting, advising, loss control engineering, risk management, claims adjusting, and public relations.

Most underwriters will agree that the E&O policy covers all activities that are related to the sale or placement of insurance but many feel that other activities present exposures not intended in the E&O policy. Often the underwriter will require either additional premium or a separate policy to cover activities such as pension or employee benefit plan preparation and accounting or tax work. Some underwriters will provide coverage for these activities for an additional premium while others exclude these activities altogether.

## Underwriting Insurance for Agents and Brokers

A typical application for agents and brokers E&O coverage requests the following underwriting information: name and address of the insured; the number of years he or she has been in the insurance business; the number of years the insured has been licensed as an agent, as a broker, or as a general agent; the names and experience of all members of the firm; the dollar amount of annual gross premium written; the states where the agency or its members are licensed; the names of all insurance companies represented; and whether the insured places business on a brokerage basis and if business is accepted from brokers or other agents.

Underwriting information also includes whether excess and surplus lines or nonstandard business is solicited and negotiated and, if so, what percentage of the total business is nonstandard and where it is placed; whether the insured specializes in any particular type or line of insurance; the claims experience under the E&O coverage; the name of the previous E&O insurer; the total number of persons handling insurance matters; the desired limit of liability and the amount of deductible; and the professional association memberships of the agency and its members. Most E&O underwriters would prefer to write agents and brokers who are members of state and/or local agents' associations and who have professional designations. Such insureds usually are more professional, have larger staffs, and frequently attend association educational programs or clinics that are designed to prevent errors and omissions.

## Typical Claims and Loss Control

The claims that might be expected under an errors and omissions policy are ones that most readers would anticipate. These include the failure to place proper coverage, failure to place any coverage, failure to renew policies, and similar claims resulting from the placement and renewal of policies. Especially in the case of the failure to renew, these losses are often the result of careless clerical work. The loss control measures presented in the next paragraph therefore emphasize office clerical practices. Less prevalent errors and omissions claims include failure to advise the insured of a cancellation and dishonesty or fraud of employees.[24]

One way to prevent errors or omissions is to set up an office management procedure for all important functions of the agency. Communications with the insured, communications with the company, and general office procedures must be well organized if errors and omissions are to be avoided. A useful checklist for effective office management in an insurance agency follows:[25]

1. Continuing education and training for the agent and for the agency staff.
2. Memo pads placed and kept near all telephones. Any agent or staff member taking a phone call should record the client's name, address, and a brief summary of the phone conversation. Any oral binders given over the phone must be recorded.
3. Duplicate diary systems for policy renewals. If one system fails, the other probably will not.
4. Careful communication of the facts to the client in those cases where coverage cannot be bound. When it is necessary to submit applications for underwriting review and when other sources of coverage (assigned risk plans or nonstandard insurers) must be used, the client should be aware that coverage does not become effective until it is approved by a home office underwriter.
5. Careful following of instructions from insurance companies. The companies are the agents' principals and the agent is obligated to follow those instructions.
6. Confirmation of all binders and all important conversations in writing.

7. Completion of forms and requests in duplicate or triplicate. One copy should be kept for diary purposes so that proper follow-up is possible.
8. Carefully informing clients when coverage is limited by endorsement. This is especially important when a renewal policy is issued with coverage more limited than that of the original policy.
9. Checking and proofreading by an experienced employee of all policies and endorsements prior to their delivery to the insured.
10. Careful study of the client's insurance needs. The agent who holds himself or herself out as an insurance expert can be held responsible if the need for some unusual coverage is not called to the client's attention.

## SUMMARY

This text has concentrated on the underwriting of the lines of insurance most often by commercial liability underwriters—auto, general liability, and workers compensation. These are not the only lines of commercial liability insurance, however. There are many "lesser" lines that underwriters occasionally see or that are underwritten by specialty insurers because of their expertise developed in that line of insurance. This chapter examines three of those "other" coverages.

The underwriting of surety bonds, especially contract bonds, is usually handled by a separate bond department at most insurers. Even if an insured approaches an insurer for all coverages, the contract bonds are usually handled separately. A traditional characteristic of contract bonds was that losses were not anticipated. In today's environment (and probably always), this expectation is not realistic. Some contractors will default, and many of the indemnity agreements backing those contractors will be insufficient to cover the losses suffered.

The appendix to this chapter is an excellent summary of factors to consider regarding the contract document itself in contract bond underwriting. It presents from the viewpoint of an attorney many factors that are considered by the contract bond underwriter.

These factors can usually be grouped into considerations about the obligations spelled out in the contract, the obligations of the surety if the contractor defaults, and considerations about the principal or contractor. This last consideration heavily emphasizes a financial analysis of the contractor and an analysis of the type and size of work projects the contractor can reasonably expect to pursue. Contract bond underwriters develop a very close working relationship with the contractors they bond, and this relationship is beneficial to both parties in terms of information exchanged and service rendered.

Professional liability insurance for physicians and surgeons is also a specialty line handled by only a few insurers. However, medical malpractice claims and the insurance to cover them are front page news. All underwriters should at least be familiar with some of the factors considered in the underwriting and the pricing of this line. Commercial liability underwriters should also be familiar with the professional liability coverage of physicians and surgeons since the underwriters may be asked to provide the nonprofessional coverage. The distinction between the two coverages is not always clear, and a doctor with inadequate professional liability insurance may look to his or her nonprofessional liability insurer for coverage on borderline claims.

Professional liability insurance for agents and brokers, errors and omissions or E&O coverage, is a less specialized line than the two others described in this chapter. Many insurers writing this line try to write as many members of a certain association or in a certain state as possible. In addition, many of the loss control suggestions made are equally applicable to the work of an underwriter. For example, confirming in writing all telephone conversations regarding coverage is something every underwriter and every producer should do. Not to do so invites problems.

This text has presented a great deal of information on commercial liability underwriting. Reading and understanding all the material in the text will not make the reader an underwriter. It must be combined with on-the-job experience and knowledge of the insurer's own guidelines and policies. An experienced commercial liability underwriter may have only found only a handful of new ideas in the text—which is really the way it should be. However, it is hoped that these experienced underwriters have also been reminded of some of the reasons behind certain guidelines, have been given some suggestions for organizing their approach to underwriting, and have gained a greater appreciation for the complexities of their job.

# Chapter Notes

1. 53 *Am. Jur.* (2d) Sec. 1, p. 512.
2. In some cases, the performance bond may also include some provision that the work will be free of liens. However, such a provision is not usually as broad as that provided by a separate payment bond.
3. Luther E. Mackall, *Surety Underwriting Manual* (Indianapolis: The Rough Notes Co., 1972).
4. Ronald C. Horn, *Subrogation in Insurance Theory and Practice* (Homewood, IL: Richard D. Irwin, 1964), p. 228.
5. Ronald C. Horn, *On Professions, Professionals, and Professional Ethics* (Malvern, PA: American Institute for Property and Liability Underwriters, 1978), p. 40.
6. National Association of Insurance Commissioners, *Malpractice Claims,* vol. I, No. 4, May 1977, pp. 16-19.
7. Jim M. Purdue, "The Law of Texas Medical Malpractice, Chapter VII: Limitations," *Houston Law Review,* vol. 11, No. 4, May 1974, pp. 828-831.
8. Purdue, Chapter VII: "Limitations," p. 835.
9. Layton v. Allen (246 Atl. 22nd 794).
10. Hays v. Hall, 488 SW 2nd 412 (Texas 1972) quoted by Purdue, "Limitations," p. 842.
11. American Institute of Insurance, *Comparative Analysis of Legislative Changes Related to Medical Malpractice,* 30 June 1975 and update, 1 September 1975.
12. George E. Hall, "The Locality Rule," *The Best of Law and Medicine '68/'70.* Selected articles from the *Journal of the American Medical Association,* 1970, p. 73. Roxanne J. Decyk and Donald J. Hirsch, "The Medical Standard of Care," *Defense of Medical Malpractice Cases,* 1977, No. 4, pp. 29-43.
13. Brune v. Belinkoff, 235 NE 2d 793 (Mass. 1968).
14. Rubsamen, *Professional Liability Newsletter,* vol. IV, No. 9, November 1972.
15. Olmstead v. United States, 277 U.S. 438 (1928); Cobbs v. Grant, 8 Cal. 3d 299 (1972); Govin v. Hunter, 374 P 2d 421 (Wyo. 1962); Berkey v. Anderson, I.C.A. 3d 790 (1969); Canterbury v. Spence, 464 F 2d 772 (1972) The District of Columbia; Wilkinson v. Vessey, 295 A 2d 676 (1972) Rhode Island; quoted and discussed by Rubsamen, *PLN,* vol. IV, No. 9, November 1972.
16. *FC&S Bulletins,* Casualty and Surety Section (Cincinnati, OH: The National Underwriter Co., July 1972), Public Liability, p. Dmp-1.
17. Osler L. Peterson, Leon P. Andrews, Robert S. Spain, and Bernard G. Greenberg, "An Analytical Study of North Carolina General Practice, 1953-54," part II, 31, *Journal of Medical Education,* 12 November 1956, p. 65.
18. Peterson et al., p. 93.
19. Peterson et al., p. 73.

20. Peterson et al., p. 84.
21. Peterson et al., p. 65 and following; also Charles E. Lewis, M.D. and Ruth S. Hassanein, M.S., P.H., "Continuing Medical Education—An Epidemiologic Evaluation, *New England Journal of Medicine,* vol. 282, No. 5, 29 January 1970, pp. 254-259 and Element R. Brown, Jr., M.D., and Henry S. M. Uhl, M.D., "Mandatory Continuing Education—Sense or Non-Sense?" *JAMA,* vol. 213, No. 10, 7 September 1970, pp. 1660-1668.
22. NAIC, *Malpractice Claims,* p. 29.
23. 192 F. Supp. 879, Wash. Dist. Ct. 1961.
24. These typical claims are based on a study by Shand, Morahan and Company of more than 800 claims reported by insured agents in 1975.
25. E. Stewart Ulrich, "A Checklist to Prevent Errors and Omissions Losses," *Underwriters Review,* February 1970.

# APPENDIX

## Understanding Construction Contracts: A Myriad of Special Clauses*

by Overton A. Currie and William E. Dorris

A contract is the primary foundation in virtually every relationship in the world of construction. The contract terms and rules of contract interpretation consequently play a crucial role in defining the duties of the parties. Familiarity with the basic rules of interpretation helps contractors, owners, [sureties], construction managers, architects, and engineers avoid problems that frequently arise during the negotiation, drafting, and performance of their contracts.

Since courts generally uphold freedom of contract, it is imperative for the parties to understand the contractual provisions. A court enforces the contractual language because it presumes that the contract accurately reflects the bargain reached by the parties. If a party later discovers that the contractual promises exceed what it actually had in mind, it will probably be too late to obtain any additional compensation. Of course, this determination usually depends heavily on the terms of the contract.

### "DURING CONSTRUCTION" PROVISIONS

#### Changes

The changes clause is one of the most significant clauses frequently found in the contract between the prime contractor and the owner.

---

*Reprinted with permission from *The Arbitration Journal,* Volume 41, Number 1, March 1986 (New York, NY) pp. 1-19.

The changes clause enables the owner to modify the plans and specifications as the need or desire arises during construction.

The most unusual aspect of the changes clause, which sets construction contracts apart from other types of contracts, is that it typically authorizes the owner to issue unilateral orders directing a deviation from the plans and specifications and allowing for an equitable adjustment to the contract for such change. In most contracts, such a unilateral order is impermissible since there is no "mutual" consent. Usually, the contractor's only remedy is to seek additional compensation if it believes that the equitable adjustment allowed by the owner is insufficient. Normally, however, an owner may not issue change orders that direct the performance of work differing materially from that contemplated in the contract documents. In other words, the changes in the work must be within the general scope of the contract.

Most construction contracts today contain a provision similar to that in Section 12.1.2 of AIA Document A201 (1976), which provides that all changes in the work shall be authorized by written change order signed by both the owner and the architect. Such provisions are valid and binding on the parties in the absence of proof of waiver or an independent contract for performance of the work, and may well prevent the contractor from recovering.[1] For this reason, the importance of the contractor or subcontractor ensuring the issuance of a written work order before performing extra work cannot be overemphasized.[2]

Generally, a court will consider evidence of words, acts, or conduct that could be construed as constituting a waiver, modification, or abandonment of the contract requirement for a written change order or some basis for application of the theory of estoppel. The various theories employed by the courts to avoid operation of this contract requirement have not always been kept distinct in decisions. The courts have used various theories interchangeably.

The general rule is, however, that a waiver or modification can be accomplished not only by express words, but also by acts or conduct of the parties that by implication waive or otherwise derogate the writing requirement. As to what particular acts or conduct are sufficient for this purpose, the decisions are inconsistent. Generally, where the work is performed with the owner's knowledge or was authorized by the owner (rather than by the design professional), a waiver or modification may be found if there are other circumstances tending to show the owner's abandonment of the contract stipulation. Similarly, where the owner has orally agreed or promised to pay additional compensation for the work in question, or has accepted the work in question upon its completion, or where the parties to the contract have entirely or repeatedly disregarded the stipulation, there may be sufficient evidence for a court to find a waiver, modification, or abrogation of the contract provision.

## Time and Scheduling of Performance

Virtually every owner on a construction project attempts to include language in its contract with the prime contractor to the effect that "time is of the essence" on the particular construction project. The purpose of such a provision is to enable the owner to assess damages against a contractor who fails to complete a project on time.

In addition to the general provision that time is of the essence, most construction contracts specifically set forth a time frame for commencement and completion of the construction project. Typically, the provision sets out that the contractor will commence performance of the work within a specified number of days after receipt of the notice to proceed from the owner. Additionally, the contract usually specifies the number of days that the parties agree is required to perform such work. Also, many construction contracts contain time extension clauses that provide for extensions to the scheduled completion date upon the occurrence of certain conditions or circumstances as specified by the clause. By including such a clause, the parties are basically stating their intention that matters beyond the contractor's control will be taken into account in adjusting the time in which the parties can expect that the construction project will be completed.

On a large construction project, monitoring progress in terms of percentage of completion and estimating percentage left to complete is a very difficult process. In order to cope with this situation, techniques such as program evaluation and review techniques (PERT), and critical path method (CPM) have been instituted to assist the contract administrator in determining the progress of the work and to aid in determining the effect of events that delay contract completion. The CPM can be particularly useful in that it offers the owner and contractor the opportunity to identify several types of work activities and monitor their progress against a schedule describing both planned duration of that activity and activity sequencing.

## Method of Payment

Since adequate cashflow is vital to the existence of most contractors, it is essential that they understand the payment provisions of their contract. These terms delineate the method by which their compensation will be computed and when they will receive payment for their work.

There are basically three methods by which the compensation a contractor will receive under the contract can be computed. First, under a fixed-price contract, the contractor agrees to do the specified work for a lump sum. The contractor must make provision in the lump sum for all contingencies during the course of performance. The only possible relief, should costs exceed the contract price, is a change order or an action for damages stemming from owner-caused delays or breaches of contract. Contracts with price escalation clauses, while more realistic in this day of fluctuating inflation rates, are still the exception rather than the rule. Normally, owners who need to fix a specific financial commitment for financing the project will utilize the fixed-price method of calculating compensation.

Second, a unit price payment clause is often generally thought to be a fixed-price contract, since the contractor is paid a fixed amount for each unit of work performed. Since the total number of units is not definite, however, the owner is not guaranteed a maximum price. On the other hand, the contractor risks the possibility that the projected cost for each unit may be higher than anticipated.

The key to successful use of unit price depends on the ability of the contractor and architect to make a reasonably accurate estimate of the number of units of work that will have to be performed. On the basis of this estimate, the contractor will compute the unit price by spreading this costs over the estimated number of units. If the actual number of units turns out to be much lower than originally estimated, however, the contractor will suffer since nonrecurring fixed costs will be higher per unit than estimated. On the other hand, if the original estimate was extremely low, the contractor may make a bountiful profit since the fixed cost per unit of work will be reduced.

Third, a cost-plus payment clause may be utilized. Under a cost-plus contract, contractors face less risk of loss, but are put in a position of trust that forces them to do their best to keep costs down. In bidding on this type of contract, competition revolves around the size of the fee, the size of the guaranteed maximum price (if one is called for), and possibly a difference in the size of allowable overhead charges. Although the fixed fee provides the contractor with some protection, it may prove inadequate to cover expenses if cost and performance time significantly exceed estimates. In such a case, contractors may claim that there has been a "cardinal" change in the contract that entitles them to an increase in their fee. Interestingly, the use of a cost-plus-a-percentage-of-cost system of contracting is prohibited in federal government procurement. The cost-plus-fixed-fee-system, however, is allowed.[3]

One of the most important provisions in the prime contract is the clause stating that the owner will make periodic progress payments to the contractor. Otherwise, the contractor must wait until after completing all the work before payment is made.[4]

One of the more significant aspects of this standard progress payment provision is that it allows payment for materials and equipment not incorporated in the work but delivered and suitably stored at the site, in addition to payment for the percentage completion of the work in place. Without such a provision, a contractor can encounter a serious cash flow problem, because most suppliers demand payment soon after delivery. The contractor will not be entitled to payment for these items until they are incorporated into the work, unless such a clause has been included in the contract.

Though owners have recognized the need of contractors to receive progress payments throughout the life of the job, they have traditionally withheld a portion of the progress payments. The normal construction contract allows the owner to withhold 10 percent of the payments to the contractor. These retained funds then become due the contractor after completion of all the work. It is argued that these retained funds protect the owner in a number of ways. First, they allegedly provide the owner with leverage to insure that the contractor completes the job. Second, it is argued that the retainage protects the owner if the work is not performed in accordance with the contract documents. Finally, the withholding of a portion of the progress payments supposedly discourages undercapitalized or financially troubled contractors from bidding on the job.

Accordingly, contractors must be aware of the existence of any retention provision in the contract. Also, they should perhaps suggest the inclusion of a clause providing for the reduction of the retention at a stage in the performance of the contract where the owner feels more secure.

## Scope of Work

The amount of profit on a project and the scope of the work are inextricably related. Accordingly, contractors must consider the exact language of the provision in their contract with the owner that delineates the scope of work. It is imperative that contractors study the plans and specifications carefully to ensure that they have considered all the work in their bids. Also, it is helpful for the contractor to understand the legal implications of the various types of specifications that may be used.

Generally, there are three types of specifications: design, performance, and proprietary. Design specifications are defined as

> ...specifications in which are stated precise measurements, tolerances, materials, in-process and finished product tests, quality control and inspection requirements, and other information. With regard to design specifications the government accepts general responsibility for design and related omissions, errors and deficiencies in the specifications and drawings.[5]

Performance specifications are the flip side of the coin. Under performance specifications, a contractor accepts general responsibility for design, engineering, and achievement of required performance. General discretion and election as to detail are left to the contractor, and performance specifications are met if the contractor's designed product meets the owner's performance criteria.

Occasionally, a contract will specify a particular name-brand product that is to be furnished and installed. Likewise, the specifications may purport to leave to a contractor the option to obtain items meeting certain requirements, but in fact may be so narrowly drafted that only a sole source can supply the desired item. These are known as proprietary specifications. A contractor who is required to furnish a particular brand-name product where the specifications were supposedly open is entitled to recover the difference in price between the article required to be furnished and that of a substituted "equal" article that would have functioned as well as the brand name required.[6] There is an obligation for the government to accept an "equal" item where the contractor can prove the functional equality.[7] Also, if the named product is properly installed but nonetheless fails to perform adequately, the courts generally hold that the contractor is *not* liable.[8]

Even if the scope of the work clause and specifications are drafted with a great deal of clarity, however, a contractor must realize that the scope of the work includes all work that is indispensable to the performance of the specified work. The fact that this indispensable work is not expressly required by the specifications is no defense.[9]

## LIABILITY PROVISIONS

### Exculpatory Clauses

Contracts frequently contain broad exculpatory clauses in which the owner disclaims any liability for the accuracy of plans, specifications, borings, and other subsurface data. Fortunately for the contractor, many courts have held that these clauses do not have the sweeping effect they are argued to have. In fact, courts normally will not allow such clauses to eliminate the relief provided to the contractor by the different site conditions clause.[10]

Furthermore, even where the contract lacks a differing site conditions clause, but does contain extensive exculpatory language, it may still be possible for contractors to recover if they can show, for example, that an independent subsurface investigation was not feasible, and that they were thus forced to rely on the information provided by the owner.[11] In one case, the county solicited bids for repairs to the piers of a bridge. Even though the contract documents required the contractor to verify all dimensions in the contract documents, the court held that to require the contractor to make diving tests to verify the information supplied by the county placed an undue burden on the contractor. Therefore, it allowed the contractor to recover the increased costs incurred due to the misrepresented conditions in the contract documents.[12]

Some states, however, take an especially hard line in upholding such disclaimers. In Pennsylvania, for example, a contractor cannot recover even when the actual conditions differ greatly from what was represented by the test borings. To recover for subsurface conditions that differ from the contract information supplied by the owner, the contractor in Pennsylvania must show that the owner knew that the test borings were incorrect. Thus, in Pennsylvania a showing of fraud may be necessary to avoid such an exculpatory clause.[13]

**Site Investigation Clause.** Bid invitations commonly require contractors to visit the site prior to compiling their bids. Construction contracts themselves also routinely require contractors to warrant that they have made a site inspection. Such a requirement does not nullify the effect of the differing site conditions clause and does not obligate contractors to discover hidden conditions at their peril.[14] A contractual requirement that the contractor make a site investigation does not obligate bidders to discover hidden subsurface conditions not ascertainable by any reasonable preaward inspection.[15] The adequacy of the site investigation is measured by what a reasonable, intelligent contractor, experienced in the particular field of work involved, could be expected to discover—not what a highly trained geologist might have found.[16]

It should also be pointed out that the term *site* investigation has generally come to mean *sight* investigation, and does not extend to making independent subsurface investigations.[17] Where a site investigation is required, however, if the contractor fails to make any investigation or if the contractor makes a careless or superficial investigation, the contractor will not be allowed to recover for any condition which could have been discovered by a reasonable investigation.[18]

**Subsurface Data.** Perhaps the most important information commonly supplied by the owner is subsurface data. Routinely, owners and their architects/engineers must consider such subsurface data when designing a project. Thus, before the bidding stage, the owner has already accumulated subsurface data through investigation and testing.

Where such subsurface data is included in the information supplied to the contractor while preparing a bid, the contractor generally has a right to rely on the accuracy of such data.[19] The rationale behind the rule of law that the owner warrants the accuracy of affirmative representations made in the bid package regarding subsurface data is compelling. The owner and architect have conducted investigations and have had the opportunity to analyze the information. On the other hand, the contractor often has severe time constraints in bidding a construction project. In addition, it is unrealistic to expect that contractors could perform their own testing of subsurface conditions to verify the data supplied by the owner. In doing so, contractors would almost assuredly incur extra costs, which, when included in their bids, would place them in a noncompetitive position.

It is in the best interests of the owner as well to encourage contractors not to load their bid with contingencies, as would be the case if the contractor could not rely upon the subsurface data supplied by the owner. In some cases, owners may have to incur additional expense based upon the differing site conditions clause where the subsurface data furnished by them is substantially different from that which is encountered by the contractor.[20] The owner, however, would not incur "contingency bidding" in every instance.

**Site Availability.** With the increased use of "fast-track" construction, contractors are frequently complaining of the unavailability of the site for commencement and orderly progression of work. Even where the fast-track method is not used, there are often several subcontractors and trades on large construction projects that need access to the same area at the same time. It is generally the responsibility of the owner's representative in charge of scheduling and sequencing on a job with multiple prime contractors to make sure that such an occurrence does not arise.

The construction process, however, is not an exact science. Where contractors claim that owners are delaying their progress by failing to make the site available for work, the owners often rebut the contractors' claims by stating that site availability problems arise on any construction project and that the contractors are unreasonable in demanding that they should always have free access to any area they desire. The courts have reacted by inquiring as to whether the owner actively interfered with the contractor's access to the job site or whether the delays encountered were of such duration that they were not contemplated by the parties at contract formation.

**No Damages for Delay.** A no-damages-for-delay provision in a contract specifies that the owner will not be liable for the effects of delay attributable to certain specified causes. This clause is another risk-shifting device. Its effect depends on the language used and on the law of the governing jurisdiction. The case of *Christiansen Bros., Inc. v. State of Washington* (1979)[21] is an excellent example of the potentially drastic impact these clauses may have on contractors. In *Christiansen Bros.,* the contractor was required by its contract with the state to perform the mechanical work on two buildings at a state university. The contractor alleged that it was delayed in completing the work under its contract due to design errors, actions against other contractors, and the lack of coordination of the various primes by the state. The contractor brought an action for damages to recover its costs resulting from the delay. The contract provided that "In no event shall any delays or extensions of time be construed as cause or justification for payment of extra compensation to contractor."

The state argued that this clause was a bar to the contractor's claim and the court agreed as it rejected each of the contractor's four arguments. The contractor had first argued that the no-damage clause was inapplicable to its suit for damages since it merely prohibited the recovery of additional compensation. The court, however, rejected this argument since it viewed the two terms, *compensation* and *damages,* as synonymous.

The contractor's second argument was that the clause should not operate to bar damages resulting from obstruction by the owner. The court conceded that active interference by an owner may be outside of the scope of such clauses, but stated that there had been no finding that the state interfered with the contractor's performance.

The court was also unreceptive to the contractor's third argument that the clause violated public policy because it was unconscionable. It held that the clause was not unconscionable, since the contractor was aware of it before submitting his bid and could have added an appropriate contingency to cover the risk.

Fourth, the contractor asserted that the clause tended to inflate the bids and should therefore be considered unenforceable as a matter of public policy. The court held that even if the bids were inflated, the clause was not rendered unenforceable, since it had the beneficial effect of allowing the state to better know the costs of a project before proceeding with construction. Accordingly, the court applied the no-damages clause to bar the contractor's suit.

Such provisions do not always constitute an absolute bar to recovery, however. For example, the New Jersey Supreme Court allowed a contractor to recover for the state's failure to provide timely access to the site, despite the presence of a no-damages clause.[22]

A number of court decisions have established that a contractor may recover in spite of the presence of such a clause in the contract, provided the delay (1) was of a kind not contemplated by the parties in the contract clause;[23] (2) was such as to amount to an abandonment of the contract;[24] (3) was the result of fraud, bad faith, or arbitrary action;[25] (4) was the result of active interference with the contractor's work on the part of the owner, or unreasonable insistence on compliance on the owner's part with a contract provision;[26] or (5) was the result of an unreasonable delay.[27]

Regarding the application of a no-damages clause, courts have adopted a policy of strict construction in determining whether the particular delay was within the contemplation of the parties.[28] Thus, a no-damages-for-delay clause will not be given effect when the delay is beyond that contemplated by the contract, or when the owner actively brings about a delay. If valid and applicable, however, such a clause can have far-reaching and expensive results and its presence or absence in the contractor should always be verified.

## Warranties

In addition to the owner's expectations that the contractor will comply with the plans and specifications on a construction project, the owner also reasonably expects the labor, material, and equipment supplied by the contract to be free from defects for a reasonable period of time. To assure that contractors satisfy their expectations in this regard, owners will seek correction of any defective materials or workmanship by asserting their rights under various "warranties." There are basically two types of warranties on which owners may depend.

**Express Warranties.** Contractors may expressly warrant that the material and workmanship furnished by them is free from defects for a specified period of time. Liability under these express warranties expands the scope of the contractor's responsibility for defective work to extend beyond the date of final acceptance and the express warranties are in addition to other responsibilities of the contractor.

Besides the express warranties that appear in the AIA documents, other warranties have been recognized by the courts. In *Burton-Dixie Corp. v. Timothy McCarthy Construction Co.* (1971), the court specifically held that the one-year warranty provision did not provide an exclusive remedy, nor did it limit the rights under the general warranty of good workmanship. The court stated:

> We agree with this construction of the contract. Article 20 is, as it states on its face, an added guarantee, inserted in the contract to extend rather than limit the contractor's liability for faulty construction. As such, it does not prescribe the owner's exclusive remedy, and it in no way impairs the contractor's general obligation to perform this contract in a proper workmanlike manner. Suing for breach of contract Burton-Dixie did not rely on the special one year guarantee. Therefore, whether the defect appeared in one year of Burton-Dixie's occupancy is immaterial to its right of recovery.[29]

Additional express warranties may be required in connection with equipment supplied by the contractor. Such specific warranties are usually spelled out under the related provisions of the technical specifications. They often are in the nature of guarantees of performance and agreements to repair defects for a specified period of time.

The express warranties required by the contract documents generally begin to run from the date of substantial completion.[30] Other special warranties may commence at delivery of the machinery or commencement of operations.

**Implied Warranties.** When there are no express warranties made by the contractor, many courts at least will imply a warranty of workmanship and materials. This implied warranty may in some instances be longer than the express warranties. Although the general repair warranty in AIA Document A201 ¶ 13.2.2 is limited to one year, the general warranty that materials are new and work is in accordance with the plans and specifications, AIA Document A201 ¶ 4.5.1, is not limited to any particular period, but rather remains in effect throughout the applicable statute of limitations.[31]

Often, contractors will be held to warrant impliedly that the materials and workmanship they supply are sufficient to pass ordinary industry standards. The contractor is usually held to this standard regardless of the existence and duration of express warranties.[32] Other states, however, hold exactly the opposite: that there is no cause of action for an implied warranty of quality of materials or workmanship.[33] The Georgia Court of Appeals [has] held that in the absence of an express warranty, there is no implied warranty in the sale of an existing new house.[34] In cases of personal injury resulting from defective material or workmanship, however, the courts are more willing to find a breach of an implied warranty.[35]

# END OF JOB PROVISIONS

## Termination

Where the scheduling and monitoring systems indicate that the contractor is performing so poorly that the owner is justified in fearing that satisfactory performance and completion will not be achieved within a reasonable time, the owner may wish to terminate the contract. As a result, owners usually include a provision in the prime contract authorizing them to terminate the contractor, to coordinate the completion of the work themselves, and to assess the cost of completion against the contractor. Obviously, it is only logical that the owner would not go to the extra effort and potential extra expense of dismissing one contractor and hiring another unless there has been a total breakdown of communication and negotiation between the owner and prime contractor.

The owner in virtually all contracts reserves a right to terminate the contractor if, in the opinion of the owner (and, in some cases, the architect), the contractor has failed to diligently pursue completion of the project. The courts strictly construe such provisions and, in any event, enforcement of such a provision is only justified where there is a material breach of contract, regardless of whether the contract fails to distinguish among particular breaches.

In addition to having the right to terminate a contractor for default, the federal government includes a clause in its contracts containing the right to terminate a contractor where such termination is "in the best interest of the government." Such a provision is unique because it allows the owner to terminate, without breaching, the construction contract regardless of the lack of fault on the part of the contractor. By including such a clause, the owner maintains the flexibility to totally abandon the contract if the construction project is no longer needed.

In addition, under the standard termination-for-convenience clause, the contractor is not entitled to recover anticipated profits on the portion of the work terminated by the government. While this clause has been used almost exclusively by the federal government in the past, the idea of retaining the right to terminate a construction contract without being liable for claims for anticipated profits by the terminated contractor is growing in favor in the private sector.

## Completion and Acceptance of Work

The date of substantial completion is often a crucial date in any construction litigation. Basically, there are two points connected with substantial completion. First, once substantial completion has been attained, the contractor is often entitled to the balance of the contract price, less the cost of remedying minor defects. Second, liquidated damages may not be assessed after this date.[36]

In many states, substantial completion also marks the commencement of a special limitation period for actions against persons performing or furnishing design, planning, supervision, observation of construction, or construction or any improvement to real property. Typically, these statutes provide an outer time limit for lawsuits for defective construction. The constitutionality of many of these statutes has been challenged because they arguably grant contractors and designers special protection. The jurisdictions are split and each state's provision must be reviewed.

When the work has been substantially completed, the owners have received essentially what they bargained for and the contractors have substantially performed their obligations. The fact that the owners have received the benefit of their bargain gives rise to the fundamental principal that after the date of substantial performance, liquidated damages may not be further assessed.[37] Since the work is usable by the owner, and is essentially what the owner contracted for, the assessment of liquidated damages would be unfair and inequitable.

Substantial completion has been defined in numerous ways and has been the subject of extensive litigation. Generally, when the owner has the use and benefit of the contractor's work and the project is capable of being used for its intended purpose, substantial completion has occurred.[38] *Substantial completion* has been defined as follows:

> The Date of Substantial Completion of the Work or designated portion thereof is the Date certified by the Architect when construction is sufficiently complete, in accordance with the Contract Documents, so the Owner can occupy or utilize the Work or designated portion thereof for the use for which it is intended.[39]

Also, upon substantial completion, contractors may recover upon their contracts and need not rely upon the equitable theory of *quantum meruit* in order to recover for work performed and materials supplied.[40]

It is a well-recognized rule of contract law that strict performance may be waived by the party entitled to performance.[41] In the context of the construction contract, this means that the owner may acquiesce in the contractor's failure to perform according to the strict terms of the agreement. Waiver is typically defined as the "intentional relinquishment of a known right."[42]

In order for owners to waive strict performance or to acquiesce in the deviation from the contract documents, however, they or their authorized representatives must be aware of the defect or the deviation. It has also been held that it is enough if owners or their authorized representatives should have been aware of the defect or deviation.[43] Whether particular acts or conduct amount to acceptance is a fact question that depends upon the circumstances of each case.

Owners sometimes attempt to avoid the effect of acceptance with a nonwaiver provision. In the absence of such a contract provision, waiver may still be implied if owners or their representatives have had an opportunity during the progress of the work to inspect and reject work or materials that obviously do not comply with the contract requirements, but failed to do so. In such a case, failure to object during the progress of the work may amount to a waiver of the defect. The mere presence of the owner or the representative at the site, however, does not necessarily constitute a waiver.[44]

Although acceptance occurs under AIA Document A201 when there has been final completion and final payment, acceptance of incomplete work can also be implied. Such an acceptance arises by analogy to UCC § 2-606(1), which provides that the purchaser of goods has accepted them when there has been a failure to reject the goods or when there is any act inconsistent with the seller's ownership. Similarly, delay or inaction resulting in a failure to reject noncomplying work within a reasonable time may constitute a constructive acceptance by the owner.

> It is also well settled that even if the existence of the defects or omissions and the cost of repairing them are proved, the person suing the contractor is nevertheless barred from recovering the cost of the defects if he accepted the work despite the patent and obvious defects or imperfections discoverable upon reasonable inspection.[45]

As a general proposition, however, mere occupation and use of a structure by the owner does not constitute an acceptance of the work as complying with the contract or amount to a waiver of defects therein.[46] This rule applies as well when the owner has taken possession of the project under the express understanding that defects will be remedied at a later date.[47]

Defects that are not apparent and that cannot be discovered until a later date (latent defects) are not accepted. This is especially true on federal construction projects.[48] It has been held, however, that latent defects in materials will not subject a subcontractor or contractor to liability, unless there is some relevant express contractual warranty. If the builder or subcontractor has purchased the materials from a reputable dealer, has no knowledge of the defect, has acted in good faith, and has exercised reasonable care and skill, there generally will be no implied warranty of fitness of the materials.[49]

Formerly, it was generally held that acceptance by the owner released a contractor from liability for injuries to a third person after the contractor had completed the work. It is now generally accepted that contractors may be liable to third parties if they have failed to exercise reasonable care in their performance of the work even after acceptance by the owner. Certainly, inspection and acceptance by the owner of a contractor's completed work is a circumstance bearing on the reasonableness of the contractor's performance.

In a nutshell, the present rule is that contractors, by the owner's acceptance, are not automatically relieved of liability for foreseeable personal injury or property damage to the owner or third party as a result of their negligence in performing the work.[50] It should also be noted that an injured third party may be able to sue long after completion of the work by the contractor. In Tennessee, for example, the time in which the suit must be filed does not begin to run until the injury actually occurs, if the injury results from a contractor's act or omission that might have proved harmless. The statute of limitations is extended because defects in a building cause no direct damages to a third party until the party is actually injured.[51]

Closely related to waiver by acceptance is the issue of whether progress payments constitute a waiver of defects. The jurisdictions appear evenly divided, with some state courts holding that partial payments will not constitute a waiver of defects, while other states hold the opposite.[52] The argument of waiver of defects by partial payment is much more persuasive when the defects were known, when owners or their representatives failed to protest, and when there was no express agreement to remedy them. Generally, however, the contract will provide that any progress payment will not constitute acceptance of any work not in compliance with the contract documents.[53]

Waiver or acceptance of defective performance by owners precludes them from refusing to pay contractors the reasonable value of the work or the price according to the terms of the contract.[54] Similarly, where owners accept the work as being in full compliance with contract, they generally cannot later maintain an action against the contractor to recover for deviations from the contract documents or recoup such damages in an action brought by the contractor for compensation.[55]

A final type of defect that the owner can waive is a contractor's failure to complete work within the specified period of time. Generally, time is stated to be "of the essence" in a construction contract and the unexcused failure to complete within the time specified is a material breach.[56] A material breach will justify termination of the contract and a refusal by the other party to continue performance.[57]

Late performance may be waived by a subsequent agreement or by conduct indicating an intention to regard the contract as still in force after the default (for example, payments for work performed after the specified completion date). The owner, however, does not, merely by accepting late performance (and waiving the right to terminate), necessarily waive the right to recover damages (including liquidated damages) suffered as a result of the delay.[58]

## THE AMBIGUOUS CONTRACT TERM

Building and construction contracts are subject to the same basic rules that govern the interpretation of contracts in general. Thus, courts lack the power to create or rewrite construction contracts for the parties, just as they lack this power in connection with other types of contracts. At the same time, a court is not at liberty to ignore the plain, clear, and unambiguous language of a contract.

Where contract language contains an *ambiguity,* whether latent or patent, however, the court has both the authority and duty to provide a reasonable interpretation through the application of certain established rules of contract interpretation. Ambiguities are frequently encountered in construction contracts. A word or phrase in a contract is considered to be ambiguous when more than one reasonable meaning may be attributed to it.

When language in a contract is clear, the parties' expressed intent, though not necessarily their actual intent, will control. Where an ambiguity is apparent or proven, however, the court will attempt to give the ambiguous language a reasonable interpretation consonant with the apparent intentions of the parties at the time the contract was executed to the extent that intention can be ascertained from the document's language.

When both parties to a construction contract submit a reasonable interpretation of an ambiguous provision, courts take their usual approach to ambiguous language; that is, the language will be interpreted most strongly against the party responsible for its inclusion in the contract. The technical name for this interpretive rule is *contra proferentem.* Its rationale lies in the notion that the party responsible for an ambiguity has no right to induce the other party to contract with it on the supposition that its words mean one thing, while at the same time it hopes that a court will subsequently adopt a different interpretation more to its advantage.

It is more important to note that *contra proferentem* is not a substitute for the technical contract interpretation rules and should only be applied as a last resort when these other rules fail to establish the contract upon which the parties actually agreed.[59]

In interpreting ambiguous language in a construction contract drafted by the owner, the court initially determines whether a reasonable bidder in the contractor's position would have interpreted the contract language as the contract did. If the contractor's interpretation is ultimately determined to be a reasonable one, it must prevail. The contractor's interpretation only needs to be reasonable. The interpretation does not have to be the only possible one, or even the only reasonable one. It is enough that it is reasonable, even if the owner's interpretation is also reasonable.

As was observed in *Bennett* v. *United States* (1967):

> To prevail . . . it is not essential that plaintiff demonstrate his position to be the *only* justifiable or reasonable one. A specification susceptible to one or more interpretations, each interpretation found to be consistent with the contract's language and the parties' objectively ascertainable intentions, becomes convincing proof of an ambiguity; the burden of that ambiguity falls solely upon the party who drew the specifications.[60]

Nonetheless, a contractor does have an obligation to seek a clarification of patent ambiguities or inconsistencies that appear in the bid *documents.* For example, in *Beacon Construction Co. v. United States* (1963), where the bid documents contained a clause requiring prospective bidders to inform the contracting officer of discrepancies in the plans and specifications, the court held against a contractor who failed to comply with that requirement and later sought to rely on an ambiguity. The court stated:

> The bidder who is on notice of an incipient problem, but neglects to solve it as he is directed to do by this form of contractual preventive-hygiene cannot rely on the principle that ambiguities in contracts written by the Government are held against the drafter. . . . Even more, the bidder in such a case is under an *affirmative obligation. He "should call attention to an obvious omission in the specification, and make certain that the omission was deliberate, if he intends to take advantage of it."* . . . If the bidder fails to resort to the remedy proffered by the government, a patent and glaring discrepancy (like that which existed here) should be taken against him in interpreting the contract. *We do not mean to rule that, under such contract provisions, the contractor must at his peril resolve any possible ambiguity prior to bidding; what we do hold is that, when he is presented with an obvious omission, inconsistency or discrepancy of significance, he must consult the Government's representative if he intends to bridge the crevasse in his own favor.* Having failed to take that route, plaintiff is now barred from recovering on his demand (emphasis added).[61]

A contractor is not allowed to "lie in wait" if there was an opportunity for clarification. So this rule that the interpretation of the party who did not write the provision will prevail requires (1) a latent ambiguity and (2) a reasonable interpretation.

It should be noted, however, that the general ambiguity rule may not be applicable where the party responsible for the ambiguity is a public body.[62] Fortunately for the contractor, the more prevalent rule is that a public body should be treated the same as any other contracting party in interpreting an ambiguous contract situation.[63]

The court, rather than a jury, is responsible for contract interpretation. It is only when ambiguities remain after all rules of interpretation have been applied that the jury is called upon to determine what the parties meant by their agreement. The jury also makes determination regarding necessary items which were initially omitted from the contract.

## CONCLUSIONS

In summary, precise and well thought-out contract provisions will guide all of the parties—contractors, owners, architects, engineers, and project managers—smoothly through the construction process. Although every contingency, delay, and disaster cannot be anticipated in preparing a construction contract, the foregoing clauses and provisions have been widely accepted both in the industry and in litigation and arbitration.

# Appendix Notes

1. See Plumley v. United States, 226 U.S. 545 (1913); 13 Am Jur. 2d, Building and Construction Contracts, § 22 (1964).
2. For example, in Environmental Utilities Corp. v. Lancaster Area Sewer Authority, 453 F. Supp. 1260 (E.D. Penn. 1978), a contractor was not allowed to recover for extra work performed because he did not have written work orders.
3. See 10 U.S.C. § 2306(a) and 41 U.S.C. 254(b).
4. See, for example, Appeal of Emsco Screen Pipe Co., ASBCA No. 11917, 69-1 BCA ¶ 7710 (1969).
5. Blount Brothers Construction Co., ASBCA No. 6172, 1962 BCA ¶ 3300 (1962).
6. Comptroller General unpublished opinion B. 165555 (January 24, 1969).
7. Farnsworth & Chambers Co., Inc., ASBCA No. 4990, 59-1 BCA ¶ 2174 (1959); Superior Fuse and Manufacturing Co., ASBCA No. 6585, 61-2 BCA ¶ 3226 (1961); and Algernon Blair, Inc., GSBCA, 67-2 ¶ BCA 6453, *aff'd on reconsideration* 68-2 BCA ¶ 7343 (1968).
8. Wood-Hopkins Contracting Co. v. Masonry Contractors, Inc., 235 So. 2d 548 (Fla. App. 1970); and Seattle School District v. King Plumbing and Heating Co., 265 P. 463 (Wash. 1928).
9. See, for example, Ambrose-Augusterfer Corp. v. United States, 394 F.2d 536 (Ct. Cl. 1968).
10. See Metropolitan Sewerage Commission v. R.W. Construction, Inc., 241 N.W.2d 371 (Wis. 1976). *Contra,* Cruz Construction Co. v. Lancaster Area Sewer Authority, 439 F. Supp. 1202 (E.D. Pa. 1977). For example, in Woodcrest Construction Co. v. United States, 408 F.2d 395 (Ct. Cl. 1969), the Court of Claims allowed a contractor to recover under the changed conditions clause in spite of extremely broad exculpatory provisions in the contract.
11. See Robert E. McKee v. City of Atlanta, 414 F. Supp. 957 (N.D. Ga. 1976).
12. Raymond International, Inc. v. Baltimore County, Maryland, 412 A.2d 1296 (Md. App. 1980).
13. See Montgomery v. Philadelphia, 139 A.2d 347 (Pa. 1958); Cruz Construction Co. v. Lancaster Area Sewer Authority, *supra* note 10; and Eastern Tunneling Corp. v. Southgate Sanitation District Arapohoe County, 487 F. Supp. 109 (D. Colo. 1979).
14. Farnsworth & Chambers Co. v. United States, 171 Ct. Cl. 30 (1965).
15. Warren Painting Co., Inc. ASBCA No. 18456, 74-2 BCA ¶ 10,834; John G. Vann *et al.* v. United States, 190 Ct. Cl. 546, 573 (1970) and Maintenance Engineers, ASBCA No. 17474, 74-2 BCA ¶ 10,760 (1974).
16. Stock & Grove, Inc. v. United States, 493 F.2d 629 (1974).
17. See, for example, Condon-Cunningham, Inc. v. Day, 258 N.E.2d 264 (Ohio Misc. 1969).

18. See Sasso Contracting Co. v. New Jersey, 414 A.2d 608 (N.J. App. 1980).
19. See Woodcrest Construction Co. v. United States, *supra* note 10; and Robert E. McKee v. City of Atlanta, *supra* note 11. *Contra,* Cruz Construction Co. v. Lancaster Sewer Authority, *supra* note 10.
20. Even where there is no differing site condition clause, a contractor may also have a recovery against the owner based upon a breach of warranty of owner-furnished information or a misrepresentation theory. See Robert E. McKee v. City of Atlanta, *supra* note 11.
21. 586 P.2d 840 (Wash. 1979).
22. Franklin Contracting Co. v. New Jersey, 365 A.2d 952 (N.J. 1977).
23. Sheehan v. Pittsburgh, 62 A. 642 (Pa. 1905); Pittsburgh Construction Co. v. Dayton, 237 F. 305 (6th Cir. 1916); and Grant Construction Co. v. Burns, 92 Idaho 408, 433 P.2d 1005 (1968).
24. American Pipe & Construction Co. v. Westchester County, 292 F. 941 (2d Cir. 1923).
25. Maurice L. Bein, Inc. v. Housing Authority, 321 P.2d 753 (Ala. App. 1958); and American Bridge Co. v. State, 283 N.Y.S. 577 (1935).
26. John T. Brady & Co. v. Board of Education, 226 N.Y.S. 707 (1928); De Riso Bros. v. State, 293 N.Y.S. 436 (1937); Gasparini Excavation Co. v. Pennsylvania Turnpike Commission, 187 A.2d 157 (Pa. 1963); Housing Authority of the City of Dallas v. Hubbell, 325 S.W.2d 880 (Tex. 1959); and John E. Green Plumbing & Heating Co., Inc. v. Turner Construction Co., 500 F. Supp. 910 (E.D. Mich. 1980).
27. Brady v. Board of Education, *supra* note 26; and Hawley v. Orange County Flood Control District, 27 Cal.Rptr. 478 (Cal. 1963).
28. Wells Bros. Co. v. United States, 254 U.S. 83 (1920); Ericks v. Edmonds School District, 125 P.2d 275 (Wash. 1942); and Ace Stone, Inc. v. Township of Wayne, 221 A.2d 515 (N.J. 1966).
29. 436 F.2d 405 (5th Cir. 1971), at 410-411. See, also, Houston Fire and Casualty Insurance Co. v. Riesel Industrial School district, 375 S.W.2d 323 (Tex. Civ. App. 1964).
30. AIA Document A201 ¶ 9.8.1.
31. Moore v. Werner, 418 S.W.2d 918 (Tex. Civ. App. 1967).
32. Burton-Dixie Corp. v. Timothy McCarthy Construction Co., *supra* note 29.
33. See National Hills Shipping Center, Inc. v. INA, 320 F. Supp. 11 (S.D. Ga. 1970).
34. Walton v. Petty, 107 Ga. App. 753 (1963); and Reynolds v. Wilson, 121 Ga. App. 153 (1970).
35. See Schipper v. Levitt and Sons, Inc., 207 A.2d 314 (N.Y. 1965) (warranty of habitability implied when child injured by hot-water heater in new home). See, also, Groover v. Magnavox Co., 71 F.R.D. 638 (W.D. Pa. 1976) (implied warranty of habitability recognized in certain situations).
36. Continental Illinois National Bank v. United States, 101 F. Supp. 755 (Ct. Cl. 1952).
37. *Restatement of Contracts* (First), § 302.
38. See Neel v. O'Quinn, 313 So. 2d 286 (La. App. 1975); Royal Ornamental Iron, Inc. v. Devon Bank, 336 N.E.2d 105 (Ill. App. 1975); Ocean Ridge Development Corp. v. Quality Plastering, Inc., 247 So. 2d 72 (Fla. App.

1971); Southwest Engineering Co. v. Reorganized School District, 434 S.W.2d 743 (Mo. App. 1958); and Reynolds v. Armstead, 443 P.2d 990 (Colo. 1968).

39. AIA Document A201 ¶ 8.1.3.
40. See 13 Am. Jur. 2d, Building and Construction Contracts, § 41,110; and Cox v. Fremont County Public Building Authority, 415 F.2d 882 (8th Cir. 1969).
41. See, generally, J. Calamari and J. Perillo, *Contracts,* § 11-37 (1977). Commercial Contractors, Inc. v. U.S.F. & G., 524 F.2d 944 (5th Cir. 1975).
42. See 28 Am. Jur. 2d, Estoppel and Waiver, §§ 154 *et seq.*
43. Cantrell v. Woodhill Enterprises, Inc., 160 S.E.2d 476 (N.C. 1968).
44. See Southern Patio, Inc. v. Varnado, 153 So. 2d 924 (La. App. 1963); 17A C.J.S., Contracts, § 514(1); and Florida Ice Machine Corp. v. Branton Insulation, Inc., 290 So. 2d 415 (La. App. 1974).
45. Florida Ice Machine Corp. v. Branton Insulation, Inc., *supra* note 44, at 418.
46. Elliott v. Caldwell, 45 Minn. 357 (Minn. 1890); 107 A.L.R. 1411.
47. Mitchell v. Carlson, 313 P.2d 717 (Mont. 1957).
48. Kaminer Construction Co. v. United States, 488 F.2d 980 (Ct. Cl. 1973).
49. See Annotation, 61 A.L.R.3d 792.
50. Johnson v. Oman Construction Co., Inc., 519 S.W.2d 782 (Tenn. 1975); see, also, 41 Am. Jur. 2d, Independent Contractors, §§ 49-50 (1968).
51. Vason v. Nickey, 438 F.2d 242 (6th Cir. 1971).
52. See Annotation, 66 A.L.R.2d 570.
53. AIA Document A201 ¶ 9.5.5.
54. Milaeger Well Drilling Co. v. Muskego Rendering Co., 85 N.W.2d 331 (Wis. 1957).
55. Guschl v. Schmidt, 63 N.W.2d 759 (Wis. 1954).
56. State Highway Department v. Hall Paving Co., 194 S.E.2d 493 (Ga. App. 1972).
57. 17 Am. Jur. 2d Contracts, § 446.
58. DeSomber v. Bickel, 118 N.W.2d 868 (Wis. 1963). *Contra,* Kaltoft v. Nielsen, 106 N.W.2d 597 (Iowa 1960).
59. See Broyles & Broyles, Inc., GSBCA 5694, 81-1 BCA ¶ 14,969 (1981).
60. 168 Ct. Cl. 61 (1967).
61. 314 F.2d 501 (Ct. Cl. 1963).
62. See, for example, City of Granville v. Kovash, Inc., 118 N.W.2d 354 (N.D. 1962), which held that a contract between a municipality and a private contractor should be construed against the contractor for public policy reasons, even though the contractor had no hand in its drafting.
63. Terminal Construction Corp. v. Bergen County, 113 A.2d 787 (N.J. 1955).

# Bibliography

"Accident Victims Win $1.7 Million Judgment." *Minneapolis Star,* 25 September 1974, p. 159.

*Analysis of Workers Compensation Laws.* Washington, DC: U.S. Chamber of Commerce, 1989.

Anderson, Ronald A. and Kumpf, Walter A. *Business Law.* 10th ed. Cincinnati, OH: Southwestern Publishing Company, 1976.

*Best's Loss Control Engineering Manual.* Oldwick, NJ: A.M. Best Company, 1976.

*Best's Underwriting Guide.* Oldwick, NJ: A.M. Best Company, 1975.

Bickelhaupt, David L. *General Insurance.* 9th ed. Homewood, IL: Richard D. Irwin, 1974.

*Commercial Lines Manual* (1985), Division One—Automobile, Section II. Additional pages, 1st ed., January 1987. New York: Insurance Services Office.

*Commercial Lines Manual.* "Classification Table." Note 3, p. CS-49. 2nd ed., January 1987. New York: Insurance Services Office, 1987.

*Comparative Analysis of Legislative Changes Related to Medical Malpractice.* 30 June 1975 and update, 1 September 1975. American Insurance Association.

Coombs, Eugene G., Jr. "Parental Immunity is Quashed When Parent has Coverage." *The National Underwriter,* Property & Casualty Insurance Edition, 5 March 1976, p. 20.

Decyk, Roxanne J. and Hirsch, Donald J. "The Medical Standard of Care." *Defense of Medical Malpractice Cases,* 1977, no. 4.

Donaldson, James H. *Casualty Claim Practice.* 3rd ed. Homewood, IL: Richard D. Irwin, 1976.

*Experience Rating Plan Manual.* Boca Raton, FL: National Council on Compensation Insurance, 1984.

*FC&S Bulletins,* Casualty and Surety Section. Cincinnati, OH: The National Underwriter Co., July 1972.

Gilmore, Grant and Black, Charles L., Jr. *Law of Admiralty.* Mineola, NY: Foundation Press, 1975.

*Guidelines for Determination of Claims under Amended Longshoremen's Act.* Program Memorandum No. 58, 5 August 1977. U.S. Department of Labor, Office of Workers Compensation Programs.

*Journal of the American Medical Association,* 1970, p. 73.

Hall, George E. "The Locality Rule." *The Best of Law and Medicine '68/'70.*

Heinrich, H.W.; Peterson, Dan; and Roos, Nestor. *Industrial Accident Prevention.* 5th ed. New York: McGraw-Hill Book Company, 1980.

Horn, Ronald C. *On Professions, Professionals, and Professional Ethics.*

Malvern, PA: American Institute for Property and Liability Underwriters, 1978.

_______. *Subrogation in Insurance Theory and Practice.* Homewood, IL: Richard D. Irwin, 1964.

*Kansas Workmen's Compensation Carriers and Self-Insurers Information Letter.* Kansas Division of Worker's Compensation, March 1979.

Kulp, C.A. and Hall, John W. *Casualty Insurance.* 4th ed. New York: Ronald Press Co., 1968.

Larson, Arthur. *Workmen's Compensation for Occupational Injuries and Death.* Desk Edition. New York: Matthew Bender & Company, 1980 and 1981.

Lorimer, James J.; Perlet, Harry F., Jr.; Kempin, Frederick G., Jr.; and Hodosh, Frederick R. *The Legal Environment of Insurance.* Vol. II. 2nd ed. Malvern, PA: The American Institute for Property and Liability Underwriters, 1981.

Mackall, Luther E. *Surety Underwriting Manual.* Indianapolis: The Rough Notes Co., 1972.

Malecki, Donald S.; Horn, Ronald C.; Wiening, Eric A.; and Donaldson, James H. *Commercial Liability Risk Management and Insurance.* Vol. I. Malvern, PA: American Institute for Property and Liability Underwriters, Inc., 1978; 2nd ed., 1986.

*Malpractice Claims,* vol. 1, no. 4, May 1977. New York: National Association of Insurance Commissioners.

"Michigan Can Be Sued Over Drowning." *Business Insurance,* 12 May 1980, p. 80.

Millus, Albert J. and Gentile, Willard J. *Workers' Compensation Laws in Insurance.* New York: Roberts Publishing Corporation, 1976.

Millus, Albert J. and Manes, Joseph F. *The Longshoremen's and Harbor Workers' Compensation Act and Its Extensions.* New York: The Roberts Publishing Corp., 1978.

*New York Manual of Rules, Classifications and Rates for Workmen's Compensation and Employers' Liability Insurance.* NY: New York Compensation Insurance Rating Board.

Noel, Dix W. and Phillips, Jerry J. *Products Liability in a Nutshell.* St. Paul: West Publishing Company, 1974.

"$128 Million Awarded in Pinto Crash." *The Philadelphia Inquirer,* 8 February 1978, p. 1-A.

Peterson, Osler L.; Andrews, Leon P.; Spain, Robert S.; and Greenberg, Bernard G. "An Analytical Study of North Carolina General Practice, 1953-54," part 2, 31. *Journal of Medical Education,* 12 November 1956, p. 65.

*The Product-Safety Function: Organization and Operations.* New York; The Conference Board, 1979.

Prosser, William L. *Torts.* 4th ed. St. Paul, MN: West Publishing, 1971.

"Public Liability." *Business Insurance,* 19 February 1978, p. 82.

Purdue, Jim M. "The Law of Texas Medical Malpractice, Chapter VII: Limitations. *Houston Law Review.* Vol. 11, no. 4, May 1974.

*Relevant Court Decisions.* A.M. Best Co., August 1977.

*The Report of the National Commission on State Workmen's Compensation Laws.* July 1972.

Rubsamen. *Professional Liability Newsletter,* vol. 4, no. 9, November 1972.

"Schedule Rating." *Casualty Individual Risk Rating Plans—Workbook.* New York: Insurance Services Office, 1976.

"Sovereign Immunity." *Business Insurance,* 10 December 1979, p. 82.

*Statutes Affecting Liability Insurance.* 17th ed. March 1977. American Insurance Association.

Ulrich, E. Stewart. "A Checklist to Prevent Errors and Omissions Losses." *Underwriters Review,* February 1970.

"What's Bright Yellow and Basically Safe?" *Journal of American Insurance,* vol. 56, no. 2, Summer 1980, pp. 6-8.

Williams, C. Arthur, Jr. and Heins, Richard M. *Risk Management and Insurance.* 3rd ed. New York: McGraw-Hill Book Company, 1976.

*Workers Compensation Insurance Basis of Premium—Payrolls vs. Manhours.* 19 June 1978. New York: National Council on Compensation Insurance.

# Index

## A

## B

# C

# D



# E

# F



# G

## J



## L

# M



# N

## O



## P

## Q



## R

# S

# T

## U

## V



## W



## Y